The Syncretic Religion of Lin Chao-en

Neo-Confucian Studies
  sponsored by
The Regional Seminar in Neo-Confucian Studies
  Columbia University

Buddhist Studies and Translations
  sponsored by
*The Columbia University Seminar in Oriental Thought
and Religion*
  with the cooperation of
The Institute for Advanced Studies of World Religions

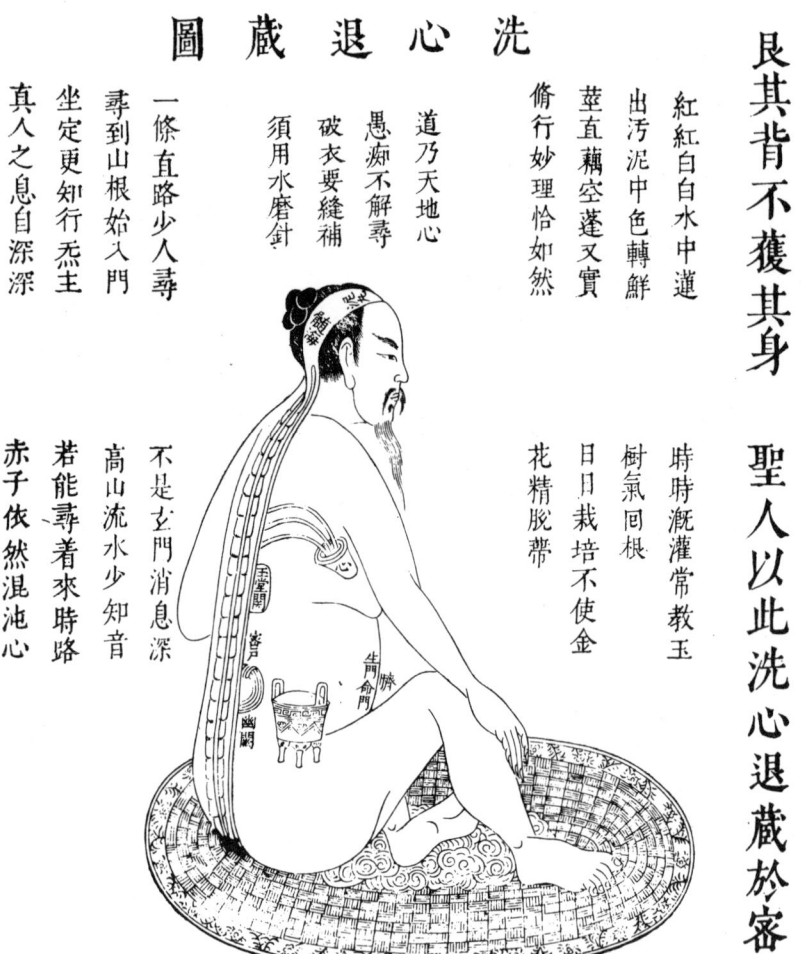

An adept seated in the meditative posture of *ken-pei* (stilling in the back) as taught in the *Hsing-ming shuang-hsiu wan-shen kuei-chih* (The revealed doctrine of the dual cultivation of Nature and Life as taught by the myriad spirits), a seventeenth-century work attributed to Yin Chen-jen. The same method is taught by Lin Chao-en in his nine stages of mind-cultivation.

The Syncretic Religion of Lin Chao-en

JUDITH A. BERLING

New York   COLUMBIA UNIVERSITY PRESS   1980

Copyright © 1980 Columbia University Press
All rights reserved.
Printed in the United States of America

Columbia University Press
New York   Guildford, Surrey

Library of Congress Cataloging in Publication Data

Berling, Judith A
The syncretic religion of Lin Chao-en.

(Neo-Confucian studies) (Buddhist studies and
translations) (IASWR series)
Bibliography: p.
Includes index.
1. Lin, Chao-en, 1517–1598. 2. Confucianists—
China—Biography. 3. China—Religion. I. Title.
II. Series: Neo-Confucian studies. III. Series:
Buddhist studies and translations. IV. Series:
Institute for Advanced Studies of World Religions.
IASWR series.
BL1875.L56B47   299'.51261'0924[B]   79-25606
ISBN 0-231-04870-X

*The Western Inscription says,
"All people are my brothers and sisters."
Therefore if one takes physical parents as parents,
then those born of the same parents are my brothers.
But if one takes heaven and earth as one's parents,
then all who are born of heaven and earth are also my brothers.
As for Buddhist and Taoists, can they live outside of heaven
and earth? If they cannot live outside of heaven and earth,
who are they if not of my mother's womb,
if not my brothers?*

                LIN CHAO-EN

Neo-Confucian Studies, Board of Editors
Irene Bloom
Wing-tsit Chan
Wm. Theodore de Bary

Committee on Buddhist Studies and Translations
Wm. Theodore de Bary
Yoshito S. Hakeda
Frederic Underwood
Alex Wayman
Philip B. Yampolsky

IASWR Series

Buddhist Monastic Discipline: The Sanskrit Prātimokṣa Sūtras of the Mahāsāmghikas and Mūlasarvāstivādins, by Charles S. Prebish (The Pennsylvania State University Press).

Sūtra of the Past Vows of Earth Store Bodhisattva, tr. Heng Ching

Avatāra: The Humanization of Philosophy Through the Bhagavad Gītā, by Antonio T. de Nicolás (Nicolás Hays, Ltd.)

The Holy Teaching of Vimalakīrti: A Mahāyāna Scripture, tr. Robert A. F. Thurman (The Pennsylvania State University Press).

Scripture of the Lotus Blossom of the Fine Dharma (The Lotus Sūtra), tr. Leon Hurvitz (Columbia University Press).

Hua-yen Buddhism: The Jewel Net of Indra, by Francis H. Cook (The Pennsylvania State University Press).

A Buddhist Leader in Ming China: The Life and Thought of Han-shan Te-ch'ing, by Sung-peng Hsu (The Pennsylvania State University Press).

The Syncretic Religion of Lin Chao-en, by Judith A. Berling (Columbia University Press).

CONTENTS

	Preface	*xiii*
CHAPTER ONE.	The Problem with Syncretism	1
CHAPTER TWO.	Syncretism and Sectarianism in Early China	14
CHAPTER THREE.	The Heyday of Syncretism	32
CHAPTER FOUR.	Biography of Lin Chao-en	62
CHAPTER FIVE.	The System of Mind-cultivation	90
CHAPTER SIX.	The Nine Stages	145
CHAPTER SEVEN.	The True Transmission of the Three Teachings	195
CHAPTER EIGHT.	The Legacy of Lin Chao-en	220
APPENDIX A.	Sources for the Study of Lin Chao-en	239
APPENDIX B.	*Lin-tzu sheng-hsüeh t'ung-tsung san-chiao kuei-ju chi*	246
APPENDIX C.	*Lin-tzu ch'üan-chi* (1606)	248
APPENDIX D.	*San-chiao cheng-tsung t'ung-lun*	254
APPENDIX E.	*Lin-tzu ch'üan-chi* (1631)	258
APPENDIX F.	Alphabetical List of Titles	260

Abbreviations and Conventions   264
Notes   265
Glossary   317
Selected Bibliography   327
Index   339

CONTENTS

PREFACE

We sometimes study religions as though they were isolated entities with clearly defined boundaries. However, religions in history are also part of a process of change; tradition, belief, and practice are constantly being redefined in light of cultural changes, intellectual trends, and personal and communal life experiences. The dynamics of religions tend to be syncretic, reacting to and absorbing into themselves elements from other religions and philosophies. As G. Van der Leeuw has written, "Every historic religion, therefore, is not one, but several; not of course as being the sum of different forms, but in the sense that diverse forms had approximated to its own form and had amalgamated with this."[1] Syncretism is fundamental to the dynamic of religious interaction through time.

To understand the nature and function of syncretism in religious interaction and change, there is no better place to look than China. In China, three great traditions (Confucianism, Buddhism, and Taoism) dominated almost the entire spectrum of religious history, and numberless popular cults and foreign religions had their day. The history of Chinese religion is a history of positive and negative religious interactions. Religious pluralism produced both broad waves of religious interaction and religious thinkers who were self-consciously syncretists. They advocated syncretism as a principle through which one might best recapture and attain the essence of the religious experience. Thus in China we can study syncretism not only as a force in the religious dynamic but also as a principle which shaped the lives and thinking of religious figures. This book will study one such figure in depth, using his case to explore the meaning and function of the phenomenon we call syncretism.

Studies of Sung and post-Sung religion in China are a relatively new field, especially in the West, and a highly specialized one. Most scholars specialize in Buddhist, Confucian, or Taoist studies, and with good reason, for each has its own rich literature and traditions. I have endeavored to make this book accessible to those who are not specialists in these fields, for Lin Chao-en represents much broader trends in the history of religion in China, and in the world. The book has two levels of annotation. On broader issues, I have mentioned basic and readable English-language sources (when available) for those readers with limited backgrounds in Chinese religion. On issues related to the specialized research of this book (Chinese syncretism, Inner Alchemy Taoism, Ming Neo-Confucianism), I have provided more extensive sources in European and Asian languages, as well as references to primary sources in Chinese, for the sake of other specialists in the field.

This book could not have been completed without the generous help of many institutions and individuals, to whom I express my gratitude. The Danforth Foundation's Kent Fellowship and Columbia University's International Travel Grant funded research in Japan; the Research and Graduate Development division of Indiana University awarded a typing grant which speeded the completion of the manuscript.

I am grateful to my teacher Wm. Theodore de Bary for his penetrating criticisms; to Wing-tsit Chan for the care with which he read my original drafts; to Wu Pei-yi and Julia Ching for advice on unresolved problems of translation; to Philip Yampolsky for assistance on bibliographical problems; to Sakai Tadao and Mano Senryū for guiding me to primary sources in Japan; to Michel Strickmann, Leo Lee, and Nathan Sivin for their helpful criticisms of my manuscript; to Howard Berkowitz for being my "reader outside of the field"; and to many friends and colleagues (notably, Irene Bloom, Catherine Swatek, Collett Harris, William May, Samuel Preus, David Smith, Eugene Eoyang, and Mark Macwilliams) and my family, for aiding and supporting me in countless ways.

The Syncretic Religion of Lin Chao-en

CHAPTER ONE

THE PROBLEM WITH SYNCRETISM

Syncretism is central to the religious life of the Chinese. There is little dispute about that. Yet scholarly discussion of the role of syncretism in Chinese history has been curiously vague and imprecise. Over fifty years ago, W. E. Soothill described the religious style of the Chinese:

> While a few of the laity devote themselves, some solely to Buddhism, some solely to Taoism, the great mass of the people have no prejudices and make no embarrassing distinctions; they belong to none of the three religions, or, more correctly, they belong to all three. In other words, they are eclectic, and use whichever form best responds to the requirement of the occasion for which they use religion.[1]

Henrik Kraemer echoed Soothill's view:

> One of the best-known features of Chinese universism is that the three religions—Confucianism, Buddhism, and Taoism—are virtually treated as one. The religious allegiance of the average man is not related to one of the three religions. He does not belong to a confession or creed. He participates *unconcerned as to any apparent lack of consistency*, alternatively in Buddhist, Taoist, or Confucian rites. He is by nature a religious pragmatist. [Italics added.][2]

Similar generalizations have been repeated by such authorities as Henri Maspero, C. K. Yang, and Hajime Nakamura.

2   THE PROBLEM WITH SYNCRETISM

The last has written: "This arbitrary syncretism had a great influence on the common people, and is one of the striking characteristics of modern Chinese religions."[3]

In the eyes of some, one happy consequence of this syncretic outlook was a record of religious tolerance which put to shame the bloody history of religious wars and persecutions in the West.[4] To counter such idealized views of the history of religion in China, J. J. M. de Groot wrote *Sectarianism and Religious Persecution in China* (1903–4), tracing the rich history of sectarian controversies and governmental measures to control or stamp out religious movements.

Are we to believe, then, that China was divided into two camps, the syncretists and the sectarians? Such a solution would be too simple, for those who most roundly denounced other sects can often be shown to have dabbled in the very religions they denounced. A famous case in point is Chu Hsi (1130–1200), the great architect of Neo-Confucianism in the Sung (960–1279).[5] Although he attacked Buddhism and Taoism and warned his students to avoid their pitfalls, his thought owed a debt to these very traditions. Moreover, he wrote instructions on the Taoist practice of breath control and annotations to two important works of religious Taoism.[6] On the other hand, as we shall see in the course of this study, those who advocated the unity of the Three Teachings (Confucianism, Taoism, and Buddhism) often called for reform—even governmental control—of heterodox practices. Thus sectarians exhibit syncretic behavior, and vice versa. Whatever the relation of syncretism and sectarianism in Chinese history, they were not clearly opposing forces.

There are, in fact, several problems with these generalizations about syncretism in Chinese religion. Who is the "average man" to whom these generalizations refer? If the three religions were treated as one, what was the cause of religious persecutions and the debates over orthodoxy and heterodoxy reviewed by de Groot? What were the beliefs, practices, and rituals of the three religions which the hypothetical average man practiced, "unconcerned as to any lack of consistency"? Could he indeed be unconcerned when such practices were denounced as heterodox? Is syncretism, as the comments seem to suggest, an indiscriminate, aimless, purely pragmatic combination of practices and ideas? What would be the purpose of such pragmatism? Broad generalizations tell us little about the role and nature of syncretism in Chinese religion. They must be set aside until much more is known.

To clarify our understanding of the role of syncretism in Chinese history, it is necessary to study specific instances of syncretism in their historical and social contexts. To that end, this book will focus on the Ming dynasty syncretist Lin Chao-en (1517–1598). As a member of a prominent scholar-official family, Lin Chao-en was educated to take government examinations and become an official, but he abandoned that career to devote himself to attaining the enlightened mind of the sage. After a long search, he achieved insight into the true understanding of mind as taught by all Three Teachings. This spiritual breakthrough was accompanied by a call to teach the truth of the mind to others. Assuming the title Master of the Three Teachings, he established a religious organization which came to include members of all three religions and all social classes. His followers continued to venerate him after his death; the sect is active even today among Chinese in Southeast Asia.

Lin Chao-en was a syncretist both in his personal religious vision and in his role as a religious teacher. He lived in the Ming dynasty (1368–1644), when syncretic forces flourished. The unity of the Three Teachings was proclaimed by millenarian sects at the popular level, by the intellectual giants of the age, and even by the Imperial Founder, Ming T'ai-tsu (r. 1368–1398). Never before or since in Chinese history did syncretism have so open and pervasive an impact on all levels of the religious imagination. Lin Chao-en and his age, then, manifest syncretism in its clearest and most detailed form in Chinese history. Study of them should go a long way toward clarifying the dynamics of syncretism. However, before turning to Lin Chao-en and the Ming, we must deal with the knotty problem of syncretism itself.

4   THE PROBLEM WITH SYNCRETISM

IN DEFENSE OF SYNCRETISM

Syncretism is a misunderstood word; it has come to have a distinctively bad odor which is the result of an unfortunate history. Syncretism has often been viewed as perfidious, random, corrupting, or superficial.

Syncretism looks perfidious when viewed against the backdrop of the credal and exclusivistic style of religion which dominated Western history. In Western theological disputes syncretism "was generally regarded as a betrayal of principles, or as an attempt to secure unity at the expense of truth."[7] In the West, where religions frequently clashed over doctrinal, hermeneutical, and ritual issues, an attempt to reconcile doctrines across sectarian lines was tantamount to religious treason. The syncretist was a suspicious character, like a double agent whose loyalties and commitments were profoundly questionable. If one starts from the assumption that religious groups have clear doctrinal boundaries and mutually exclusive memberships, then syncretism challenges the territorial system worked out by competing religious groups. However, the territorial model is not suitable for all cultures. In China, for instance, religions tended to be neither credal nor exclusivistic; belief, practice, and membership in more than one religion was possible, in most cases without censure of any sort. Where religions are not mutually exclusive, syncretism need not be a betrayal. It is simply inappropriate to project Western value judgments about syncretism onto all world religions.

The charge that syncretism is random fails to distinguish it from eclecticism. In this view, syncretists juxtapose beliefs and practices, unconcerned about inconsistencies. Syncretism is then meaningless; it represents no rational, coherent pattern of religious belief or behavior. Like good Methodists who practice Hatha Yoga for health and beauty, syncretists are unaware that they are living with two religious world views. In study of traditional cultures, such as China, this view has come from the inability of scholars to perceive any pattern or meaning in what seemed a religious hodgepodge. Sometimes no order exists, but I would argue that true randomness should be differentiated from syncretism; I term the former eclecticism. Eclecticism is idiosyncratic or whimsical, a bold openness to experimentation. Syncretism, on the other hand, attempts to reconcile elements from more than one religion. The reconciliation may not be apparent to observers unless they understand the way in which elements have been altered to fit their new context. This distinction between eclecticism and syncretism may seem arbitrary, but it is useful for the study of religion, for it distinguishes two unrelated but often confused forms of religious thought and behavior.

A third view rejects syncretism as corrupt, lacking in intellectual or doctrinal integrity. It is "unity at the expense of truth." Syncretists are confused, deluded, and simpleminded; their ideas corrupt and distort religious tradition. They fall into this error because they are attempting to reconcile the irreconcilable. Such a view is held by Richard Gombrich in his book on Singhalese Buddhism. He denies that Singhalese Buddhism is "corrupt" or "syncretistic" (note that the two are identified) since Hindu and local deities have been integrated into the structure of the Buddhist pantheon and are not seen as incompatible with Buddhist doctrine; whereas of some modern efforts to assimilate Western ideas with Buddhism he says, "This is syncretism, because it shatters the Buddhist framework."[8] The main difficulty with Gombrich's view is that it begs the question of who defines orthodoxy. Do those involved in East-West syncretism see it as shattering the Buddhist framework? Did the assimilation of Hindu and local deities have no impact on Buddhism? In both cases it would be more instructive to examine the impact of syncretism, the changes it produced, than to make a value judgment about its success, especially against a norm which is not adequately defined.

This view, carried to an extreme, would deny the fact of religious change. Religious synthesis would be valid only when it integrated disparate elements from two traditions while fully retaining their original definitions, overtones, connotations, and associations. By that standard, ordinary syncretism is an impoverishment of tradition. However, syncretism is a process of religious interaction and change. Any interaction, such as a dialogue, subtly modifies terms and symbols as they move from one symbolic context to another. In fact, they must be changed in order to fit into their new context. Likewise, religious symbols and ideas are modified through interaction, taking on new meanings and discarding old ones. The changes may take the direction of greater complexity and profundity or of simplification. To be properly understood, syncretism must first be evaluated in the light of its internal coherence, and only then measured against the yardstick of tradition or philosophical profundity.

A fourth view sees syncretism as superficial largely because syncretists are would-be peacemakers who promote doctrinal reconciliation with wishful thinking. In their attempt to reconcile the irreconcilable, syncretists resort to slogans or sweeping generalizations which reflect heart more than head, principle more than doctrine. They are troubled by religious polemic and dogmatism and yearn for a world of mutual understanding, tolerance, and unity. Thus they proclaim the unity of all faiths and assert that "all is one," ignoring the distinctive world views and beliefs of differing traditions and groups. In discussions of Chinese syncretism, these sweeping and virtually meaningless slogans have often been brought forward as paradigms of syncretic thought:

> The teachings are three, but the Way is one.
> Confucianism is the sun; Buddhism is the moon; Taoism is the stars.
> Confucianism governs the state; Taoism governs the body; Buddhism governs the mind.

These slogans do not inform us about syncretism; they are little more than a call for harmony or peaceful coexistence. However, there is a difference between syncretic slogans and statements which exhibit syncretic attitudes and reconciliations; the latter show *how* various religious elements are reconciled instead of merely proclaiming their essential unity or their broadly complementary functions.

The general objections to syncretism, then, reflect the polemical history of Western religions and intellectual predilections for purist or elitist philosophies. They ignore the etymology of the term, syn-cret-ism; this derives from a historic incident in which the citizens of Crete overcame internal disputes and banded together to face a common enemy.⁹ In the etymological paradigm, views were reconciled not in an arbitrary or irrational way, but to serve a purpose—survival. Likewise, religious syncretism is not arbitrary or irrational, but serves a religious function. One must start from the assumption that syncretism serves some positive religious role before one can understand it as a meaningful category. Not all would agree that this is possible; historian of religion Robert Baird has attempted systematically to demonstrate that syncretism is irredeemable as a technical category in the study of religion.[10]

Baird defines the task of the historian of religion as the accurate description of the ultimate concerns of the human past. He objects to the category of syncretism on several grounds: (1) It is used in conflicting ways, even by one author. (2) The search for historical origins is pointless because there is no room for a first cause. "The historian must jump into the stream of history somewhere if he is to study anything."[11] (3) The process of borrowing, blending, and influencing is equally part of all religions, so that to call them syncretistic says nothing distinctive about them. (4) The term is, in most cases, used when conflicting ideas or practices are brought together without benefit of consistency. If true harmony is achieved, contends Baird, the word "synthesis" would do as well. (5) Finally, the concept "syncretism" itself is irrelevant to those inside those faiths. Thus, this category can only serve to widen the gap between the observer and the subject of the study, and it should be dropped from the lexicon of serious scholars.

It is possible to meet Baird's objections. First, the lack of a clear definition for syncretism does not mean that no such definition is possible; I will attempt one below.

Second, while the search for origins can degenerate into pointless pedantry, it would be naïve and antihistorical for scholars to ignore the immediate forces and influences which have shaped the articulation of religious thought at a specific point in history. There is, after all, a context from which religious consciousness emerges; understanding that context is essential to the sort of accurate description and understanding which Baird himself advocates. It is not a search for first causes.

Third, it is true that the sheer fact of borrowing, blending, and influencing is in itself insignificant and even trivial; failure to recognize that fact has detracted from studies of syncretism. However, it is not trivial to analyze *what* has or has not been borrowed or blended, and *what* has or has not influenced specific religious thinkers at specific points in history. It is not the fact of borrowing, but the *selectivity* and *intention* of borrowing that add to our understanding of religious thought.[12] Further, the universality of syncretism, far from devaluing it, suggests that it is a vital force in the dynamics of religious change.

Fourth, Baird contends that syncretism is essentially failed synthesis. Synthesis, however, is an overly exacting ideal. A synthesis of all elements of two traditions is almost inconceivable; two world views and symbol systems cannot be neatly melded into a whole. To the charge that syncretism represents unreconciled conflict, I would argue that the conflict is in the eye of the observer, not of the syncretist. Syncretists either combine ideas and practices in which they perceive no conflict or they reconcile them by redefinition. If the observer sees conflict, it is because he fails to recognize how borrowed elements have been redefined.

Finally, it is true that syncretism is a heuristic construct of the historian of religion. There was certainly no such term in traditional Chinese religious thought. However, borrowing, integration, and influence did not go unnoticed; the three religions were not "treated as one" to that extent. There were concepts such as the integration of the Three Teachings (*san-chiao ho-i*), the reconciliation of the Three Teachings (*san-chiao t'iao-ho*), and slogans like "three doctrines, one way" (*chiao san tao i*). Further, because there were always critics, syncretists such as Lin Chao-en were repeatedly called upon to defend or justify their stand. Insofar as this was an articulated position which they defended in principle, it is simply not true to say that syncretism was irrelevant to them.

I have attempted to meet both the general and the scholarly

objections to syncretism as a category; it remains to propose a definition which can serve as a useful tool for this study.

TOWARD A DEFINITION OF SYNCRETISM

Syncretism may be tentatively defined as the borrowing, affirmation, or integration of concepts, symbols, or practices of one religious tradition into another by a process of selection and reconciliation. Syncretic borrowing may not be entirely conscious, but it is not a hypocritical manipulation. As one scholar put it, the "subjective experience of the truth of syncretistic eclecticism must not be overlooked."[13]

Syncretism is here defined as a religious category. There may be analogous forms of syncretism, in politics and philosophy, for instance, in which parties incorporate ideas from other systems of thought. These share a certain psychological tension, since (from another's point of view) the syncretist often seems to be violating his or her fundamental values. However, the proposed definition takes into account only religious syncretism. Let me first clarify what I mean by "religious." For the purposes of this study, I will adopt Streng's definition of religion as a "means of ultimate transformation," with his qualification that religion has transcendent or ultimate dimensions, personal or experiential dimensions, and traditional or cultural dimensions.[14] This definition is not culture-bound, projecting one form of religiosity as the universal standard for judging religion. In China alone, there is such a variety of religious praxes that one needs a very broad rubric to encompass all that is religious. The definition distinguishes between tradition (the cultural, objective, observable legacy of communal religious experience) and personal experience of religion and the ultimate. Such a distinction is useful for this study, for syncretism is a reformulation of traditions in personal religious experience which is sometimes reincorporated into tradition as a whole.

Syncretism, as opposed to eclecticism, assumes a firm basis of religious authority. It is not simply a random juxtaposition of elements into an idiosyncratic whole, but the incorporation of various elements into a home tradition. Most commonly syncretism is an enrichment and reinterpretation of the syncretist's lifelong religion, building on traditional forms of authority to verify the orthodoxy of the new vision. Occasionally, the syncretist breaks off to found a new tradition, but he or she must still rely on traditionally recognized forms of authority to authenticate religious experience and expression. Religious traditions vary in their degrees of centralization and systematization; they also have looser or more rigid orthodoxies. Many, in fact, have several levels of orthodoxy; orthodoxies defined by the state, orthodoxies defined by the intellectual or ecclesiastical elite, orthodoxies defined by the intellectual and religious trends of the time. It is the existence of these orthodoxies which makes the selection and reconciliation process necessary for syncretists. Syncretists are not trying to step outside the bounds of tradition; they are trying to reform it or to recapture its essence. Syncretists must therefore reconcile their borrowing in terms they can defend as "orthodox."

The dynamics of syncretism suggest yet another dimension of orthodoxy, which might be termed internal or gut orthodoxy. Any tradition has an orthodoxy defined by external forces; there is also, however, an internalized sense of the core of tradition that varies with each individual. Part of the dynamic of religious change is that individuals come to feel that the tradition as they received it has been desiccated. It no longer directly conveys the essence of religion, the sacred transformative power which alters lives. These individuals identify with the tradition, but their internalized view of "orthodoxy" may differ somewhat from the view of their age; their religious discontent opens them to new definitions, images, and symbols which can reform and revitalize tradition. The more they borrow and the greater the impact these borrowed elements have on the home tradition, the more syncretists will be concerned with orthodoxy. They have internalized boundaries which they dare not go beyond for fear of losing their religious identification. The closer they come to these boundaries, the more important it is to proclaim their loyalty and the rightness of their vision. The notion of internal orthodoxy helps explain why syncretists often vehemently attack heresy and errors. The psychology is that of a boundary situation; there is an inherent tension, a threat of disloyalty, when tradition is being reformed or redefined.

Although syncretism does not shatter traditions, it does change them, sometimes radically. The impact of syncretism depends on the extent of the borrowing and the centrality of the elements borrowed. The first is quantitative; how much is borrowed from outside? Are merely a few isolated practices or ideas borrowed, or a substantial body of new material? In the former case, the new ideas can be reconciled or "tucked into" tradition with little or no impact, while in the latter even after reconciliation the tradition will have a strikingly new face. The second is more qualitative; how central to the religious vision and practice of the tradition are the elements borrowed? Does the borrowing, in fact, represent a new turn, a new emphasis, in the definition of core belief and practice? One element, such as meditation, can make an enormous difference to the religious nature of a system; it has extensive ramifications which the tradition will have to digest.

Syncretism may take place at the conceptual level or at the level of ritual or practice. Where a tradition has a well-defined orthodoxy, the tendency will be for borrowing to begin at the level of individual practice by means of what one scholar calls "substitution." In substitution, a religious habit from another tradition may replace one of like function in the home tradition. One example is the practice of Indian Christians who touch sacred icons or pictures as an act of devotion which allows them to sense the divine presence.[15] Since the function is a familiar and acceptable one, there is less danger of feeling the threat of heresy than might occur in the borrowing of ideas.

It is difficult to imagine a historical situation in which a person or group would set out systematically to integrate *all* aspects of two religious traditions. The result would be a cumbersome, hybrid monster. Rather, syncretism tends to be highly selective, and the patterns of selectivity reflect the particular religious needs and interests of the syncretist and the historical and cultural nexus against which they emerged. The pattern of selectivity is much more significant than the mere fact of borrowing.

Aside from selectivity, syncretism requires that borrowed elements be reconciled, sometimes radically reinterpreted, to accommodate them to the world view and doctrines of the home tradition. Van der Leeuw calls this reconciliation "transposition."[16] One might also use a linguistic metaphor and call it "translation." At first glance, translation may seem to be arbitrary, superficial, or downright distorting; however, it is not the intention of syncretists to maintain the integrity of the borrowed idea in terms of its original tradition. Their task, rather, is to reform, illuminate, or revivify their own religious vision within the rules and framework of their tradition. What is intellectually significant is not the synthesis of world views, but rather the evolution of religious vision, and the modulation of a tradition and its orthodoxy.[17] Syncretists are not usually ecumenical diplomats seeking peace between warring traditions; they are religious persons seeking to respond to new religious tensions and needs.

Religious borrowing may or may not be consciously syncretic. What to the observer seems a syncretic adaptation may be perceived by participants as emerging naturally from within their tradition. One might cite, for example, the practice of self-cultivation through quiet sitting and the metaphysical speculations on the mind among Sung Neo-Confucians, who felt themselves to be revitalizing their own tradition as a reaction against Buddhist and Taoist excesses. To the historian of religion, the syncretic debt of the Neo-Confucians is clear; yet that debt would have been indignantly denied by many Neo-Confucians. Identifying the syncretic debt does more than label the origins of the ideas, and it certainly does not undermine their validity in the Confucian tradition. It helps rather to clarify how the process of arming themselves against the "errors" of Buddhism transformed and broadened their religious vision. It helps to clarify the historic affinities between Neo-Confucian thought and certain overtly syncretic strains which emerged at the same period in the Taoist school. Finally, it helps us to understand how a few centuries later some who followed in the line of Neo-Confucians could begin to interpret their heritage in overtly syncretic ways, while considering themselves "orthodox" followers of Neo-Confucianism.

The definition proposed above covers a wide variety of phenomena, from unconscious borrowing to elaborate and well-articulated syntheses of two or more traditions. The reader may question whether it is useful to propose so broad a category. It may be that this definition will prove to be in need of further clarification and narrowing over the long run. However, I believe it would be premature to narrow it arbitrarily at this point. One reason is that advocates of the reconciliation of the Three Teachings in China, including Lin Chao-en, cited historical precedents for their stand which included all manner of borrowing, influence, unconscious debts, and so forth. Since they viewed these as a loose "tradition" of Three Teachings thought, it is useful for us also to view them in that light. Further, since these phenomena have not, for the most part, been rigorously studied in a syncretic framework, it is difficult at this juncture to judge which cases are the most fertile for illuminating patterns of religious interaction. There is clearly a difference between the isolated borrowing of a ritual and a clearly articulated synthesis of significant doctrinal elements. However, it is likely that borrowing in some cases paved the way for a more thoroughgoing synthesis, or that the same historical situation shaped both the limited and the more radical form of syncretism. Study of the differences can shed light on the religious issues of the day.

CHAPTER TWO

SYNCRETISM AND SECTARIANISM IN EARLY CHINA

Religious pluralism has been the norm in China. Over the centuries patterns of interaction and modes of thought have evolved by which the Chinese dealt with this situation. While the apogee of full-blown syncretism—Three Teachings cults, Three Teachings halls, articulated and detailed accommodations of the three religions—occurred between the Sung (960–1279) and Ming (1368–1644) dynasties, the patterns of thought and interaction had developed during preceding centuries in an interplay of competitive and accommodative impulses. In vying for privileged positions in sectarian competition, each of the three traditions was led to syncretism. Thus, sectarian motives led to syncretic activity. A history of syncretism is beyond the scope of the present volume.[1] This chapter will paint in broad strokes some of the early patterns of religious interaction which set the stage for later syncretism.

THE CLASSICAL PERIOD: TRANSMITTING THE WAY OF THE ANCIENTS

The Chou dynasty (1122–256 B.C.E.) was founded on a type of ritual feudalism which combined ancestor and nature worship. At the pinnacle was heaven, the first ancestor and ruler of all nature. Only the king of Chou could worship heaven directly, for he was the "Son of Heaven." Local rulers worshiped their first ancestors, who were the lords of their domains, and the nature spirits who dwelt in their lands. As their ancestors and nature spirits paid deference to heaven in the spiritual hierarchy, so these rulers deferred to the king of Chou. The hierarchies of the spirit world, the ritual world, and the political world mirrored each other in a divine symmetry. Over the centuries, however, the political and military balance of power shifted dramatically until by 771 B.C.E., when the capital was moved east, the Chou king controlled the political order in name only; he had become a ritual rubber stamp, giving *ex post facto* sanction to changes in boundaries, alliances, and rulers. The symmetrical heavenly order was in disarray. So was the political world. Small states were annexed or forced into unfavorable alliances. Rulers were unseated by intrigues. Any semblance of stability was impossible in the atmosphere of intense competition. Political debate was dominated by a single question: who would be able to reunify China, and on what basis could he restore a stable government and society?

One side of the debate argued that the strongest and wealthiest ruler most skillful at military and political strategy and social control would be the inevitable victor. Such thinking spawned the Realist or Legalist school, advocates of law and order, strong and stable government, tightly regulated social institutions, and strict and swift punishments. Since the religious foundations of Chou sovereignty had been discredited by the events of recent history, they considered it necessary to dispense with outmoded values and to think pragmatically about the problems before their eyes. However, two other sides of the debate looked back through the morass of the present to ancient religious values for a better way. They in effect radically redefined their religious heritage to found the traditions we call Confucianism and Taoism.

Confucius was quite emphatic about his reliance on tradition. He said, "I transmit but do not create. I believe in and love the ancients."[2] He looked to the paragons of the early

Chou, studying them assiduously for their moral lessons. The virtue of the Chou and the heart of the way of heaven was to be found, he thought, in *li*, ritual.[3] *Li* originally meant sacrifice; through sacrifice the ruler became a channel for the ruling power of the spirits. However, in the Chou, *li* also referred to the court ceremonials which gave visible form to the spiritual and political hierarchy. The rituals were, in the mind of Confucius, the basis of the harmony and order of the early Chou. Confucius further expanded the definition of *li* to encompass all social rituals; they became for him the definition of civilized and moral behavior appropriate to all social roles as defined in the five relationships: parent-child, ruler-subject, husband-wife, elder-younger, friend-friend. Thus social courtesies, ancestor worship, filial piety, and basic civilized behavior had external forms in ritual. The external behavior had to be balanced by internal moral attitudes, such as humanity, righteousness, trustworthiness. Ritual was the symbol of civilized behavior; it was the means through which learning and wisdom could be translated into action; it was the outer manifestation of the character of the good man. The promise of a harmonious social order rested on the base of personal moral cultivation. In his understanding of ritual, Confucius went far beyond a slavish imitation of the Chou; he looked to tradition to find its essence and in turn redefined tradition and revivified it in terms of this new understanding. The way of the ancients took on a new face and form in the teachings of this man.

Lao Tzu and Chuang Tzu, the founders of Taoism,[4] also looked to the past, but for them the lesson of the past was not embodied in the achievements of Chou civilization. We know little about the ineffable Lao Tzu,[5] but it is significant that Chuang Tzu came from a state inhabited by descendants of the earlier Shang dynasty (1523–1122 B.C.E.), which had been conquered by the Chou.[6] He harbored no special affection for the decaying Chou state. But the problem was not just with the Chou. Lao Tzu and Chuang Tzu looked back to a Way that was not embodied in the classics of human learning or in the advances of human society; they looked rather to a simpler time when humans had lived in harmony with the natural world untainted by the so-called glories of learning and civilization. The present mess, they felt, was simply the natural result of misguided attempts to establish human society and civilization as superior to the Way of nature.

As Confucius had radically redefined *li*, Lao Tzu redefined the term Tao. "Tao" meant basically way or path; secondarily it meant method, principle, and moral teaching. Lao Tzu looked beyond all these "ways" to the one, original Way, the source and sustainer of all life. The Way or Tao was the source of all, and its movements in the world could be most clearly seen in nature. It was the simple, spontaneous, yet ordered actions of nature; it followed what was natural rather than trying to improve on it. The Way required humans to acknowledge that their individual and collective lives were not the center of reality but only part of a larger whole. Only by conforming to and flowing with the stream of the Tao could real stability and power be attained. Because the fundamental symbols for the Tao were natural symbols, one might say that the early Taoists radically redefined the ancient tradition of nature worship, although in this case the redefinition was radical indeed.

Thus both Confucians and Taoists established their traditions as we know them by reformulation of tradition in light of the present. Even these "founders" did not see themselves as creating a new vision. They looked to their ancient heritage. Likewise, throughout Chinese religious history, radical religious innovations were expressed and experienced as a recapturing of the wisdom of the past.

The major pattern of interaction during the period of classical philosophy was debate. Advocates of all schools vied for the ears of rulers, hoping for a chance to test their theories in the political arena. Their writings illustrate how aware they were of rival positions, and how eager to demonstrate the advantages of their own. The lively competition produced more than nasty jibes; many adopted ideas from other schools to strengthen their positions. Nonaction (*wu-wei*), for example, was used alike by Legalists, Taoists, and Confucians to illustrate the power of their ideas for instituting a stable society.

There is some debate as to whether nonaction originated

among the Legalists or the Taoists,[7] but its broadest religious meaning was certainly Taoist. To the Taoists, nonaction was action in accordance with the Tao. It was not self-centered, scheming, manipulative, or acquisitive action. It was not aggressive or contentious. It was relaxed, effortless, selfless. It flowed with the Tao, letting Tao act through the self. It was not the self but the Tao which acted, and hence the action was always fruitful.

> The Tao never acts yet nothing is left undone.
> Should lords and princes be able to hold fast to it,
> The myriad creatures will be transformed of their own accord.[8]

Nonaction was the best, most powerful action, for the Tao was the basis of the natural self-transformation of things.

For the Legalists, nonaction was a powerful political strategem. The ruler, to insure his continued strength, should never show his hand in overt action. He should rather follow nonaction, withdrawing from the public eye and letting his ministers act in his stead. Nonaction let him see the true minds of his subjects; if he did not show his hand, others would constantly have to show theirs without knowing what he wanted. Nonaction could enhance his mystique, keeping him remote from the prying eyes of potential rivals; being remote, he would not display human foibles and vulnerabilities. Nonaction also could insure the impersonal and just application of laws; if he were inaccessible as a ruler, no one could curry favor to seek special dispensation from punishments and regulations. Nonaction could keep the ruler one step removed from the political fray; the ministers would bear the brunt of political problems. The best way to remain king of the mountain would be to avoid challenges; if he fought all his battles personally, he would soon be exhausted and vulnerable.

For the Confucians, nonaction represented the efficacy of ritual when each person assumed his or her proper role.

> Confucius said, "To take no action and yet have the empire well governed, Shun was the man. What did he do? He merely made himself reverent and correctly faced south."[9]

By facing south, the sage ruler Shun assumed the correct ritual position of the ruler; since he did so reverently and correctly, government and the ordering of society were effortless. To Confucians, ritual was a civilizing influence that allowed each person to fulfill his role and work with others without friction.[10] It is particularly striking that Confucius co-opted the notion of *wu-wei*, since he was an advocate of dynamic moral action and civilizing effort. He could simply have attacked the notion as morally irresponsible. Instead he borrowed it to enrich his position about ritual, arguing that ritual was not as forced and unnatural as Taoist critics suggested. This strategy was effective; it mitigated the impression of a society constantly consulting the ritual classics and nervously weighing the proper course of action by positing a counterimage of a civilized world in which decorum flowed naturally and effortlessly from the font of moral character.

Thus from very early times, Confucianism and Taoism defined themselves in dialogue with each other and with the past. Synchronic dialogue, such as the debate on *wu-wei*, and diachronic dialogue between present and past constantly enriched Chinese religious traditions.

HAN:
ONE WAY UNDER HEAVEN

After centuries of disorder, China was finally unified under a central government in 221 B.C.E. After a brief and violent dynasty which discredited the Legalist position in Chinese eyes, the Han dynasty (200 B.C.E.–220 C.E.) elevated Confucianism to be the state ideology, a position it held until 1911. The establishment of a centralized empire encompassing a territory far greater than had ever been under Chinese influence had its impact on Confucianism, indeed on all Chinese religious thought. Suddenly "all under heaven," the vast part of the known world, was the dominion of Chinese civilization, and the standardized script, weights, measures, and axle lengths (which made the roads accessible to all) allowed for unprecedented cultural unity. As man's world had become rationalized and ordered, so it seemed that the entire cosmos, physical and spiritual, was the product of rational and orderly forces. In their exhilaration at their social and cultural achievements, Han intellectuals believed that they could understand, indeed could map or chart, these orderly principles. All reality was the product of these forces and reflected the rational order.

The optimism of Han intellectuals made the cosmic order seem all-inclusive. It was not that things, events, thoughts, and feelings had to live up to some rigorous standard of rational law to be seen as real; it was rather that the cosmic principles had to be broad enough to account for all experience: material, historical, emotive, intellectual, and spiritual. Likewise, all ideas, even religious ideas, with a shred of veracity were a part of the Way of heaven.[11] Taoism and Confucianism, along with a variety of more magical or spiritualistic religious beliefs, each took its place in the world view. The differences were not obliterated, but whatever effectiveness they had was now seen to derive from the same inclusive cosmic order. This belief in the unity of the Way of heaven established a foundation for syncretic thought; unless religious ideas could be shown to be outright fantasies, they had some claim on truth, even if a distorted or partial truth. Distortion or partiality could be rectified; the believer was seldom called upon to choose one god or one truth over all others. The Way of heaven included all truths of man.

Another legacy of the Han period was a distinctive mode of thought which allowed the Chinese to relate and reconcile widely diverse phenomena and ideas by establishing chains of correspondence. Reconciliation by chains of correspondence was pivotal to much syncretic thought in China, including that of Lin Chao-en. Han thinkers celebrated the cosmic order represented in its simplest form by the triad of heaven, earth, and man. The most visible manifestation of cosmic order was the regular movements of the heavenly bodies. The order of the natural world on earth mirrored the heavenly order; the tides, the seasons, and the cycles of animal and vegetable life followed the movements of heaven. Likewise the human world, whether the external social world which lies between the realms of heaven and earth or the internal world of the body and thought, had to reflect that order if humans were to remain in touch with the only real basis for order in the world. The Han philosophers believed that humans could understand and follow that order; the ruler was to be the pivot uniting the realms of heaven, earth, and man and holding them in their perfect balance.

Perfect moral and cosmic order had to embrace all reality. The broad pattern was not a problem; as long as the Han empire remained stable, the general correspondence of the realms of heaven, earth, and man seemed an obvious truism. But it was more difficult to integrate the panorama of the real world—including moral values, human feelings, plants, animals, human endeavors, musical notes, and colors—into a neat and symmetrical schema. To accomplish this, Han thinkers looked to older principles for identifying the basic forces in the universe. Yin and yang and the Five Phases had first been united in a primitive cosmology by one Tsou Yen, two hundred years before the Han. Yin and yang represented all the fundamental polarities of reality: light and dark, movement and rest, male and female, filled and empty, dry and moist, etc. The Five Phases [12] (*wu hsing*), Wood, Fire, Earth, Metal, and Water, were systematized to represent the phases through which things and forces in the world combined to create and destroy things; they were not static elements which defined the material constituents of the universe, but rather that through which change moves and flows. The eight trigrams and sixty-four hexagrams of the *Book of Changes* (*I ching*) dated from antiquity; in the Han they were systematized to represent more minutely the forces and cycles of change. Since the models were the movements of the plants and the agricultural year, change was understood as a cyclical rather than linear process. Even within what seems to be a linear development, such as an individual life or the tenure of a ruler, there are many cycles and many beginnings. Yin and yang, the Five Phases, the trigrams and hexagrams, were correlated with each other and with astrological signs, musical notes, colors, flavors, feelings, virtues, animals, birds, seasons, organs of the body, and all other phenomena. The detailed systems of correspondence need not detain us here; what is important is the mode of thought involved.[13]

Let us take an example. In the Chinese system, *hsin* (heart and mind) corresponded to the phase of Earth. The relationship is expressed in the Chinese phrase *hsin t'u yeh*, which is translated "mind is Earth." However, the phrase does not imply, as the English translation does, a logical *identification* between mind and Earth; it implies rather an association based on a chain of correspondences which is understood but not expressed in the statement. The phase Earth is associated with the center among directions; likewise the heart is considered central among the five organs, in a functional if not a spatial sense. In the case of this association, it is relatively simple to identify the justification for the correspondence, but in many cases the chain of correspondence was accepted even when the thinker could not articulate its basis. It became a customary way of relating things.

Han thinkers were not fussbudgets who created the correspondences to tidy up the universe and put everything in its proper little nook. In their eyes understanding the correspondences clarified the cosmic principles behind all processes and phenomena, and thus allowed humans to understand and control them. Through them the secrets of the universe could be controlled at the source. The power made available through understanding the cosmos was illustrated in the mystique of the emperor, who was the pivot of the triad of heaven, earth, and man, and thus responsible for upholding the entire cosmic order. It was also illustrated in the theories of the Han alchemists, whose systems were readapted by later Taoists and from them by Lin Chao-en.

The classic of Han alchemy was the *Chou-i ts'an t'ung ch'i* (The homology of the triad in the *Book of Changes*).[14] It applied the trigrams and hexagrams of the Changes along with their various correspondences in Han thought to three areas: government, cultivating human nature, and the preparation of the elixir of life. Each section of the book was divided into these three areas, although the three were said to be mutually illuminating. They were all modeled directly and literally on the laws of movement in the *Book of Changes*. The alchemical laboratory was a microcosm of nature and the cosmos, and the creation of the elixir of life drew on the secrets of creation in nature. The timing of each stage of the process was rigorously modeled on the cycle of change and the movements of the heavens; the mixing of ingredients and balancing of opposing forces such as heating and cooling the elixir followed the principles of the Five Phases. The elixir bestowed life because it "stole" the secrets of creation and checked the forces of destruction.

The system of correspondences developed by Han thinkers both reflected their exhilaration with the power of human culture and gave them a means to solidify and extend that power. It also gave them a means for reconciling diverse ideas within the all-embracing Way, which was used to advantage by later syncretists. For instance, a Buddhist attempting to reconcile the five moral precepts of Buddhism with Confucian moral values used the Han system of correspondences as a bridge between the two religions:

> Concerning the teachings, there are five precepts. Not to kill is paired with the east, the east is Wood, and Wood is based on humaneness. The meaning of humaneness is to preserve life. Not to steal is paired with the north, the north is Water, and Water is based on knowledge. The one who knows does not steal. Not to commit adultery is paired with the west, the west is Metal, and Metal is based on righteousness. The one who is righteous does not commit adultery. Not to drink intoxicating liquor is paired with the south, the south is Fire, Fire is based on propriety. Propriety means to be protected against committing faults. Not to tell lies is paired with the center, the center is Earth, Earth is based on trustworthiness. The one who tells lies is cunning, perverse, and double-headed; he is not in conformity with rectitude. The one who is upright is not biased or perverse.[15]

By using the system of correspondences, the Buddhist could associate the five precepts with the five virtues without claiming that they were logically identical.

THE PERIOD OF DISUNION: BUDDHIST ACCOMMODATIONS AND ACCOMMODATIONS WITH BUDDHISM

After the fall of the Han in 220 C.E., China fell into a long period of disunion; it was not reunited under one government until 589. The collapse of the great empire which had been "all under heaven" also undermined the naïve faith in the ability of human reason to grasp the order of the cosmos. A new movement in Taoism, called Neo-Taoism in Western scholarship, denied that the Tao ordered the world or was the basis of any reliable natural or moral laws; Tao was Nonbeing (*wu*) and simply followed the natural or spontaneous (*tzu-jan*), behind which was no eternal or transcendent order. The disillusionment of a dream lost also opened many intellectuals to Buddhist notions of suffering and the emptiness of ordinary reality.

During the long centuries of disillusionment, Confucianism, Taoism, and Buddhism vied for the hearts and minds of the Chinese. The three religions competed for adherents, but even more importantly for the patronage and support of the imperial court and local notables. The stakes were real: money; influence; support for temples, scholarship, and rituals; even political power. They were also in a sense spiritual, for each religion had its own social ideals; only with the support of the court and officials could these be realized. The state intensified the competition between religions by its assumption that it had the right to control religious institutions and to define acceptable religious practices. There was no concept of separation of church and state in China. A religion whose adherents offended the government might be legally proscribed and its books burned; adherents of opposing views frequently recommended such measures. Thus competition for official support and patronage had a strong influence on syncretic and sectarian attitudes in the history of Chinese religion.

Given this situation, foreign religions seeking to gain a foothold in China were forced to engage in what might be called acculturative syncretism, accommodating themselves to the beliefs and practices of Chinese culture. When Buddhism first entered China, the Buddha was worshiped as another form of Lao Tzu; the Chinese did not yet understand that he represented a distinctive doctrine. An early Buddhist apologist sought an audience by defending his doctrine on Confucian grounds. When asked why, he replied, "It is because *you* know the contents (of the classics) that I quote them. If I should speak about the words of the Buddhist sutras and explain the essential meaning of Nirvāṇa, it would be like speaking about the five colours to the blind, or playing the five tones to the deaf."[16] Further, early translations of Buddhist writings often used the device of matching meanings (*ko-i*), using native, often Taoist, philosophical terms as "matching" very loose translations of the Sanskrit terms; this was a variation of reconciliation by correspondence, discussed in the last section. As verbal and philosophical equivalents, these "matchings" were misleading and caused considerable confusion, but they were an attempt by the Chinese to understand Buddhism in the religious terms most meaningful to them.

Buddhist attempts at accommodation illustrate the problems of the syncretic transposition and translation of ideas discussed in chapter one. The Buddhists faced not only the considerable problem of translating Sanskrit into Chinese (usually through at least one central Asian language as an intermediary), but also of translating a radically different religious world view which reflected a different culture. Linguistic, cultural, and historical problems intertwined to complicate the task.[17] Buddhism had arisen at roughly the same time as Confucianism and Taoism in response to a very different religious debate in India. Indians at that time saw life as suffering, the product of endless rebirths, an unending wheel of change and repetition. They sought liberation from the world of suffering and rebirth in the Absolute, the eternal, unchanging real. The Buddhists broke off from the Hindus in this debate by denying the existence of an Absolute; liberation, they claimed, came in the realization of the impermanence and interdependence of all reality, all things and selves. They agreed with dominant Hindu schools, however, that liberation required a life of renunciation of the world and its pleasures to seek religious fulfillment.

These ideas were not merely new to the Chinese; they ran directly counter to Chinese religious assumptions. The Chinese saw the world as real and potentially the perfect embodiment of the Way. They believed in the eternity of change, but saw change as governed by the cosmic laws of the Way of heaven. Change was to them rational and ordered, not a curse from which they had to be liberated. They affirmed the reality of all things, seeing them as products of the cosmic laws. Finally, they saw no need of renouncing this world or this life; rather, they felt that affirming this life was the highest form of religious acceptance. To be sure, Confucian and Taoist views of the affirmation of this world differed, but both were affirmations of a reality here and now.

Thus the Buddhists faced not only the problem of finding precise linguistic equivalents; more important, they had to find terms in Chinese which would convey the religious meaning and connotations of their words. The process was further complicated by the fact that almost eight centuries of debate and commentaries had complicated Buddhism by the time missionaries arrived in China; it was not the pragmatic and simple sermons of the historical Buddha which were being translated, but the far more technical and sophisticated philosophical speculations of later Buddhist schools.

The Mahāyāna Buddhists, who advocated universal salvation aided by the compassion of myriads of Buddhas and Bodhisattvas, had reason not to be discouraged by the obstacles facing their propagation of the faith. They had developed the notion of skillful means (*upāya*), which averred that the historical Buddha had tailored his teachings to the abilities of his audience to hear and understand. He had deliberately held back some of the higher truths of Buddhist law in order to reach his audience. Following the Buddha's skillful means as a model, the Mahāyānists saw doctrine as a means to an end, which was enlightenment; in moving people toward that end, it did not matter if the means were less than accurate or even slightly misleading. The aim was to stimulate interest in and attention to the truths of the Buddhist way; the "packaging" was less important. Hence although the practice of "matching meanings" did violence to orthodox Buddhist doctrine, it started a religious dialogue which was the first step in propagating Buddhist truths. This dialogue in turn enriched the Taoist tradition by stimulating speculation on change and Nonbeing.

The Buddhists also had to alter their practices to gain a foothold in the religious life of the Chinese people. The best example is their prominent role in funeral and memorial services. Since Buddhists denied the existence of the soul, it seems bizarre that they should preside over prayers for the comfort of the soul. However, this practice accommodated the Buddhist religion to the deeply entrenched Chinese belief in ancestor worship, and it gave Buddhists a role in the most powerful religious moments of Chinese life. Funeral sermons often exemplified acculturative syncretism; they would begin and/or end with a Buddhist statement of the ultimate emptiness of all souls, but the middle portion treated the souls as though they existed to assist mourners in their profound grief.

The intense rivalry between Buddhism and Taoism during the period of disunion stimulated a form of religious borrowing which might be called "adversary syncretism." In vying for support, Buddhists and Taoists co-opted all elements which might enhance their stand as long as they could be reconciled in any way with their own tradition. A famous example of adversary syncretism is the *hua-hu* (conversion of the barbarians) controversy, in which each side forged scriptures which became increasingly "ancient" and "authoritative." The Taoists claimed that Lao Tzu had gone to India to become the historical Buddha Gautama; in teaching Buddhism, he was trying to convert the Indians to Taoism. Thus Buddhism was nothing but a slight distortion of Taoism, and subordinate to its mother tradition. The Buddhists, on the other hand, claimed that Lao Tzu had left China in disillusionment and was converted by the Buddha. Originally the legend was a Chinese attempt to honor the Buddha by giving him a historical link with the Chinese sages, but it later became a ground for polemical battles. In the course of this controversy, each side adopted many deities from the other side into its pantheon (in properly subordinate positions, of course) and plagiarized the writings of the other side to assimilate concepts and rituals into their spiritual territory.[18] The motivation may have been more sectarian than syncretic, but the borrowed elements were integrated into the host traditions and made of them a richer religious store. Moreover, the borrowed items were selected and reformulated to bring them within the accepted limits of the host tradition. The historical fact of competition caused both sides to reexamine and redefine their religious boundaries.

In the atmosphere of competition those schools under most direct attack resorted to what might be termed "defensive syncretism." When schools in favor attacked their religious rivals, the defendants had to argue their case in terms of predominant religious values. Defensive syncretism is related to acculturative syncretism; but in this case the problem was less accommodation to a new culture than accommodation to the dominant values of the day. To give but one example, when Emperor Wu of the Northern Chou (561–580) was about to persecute Buddhism, the monk Tao-an (dates unclear) wrote the *Erh-chiao lun* (On the two teachings) in defense of the legitimacy of Buddhism. Since the attack came from Confucians, Tao-an argued that Buddhism and Confucianism were not in conflict but rather occupied complementary spheres, governing respectively the inner and outer aspects of life.[19]

Through the long period of disunion, then, Buddhism established its foothold in Chinese culture. Syncretic interactions took acculturative, adversarial, and defensive forms. Sectarian competition and syncretic interaction played off against each other as the Three Teachings sought to find their place in the religious order. In the process all the traditions were considerably enriched.

T'ANG: SYNCRETISM AND SECTARIAN RIVALRY

Religious competition perhaps reached its height, and certainly its most institutionalized form, in the T'ang dynasty (618–907). The T'ang was the second great unified dynasty, representing a flowering of the power and culture of Chinese civilization. Religiously, it was complex. Because it was centralized and stable, the Confucian scholar-officials were powerful in the court and bureaucracy; Confucianism remained the state religion and Confucian classics were the basis of the state examinations. However, it was also a golden age for Buddhism and to some extent for Taoism. By the T'ang, Buddhism had established a firm foothold in Chinese culture. The Chinese had assimilated and sinified Buddhism, making their own sense out of its vast legacy. Chih-i (538–597), the founder of the T'ien-ta'i school of Mahāyāna Buddhism, building on the notion of the Lotus Sutra that all Buddhist teachings represented the one vehicle of Buddhism (although with varying degrees of completeness), classified the various schools and scriptures of Buddhism into a coherent system based on rational principles.[20] This syncretism within Buddhism opened the way for syncretism with other schools of Chinese thought. The T'ien-t'ai school was also the first of the uniquely Chinese schools of Buddhism, in which Buddhist learning, ritual, and practice flourished. During the T'ang period Buddhist monasteries and universities were lavishly supported by wealthy families and the court. In addition to supporting Buddhism, the imperial family considered itself to have a special relationship to Taoism. Its surname was Li, the purported surname of Lao Tzu's descendants. Privately, many T'ang emperors sponsored Taoist rites and supported Taoist temples. Thus all Three Teachings were active and influential at court.

The lively competition of the times was institutionalized in the Three Teachings debates at court. This series of confrontations took place intermittently, often on auspicious occasions like the emperor's birthday. Famous proponents of each school were invited to debate specified issues to establish the supremacy of their faith. Debates were often tense, as indicated in disputes over seating and ritual precedence. The Taoists were at a disadvantage, since their knowledge of Buddhism seems still to have been influenced by now-outmoded "matching" translations, such as *wu-wei* for Nirvāṇa or Tao for *bodhi* (enlightenment).[21] Repeated Taoist failures humiliated the Taoists and pointed to the need for revitalization of their intellectual tradition. Debates were sometimes followed by lighter diversions, such as farcical Three Teachings dramas, in which all schools were caricatured.²² These presumably served to defuse tensions. Although these diversions suggest a lighter side to the occasions, the involvement of eminent Confucians such as the poet Po Chü-i (772–846) in the debates suggests that they were not without intellectual pretensions.²³

These ritualized debates were hardly the basis for an in-depth ecumenical dialogue, but one scholar had concluded that "by virtue of such practices as the debates of the Three Teachings in the T'ang, the understanding and confluence of the Three Teachings progressed to the extent that failure to understand the doctrines of each of the other schools was a hindrance to the propagation of one's own doctrine."²⁴ The very fact of competition kept information flowing.

The strength of Buddhism in the T'ang alarmed some Confucians; they saw in the economic power of temples and the popular influence of Buddhist devotionalism a direct challenge to Confucian moral and social values. Han Yü (786–824) wrote his famous memorial on the Buddha's bone in reaction to a great processional in which this relic was to be displayed in the Chinese capital. Such was the Buddhist fervor of the times that throngs of believers lined the streets to view the procession, some even wounding themselves as a sign of their Buddhist piety. Han Yü asked the emperor to put an end to such displays and to curb the power of Buddhism:

> Now Buddha was a man of the barbarians who did not speak the language of China and wore clothes of a different fashion. His sayings did not concern the ways of our ancient kings, nor did his manner of dress conform to their laws. He understood neither the duties that bind sovereign and subject, nor the affections of father and son. If he were still alive today and came to our court by order of his ruler, Your Majesty might condescend to receive him, but it would amount to no more than one audience in the Hsüan-cheng Hall, a banquet by the Office for Receiving Guests, the presentation of a suit of clothes, and he would then be escorted to the borders of the nation, dismissed, and not allowed to delude the masses. How then, when he has long been dead, could his rotten bones, the foul and unlucky remains of his body, be rightly admitted to the palace? . . . Your servant is deeply shamed and begs that this bone be given to the proper authorities to be cast into fire and water, that this evil may be rooted out, the world freed from its error, and later generations spared this delusion.²⁵

It would seem that Han Yü was a pure sectarian, arrogantly anti-Buddhist. Not so. Han Yü had warm relations and discussions with Buddhist monks. There was a distinction between his public puritanical stance, which was concerned with keeping the masses from error and the government and social values from degeneracy, and his private stance, in which he felt free to explore Buddhist views with respect. Many Confucians followed Han Yü in being highly critical of the social aspects of Buddhism while privately admiring some of its intellectual ideas.

The Buddhists did not fail to respond to Han Yü's attack. Tsung-mi's (780–841) defense exemplified an interplay of sectarian pride and syncretistic accommodation. To him, all religions were part of the all-embracing Buddhist way. Within that way he ranked them according to the completeness of their understanding of truth, with Confucianism and Taoism at the bottom. More striking than this normative ranking, though, was the syncretic view of the complementarity of teachings.

> Confucius, Lao Tzu, and Shākya Buddha were perfect sages. They established their teachings according to the demands of the age and the needs of various beings. They differ, therefore, in their approach. Buddhist teachings and non-Buddhist teachings, however, complement each other; they benefit people, encourage them to perfect all good deeds, clarify the beginning and end of causal relationship, penetrate all phenomena (*dharma*), and throw light on [the relationship] between root and branch by which all things come into being. Although the teachings reflect the intentions of the sages, differences exist in that there are real and provisional doctrines. Confucianism and Taoism are provisional doctrines; Buddhism consists of both real and provisional doctrines. In that they encourage the perfection of good deeds, punish wicked ones, and reward good ones, all three teachings lead to the creation of an orderly society; for this they must be observed with respect.[26]

Even at the height of religious competition, the stage was set for the more full-blown syncretism of following periods.

CHAPTER THREE

THE HEYDAY OF SYNCRETISM

The dialectic of sectarian and syncretic forces in the long period from the political debates of the Chou to the Three Teachings debates of the T'ang established fundamental patterns of interaction which continued to influence the religious dynamic throughout Chinese history. However, the dominant pattern of competition for religious and intellectual influence put definite limits on syncretic impulses in this period; syncretism tended to serve sectarian ends.

During the Sung (960–1279), Yüan (1260–1368), and Ming (1368–1644) dynasties, however, syncretism became an increasingly powerful force, a positive ideal in its own right. During this period images of the Sages of the Three Teachings were enshrined in many temples, and Three Teachings halls dotted the countryside, particularly in the South.[1] The efflorescence of syncretism was stimulated by a variety of factors. The Sung was a period of considerable religious change; Confucians, Buddhists, and Taoists all reexamined and redefined the core of their traditions. The changes in the three religions manifested a confluence of religious concerns and ideas. As the three reformulated their traditions in light of similar questions, dialogue and positive interaction were greatly facilitated. The religious changes of the Sung and Ming shaped the heritage on which Lin Chao-en drew, and his syncretism exemplified clearly the confluence of religious thought. This chapter will give a broad and interpretive overview of developments in Sung and Ming religion which contributed to the climate for syncretism. The conclusions are tentative, since much research remains to be done on these periods. For lack of knowledge, unfortunately, Yüan developments will not be discussed; scholarship has not even begun to scratch the surface of Yüan religion.

SUNG:
THE NEW FACE OF
THE THREE TEACHINGS

Buddhism

Changes in Buddhism were the result of a series of persecutions at the end of the T'ang. The most famous of these in around 845 razed countless temples, melted down images, and decimated the ranks of monks and nuns. The great ritual and philosophical sects of Buddhism, dependent on monasteries, libraries, and images, were fundamentally destroyed. The sole survivor was the Ch'an school of meditation, which claimed that rituals, images, and scriptural studies were secondary to the main practice of meditation leading to enlightenment. Ch'an survived because it could survive anywhere and under most conditions; Ch'an Buddhists needed only a place to sit and a qualified teacher.

The elevation of Ch'an to be the transmitter of Buddhism opened the whole of Buddhist tradition to reexamination. Since Ch'an Buddhists refused to see any particular scripture, doctrine, or ritual as the special repository of Buddhist truth or power, they were not disposed to accept whole and unquestioned the minute philosophical, scriptural, and ritual commentaries which were the product of specialized Buddhist scholarship in other schools. The intellectual streamlining of tradition under Sung and post-Sung Ch'an has often been viewed as a decline in Buddhism.[2] However, the pressures on Buddhists at this time were for simplification. The great centers of learning and ritual were no more; Buddhists had to find the vigor of their religion in a simpler and more modest style of religious life. Moreover, with all Buddhists thrown together in the Ch'an school, the central issues which had divided the schools had to be debated once more or set aside. There was no opportunity to pursue finer points of variation. Since Buddhism had lost its intellectually dominant position, those who chose Buddhism could not do so because it was stylish; they had to understand and affirm the core of the Buddhist vision. Finally, if Buddhists were to appeal to the religious public without elaborate ritual and iconographic trappings, the Buddhist message would have to be simple, direct, and forceful.

The simplification of Buddhism, in fact, may have made it a more accessible intellectual influence on non-Buddhists. Because the Ch'an monks themselves were reexamining tradition and scriptures relatively unencumbered by earlier sectarian differences, it was also easier for non-Buddhists to have access to contemporary Buddhist thought. There was no longer a wide intellectual gap between monks who had spent a lifetime in a great Buddhist center of learning dominated by a specialized school and laymen who were interested in the issues raised by Buddhism but were lost in the philosophical technicalities. As learning within Buddhism became more selective and more pragmatic, the layman could establish a dialogue in which he could selectively and pragmatically cull ideas and inspiration from Buddhism. Thus the simplification created opportunities for syncretic interaction.

Sung and post-Sung Ch'an, then, became more flexible. One manifestation was the odd marriage of Ch'an meditation and the recitation of the name of Amitābha (*nien-fo*), the hallmark of the Pure Land school of Buddhism. At first glance Ch'an and Pure Land seem irreconcilably at odds. Pure Land taught that the power of sin was so great that most people could not save themselves; they had to rely on "other power," the active compassion of Buddhas and Bodhisattvas. If sinners could be made to fear the tortures of hell, they could call in faith on the name of Amitābha, who had promised that he would cause them to be reborn in the Pure Land paradise, where they would hear and understand the Buddhist teaching.³ Ch'an Buddhism, on the other hand, was the school of "self power," insisting that Buddhism was not an easy path; it required commitment, discipline, and courage. No one could achieve enlightenment for you; you had to do it yourself. Yet in the Sung when Ch'an monks found themselves the sole transmitters of Buddhism, they had to soften their stand somewhat. After all, they were Mahāyānists who believed in universal salvation, and not everyone was suited for the extreme rigors of Ch'an discipline. Thus they made recitation of the name a simple form of lay meditation which could be practiced in all situations.⁴ The purpose of Ch'an recitation of the name was not to be reborn in a paradise; the Pure Land was redefined as an inner purity resulting from inner luminosity or enlightenment. The Sixth Ch'an Patriarch Hui-neng (638–713) had defined it in this way:

> Let the Tathāgata of enlightenment within your own mind-ground release the luminosity of great wisdom, shine upon the six gates, and with its purity destroy the six heavens of the world of desire (kāma-dhātu). [If your own nature illuminates inwardly] the three poisons will be cast aside and hell will at once be destroyed. If inside and outside are clear, this will be no different from the Western Land. If you don't carry out this practice, how will you be able to reach there?⁵

The flexibility and pragmatism of Sung Ch'an helped it to represent Buddhism in general and facilitated positive interaction with other religions.

Confucianism

If the changes in Buddhism were the result of persecutions in the late T'ang, the transformation of Confucianism responded to events within the Sung. The Confucian scholar-official class had carried the burden throughout Chinese dynastic history of maintaining the cultural legacy, moral fiber, and social integrity of the state. With Buddhist influence at court diminished, Confucians had the ear of the emperor and his counsellors. Yet they encountered serious problems in fulfilling their responsibilities.

The first blow to Confucian confidence was the failure of a reform movement headed by Wang An-shih (1021–1086).⁶

Wang and his colleagues had set out with great energy and moral fervor to right the inequities in Chinese government, moving the bureaucratic system closer to its Confucian ideal. Unfortunately, they were insensitive to the unsettling impact of these reforms on entrenched bureaucratic interests, and they were somewhat tactless in their methods. When the reform movement failed, many Confucians blamed the inadequate moral cultivation of Wang and the reformers. Confucians had failed to reform themselves, much less the world.

Hard on the heels of the first blow came an even greater one, the loss of North China to the Jürched barbarians in 1126. Confucians in the South saw the loss of the North as evidence of their moral failure; it demonstrated to them the urgent need for a revitalization of the Confucian tradition. Some sought a solution in a reexamination of the lessons of history. Others sought to recapture the moral dynamism of Confucianism in such a way that it could be translated into effective action. These latter founded the movement we call Neo-Confucianism.

Chu Hsi forged the reflections of the early Neo-Confucians, especially the Ch'eng brothers, into a coherent system known as the Ch'eng-Chu school.[7] Searching for the key to moral cultivation in the Confucian tradition, he bypassed centuries of commentaries on the classics and histories to redefine the core of tradition, elevating the Four Books (*Analects* of Confucius, *Mencius, Great Learning, Doctrine of the Mean*) to be the starting point for all Confucian studies. The last two were originally sections in the *Classic of Rites,* but Chu singled them out, because of their theories of moral cultivation, as equal in value to the sayings of the founders of the tradition. He also turned to the commentaries on the *Book of Changes,* in which he found the means to systematize metaphysical or cosmological speculations which could establish a solid basis for moral speculation.

The classical Confucians had sought to transform men into gentlemen or superior men (*chün-tzu*), men of refinement and moral integrity. They realized that external acts alone were not sufficient to make men good; so-called "good" acts performed out of fear of punishment or for personal gain were not the acts of a gentleman. Thus from the beginning, Confucians recognized two sides of practice, the inner and the outer: self-cultivation to perfect the moral nature and external actions to fulfill duties to family, community, and state. These two were not unrelated, for they supported and nurtured each other; they represented a balance that had to be maintained.[8] In early Confucianism cultivation was a process of learning from past models, ethical self-reflection, refinement through cultivation of the arts, and effort of will to control the emotions and bad tendencies.

Sung Neo-Confucians elaborated the basis of moral cultivation; the term took on new levels of meaning, a deepened spirituality.[9] The goal of self-cultivation was no longer to become the gentleman but the sage, a fully realized human being in a state of unity with heaven, earth, and all things. The sage was man transformed and realized so that the radiance of his mind could penetrate and illumine the natural and human realms. The sage no longer sought merely to apply the will to act in accordance with innate good nature as he approached each situation, but to transform his mind to the point that in any situation his mind would immediately apprehend the principles of moral nature and spontaneously act in accordance with them. He did not merely moderate feelings to accord with the Mean, for he had attained the state of equilibrium (or Mean) which had existed before the emotions had arisen (*wei-fa chih chung*).[10]

To attain this original pristine state, one had to return to the heavenly endowed nature (*hsing*), which was moral principle (*li*). All things in the world have their principles; when actions accord with principle the world is perfectly ordered according to the laws of heaven. The problem with human beings, according to Chu Hsi, was that the human mind is subject to two forces. The mind of heaven and earth (*t'ien-ti chih hsin*) follows innate human nature and therefore principle; it is the true mind. However, the mind of material endowment (*ch'i-chih chih hsin*) follows material force (*ch'i*) and hence is subject to the habits, dispositions, talents, and feelings of the individual; these tend to obscure principle and therefore human nature. The devolution and fragmentation of mind from its original union with principle was represented in the Diagram of the Great Ultimate, which was believed to embody the cosmological principles of the *Book of Changes*.[11] To return to the Great Ultimate and achieve sagely mind one had to investigate the moral principles of all things, including the self, and accord the actions with them. In this way the mind of material endowment and the mind of heaven and earth would be fused; mind and human nature would act in harmony.

The Ch'eng-Chu system exhibited a debt to both Buddhism and Taoism. Several central issues for this school had long histories of Buddhist reflection: the religious function and nature of internal spiritual harmony, the origins and impact of mental evils, the mystical luminosity and vastness of the pure mind. Neo-Confucian cosmology owed a debt to Taoism, for the Diagram of the Great Ultimate was derived from a Taoist source.[12] However, while the early Neo-Confucians were greatly influenced by the other traditions, they were not avowedly syncretic. Their sense of internal orthodoxy was very strong; they saw themselves as establishing a Confucian bulwark against the dangers of the other traditions. Chu Hsi was very leery of the dangerous and seductive ideas of the Buddhist; he warned, "A student should forthwith get as far away from Buddhist doctrines as from lewd songs and beautiful women. Otherwise they will soon infiltrate him."[13] He accused his Neo-Confucian rival of the School of Mind, Lu Hsiang-shan (1139–1193), of Buddhist influence; Lu countered by calling Chu a Taoist.[14] Despite their common ground with Buddhists and Taoists of their day, because of the radical reexamination they were undertaking, the Neo-Confucians were extremely concerned that their ideas maintain the integrity of the Confucian tradition. The memory of Buddhist dominance during the T'ang had not faded; they wanted to revive their tradition, not discard it.

Taoism

After the loss of the North to the barbarians, some Confucian intellectuals in the South established Neo-Confucianism. Those who were left in the North were cut off from this development. Many, although educated Confucians groomed for public service, refused to serve a barbarian dynasty, choosing instead to live as hermit contemplatives. Some of these founded a new form of Taoism, known as Inner Alchemy (*nei-tan*). Because of their Confucian education, these men were not comfortable with many of the external religious trappings of ritual Taoism—the pantheon, charms and amulets, quasi-shamanistic rituals—and with the quest for immortality, which had dominated some forms of religious Taoism since the Han dynasty (200 B.C.E.–220 C.E.). Thus they were the natural intellectual leaders of a new contemplative and meditative school that had been taking shape in T'ang Taoism.

The influence of the Confucian backgrounds of the early Inner Alchemists is apparent in the founder of the Northern or Golden Elixir (*chin-tan*) school, Wang Che (1112–1170).[15] A scion of a wealthy Hopei family, he had studied for the *chin-shih* degree and excelled in martial arts. When the Jürched forces were pacifying Hopei, he joined a group of recluses rather than serve the regime. Tradition has it that in 1159 he met Lü Tung-pin (1154?–1269?), who transmitted an oral secret which established the *chin-tan* line of transmission.[16]

The teaching established by Wang Che had a strong ethical base. It returned to a simple, reclusive style of Taoism, as opposed to the arts of magicians and immortals. It emphasized the elimination of desires, including basic desires for food, sleep, and sex, through ascetic discipline, such as learning to endure heat and cold. He advocated a strict ascetic form of meditation, sitting in a closed room until one's "nature filled up heaven and earth." He gathered followers and established meeting halls which were overtly syncretic; the names often included an affirmation of the Three Teachings. The syncretic color of his school is also suggested by the fact that he recommended for study books from all three religions.[17] Thus his Taoism drew on many Confucian elements, and affirmed the unity of the Three Teachings.

Inner Alchemy Taoists redefined Taoist tradition and practice by turning back to the abstruse texts of the alchemists. They were not so much interested in the herbal and experimental alchemy of men like Ko Hung (283–343) and T'ao Hung-ching (456?–536).[18] Rather, they went back to the original classics of the tradition, like the *Ts'an t'ung ch'i* (Homology of the triad), which were based in the Han system of cosmology and correspondences. In the Han theory of alchemy they saw a basis for the fundamental transformation of man. In the *Ts'an t'ung ch'i*, the alchemical process, the inner life of man, the world, and the heavens were all homologies of the cosmic order. These correspondences had been used for centuries in a variety of alchemical regimens for preserving vitality and gaining longevity, but in Inner Alchemy they were applied to mind-cultivation with the goal of mystical union with the Tao through contemplation. The Inner Alchemists created a Taoist school of meditation, using the language and symbols of alchemy to represent the process of inner transformation.

In so doing they went beyond reacting defensively to the Buddhist challenge. Like the Neo-Confucians, they responded in a positive way to the issues Buddhists had raised about obstacles to spiritual realization and the means to overcome them. They sought in the alchemical texts of their own tradition a basis for attaining a religious experience of mystic union with the Tao which they felt had been lost in the emphasis on external religious practices in traditional sectarian Taoism.[19] They could not accomplish this without a broad debt to Buddhism, and they were not unaware of that debt. The early Inner Alchemists were openly syncretic, seeing no essential difference between achieving Buddhahood and becoming a sage-immortal. For instance, Po Yü-ch'an (1134?–1220?) organized the Southern or Perfect Realization (*ch'üan-chen*) school into a religious sect.[20] His writings drew generously on ideas of all religious schools, openly advocating the unity of the Three Teachings.[21] His intellectual and syncretic breadth make his one of the clearest articulations of Inner Alchemy thought.

THE SUNG SYNCRETIC VISION

Religious changes in the Sung exhibited a convergence of interest in the mystical vastness and luminosity of the original untrammeled mind. Confucians and Taoists, drawing direct or indirect inspiration from Buddhism, elaborated theories about the cosmological or metaphysical basis of the purity of original mind. They also discussed the sources of mental obstruction and the means to remove those obstructions. The similarities of concern did not escape Sung religious thinkers, some of whom claimed that Confucianism, Buddhism, and Taoism taught essentially the same process of mind-cultivation. They did not attempt a unification of the three processes into a single system, but rather claimed that they were three fundamentally identical paths with the same goal.

Li Tao-ch'un (dates and biog. unknown), a disciple of Inner Alchemist Po Yü-ch'an, exemplified this form of Sung syncretism. He was the earliest of a group—it cannot be called a school since there was no historical consciousness of unity among the members—of Inner Alchemy thinkers exhibiting marked affinities for Confucian categories of thought.[22] He was also steeped in Buddhist categories and terminology. Thus he had the philosophical breadth to articulate the syncretic confluence of Sung thought from a Taoist point of view.

Li Tao-ch'un's vision of the convergence of the Three Teachings was elaborated in his essay *Chiao-wai ming-yen* (Perspicacious sayings outside the written doctrine). In discussing the core of the teachings of the three religions, he carefully selected terms which, while representative of the school under discussion, avoided abstruse technicalities and highlighted shared concerns. Thus his selection suggests a possible basis for dialogue between Inner Alchemy Taoists and contemporary Buddhists and Confucians. I will include and discuss key portions of the essay here not only because it is a succinct representative of Sung syncretism but also because the particular terminology he selected, particularly that for Confucianism, was also central to the syncretic synthesis of Lin Chao-en.

The first half of Li's essay argued that Buddhism, Taoism, and Confucianism all teach that all things in the world are empty illusions, being simply products of the mind. Even in Confucianism,

The man of extended knowledge is sincere, enlightened, quiescent, and calm. Therefore he understands what arises and extinguishes incessantly is illusory form; what makes distinctions and inequalities is the deluded mind; what change and are never stable are the ages of past, present, and future; what are destroyed and do not endure are events and affairs.[23]

Li's argument was Buddhistic; even the extension of knowledge and investigation of things were drafted to serve the Buddhist purpose of exposing the illusory and impermanent nature of things. Li ignored the fact that for Sung Neo-Confucians investigation of things was examination of principles which were unchanging moral truths. Principles revealed the basis of enduring reality; they did not expose the illusory nature of all phenomena. He saw Confucianism through Buddhist eyes.

According to Li, if the Three Teachings see that the empty illusions of the world are merely products of the mind, then liberation from them can only be achieved by mind.

If we consider these, the Three Teachings are only a question of the mind. Production and transformation [of all illusory things] come from the mind; going beyond production and transformation also comes from the mind.[24]

Having established the importance of mind-cultivation as the center of each of the Three Teachings, he went on to describe each school's theory of mind-cultivation. His discussion of Buddhism stressed Ch'an concerns with strict discipline, the cutting off of the stream of consciousness in which thoughts and the world constantly arise and extinguish, and the simultaneous cessation of self, body, mind, and all things. He also, however, drew on the notion, stressed in T'ien-t'ai Buddhism, that meditation entailed stopping of the flow of consciousness through concentration while simultaneously contemplating the emptiness and transitoriness of all things through intuitive insight.[25] His statement was a straightforward and not overly technical description of Mahāyāna Buddhist views of mental discipline.

THE HEYDAY OF SYNCRETISM   43

The essentials of studying Buddhism lie in manifesting the Buddha-nature. Now if one wishes to manifest the Buddha-nature, he must first use the determined will to overcome the force of habit and custom, and the strength of strict observance to maintain clear enlightenment. After that one can illuminate and vanquish all sorts of empty delusions so that the mind will not be attached to things and the thoughts will not be the lackeys of the emotions.

Thoughts are the roots of vexations; the mind is the seed of the dust of mental objects.[26] As the thoughts arise, so do the various vexations. When thoughts cease, then the various vexations also cease. When the mind arises, then the physical and mental objects arise; when the mind is extinguished, then the various objects are extinguished. Thoughts arise and immediately cease; they always arrive at the point of arising and extinction through the self-mind. When even extinction is still, when extinction constitutes bliss, this is to see the Buddha-nature.

The reason that students today are unable to see the Buddha-nature is that they are obstructed by the double obstacle of things and their principles.[27] Unless one has great insight in contemplation he cannot remove the obstruction of principles; unless one has great concentration [in stopping thoughts through meditation] one cannot cast off the obstruction of things.

Great insight in contemplation means the wisdom of judgment;[28] great concentration means powerful discipline. If the wisdom of judgment has been mastered, then all principles are seen to be empty; if powerful discipline has been mastered, then all things will be [seen as] empty.

To understand thoroughly the great emptiness of the three emptinesses [of self, things, both self and things] and to understand the ultimate truth which is the single truth: this is the ultimate of great insight [in contemplation]. Simultaneous [mental] cessation of the self, body, mind, world, affairs, thoughts, cares, emotions, and consciousness is the ultimate of great concentration. Who but one of the most supreme widsom would be able to partake of this?[29]

Li's discussion of Taoist mind-cultivation entirely avoided the abstruse and technical symbolism of alchemy. It dealt in a more general way with the need to cut off emotions and discriminating thoughts and cultivate profound mental quiescence. While the Inner Alchemy system tended to stress the reversal of life forces to return to and re-create the original self,[30] behind every phase of that process is the power of meditation and the suspension of the normal flow of consciousness. Li's description highlighted the meditative and contemplative aspects of Inner Alchemy.

The study of Taoism lies in preserving the nature. Now if one wishes to preserve the nature, he must first cut down the host of demons with the wisdom sword and dissipate the six desires with the fire talismans.[31] Next, by power of meditation he forgets the emotions, cuts off deliberations, releases bonds of vexation, and purifies the mind.

When the mind has been purified, the bonds released, deliberations cut off, and emotions forgotten, this is what is called preserving the nature. When the true nature is preserved then there will be no production or transformation.

Today's students are in the grasp of emotions and discriminating consciousness. If one wishes to do away with emotions and discriminating consciousness, he must first cast off the mind of arising and extinction. If the mind does not undergo arising and extinction and the body does not undergo arising and extinction, this is the state of concentration.

To do away with the mind of arising and extinction, one must start from the cumulative practice of no-thought. When that has been sufficiently mastered, one can achieve the state of dreamlessness. When quiescent concentration without thought has been sufficiently mastered, one can then arrive at the state of nonarising [or: no birth].

Dreamlessness is the great task immediately before us, and no-thought is the long-range great task. If there is no arising, there is no production; if there are no dreams, then there is no transformation. If there is no production or transformation, then there will be no arising or extinction. Who but the most eminent adept would be able to partake of this?[32]

In his discussion of Confucian theories of the mind, Li avoided Confucian metaphysical theories. He drew instead on their blueprint for transformation of self and the world in the *Great Learning*, and discussed the discipline of "forgetting" taught in the *ken* hexagram of the *Book of Changes*. The "forgetting" discussed in this passage was forgetting both things and the self, a discipline taught by the classical Taoist Chuang Tzu.[33] Li probably called it Confucian because of Neo-Confucian Ch'eng Hao's (1032–1085)[34] discussion of forgetting in his discussion of *ken*; Ch'eng wrote:

> Instead of looking upon the internal as right and the external as wrong, it is better to forget the distinction. When such a distinction is forgotten, the state of quietness and peace is attained. Peace leads to calmness and calmness leads to enlightenment.[35]

It seems that Li took Ch'eng Hao's statement and gave it a new twist so that it suggested the cessation of mental activity in a meditative state.

> The essentials of Confucian study lie in perfecting the nature. Now if one wishes to perfect the nature, it lies in clarifying bright virtue, which [in turn] lies in stopping at the highest good. After one knows where to stop, then one can be settled.[36] Being settled, one is able to forget things and the self.
>
> In the commentary to the *ken* hexagram it is said: "Stilling in the back, he does not apprehend his body. Moving in the chamber, he does not see the people. No blame."[37] Stilling in the back means to forget his mind. Not apprehending the body means to forget the self. Moving in the chamber and not seeing the people mean to forget things. When these three have been forgotten, what blame can there be? This is the ultimate of knowing where to rest.
>
> Knowing where to rest, one can therefore forget things and the self and perfect the principle of nature [within the self]. This is called perfecting the nature.
>
> The reason that men of today cannot perfect their natures is that they are bound by [the concepts of] body and mind. Having these bonds, they are obstructed. They must achieve firm resolve by means of decisiveness. Having firm resolve, one is able to forget things. Having decisiveness, one is able to forget the self. When things and the self have both been forgotten, then the perfection of nature and the attainment of destiny are established. Who but one of divine virtue and sagely achievement would be able to partake of this?[38]

In his syncretic vision Li viewed the Confucian, Buddhist, and Taoist views of mind as sharing a concern for the cessation of ordinary mental activity in meditation so that the obstacles and shackles of the mind could be removed. His selective interpretation played down real and serious areas of contention between the schools on such issues as Being and Nonbeing and the status of moral values. However, he highlighted the common ground on which exchange of ideas could take place.

If the doctrine of the harmony of the Three Teachings enjoyed a certain degree of success in the Sung, it was still in tension with very powerful sectarian attitudes among some of the most powerful thinkers of the time. Syncretic impulses did not achieve full strength, particularly among the Neo-Confucians, primarily for doctrinal reasons. One major doctrinal impediment was the Neo-Confucian concept of principle (*li*) as eternal and immutable. Principle was inherent in things in the objective world, a concrete standard which transcended the mind and could transform its inner structure.[39] This was a major source of contention, since Buddhists viewed Neo-Confucian principle as mere rationality, an obstacle to enlightenment. From his Buddhist and Taoist perspective, Li Tao-ch'un had to redefine the meaning of principle to accord with his syncretic vision. On the other hand, Neo-Confucians objected to the Buddhist doctrine of the emptiness of external things and affairs as denying the existence of moral principles. Such a denial posed a basic threat to the foundations of personal morality and the social order.

THE MING CONTEXT FOR SYNCRETISM

In the early Ming the social and intellectual obstacles to syncretism were greatly reduced. The rich variety and complexity of syncretic impulses in this period form the immediate context of religious interaction which shaped Lin Chao-en's syncretic vision.

Syncretism found a measure of imperial sanction in Ming T'ai-tsu's pronouncements on the Three Teachings. Coming from the pen, or at least under the seal, of the founding father of the dynasty, these statments took on an air of inviolable authority. They could be and were cited by advocates of the unity of the Three Teachings as a source of official legitimacy.

Although T'ai-tsu wrote several essays dealing with the Three Teachings, the substance of his position was contained in the *San-chiao lun* (On the three teachings).[40] The essay claimed it was misleading to assert that the Way is the province of Lao Tzu, Confucianism of Confucius, and Buddhism of Śākyamuni. The Way, rather, is an indispensable part of daily living, and is embodied in the Confucian virtues of humanity and resoluteness. The true Way or Tao is not to be confused with the practices of those whom the world calls Taoists. Buddhism and Taoism are subtle and spiritual, while Confucianism is forthright and solid. Men of small intellect have opposed Buddhism and Taoism on the grounds that they harm the nation and incite the masses, and the greatly ignorant have claimed that the adherents of these two schools were merely those who clung to life in their fear of death. Both these positions fail to demonstrate an understanding of the situation of the Three Teachings. Confucianism is the Way of yang or manifest virtue. It can be relied upon for countless generations and is the culmination of this-worldly doctrine. Taoism and Buddhism are yin, or hidden virtue, and are secret aids of the kingly Way. One needs both the manifest (yang) and the hidden (yin), for together they comprise the Way of heaven.

T'ai-tsu wrote elsewhere that the unchanging Way was made up of the three bonds and the five constant virtues (*san-kang wu-ch'ang*). When the Chinese people ceased to follow the Way, the sage Śākyamuni was born in the West. The Way he taught was none other than the unchanging Way.[41]

T'ai-tsu's affirmative attitude toward Buddhism and Taoism should be viewed in light of three factors: (1) his personal background as a Buddhist before his ascension to the throne, (2) his appointment of monks well versed in Confucianism to official posts in the early years of his reign before he had earned widespread support among scholar-officials, and (3) his concern that people of all persuasions be included in and lend support to the moral consensus of his dynasty.[42] While his motives were largely political, his affirmation of the Three Teachings lent weighty support to syncretic forces in society.

It would be misleading to cite T'ai-tsu's espousal of the harmony of the Three Teachings without also noting the counterbalancing policies of the Ming government, beginning in T'ai-tsu's reign, to control and limit the activities of Buddhists and Taoists. Such policies were entirely consistent with the assumptions behind T'ai-tsu's syncretic pronouncements; the selectivity of his affirmation of Buddhism and Taoism suggests that his syncretism was political. The Three

Teachings were valued insofar as they supported the kingly Way, that is, insofar as they supported the central government in maintaining social unity and order. As the main ideological support of the emperor's supreme role, Confucianism occupied a primary position. Indeed, even the monk-officials were not allowed to serve *as monks;* they had to grow their hair and don Confucian robes before being invested with their official responsibilities.[43] The government was suspicious of any elements of Buddhism and Taoism which would not support the "kingly Way." Throughout the dynasty a steady stream of edicts attempted to stem the economic power and potentially subversive activities of Buddhists and Taoists. For centuries, Confucian scholar-officials had frequently memorialized about the dangers posed by Buddhists and Taoists. In large part, they opposed the diversion of wealth into opulent temples and the tax shelters which religion provided for the shrewd entrepreneur. They were never able to reconcile themselves to monasticism, which seemed a direct threat to the familial and social values which were the basis of Chinese civilization; it was, in their terms, a moral outrage when a son deserted his family responsibilities to follow the religious life. Moreover, they linked Buddhist and Taoist cults with rebellions. As far back as the Han dynasty, and increasingly from the Sung on, millenarian cults and secret societies had been linked with uprisings and rebellions. Nervous scholar-officials came to see a potential rebellion in every religious gathering. Recent scholarship shows that persecution and harassment by an overly nervous government often drove peaceful groups to rebellion; treated as rebels, they were often forced to rebel for their own protection. But even the most staid and conservative Buddhist and Taoist groups were always under government scrutiny and control; the court recognized no separation of church and state, and frequently exercised its prerogative to keep watch over religious groups.[44] If advocates of syncretism could cite T'ai-tsu's essays for imperial sanction, their critics could cite the social evils of Buddhism and Taoism with which the laws were trying to cope.

Confucianism and Syncretism

T'ai-tsu's affirmation of the unity of the Three Teachings meant that "official orthodoxy" was no longer rigidly Confucian. Moreover, the ascension of the School of Mind in the early Ming created a new openness among Neo-Confucians on the problem of "orthodoxy." During the Sung the lines between "orthodoxy" and "heterodoxy" had been firmly drawn because of the philosophical antipathy between the Sung Neo-Confucians and the Ch'an Buddhists and Taoists over the primacy of principle or mind. Neo-Confucians held that there was in the human mind an inherent tension between human nature, which was equivalent to fixed moral principle, and emotions, which tended to act against that principle. The mind could follow either principle or emotion; the study of objective principle in all things was the key to the transformation of the mind. For the Ch'an Buddhists, on the other hand, mind was primary, the integrating and unifying substance of life, controlling the entire function of human existence and beyond the limitations and dichotomies of good and evil.

Neo-Confucians of the early and mid-Ming were increasingly troubled, as Lu Hsiang-shan (founder of the School of Mind) had been in the Sung, by the tension between mind and principle. This tension seemed to inhibit spontaneity and undermine any hope for moral dynamism. They saw the potential for true moral dynamism in the natural, vital spontaneous mind unconstrained by the demands of the search for objective principle. Asserting the primacy of the dynamic mind as the source of principle, Wang Yang-ming (1472–1529), the giant of the Ming School of Mind, taught the doctrine of innate good-knowing (*liang-chih*).[45] Through the active faculty of good-knowing, the mind had the power directly to intuit principles in every situation; the sagely mind, in other words, was already fully present in each individual. Good-knowing relied on independent judgment, not on established external norms. It was ultimately beyond the distinctions of good and evil, for Wang Yang-ming "meant to encourage the undertaking of any act with one's whole energy, without the loss of vitality" from overscrupulousness or inhibitions.[46] No extraordinary effort of self-cultivation or self-reflection was necessary before the sagely mind could be activated. One learned about the sagely mind by using it; knowledge and action were two sides of the same thing.

Wang Yang-ming was open to other traditions; he taught that any idea consonant with the goal of realizing the inherent good of the mind, even an ideal from a so-called heterodox school, was to be embraced. "If learned correctly, even a heretical teaching could be useful in the world, but if learned incorrectly, even Confucianism would be accompanied by evils."[47] As long as it aided the extension of the faculty of good-knowing, any teaching was acceptable. Principles in the mind did not have to conform to external standards of orthodoxy; the mind was competent to judge the spiritual or moral function of an idea. The School of Mind removed major intellectual obstacles to a more open Confucian dialogue with Buddhists and Taoists. From the rise of the Wang Yang-ming school through the sixteenth century, syncretism reached the apogee of its intellectual influence.

The new openness to Buddhism and Taoism was prominent throughout the School of Mind, but particularly so in the left-wing T'ai-chou school, named after the home region of its founder.[48] This school followed Wang Yang-ming, but they did not share his concern for balancing the thrust toward moral dynamism and affirmation of the innate faculty of good-knowing with the more cautious emphases on study and self-reflection in the Ch'eng-Chu school. The T'ai-chou thinkers stressed the universality of sagehood; the streets, they claimed, were full of sages. They denied the need for gradual and deliberate cultivation, and challenged everyone to affirm and activate the innate sagely mind. If Wang Yang-ming identified knowledge with action, the extremists of the T'ai-chou school elevated action over knowledge. They themselves were quite untrammeled by social conventions. Wang Ken (1483–1541), a salt dealer who had experienced enlightenment many years before he accepted Wang Yang-ming as his teacher, used to dress up like the sages and ride around in a cart designed like that of Confucius to teach the sages in the streets. His eccentricities caused such a stir that Wang Yang-ming had to restrain him.⁴⁹

Many members of the T'ai-chou school saw no obstacle to simultaneous study and practice of Confucianism, Buddhism, and Taoism. The founder of the school, Wang Chi (1498–1583), wrote, "Confucians of today do not know that what the Buddha taught is fundamentally the great path of us Confucians."⁵⁰ Chou Ju-teng (1547–1629) argued that Confucianism and Buddhism needed each other: Confucians make Confucianism shallow by ignoring the potential contributions of Buddhist thought, and Buddhists lose their breadth and relevance by being closed to the problems of good government.⁵¹ Yang Ch'i-yüan (1547–1599) argued that Buddhism was not heretical, since the inner spirit of Buddhism had existed in China long before the outer traces were transmitted from India during the Han.⁵² Yang was enough of a Buddhist to style himself "monk" in some of his writings.⁵³ He also asserted that all Three Teachings were important aspects of heaven's love for the people.

Yüan Tsung-tao (1560–1600), turning the tables on the Sung critics of Buddhism, went so far as to claim that Buddhism was necessary for a proper understanding of Confucianism itself: "It is not irresponsible to assert that we can understand Confucianism for the first time only after we have studied Ch'an."⁵⁴ Chiao Hung (1541–1620) also believed in using Buddhism to understand Confucianism.⁵⁵ He charged that Chu Hsi had missed the cardinal meaning of Confucianism because of his fear of Ch'an and his unwillingness to use Buddhist ideas as an aid in elucidating the truth. Since Buddhism dealt with problems of human nature and destiny, it was not incompatible with the Chinese tradition. Sages of antiquity had made no distinctions between orthodoxy and heterodoxy, for they had understood the true meaning of the Tao. Chiao Hung used the Taoist concept of the transcendent Way to reconcile Confucianism and Buddhism: the doctrines may be different, he argued, but they are mere images of the imageless Way, which is transcendent and beyond words.⁵⁶ The Way is one and undivided; one cannot combine the

Three Teachings because their Way is already one. "The Way does not exist as three. It does not become three [in spite of our attempt to] make it three."[57]

The members of the T'ai-chou school cited above affirmed the value of Buddhism and Taoism insofar as they aided in the perfection of innate good-knowing, but they did not go on to question Confucian social and political values. In those spheres Confucianism was still the standard. However, one extreme offshoot of the T'ai-chou school, Li Chih (1527–1602), was driven by his disillusionment with the social and political values of his day to embrace a radical syncretism designed to expose the complacent hypocrisies of Confucians.[58] Like others of his day, Li cited the writings on the Three Teachings of Ming T'ai-tsu as an authority for his syncretic outlook:

> The Sages of the Three Teachings are heroes who stand firmly on earth and reach to heaven. Clearly there is no room for differences. Therefore it is said, "There are not two Ways under heaven; the sage or worthy does not have two minds." Our eminent Founder united the world and established the domain. He respected Confucius, Lao Tzu, and Śākyamuni as though they were one person. Therefore in the *Collection of Imperial Writings,* he often speaks of the Sages of the Three Teachings. And he often uses these two statements [i.e., the above quotation] to judge them in order to show that they are not different. Now the Way is identical with the mind, so how can there be any differences? Not even ignorant men and women, not even insects and plants, can go outside the purview of this Way and this mind. How much less the Sages of the Three Teachings? Even if one wished to have two Ways or two minds, one would not be able to do so.[59]

Li Chih was highly critical of sectarian tendencies, noting the failure of attempts throughout history to eradicate any of the Three Teachings by means of persecution. To this point he can be said to be in general agreement with the position of Ming T'ai-tsu and members of the T'ai-chou school. However, there was also a profoundly antisocial cast to Li Chih's syncretic thought; he found in the Three Teachings a basis for his strident refusal to conform to the expectations and values of his day. He felt that the sages of the Three Teachings agreed in their contempt for wealth and rank; they were united in "their seeking for the Way in order to be delivered from this world, for only by escaping the world can they avoid the sufferings of wealth and rank."[60] Li Chih felt that the Ming world of scholar-officials was so corrupt and contaminating that the true seeker had no choice but to become a monk. He argued that only through Buddhism could one achieve deathlessness, true self-realization:

> Therefore those who discuss the Three Teachings cannot discuss them with a narrow mind, cannot discuss them with a partial mind [a mind of love and hatred]. Only when one has calmed his mind, and considered their ultimate merits, can he know that the contemporary students of Confucianism have achieved no more than handing down achievements and fame. Those who study Taoism have achieved no more than the attainment of life. But those who study Buddhism, when they achieve their results, are able to cut off birth and death, ultimately achieve Nirvāṇa, and save all sentient beings so that all will perfect true enlightenment. Therefore I have used the analogy that Confucianism is applicable to China. Taoism is applicable to perfected human beings. Buddhism is applicable to the *dharma* of the realm of ultimate emptiness. Confucianism is like governing a single household; its authority can be applied within its boundaries and walls, but outside them it can summon no support. Taoism is like governing a district; instructions reach everywhere within the four boundaries, but outside them one cannot control. Buddhism is like having all within the four seas as one's domain. The ruler leads all the men under vast heaven, and there are none who are not his subjects. The rites, music, and campaigns all emanate from his person.[61]

Confucian critics of Buddhism had often denigrated it as dealing only with the individual and ignoring the state. Li Chih no doubt chose his jurisdictional analogy to needle the detractors of Buddhism. Having overturned the usual order of priority, he added insult to injury by claiming that men must become Buddhists in order to escape the present world, contaminated as it was by Confucian hypocrites and phonies. He himself entered a temple and was finally imprisoned for publishing virulent attacks on Confucian morality and historiography; he ended his life in a suicide of protest.

Li Chih's vision of the unity of the Three Teachings was ultimately related to his search for the innocent childlike mind, even at the cost of withdrawal from the social order. His Ming and Ch'ing critics saw in his thought a profound threat to the moral foundation of Confucian society.

Li Chih represented the most socially radical strain of syncretic thought in the T'ai-chou school. At the other end of that spectrum was Kuan Chih-tao (1536–1608).[62] Kuan Chih-tao was alarmed by the "freer" currents in the T'ai-chou school. For instance, he felt that the popular lectures sponsored by men like Wang Ken were dangerous and might arouse social unrest. Seeking to temper what he felt was excessive self-indulgence on the part of those who advocated the doctrine of good-knowing as being "neither good nor evil," he turned to Buddhism for aid in removing these vices and reestablishing Confucian ethics, particularly social ethics, on firmer ground. He advocated a doctrine of humble, strict self-reflection, asceticism, meditation, and repentance, "searching into the fountainhead of human evil in the depths of the mind."[63] He saw in Buddhism and Taoism as well as in Confucianism the truth expressed in the *Doctrine of the Mean* that the Way involved cultivation of the moral nature.

Kuan praised Ming T'ai-tsu for seeing beyond the sectarian attitudes of the Sung Neo-Confucians to the shared principles of the Three Teachings, and charged that earlier critics had attacked the surface but not penetrated to the marrow of Buddhism and Taoism. He believed that all Three Teachings could be marshaled to support strict moral cultivation.

Despite syncretic currents in the School of Mind, several thinkers of the early Ming adamantly opposed the growing influence of Buddhism, and sought to reaffirm what they took to be the orthodox line of Confucianism. Hu Chü-jen (1434–1484) had emerged as an early champion of Ch'eng-Chu orthodoxy, battling against Buddhist and Taoist influences on contemporaries such as Ch'en Hsien-chang (1428–1500).[64] Hu criticized the lack of moral discipline among Buddhists and their denial of the reality of things and their principles. Around 1525 Chan Ling (dates unclear) wrote *I-tuan pien-cheng* (The rectification of heresy), an "orthodox" attack on the syncretic tendencies of the early Ming.[65] Chan himself was a minor official holding teaching posts at the subprefectural level. He was an adamant defender of Confucianism against the evils of Buddhism, which he hoped to drive away once and for all through a comprehensive attack on all levels.

Lo Ch'in-shun (1465–1547), an advocate of Ch'eng-Chu orthodoxy, debated Wang Yang-ming in a series of letters.[66] Lo had studied Buddhism, but he found it philosophically unsatisfying. He wrote detailed philosophical criticisms of Buddhist doctrines, claiming that Buddhists did not understand ultimate truth. His arguments, unlike those of Chan Ling, were not simply a rehash of Han Yü's diatribes, but an intellectual and philosophical critique.

Although the Confucian affirmation of Buddhism and Taoism was by no means unanimous, there was lively and open debate within Confucianism on the merits of these doctrines. Confucian interaction with the two schools was more open and better informed than ever before.

Taoism and the Three Teachings

The syncretic strain in Ming Taoist writings is represented in Yin Chen-jen's (dates unclear) *Hsing-ming shuang-hsiu wan-shen kuei-chih* (Revealed doctrine of the dual cultivation of nature and life store taught by the myriad spirits). A drawing of the Sages of the Three Teachings, with Buddha in the center, Lao Tzu on the left, and Confucius on the right, opens the book.[67] Yin Chen-jen wrote that the practice of the Way in all Three Teachings was the cultivation of the true mind of man:

> If you wish to cultivate long life you must know the source from which you were given life. If you wish to seek deathlessness, you must understand the men who have not died. Therefore it is said, "Only a man who can recognize men who have not died can escape death." The Taoists call deathless men Iron Men, and the Buddhists call them Diamonds, but these refer to the wondrously enlightened original true mind of people in this world.
>
> This mind is spiritual, without darkness, always wise. Its substance neither arises nor is extinguished; its aspects do not go or come, and it is traced back before the state of heaven and earth. None can know its beginnings. It ends after heaven and earth end, and none knows its end. It is so high there is nothing above it, so wide one cannot reach its outer limits, so deep nothing is below it, so profound it cannot be fathomed. Heaven and earth rely on this to cover and support; the sun and moon rely on this to shine; the sky relies on this to be vast, and the myriad spirits rely on this to go through their transformations.
>
> The great Sages of the Three Teachings taught men to practice the Way; it was to practice this. Achieving immortality or Buddhahood is

this. . . . The two paths of sage and ordinary man divide from this, and there is no other road which goes beyond life and death.[68]

The *Hsing-ming shuang-hsiu wan-shen kuei-chih* dealt mainly with the technicalities of specific methods of self-cultivation. It seems to have been a manual for Taoist adepts. Thus while its outlook is syncretic, it was too technical to have a broad appeal to non-Taoists.

Perhaps the most far-reaching Taoistic contribution to syncretic accommodations with Buddhism and Confucianism was the work of Yüan Huang (1533–1606). Yüan Huang came from a former scholar-official family which had turned to the practice of medicine after being barred from holding office for political reasons.[69] He was not encouraged by his family to take the examinations. Moreover, early in his life a Taoist fortune-teller predicted that he would never hold office. However, a Buddhist monk named Yün-ku (identity unclear) persuaded Yüan to abandon his fatalism in favor of belief in the science of moral retribution. Yüan vowed to do three thousand good deeds if heaven would grant him a son and ten thousand for a *chin-shih* degree. He kept a ledger of merits and demerits (*kung-kuo ko*) in his study, faithfully recording his good and bad deeds. His faith in the system was confirmed when he got both the son and the degree. After some years in office, he spent the last ten years of his life writing. He contributed to the publication of a Buddhist canon, and was well known for a simple *Primer on the Four Books* (*Ssu-shu hsün-erh su-shuo*) and manuals on taking examinations. He also wrote encyclopedias for daily use and morality books.

The tradition of morality books had its origins in Taoism, but Yüan Huang's books also included Buddhist and Confucian elements. Morality books grew in numbers and in popularity in the Sung and Ming dynasties. They were simple and practical, defining exemplary behavior and warning against common moral failings in the various roles and occupations of Chinese society. Often they dramatized their points by describing the lives and moral retribution of models and antimodels. During the Ming a number of morality books were written and distributed by members of the imperial family; through these publications the royal house won itself religious merit while reinforcing the social values which would keep society stable under their rule.[70] For individuals like Yüan Huang, morality books were a concrete way of defining daily moral obligations and of measuring progress in moral cultivation. The books generally combined Confucian social morality with Buddhist reverence for life and Taoist moderation of desires to preserve health and vitality. Yüan's morality books appeared to have strong Buddhist influence, but his interpretation of quotations from Buddhist sutras was often quite Taoistic;[71] Taoism was the tradition which defined his "internal orthodoxy." He maintained throughout his life a strong interest in Taoism, vowing at one point to attain the elixir with the aid of the immortals and the sages. Yet, he was a *chin-shih* and a student of Wang Chi; his Confucian training showed in his vigorous emphasis on moral action.

Yüan Huang's career and his writings exemplify well the strongly syncretic trend in the early Ming. Like many others of the period, he reinterpreted and combined elements from earlier traditions to fit the religious mood of the day; he transformed the doctrine of moral retribution, which had traditionally been based on the belief in the retributions administered by the gods in the heavenly bureaucracy, into a demythologized ethical science.[72]

Buddhists and the Three Teachings

Although in the early Ming Neo-Confucians turned to Buddhist ideas in resolving the tensions in their philosophy, they did not do so under the influence of great Buddhist scholars. They turned instead to Buddhist sutras, particularly the *Leng-yen ching* (*Surāṇgama*), for new insights into the problem of the mind.[73] Ironically, the rise of the School of Mind created a climate which in turn led to a new vigor in Buddhism, manifested in the appearance of several prominent Buddhist thinkers.

As a youth interested in a monastic vocation, Han-shan Te-ch'ing (1546–1623) had been troubled by the absence of eminent monks in his age and the low esteem in which monks were held.[74] The abbot into whose care he was entrusted evidently shared this concern, and educated the lad for a Confucian career, feeling that he was too talented to waste his life as a monk. Despite everything his monastic calling was strengthened; he modeled himself on the eminent monks of the past, becoming one of the leaders of the new Buddhism.

The new Buddhism was not a revival along sectarian lines. The predominant trend was for a combination of Ch'an and Pure Land beliefs, with some T'ien-t'ai elements. It was also marked by syncretic accommodation with Confucian and Taoist ideas. Te-ch'ing, as we saw above, had received a Confucian as well as a Buddhist education, and he had also written on the Taoist classics. He saw common ground in the Three Teachings in that they all taught the evils of desires and sought to break the hold of egoism. He argued that Buddhist precepts for discipline taught the virtues of humanity and filial piety, and that the vow of the Bodhisattva showed the concern of the Buddhist for the affairs of this world. Yet despite all the common ground, Te-ch'ing's philosophy placed Buddhism at the top. The Sages of the Three Teachings, he argued, taught men according to their several capacities: Confucianism represented the human vehicle, Taoism the heavenly vehicle, and the Bodhisattva the vehicle which transcended them both. Confucianism was suitable for teaching ethics, Taoism for getting men beyond desires, and Buddhism for completing their transformation.[75]

The monk Tzu-po Ta-kuan (or Chen-k'o; 1544–1604) saw in the revival of Buddhism an alternative to the political, intellectual, and spiritual corruption of the day. In this view he was following in the footsteps of two men: (1) the Sung monk Ta-hui Tsung-kao (1089–1163), who had seen Ch'an as a violent energy which could cut down the established values like a violent wind,[76] and (2) Li Chih, who had chosen Buddhism as a protest against the corruption and hypocrisy against which he so vociferously inveighed. Like Li Chih, Ta-kuan ended his days by a suicide in prison.[77] Though a confirmed Buddhist, Ta-kuan was anything but a quietist; like the Neo-Confucians, he placed very high value on dynamic moral activity. Toward the end of his life, like Li Chih, he turned to more and more virulent criticism of the social order, finally coming to see himself as a Dharma King whose mission it was to reform the world.

Ta-kuan was sympathetic with the School of Mind, but he saw Buddhism as the fountainhead of that school. While he respected much of the teaching of the Wang Yang-ming school, he nevertheless felt that they had stopped halfway to enlightenment, and still lived fettered to the ties of the world.

However, if Ta-kuan emulated Li Chih in his anger against the social order, another Buddhist, Yün-ch'i Chu-hung (1532–1612) was highly critical of Li Chih's self-indulgence and selfishness; he claimed Li had perversely used Buddhism as a means to escape his proper place in the world.[78] Chu-hung did not feel called upon to denounce the present social order; he was a syncretist and a peacemaker.[79]

He was opposed to excessive sectarian rivalry; while admitting that a certain amount of controversy had been inevitable between Buddhists and Confucians, still, looking with an open mind, "one will see that Buddhism and Confucianism, far from embarrassing each other, complement each other."[80] His support for this statement was singular: the fear of rebirth in hell was an impetus to the reform of a lawbreaker whom the law fails to apprehend, and, on the other hand, the law of the state aids the church in punishing monks who cannot be controlled through monastic discipline alone. Hence the Buddhist church and the state aid each other.[81]

Chu-hung tried to reconcile the Buddhist and Confucian schools through their shared moral values, particularly their reverence for life. However, he argued that Buddhist morality was more far-reaching and demanding than Confucian morality. Confucianism was concerned with the good of society, and Buddhism with Good in its absolute sense; they needed each other.[82]

In his attempts to reconcile the worlds of the secular and the sacred, Chu-hung became a prominent advocate of lay Buddhism; his teaching was a mixture of Ch'an and Pure Land with a strong, almost Confucian emphasis on moral effort in this world. Lay Buddhism was institutionalized in Associations for the Releasing of Living Things (*fang-sheng hui*), which promoted vegetarianism. But it need not take on institutional form; Chu-hung urged wives, officials, or anyone in any secular role to take the vow of the Bodhisattva and practice Buddhist precepts in their everyday lives. His advice to lay Buddhists was pragmatic, allowing accommodation for the real responsibilities that secular life might entail, so that, for instance, "performing good deeds was here skillfully identified with the Confucian ideal of an upright official."[83] Enlightenment could be attained by laymen in the midst of the world. His advocacy of lay Buddhist ideals laid "a theoretical foundation for the absorption of Buddhism into the personal lives of the literati-official class."[84]

The Ming, then, was a period highly conducive to syncretic impulses. Ming T'ai-tsu's affirmation of the Three Teachings stimulated syncretic impulses in Buddhism and Taoism, often in forms, such as lay associations and morality books, which focused on the religious needs of laymen; this trend narrowed the gap between themselves and the Confucians. With the rise of the School of Mind, the Confucians were more than ever open to the ideas and lessons from other traditions; their emphasis on dynamic moral action over study and reflection extended the sagely Way beyond scholars to encompass men and women in the streets. The lessons and values of tradition were questioned as never before; syncretists sought moral rearmament through the combined spiritual vitality of the Three Teachings or through the exposure of hypocrisy and corruption caused by narrow views.

Lin Chao-en exemplified the syncretic impulses of his age perhaps more than any figure so far considered, for he "was the first to promulgate formally the principle of the amalgamation of the Three Teachings as a single philosophical entity in which the three of them could still exist."[85] He was also the first to establish a single religious organization for people from all religions and all walks of life based on the unity of the Three Teachings and their shared doctrines of mind-cultivation. His system of mind-cultivation integrated elements from all three religions into a single practice; yet he believed that its essentials could be adequately explained in terms of any one of them. Finally, he firmly believed that the true Way of heaven must be broad enough to encompass all doctrines and accessible to all people, regardless of their social status or their innate talents and capabilities.

CHAPTER FOUR

BIOGRAPHY OF
LIN CHAO-EN

THE EARLY YEARS

Lin Chao-en was born in 1517 in P'u-t'ien, Fukien, the second son of his father Wan-jen.[1] P'u-t'ien was known for the success of its sons in the government examinations.

> In the Ming at every provincial examination P'u-t'ien took half of the places of all Fukien, and at the Metropolitan examination they always won one-third of the places above the quotas. Few areas in the realm could match their ability to have successful *chin-shih* among grandfather and grandson, father and son, elder and younger brothers and cousins within one family.[2]

No family in P'u-t'ien was more successful in this regard than the Lins.[3] Over its long history this clan had produced many officials of distinction, including Chao-en's grandfather, Lin Fu (1474–1539), whose service in economic administration, the Ministry of War, and the Censorate must have been a model for Lin Chao-en's generation.[4]

During his early years Lin Chao-en was groomed to carry on the family tradition by taking the governmental examinations and following an official career. He entered school at the age of six Chinese years.[5] Although he was not particularly brilliant at first, by the age of sixteen he had earned such a high reputation that a superintendent of education kept a collection of his essays, which were later published.[6] In 1534 Lin was awarded his *hsiu-ts'ai* degree, the first of three degrees which qualified candidates for official service. By 1540 he was ranked first among the local students.

Very little else is known of Lin's early years, except that he reportedly began his philanthropic activities at an early age, giving money to the poor whenever he went out. When questioned by his mother about this, he replied, "The world has a surfeit of suffering. It is the Way of heaven to help those who do not have enough."[7]

Lin Chao-en's emergence into young manhood was clouded by events of a more somber nature. Married at eighteen, he lost his wife within a year. He remarried shortly thereafter, but more losses were to follow. His grandfather died in 1539, and his father followed in 1544. In 1546 he lost his uncle Wan-ch'ao, only eight years his senior and the rising star of the family.[8] Lin Chao-en was then thirty years old.

Shortly after the death of his uncle, Lin had a curious dream. In it he rolled three dice which came up 4:4:1, but the "1" rolled a long time before it finally came to rest. Some suggested that the dream portended success in the three examinations leading to the *chin-shih* degree. Lin Chao-en evidently did not see it that way. During that same year, he visited Lo Hung-hsien (1504–1564), a scholar of the school of Wang Yang-ming, to request a funerary inscription for Lin Wan-ch'ao.[9] Before he returned home, he had decided to abandon his studies for the government examinations, thus forfeiting any chance for an official career. Lin wrote that his decision stemmed from his realization of the emptiness of his much acclaimed talents:

> When I was studying for the examinations, I wrote two essays: "On Holding to the Mean," and "On the One Thread." At the time everyone said that my writing captured the principles handed down from Yao, Shun, and Confucius. Delighted, I too thought I had grasped them. A year or two later, I suddenly realized that when I tried to embody what I had written in my actions, I did not understand what the words meant. They merely reflected the dregs of the ancients.[10] It was not only that I was deceiving others with them; I was also deceiving

myself. Bitterly reproaching myself, I abandoned examination studies and took up the Way of sages and worthies, determined to seek the means to realize it in myself, obtain it in my mind, and manifest it in my actions. How could I dare to devote myself once more to reiterating mere words?[11]

Lin's complaint was that his education had not resulted in personal moral growth. Those overseeing his education lauded his talents, but in Lin's view all these reputed talents were merely a matter of literary style. The inner man had not been educated.

Lin was not alone in his concerns. Similar indictments of the superficiality and pedantry of education in the official schools had led to the establishment of private academies whose founders sought to restore the Confucian ideal of educating the whole man, the moral man. The public schools, it was felt, were merely preparing students for exams; in them, tradition was taught as a set body of knowledge and opinions rather than as a living moral way.[12] Lin Chao-en had come to feel that examination studies and moral studies were irreconcilable.

The decision to abandon examination studies grew out of an emotional and spiritual crisis of some depth. In the above quotation, he denounced his former views as deceptions, lies; he expressed an urgent need to define and live "real" values. This need may have been stimulated in part by his repeated bereavements, which deprived him of his immediate family models. He and his brothers now bore the full responsibility of carrying on the family name; there were no elders to provide guidance, support, and contacts with influential scholars. The actual decision to abandon hopes for an official career may also have been influenced by his meeting with Lo Hung-hsien, who had retired from official life for reasons of principle to pursue a life of scholarship.[13] The Confucian's call to public service was strong, but Lo Hung-hsien was one of a growing group of serious-minded Neo-Confucians in the Ming who had come to feel the tension between the harsh realities of politics and the moral ideals of the Confucian. However, if at one level Lin's decision was a renunciation of the route to government service, it was first and foremost a decision *for* the study of the sagely Way. He was seeking the truth which would lead to spiritual transformation, for a Way which he could "realize in his self, obtain in his mind, and manifest in his actions." The decision began a period of intense spiritual search which lasted for over ten years.

THE PERIOD OF SEARCH

Lin Chao-en's search led him in many directions; he earnestly sought instruction from all who studied the Way, whether they were Confucian, Buddhist, or Taoist. For a time he had a companion in his search, one Cho Wan-ch'un (dates unclear), a local eccentric of the Taoist type. In 1548 Cho visited Lin and suggested to him that the dice in his dream represented the ninefold refined elixir (*chiu-huan tan*), since $4+4+1=9$.[14] This elixir, said Cho, was the "advanced degree" of the realized man (*chen-jen chin-tzu*); by this play on words, Cho suggested a Taoist alternative to sterile Confucian studies.[15] Being open at that time to all paths of the Way, Lin was delighted with this interpretation. For the next several years these two men became inseparable companions, roaming about the countryside, discussing the secrets of the Way, drinking and versifying. They came to be known as Wild Cho and Crazy Lin.

Cho Wan-ch'un had lost his father when he was six and his mother when he was eight.[16] Having no relations to provide for him, he took to begging in the streets. Eventually he became so skillful at fortune-telling that local notables vied to entertain him with feasts and gifts. Lin Chao-en, however, claimed that Cho cared not a whit for all these riches: "He had not a pint or peck of provisions, yet when others invited him, he went only under duress, even to a banquet of the most sumptuous delicacies. He did not own an inch of property, but whenever he received a gift he immediately gave it to someone else."[17]

Cho practiced a form of ascetic self-cultivation. He slept on the rocks among the hills, even in the bitterest cold. He once demonstrated his attainments in self-cultivation by bathing in an icy mountain stream during midwinter before a party of assembled monks.[18] He lived a celibate life, steadfastly resisting Lin's pressure on him to marry.[19] Cho Wan-ch'un completely neglected his personal appearance. His hair was disheveled, his feet bare, and his clothes coarse and unconventional. He was oblivious to the conventions of social decorum, even in his relations with the rich and powerful. In short, he represented a "type" of Taoist eccentric, known for outrageous behavior, magical powers, and prophetic skills.[20]

Cho Wan-ch'un seems to have introduced Lin to Inner Alchemy Taoist thought. Together they composed the *Wu-yen lu* (Record of the dialogues). The dialogues contain a fragmentary exploration of the Inner Alchemy homologies of the natural order, the heavenly order, and the inner workings of all living things (including man) governed by the laws of the *Book of Changes* and the Five Phases. These homologies and the technical language of the Inner Alchemy tradition later became important elements in Lin Chao-en's synthesis. However, the intellectual content of the *Wu-yen lu* was hardly a systematic exposition of the Inner Alchemy system; it served as a precursor to Lin's later adaptation of Inner Alchemy only in the most general sense.

The period of companionship with Cho Wan-ch'un was thus only a part of the search. Cho opened Lin to new ideas and to a new style of thought, but he was not his teacher. This is clear from the format of the dialogues, in which they were depicted as a kind of team. Cho offered terse, obscure answers to students' questions about the workings of the Way or the technical language of self-cultivation, and Lin elaborated Cho's statements with fuller theoretical explanations. Neither deferred to the other, and Lin was by far the more articulate. Thus while Cho was an important influence, Lin never accepted him or any other man as his teacher. He sought a teacher among all traditions, but never found one.

He went to a teacher of the Ch'eng-Chu tradition of Neo-Confucianism, who urged him to investigate the principles of everything in the world by means of deliberation, viewing their manifestations in affairs, and by studying and attending lectures. Lin objected that such minute investigation of external things was an impossible and endless task which would never lead to an understanding and realization of the sagely mind.[21] Lin's criticism of Ch'eng-Chu Neo-Confucianism echoes the views of the School of Mind. In his youth Wang Yang-ming had set out to investigate the principles of all things, beginning with the bamboo in his garden. After some weeks he was physically and mentally exhausted but no closer to the truth. Thus he rejected exhaustive investigation of the principles of external things as both debilitating and fruitless.[22]

Lin Chao-en also visited a Taoist master who wanted to teach him the arts of eternal life. Lin asked him about the root of heaven and earth, the state before the creation of things to which the "realized man" aspired to return.[23] The Taoist advised him first to master the technical symbols and terms of alchemy.

> My dear sir, if you wish to study the Way, you must first differentiate what are lead and mercury, the dragon and the tiger, the measures of the hexagrams and lines, advancing and withdrawing, adding and extracting, the proper year, month, day, and hour [for each step]. When these are all clear in your mind, and you have obtained their essential and subtle points, only then can I tell you about . . . the [state] before heaven and earth.[24]

Lin objected that to begin with such discriminations would only fragment the mind. The Taoist also urged upon him several methods of breath control, but Lin retorted that to start with breath control was to put the cart before the horse: the quiescent mind should control the breath and not vice versa.

He also turned to a Ch'an master, but became disillusioned when the master praised Lin's undiscerning repetition of Ch'an clichés as true understanding. The Ch'an master also wished to talk about techniques and practices: sitting in meditation, study of sutras, abstinence from meat and strong drinks. Lin objected that all practices should be understood in terms of their benefits for mind-cultivation, but the master was unable to explain them in those terms. Again, Lin's experience echoes the frustration of other scholars of his day. Before Te-ch'ing and Ta-kuan, Buddhists lamented the intellectual aridity of the Ch'an tradition. There was some vitality to practice, but Buddhism lacked the intellectual giants of earlier periods. Scholars of other schools turned to Buddhist scriptures, but not to living Buddhist teachers.[25]

Finally, he attended lectures at an academy, where the master taught the essentials of the left wing of the School of Mind. Since originally the mind was rectified and the will sincere, there was no need to apply effort to return them to that state; one need only let them manifest their essential natures. Lin countered that although the mind and will may have been originally pure, they were in fact not pure in the actual lives of ordinary beings; without effort there would be no means to return to the original, essential nature of man.

Lin's search for the sagely Way was a search for the key to the sagely mind. He turned to all three traditions in his search and found them all wanting. The Confucians of both the Ch'eng-Chu tradition and the extreme School of Mind had failed, in Lin's eyes, to provide a realistic method of self-cultivation. Taoists and Buddhists, on the other hand, had spoken only of techniques and failed to provide for Lin a theoretical basis for relating those techniques to the understanding of true mind. His search was frustrated at every turn. He lamented,

> But I do not know the means to rectify the mind and make the will sincere. It troubles me sorely, and I feel like a poor man with nowhere to turn. Indeed, it can be said that to this day I have sought the mind of the Way diligently. How could it be the will of heaven not to show its love of the Way and look upon my spark of true mind which does not backslide?[26]

Although he had to wait for many years, the breakthrough finally came.

THE CALLING

Within ten years,[27] I was fortunate to meet an enlightened master who pitied and instructed me. He directly pointed to this sagely mind, and all the words he spoke to me were from the Four Books and the Five Classics.[28] He said, "Since the time of Confucius and Mencius these books have been obscured by interpretations and have remained unclear to this day." Moreover, he repeatedly discussed for me the subtle principles regarding stilling in the back and moving in the chamber.

When he was about to leave, he spoke to me again, saying, "You are not an official. If you do not have the means to verify this, who will be able to follow and believe it?"

I said, "With what shall I verify it to bring others to believe?"

"Verify it with illness. If the illness is cured, they will believe."

"But how am I to cure people's ills?"

The master said, "When you were young did you not recite the writings about the fullness of the body and the plumpness of the countenance?[29] A full body comes from a broad mind, and plump countenance is rooted in the mind. Even more the yellow center (*huang-chung*) of the *Book of Changes*,[30] when its regularizing influence reaches the cavities of the body, is sufficient to extend its wondrous effects to the four limbs. You need only maintain your resolve and do no violence to your vital force,[31] and illness can be cured."

I said, "I beg to inquire the method."

"Medicine is the will, and the method rests firmly in your own mind."[32]

Lin's account of his meeting with the enlightened master merits close examination. First, there is the problem of the enlightened master himself. In general, Lin Chao-en's chronological biography (*nien-p'u*) is generous in detail; it provides names, dates, and places which can be verified in Lin's letters or essays or in dated colophons by immediate disciples.[33] Yet this source yields no clue as to the time and circumstances of this meeting or the identity of the master. Another biography, which includes hagiographical legends that grew along with Lin's fame as a religious teacher, provides a somewhat different version of the so-called meeting. In that account, at the end of his long search Lin dreamed that he saw Confucius, who imparted to him the secrets of the *Analects*, saying that because these secrets had been beyond ordinary knowledge he had not spoken of them but transmitted them to Lao Tzu and Śākyamuni, who interpreted them in terms of their own doctrines.[34] The facts are not entirely clear. Since the first account is in Lin's words, it should reflect his version of the event. However, the lack of concrete detail in it suggests that the enlightened master may have been "met" in a dream or vision, but that Lin himself was too modest to name the sage. Such a hypothesis also accords with Lin's inability to find a teacher among the Three Teachings; he was called upon to revive a lost line.

Meeting with an enlightened master has carried rich religious connotations in Chinese history. First, it suggested transmission of learning. Han Confucians spoke of the enlightened master as one who could clarify and transmit true knowledge.[35] Second, in Buddhism the need for enlightened instructors was intensified by the Buddhist view of the increasing weakness and ignorance of people in the days of the vestigial law (mo-fa, J. mappō). The Pure Land school of Buddhism taught that during this final period people could achieve salvation only through faith in the saving power of the Buddha, their minds and wills being too weak to achieve salvation on their own power. As the world moved further into this age of ignorance, even the leap of faith was too much for most, save for those who met an enlightened master to lead them past their karmic obstacles to faith.[36] Third, meeting with an enlightened master suggested the Ch'an Buddhist doctrine of direct and wordless transmission. In Ch'an, Truth was held to be transmitted directly from mind to mind by "direct pointing" (chih-chih), without reliance on externals such as the written word. Having abandoned the traditional external sources of Buddhist authority, Ch'an Buddhists required that the enlightenment experienced be verified or sealed by a master, thus insuring that the monk's experience was that of the true doctrine transmitted directly from mind to mind from Śākyamuni himself through the Ch'an line of transmission.[37] Thus one had to meet a true master before transmission could be effected. Fourth, meeting an enlightened master suggested transmission of secret teachings. In Inner Alchemy Taoism the secret techniques and doctrines had to be imparted directly as the oral secret (k'ou-chüeh) of a true master. Without such instruction, the student was apt to misinterpret the teachings and fall into error. When the Way was lost, only by meeting an enlightened master could one hope to restore the real meaning of the written traditions.[38]

Lin's account of his meeting with the enlightened master drew on all these connotations. The master transmitted instruction to him by means of direct pointing (*chih-chih*) to the secrets of the *Analects,* lost since the days of Mencius. He also taught him the secret of implementing these teachings and techniques for bringing others to believe it. Thus he could revive the Way, pointing to the true understanding of the classics, that would lead to personal realization of the sagely Way.

The secret method imparted to Lin Chao-en in his vision was the *K'ung-men hsin-fa,* the Confucian system of mind-cultivation.[39] This method rested on the techniques of stilling in the back and moving in the chamber, terms drawn from the commentary to hexagram 52 of the *Book of Changes.* The theme of the hexagram is bringing the mind to rest in its proper place. This hexagram, and the application of these techniques to a system of self-cultivation as elaborated in Lin's nine stages, will be discussed in detail in the next chapter. Here we need only note that his system was also heavily indebted to Taoist and Buddhist meditative techniques. Lin transcended the problems he had perceived in the teachings on the mind prevalent in the three traditions by integrating Buddhist and Taoist techniques with Confucian theory; the Buddhist and Taoist techniques gave the Confucian ideal of sagely mind a means of application, while Confucianism gave meaning to Buddhist and Taoist techniques.

Lin's vision of the enlightened master was above all a religious call to teach and save men. The long search not only led to a breakthrough which revealed the key to achieving sagely mind but also gave him a new direction for his life. He was to impart the truth he had received, thus reviving the transmission of the Way.

However, Lin's account of his calling also revealed his doubts about his fitness for his exalted vocation. He was called to be a teacher of the true Way, but being neither an official nor a holder of an advanced degree, he feared he would be ignored and discounted. Hence the need for healing to lend authority to his understanding of the doctrine of mind.

Healing had been an important factor in the spread of Buddhism and Taoism in Chinese history, particularly at the popular level. Illness, like drought or famine, was considered a sign of the irruption of evil forces which upset the order of nature, society, and human life. Illness was disequilibrium; restoration of order was healing. In religious healing, priests evoked spiritual authorities against these forces. The methods varied, depending upon the religious outlook of the priest, but they relied on the support of a hierarchy of spiritual powers or at least could be explained in spiritual terms. These powers could be marshaled through the recitation of sutras, the conversion of unbelievers, the knowledge of the names of gods used in rituals or spells, drugs whose powers had been taught by the gods, or symbolic rituals. In Chinese classical medicine, on the other hand, illness was viewed as a disturbance of the delicate balance of inner workings of the body, caused by disruptive forces (*hsieh-ch'i*). Health was achieved by restoring the inner balance of the vital forces or configurational energies within the body through means which could be explained in terms of the internal cosmos governed by yin and yang, the Five Phases, and other cosmological forces. The ritual and classical traditions borrowed from each other so that, for instance, we see ritual remnants in some classical cures. There does, however, seem to be a legitimate distinction in terms of the principles by which the healer understood the cure to be effective, the principles representing distinctive world views.[40]

Although Lin used healing as a support for his religious teaching, his theory of illness drew more upon the classical tradition of medicine than the popular tradition of religious healing. He did not rely on drugs, charms, liturgies, or divine agencies, but on correcting imbalances of vital forces, which he interpreted in a moral sense. Good deeds were held to produce healthy yang forces, while evil deeds produced unhealthy yin forces. An excess of yin produced the imbalance of vital forces in the body. This, said Lin, was Chu Hsi's doctrine of dissolving imbalanced vital forces (*hsiao-shuo pu-cheng-ch'i*).[41]

Lin's healing method will be discussed in detail in a later chapter. Suffice it to say that he used a simplified classical

Confucian theory of healing to lend authority to his religious teaching. To my knowledge he was the only Confucian thinker of the Ming who used healing in this way.

The vision of the enlightened master, then, was a major turning point in the life of Lin Chao-en, but only gradually did he come to realize the full potential of his calling to be a teacher.

THE CONFUCIAN TEACHER

After his calling, Lin Chao-en took up his new role, rather cautiously at first. In 1551 at the age of thirty-five he accepted his first disciples, beginning with his friend Huang Chou and followed by eleven others, including his brother Chao-chü and three of his cousins. He took the first opportunity to demonstrate the validity of his method of mind-cultivation by curing Huang Chou's teenage daughter of eye trouble. Liu Hsün (dates unknown), an official of the local Censorate who had a similar affliction, was eager to try Lin's method. Not only was he cured, but he was so impressed with Lin's doctrine of the mind that he also became a disciple.[42]

However, before Lin could establish his own school another obstacle had to be overcome. The next two years were given to a struggle between Lin and the local education superintendent Chu Heng (1512–1584).[43] Chu tried by every means at his disposal to get Lin back into the official school; since Lin was an officially registered scholar, it was incumbent on him to pursue examination studies. The headstrong young Lin refused, burning his student collar before Chu Heng's gate and defying Chu to force him to return.

Lin responded to one summons as follows:

> I am not good at literary forms. Even if I were it would be mere pedantry. Several years ago I had this addiction, but now I have experienced a degree of enlightenment, and I single-mindedly value what is inner and disdain what is external, wishing to find satisfaction as an illiterate villager of the realm. . . . Let me set loose the nature of a wild deer of the mountain groves. . . . Before, when I was in school, you could have summoned me. Now I belong to the mountain groves, and

you may no longer summon me. If you wish to see me, you will have to send your officials here [to take me by force].[44]

Having chosen to follow the Way, Lin could not bring himself to return to the superficialities of training for the examinations. Chu Heng brought Lin in on a legal summons, but only after a long argument did he persuade the young man to compromise. Lin agreed to remain on the school register, but refused to study for the examinations. Chu not only accepted the compromise, but read and greatly admired Lin's writings; henceforth he was a supporter of Lin Chao-en.

Lin Chao-en survived this confrontation with authority unscathed; in truth he seems to have won Chu Heng as an ally. The young man's tone was defiant; he would not be turned aside from his path. It is interesting to note, however, that in the end he did compromise. He had followed his own conscience into the life of a man of the Way, but he was not a rebel. There was in Lin Chao-en none of the profound anger and intransigence of a Li Chih.[45] His understanding of the truth did not lead him to flout the social order. He consistently maintained that his Way was compatible with orthodox Neo-Confucian thought and society.

The issue of his status as a student in the official school resolved, Lin was free to follow his vocation as a teacher. He taught his students privately, outside the official school, to give them an education closely modeled on the principles of Confucius, combining serious classical learning with the cultivation of character. In 1554 he outlined his regulations for study:

(The course of study)
On every day with a four or nine in it [i.e., 4, 9, 14, 19, 24, 29] students should write an essay, working on it from 7 A.M. until 11 A.M. If students are studying different classics, on meeting days they should all write on the Four Books, each choosing his own topic.

In writing clarity of principle is primary, and is supplemented by lively style. . . . When one arrives at depth through inner cultivation, expressing it in words will come naturally and smoothly. Therefore it is said, "The virtuous man will be sure to express himself correctly."[46] It is well that students do not seek it simply in words.

In reading books, students should diligently recite a page and a half of the Four Books each morning, and the same amount of the classics each afternoon. Commentaries should also be carefully recited.

In the course of study students should write two formal commentaries, one disquisition, one proposal or one memorial, during each ten day period.[47]

(Meetings)

Each month on days containing a four or nine there should be an afternoon assembly in the Hall for Expounding the Classics. First the students should privately read and correct the errors in their essays for the day and then hand them in to be read. After the reading has been finished, let the students draw lots for recitation of memorized texts. Those who get the lots will recite five lines from memory. Then moving to the left each person in turn recites five lines, continuing round the circle until all texts have been recited. Next they draw lots for expounding the classics, with two students getting the lots each round. These two ask each other questions. If their explanations are unclear, another student will be elected to explain the point further. The rest of the students should sit quietly and listen and are not to make noise or misbehave. Discussion should elucidate the main text and minor notes which pertain to it, clarifying them section by section. Anyone who has questions should first record them in his record of attendance and activities, and ask about them after the lecture is finished or from time to time draw lots for an investigation of these questions. Next the students draw lots for the recitation of the specialized essay forms, choosing only three men to recite ten lines each.

(Primacy of Studies)

Each student should be provided with a record of attendance and activity, in which he records for future examination the books he has read, the number of each of the essay types he has read, and which classics and how much of each he has read.[48]

On meeting day the students come after breakfast and go home for lunch. This avoids the necessity of rotating the responsibility for planning banquets, thereby achieving simplicity and reducing complications. If a student has some business and is prevented from attending the meeting, he should submit advance written notification of that fact.

From the time that the schedule of meetings is established, students need not have social dealings outside of meeting times. As to the indispensable rites and courtesies of friends and intimates, they should be attended to on the first and fifteenth of the month, which are days of rest from study.

If the person with the lot for recitation has some other business, let him arrange for a substitute in advance.

The course of study is extremely simple. If there is something which you cannot understand for yourself, and you wish to follow another master and privately write additional essays under him and read with him such books as the Five Classics, the *Hsing-li ta-ch'üan*, and the *Tzu-chih t'ung-chien kang-mu*, so be it.[49]

(Proper Behavior)

It is the duty of all students to cast off bad habits. In private dining it is not permitted to gather outsiders and discuss the strengths and faults of others.

In speech one should value simplicity, loyalty, and faithfulness.

In clothing one should value dignity and plainness.

Students are not allowed to drink liquor and wander about the streets indulging in amusements which might disturb their minds and natures and hinder their course of study.

In study one values steadiness. It is not good to exhaust the spirit. At the height of the summer's heat, the student need not read in the evening until midnight, instead practicing quiet sitting to nurture his mind. At other times he may stop at the first drum [8 P.M.] and then practice quiet sitting to nourish his mind.

(Social courtesies)

The essay "On the Hall for Honoring the Rites" gives instructions to students for relations with outsiders. It says that if in a meeting there is some occasion for celebration or a banquet, it should be simple, and it is not necessary to kill animals for meat. At each table for four there may be five meat dishes and two vegetables, a round of noodle soup, and two plates of noodles [or buns], and one jar of wine. . . .

Shih was the personal name of the Duke of Shao, and the Duke of Chou called him Lord Shih, honoring his disposition. Later generations relied on the courtesy name (*tzu*) and observed the taboo against his personal name, and then gave him an honorific name (*hao*) to avoid the courtesy name.[50] From this day forth you should address each other by your courtesy names. A younger person should be addressed by his courtesy name, and an elder called by his courtesy name together with the appellation "elder brother." This is the custom of the ancients.

The students are truly like brothers. In sitting together they need not observe distinctions of host and guest, but simply rank themselves according to age. If that should cause inconvenience to other guests, then it can be temporarily altered.

(Pleasures)

On the first and fifteenth days of the month in the afternoon students should climb East Mountain near the city wall where there is some spot of scenic beauty, there to imitate Tseng Tien's delight in washing in the Yi and enjoying the wind among the rain altars. After supper all should go to the Hall for Expounding Classics to engage in quiet sitting or to recite a section of the Four Books or to chant a poem.[51]

The regulations depict a school aimed at grooming worthy disciples of Confucius. Lin provided a detailed program of study and literary training, based on the classics and the Four Books. He proposed regulations to limit the amount of socializing and feasting, so that the school would be more than a social club.[52] Like Confucius, he sought to instill in his students gentlemanly behavior as a part of their training. Moreover, he wanted to hold study itself in moderation, so as not to threaten health or exhaust the mind. He was concerned that students treat each other with respect but not excessive formality. Finally, he alluded to Confucius' praise of Tseng Tien in suggesting the simple pleasures of the man of the Way, enjoying a pleasant outing with friends.

In his calling, Lin's understanding of Confucian mind-cultivation had been enriched and broadened by means of a syncretic integration with certain ideas and techniques from Buddhist and Taoist traditions, but there is no trace of syncretism in the early school regulations. They make no mention of his system of mind-cultivation or his healing technique. There is a reason for this omission. Because he had just weathered the confrontation with school authorities, he was acutely aware of his ambivalent claim to the status of teacher in the eyes of society. His uncertainty about his new role put him at pains to demonstrate that his curriculum conformed to an acceptable Confucian standard. Thus in his introduction to the regulations Lin Chao-en urged his students to prepare for government service as well as pursuing the moral Way. Although he had rejected examination study and government service for himself, his school did not challenge the official view of the importance of government service. The strong Confucian tone and style of the early years of Lin's teaching is corroborated by the Confucian themes of Lin's writings known to date from this period, in particular the detailed essays on ritual.[53] In these years, his private vision was syncretic, but his public image was strictly Confucian.

THE MAKING OF
A RELIGIOUS LEADER

However, events of succeeding years altered Lin's image of himself as a teacher. There is no evidence that this alteration was sudden, blinding, or even fully conscious; it came in a series of step-by-step changes caused by external events. To Lin it must have seemed a natural evolution of affairs.

The change occurred during a period from 1556 to 1563, when the P'u-t'ien area was beset with Japanese pirate raids.[54] The raids were bloody, leaving roads and fields strewn with corpses. From 1560 on villagers and peasants were frequently forced to seek refuge in temples within the city walls; agricultural production was interrupted and food shortages became acute. As the raids continued, the corpses on the roads and the crowded refugee conditions in the town combined to cause widespread illness. When the city fell to the pirates in 1562, many died trying to escape with their families.[55]

Clearly this was a community crisis, and the human suffering engendered a spiritual crisis as well. For Lin Chao-en, it was the coming together of the man and his time, for during this time he assumed a position of spiritual leadership, not only of his students but of the community at large. He became involved in the crisis at many levels. He proposed a plan for defense of the area. He offered himself as a hostage to shame the community into paying some mercenaries they had hired.[56] He and his family and disciples were deeply involved in relief efforts, distributing food and medicine to the refugees. He was best remembered, however, for his burial of thousands of corpses left unattended because there were no relatives on hand to look after their burial and sacrifices. Here, from the Chinese point of view, was a serious matter indeed. Ancestors in Chinese religion were the source of great blessings or great misfortunes. When ancestors were properly buried and mourned, remembered, revered, and "well fed" with ritual offerings, they would bring great good fortune—sons, wealth, harvests. However, ancestors not buried, not mourned, and not "fed" became "hungry ghosts," who in their anger were a constant menace to the living, causing illness, insanity, sterility, economic failure, bad luck generally, and death.[57] These vengeful souls had to be put to rest before true order could finally be restored.

Over these years Lin Chao-en and his disciples worked steadily to bury large numbers of such dead. At first they attempted to bury them in coffins, the preferred Chinese style, but when the sheer numbers of bodies forced them to turn to cremation, Lin invited monks from as far as Peking to preside over cremation ceremonies.[58]

In the course of the burials, Lin took his first steps toward something like a priestly role; he personally composed prayers and offered sacrifices to the spirits of the dead, thus filling in for their absent descendants. In these prayers he announced to the spirits precisely what he and his disciples had done toward the burial effort, and then offered sacrifices of food and drink for the repose of their souls.[59] Finally, he held a service for the salvation of all the souls, first notifying them in a prayer:

> Acceding to the request of my countrymen, I selected by divination the fourteenth day of this month as the time for the salvation of the souls. I respectfully give advance notice to the spirits [of the dead]: All of you, male or female, high or low, old or young, those whom we have encoffined and buried; those who were lifted and cremated; whether you have been slain and your family perished so that you have no one to depend upon; whether you are from other parts, having died as travelers in P'u-t'ien; whether your bodies were carried away by the waters and have not yet been recovered: if your spirits have consciousness, I entreat you all to come at the appointed hour to the Buddhist ritual platform at the Buddha Hall on the Eastern Slope, so that I shall be able to give comfort to the spirits of the manifold souls of the dead and to deliver them, thereby in some small way fulfilling my heart's wish.
>
> [There follows a passage in which those who died by fire, by water, or in battle are comforted by the examples of famous historical figures who met similar deaths.]
>
> Among you spirits, how could you not deem it unfortunate that you were not encoffined and buried, but were cremated? I had you cremated to prevent the exposure of your remains and your rotting flesh; this is really your good fortune. How can the world be free of exposed

and rotting corpses if we do not cremate and bury them? If your spirits have consciousness, let this be a comfort to you.[60]

During the period of the pirate raids Lin Chao-en ministered to the physical and spiritual needs of the community and the spiritual threat of restless dead. He moved from his cautious beginnings as a teacher with a few students among his family and friends into the role of community leader with a philanthropic and spiritual mission. If healing had been originally a compensation for his non-official status, it had now become an integral part of his mission to serve others. Moreover, the official commendation he received for his activities during the pirate raids offset to a great extent any lingering official doubts over his not pursuing examination studies. He had gained public recognition for his service as a private teacher.

As a result of all these factors, there was a discernible shift in Lin's teaching style; he transcended his former style as a teacher in the traditional Confucian mold, and became a teacher of the religious mold, the Master of the Three Teachings. His shift in style can be seen as an expansion of his understanding of the ideal of the sage. Traditionally, the sage had to be a scholar; a moral example to his family, his students, and the world at large; and a public servant who devoted his life to upholding the social order and human ideals endorsed by Confucianism. During the pirate raids Lin fulfilled the roles of moral exemplar and maintainer of social and human order, not as an official but in his capacity as a healer, philanthropist, and minister to spiritual needs. In short, he found a new ideal of public service as an imparter of truth, a healer of ills, and a comforter of the suffering.

His shift in identity is corroborated in his writings. Shortly after the pirate raids Lin published two of his most important works, the *San-chiao hui-pien* (Joint chronicle of the three teachings) in 1562 and the *Hsin-sheng chih-chih* (Direct pointing to the mind as sage) in 1564. The first was Lin's compendium on the Three Teachings, a discussion of erroneous and correct interpretations of each of the three traditions over the course of Chinese history. It set the style for all of Lin's subsequent syncretic thought. The work reflected Lin's urge to expand his teachings further into all traditions. The second is the most important single source on Lin's system of mind-cultivation. Its appearance at this time suggests that Lin began to foresee a broader religious role in his teaching with more time given to the concrete problems of self-cultivation in the effort to realize the sagely mind within the self.

MASTER OF THE THREE TEACHINGS

As of 1563, then, Lin had assumed the role of a religious teacher. The next twenty-five years of his life were devoted to spreading the correct doctrine of the Three Teachings. He began to travel widely around southeast China, teaching along the roads and in towns at the invitation of local gentry. If his teaching efforts generated interest he deputed disciples to carry on after he left; he also sent them to answer some of the invitations he received. As his teachings spread, demand grew for the publication of his writings. From 1567 on, collections of Lin's writings were regularly edited and dispersed, and new writings were continually going into woodblock editions.[61]

By 1571 his following had grown so large that he was forced to expand his school in P'u-t'ien. When he did so, he posted new regulations for his disciples. In contrast to the earlier regulations, these make it clear that adherents of all religions and a variety of social backgrounds studied at the school.

To Scholars [registered students]:

If you can accept and uphold the Confucian method of mind-cultivation and at the same time pursue your examination studies and feel no conflict between these two, then you are my disciples, and may enter.

If you cannot accept the Confucian method of mind-cultivation, you are no different from vulgar Confucians. You are not my disciples, and may not enter.

Or, if you can accept the Confucian method of mind-cultivation, but deem examination studies an obstacle to it and lightly reject them, can you be called scholars? You are not my disciples either, and may not enter.

Those who enter must sit in the eastern lodge and not cross over into other lodges and sit with other groups.

To Farmers, Artisans, and Merchants:

If you are able to accept and uphold the Confucian method of mind-cultivation and each maintain his apportioned lot and be at peace with his regular work, then you are my disciples, and may enter.

If you cannot accept the Confucian method of mind-cultivation, then you are no different from vulgar farmers, artisans, and merchants. You are not my disciples and may not enter.

If you can accept the Confucian method of mind-cultivation but do not maintain your apportioned lots or are not at peace with your regular work, how can you be called farmers, or artisans, or merchants? You are not my disciples and may not enter.

Those who enter must sit in the western lodge, and not cross over into other lodges and sit with other groups.

To Commoners [those who fit no other category, often scholars, no longer registered as students]:

If you can accept and uphold the Confucian method of mind-cultivation and at the same time administer your households according to principle and adequately serve those above you and nurture those below you,[62] you are my disciples, and may enter.

If you cannot accept the Confucian method of mind-cultivation, but do not serve those above you and nurture those below you, can you be called [good] commoners? You are not my disciples, and may not enter.

Those who enter must sit in the easternmost lodge, and not cross into other lodges and sit with other groups.

To Taoists and Buddhists:

If you can accept and uphold the Confucian method of mind-cultivation and also recite and study the classics and scriptures and accept the precepts and discipline in the scriptures, then you are my disciples, and may enter.

If you cannot accept the Confucian method of mind-cultivation, then you are no different from vulgar monks and Taoists. You are not my disciples, and may not enter.

If you can accept the Confucian method of mind-cultivation, but do not study and recite the classics and scriptures and accept the precepts and discipline in the scriptures, can you be called disciples of Taoism or Buddhism? You are not my disciples and may not enter.

Those who enter must sit in the westernmost lodge, and not cross over into other lodges and sit with other groups.[63]

What all these groups shared was a commitment to Lin Chao-en's method of mind-cultivation. Lin insisted that this could and must be practiced in conjunction with the religious, moral, and occupational duties of each social class. It is noteworthy that Lin Chao-en requested Taoists and Buddhists to continue their religious practices and to maintain their vows, and also that he strictly prohibited any mixing of the various groups. Lin Chao-en sought to attract followers from all social classes, but the equality of men lay in their capacity for sagehood; such equality was by no means a denial of the validity of social distinctions. Lin Chao-en taught that the Way should be open to all, regardless of wealth or position. The regulations for disciples establish his concrete concern with people from all groups. However, the sources provide very scant information on those disciples who were not officials.[64] We are told that Lin taught people of all social backgrounds. On his trip to Ch'iao-yang in 1572, even the poor, the sickly, and the crippled were among the crowds that came to hear Lin Chao-en; he taught them all. None of this is sufficient to establish the actual breadth of the social base among Lin Chao-en's disciples. Lin made a concerted effort to reach all social classes; to what extent he did in fact reach peasants and artisans cannot be determined by the available evidence.

THE PINNACLE OF HIS CAREER

By around 1580 Lin had reached the pinnacle of his career. He was sixty-four years old. Wherever he went he was greeted by large crowds who were eager to hear his teachings. In the 1580s he was active in repairing temples of all three traditions. He began seriously to prepare a legacy to leave for his students. It was during this time that he wrote his commentaries on Buddhist and Taoist texts. The editing of new collections accelerated greatly. More and more disciples were sent out to teach throughout the southeast.

Lin had begun to attract some relatively eminent disciples. In 1589 he received letters from a group of scholars at the Hanlin Academy who had been instructed in his doctrine by Wang K'o-shou (dates unclear). These men were enthusiastic and proclaimed themselves Lin's unofficial disciples. When they met a relative of Lin's who was going back to P'u-t'ien, they sent a group of letters asking for further instruction in his doctrine of mind.[65]

Lin had also gained respect in scholarly circles. Tsou Yüan-piao (1551–1624), leader of the Tung-lin party, defended Lin Chao-en against detractors.[66] Keng Ting-hsiang (1524–1596) of the T'ai-chou school, who had served as a superintendent of education in Fukien, once recommended Lin to the court. In his petition, Keng advocated a broader avenue for attracting men of talent, arguing that the examination system was no longer in fact sifting out from the population all men of profound scholarship and worthy conduct who might insure wise counsel to the throne.[67] Although the petition was not accepted by the government, the very fact that Keng submitted it testifies to his respect for Lin Chao-en. Finally, Yüan Huang once visited Lin and praised the profundity and insight of his interpretation of the classics.[68]

Lin also had his enemies in official and scholarly circles. Both he and his disciples had to contend with occasional charges of heresy. However, no one was able during Lin's lifetime to sustain successfully a charge of heresy against Lin or the cult.[69]

This may have been in part because Lin was very sensitive about his public reputation for integrity and orthodoxy. Perhaps his early struggle with the authorities had taught him a lesson. Lin taught that both public and private integrity were necessary to the practice of the Way, and therefore he advocated the practice of vows to heaven. Lin offered such vows every morning before he turned to his daily business, and he required that students take vows before receiving instruction and at other points in their training.[70] The vows informed heaven of his activities and his determination to do good deeds and accomplish good works. They also served the function of bearing witness before his disciples and others of his lofty intentions and correct behavior. They constituted, as it were, a constant public testimony under oath that Lin was not using his position as a teacher for heterodox or unlawful purposes.

For example, Lin Chao-en clearly set forth the moral exigencies of his role as a leader in an early vow:

> I, your servant, Lin Chao-en, not fully aware of my limitations, presume by means of expounding the doctrine of the sagely mind to bring the errors of the Three Teachings back to the principles of Confucius in order to continue the wisdom of the past and to reform the generations to come.
> Therefore, when any student came, I declined all gifts, even trifling things such as caps and kerchiefs. This shows that I was careful in the beginnings of my intentions to practice the mind of the Way. Later, if I lacked road expenses on a long journey, then I accepted various gifts to be used for boat and carriage fees and travel expenses, or for the necessities of food and clothing; but I never used any part of them for my private profit. This is the distinction between honesty and cupidity, and I dare not fail to be pure in this regard.
> As for gifts of cloth or other material goods, in order to express their sincerity, students must conduct their social intercourse [with me] in accordance with the Way and proper ritual before I will accept gifts. Even then I do not wish to take much from them. This shows the principle of respect in social intercourse, and I dare not but follow it scrupulously. . . .
> Now my teaching does not compare with the teaching of Confucius and Mencius, and the present times also do not compare with the times of Confucius and Mencius. Furthermore, there are many, many people who avail themselves of the Way as a means to fame and profit. It is precisely for this reason that I dare to brave death to send this petition.
> If your servant is carried away by profit or acts in violation of what has been set forth in this petition, then I will be cheating heaven by cheating myself. Since heaven is a brilliantly clear mirror, how could I not be punished with death?
> I have vowed this of my own volition; if I violate it on my own volition, it is my willful sin. Who else have I to blame? I approach with fear and trembling.[71]

In the petitions Lin listed in detail the income and expenditures for travel, publishing, charity, and any building or repairs on the grounds at East Mountain, where his school was located. To give but one example:

> Your servant Lin Chao-en respectfully petitions:
> On the nineteenth day, fourth month, 1572, I went to Shao-wu. On the second day, ninth month, I returned to the county seat [i.e., P'u-

t'ien]. I still had 27 *liang*, 2 *ch'ien*, 6 *fen* of silver.⁷² In previous years when I had traveled afar and returned, I divided whatever money was left over and gave it to the poor. But because the grounds of the Hall for Honoring Confucius had not been paved with bricks, the courtyard had not been paved with stones, the walls had not been plastered, the gates were not in good repair, and there were no tiles to protect the wood against the elements, the students in the county seat felt that the extra funds should be used to repair and decorate this hall in order to accommodate students from far and near. Was not what they said better than simply to give it to the poor? I agreed to their proposal, and accordingly delegated Yao Min of Shao-wu to come to P'u-t'ien to oversee expenditures and keep an account. At the time student Hung Tzu-wen contributed 40 *liang* of silver. Monk Hui-ti of Kuang-t'a Temple and others were raising money, but when the cedar was purchased they were short 4 *liang*, 8 *ch'ien*, and were pressed for payment. I sent them that amount, and still had 64 *liang*, 4 *ch'ien*, 6 *fen*.

Again some students gave 2 *liang*, 4 *ch'ien*, 8 *fen*, and as a congratulatory present on the occasion of the beam-raising ceremony, gave 1 *liang*, 6 *ch'ien*, 2 *fen*, 5 *li*, for a total of 66 *liang*, 5 *ch'ien*, 6 *fen*, 5 *li*.

I also used 20 *liang* from income from lands set aside for charity.

First we built and covered the two doors of the Hall for Honoring Confucius; then we built two towers to the east and west, and two corridors.

All of this is in Yao Min's record of expenditures, and can be checked point by point. For that purpose I attach the sheet of expenditures and announce it in petition, that heaven may examine it.

Your servant Chao-en approaches with fear and trembling, and respectfully reports."⁷³

In these petitions Lin Chao-en kept his slate clean before the eyes of gods and men; in one petition he stipulated, "I had all the income and expenditures entered in two identical account sheets. One was kept in a public place so that students could examine it; one was stored in the home of Ch'en Tao-ch'ing."⁷⁴ In this way Lin set a moral example for the members of his cult—which, it should be remembered, included merchants. Furthermore, he placed the decisions and government of the cult under the scrutiny of heaven, subjecting his actions not merely to legal or social sanctions but to the ultimate moral sanction of heaven itself.

He also maintained a watch over the activities of his disciples on behalf of the cult. During a famine in 1594 Lin Chao-en sent grain to the public granary to be used for famine relief. When he heard that those in charge of transporting the grain were taking it for their own use, he expelled them from the organization.[75] Lin's meticulous concern over the sect's reputation for integrity was no doubt an important factor in its freedom from persecution.

THE END AND THE BEGINNING

In 1596 disciples came from far and wide to celebrate the Master's eightieth birthday.[76] From that time on, Lin withdrew from teaching activities and began in earnest to prepare for the end. He began to talk and eat less, but he still had his vital force in full measure and his color was still healthy; there was no appearance of sickness in him. He had a vision of the Masters of the Three Teachings, who enjoined him to uphold the Three Teachings and save the three schools. He announced to a disciple the time he would "return" to the state of Nonbeing.[77]

He withdrew more and more from external affairs.

> The Master from this time on was oblivious to outward forms and had returned to a state of voidness. He no longer wrote. Even when his formerly close acquaintances came to pay their respects, the Master often did not remember their names; but when he spoke with them, he always hit the absolute essential point.[78]

Toward the end of 1597 he became very weak, even losing the capacity for speech. It was an effort for him to raise his hands.

> He was not still, yet not without stillness. He was not stimulated by externals, yet not lacking stimulation. He was beyond substance, yet not without substance. He was beyond function, yet not functionless. He had no particular nature, yet was not without a nature. He was free of passions, yet not passionless. He was beyond emptiness, yet did not lack emptiness. He was beyond nonemptiness, yet was not unempty.[79]

In this state he was close to the final state of perfect unity with the void, and that moment came in early 1598, while he was surrounded by relations and disciples: "Between three and five A.M. the Master folded his hands and passed away. His hands opened and closed again. His limbs and body became soft. His hair turned black once more, and his color was light yellow [not ashen]."[80]

Some biographers, evidently focusing upon the reports of forgetfulness in the above accounts, claim that Lin died insane.[81] However, note that the above accounts report that he was lucid, although oblivious of external affairs and probably a bit senile. His disciples interpreted his withdrawal from external affairs as a turning inward, away from the discriminations of the senses to the inner contemplation of the void. The disciples' account of Lin's death is clearly hagiography, but it is unclear that the report of insanity is any more accurate. It is more likely that the latter is a misunderstanding of the meaning of the disciples' description, since the critics relied on the disciples' accounts.

What is noteworthy is that the biographers depict Lin as choosing a type of religious death, not unlike that of other religious figures in Chinese history. He predicted the time of his passing away.[82] As the end approached, he entered into a deep meditative trance, passing away in a state of pure mental concentration. Finally, the restoration of the youthful appearance of the body is a sign of great spirituality; such well-preserved bodies were worshiped as deities, as though they were temple images.[83]

One of his disciples discussed the meaning of Lin's death in his eulogy:

> When the Master first established his doctrine, he referred to Confucius, Lao Tzu, and Śākyamuni as the Masters of the Three Teachings. Today the people of the world, whether they are scholars or gentry, Taoists or Buddhists, or the countless living beings, all refer to our master as the Master of the Three Teachings.
> Now the wise man is said to have withered away.[84] In our generation, those who saw the Master rejoiced, and those who were unable to see him lamented it. Hence, we know that our Master is one with Confucius, Lao Tzu, and Śākyamuni, and he is also distinct from them. Is it the man with form and countenance who is our Master, or is it the being beyond form and countenance? At times he is in the world, a Master with form and countenance, who draws the eight trigrams,[85] achieves Nirvāṇa, and elucidates the Three Teachings. At other times

he is outside the world, a Master without form or countenance, who encloses heaven and covers earth, who penetrates mountains and rivers, who rises and sets with the sun and moon.

Being is originally produced by Nonbeing, and Nonbeing is originally without a beginning. Who can say that the Master came into life through coming into Being [i.e., birth] and died through death? Thus, who can say that to see the Master is fortunate, and that not to see the Master is unfortunate? The Master was born many times from ancient times until today, repeatedly passing from Nonbeing into Being and from Being into Nonbeing. When this life directed him toward Being, he was even more hard-working; when this life returned him to Nonbeing, he became even greater.[86]

Thus in the eyes of his disciples, at least, the death of Lin Chao-en was not an end, but a beginning in the life of the cult.

CHAPTER FIVE

THE SYSTEM OF MIND-CULTIVATION

Lin Chao-en's formative spiritual crisis resulted from his difficulties in putting into practice the ideals of Neo-Confucianism by personally embodying the sagely mind, which was the pivot of his philosophy. Lin judged every religious and philosophical concept in terms of its ability to convey the truth of sagely mind. But without praxis, without some means to actualize sagely mind, all theories and truths were mere verbiage. Lin's examination of the Three Teachings taught him that none of them by itself could show him the way out of his spiritual malaise. In his view, Neo-Confucians were long on theories but short on effective and workable praxis. Buddhists and Taoists were long on techniques, but short on attention to the sagely mind.

His search ended in a method of mind-cultivation based on the hexagram *ken*. The nine stages of mind-cultivation represented a personal synthesis of the Three Teachings that Lin regarded as both practicable and theoretically sound. This personal synthesis, arising from a deeply felt spiritual need, was in turn the basis for Lin's integration of the Three Teachings; his syncretic thought was the external elaboration of his personal religious vision. He was highly selective in his integration, producing a new system uniquely suited to his concerns; but that system must be understood in light of the theories and techniques of mind-cultivation in each of the three schools.

MIND-CULTIVATION IN THE THREE TEACHINGS

Buddhism

Buddhist meditation was not the predominant form of mind-cultivation in the Ming or in the thought of Lin Chao-en, but in many ways it had set the tone and defined the issues for Neo-Confucian and Inner Alchemy mind-cultivation.

The Buddhists from the time of their founder Śākyamuni had taught that the source of human suffering was in our ordinary habits of mind. People live their lives to maximize happiness and minimize frustration and loss. The way they live assumes that there are things to be desired and things to be avoided, and that there is a self who will benefit from happiness and suffer from loss. Yet according to the Buddhists these assumptions are false. All happiness, all suffering, all selves are impermanent and fleeting, merely temporary products of temporary causes, no more substantial or consequential than a shadow, a mirage, or a dream. They only affect us because we wrongly believe them to be real and consequential; thus the joys and agonies of our lives are in our minds. There is no one to rejoice or suffer, and no things to cause sorrow or joy. To escape delusion and achieve enlightenment, people had to alter their mental habits fundamentally through mind-cultivation.[1]

Buddhists practiced many forms of mind-cultivation. Basic monastic and moral discipline directly assaulted and purified ego-centered and desire-ridden habits of thought, feeling, and action; as adepts controlled speech and action, they also transformed patterns of thought. Early Buddhists meditated on the transience of self and things, envisioning the constant flux and extinction of the "realities" which make up our ordinary world.

Mahāyāna Buddhists greatly expanded the context of

meditational technique. They viewed the historical Buddha as simply one avatar of the cosmic Buddha, the universal and ever-present enlightenment for which all sentient beings are destined. All beings are endowed with the Buddha-nature; buried beneath their ignorance is an actual and actualizable potential for enlightenment. Moreover, the Buddha is compassionate, constantly seeking the enlightenment and salvation of all suffering beings; the embodiment of the Buddha's compassion was the Bodhisattva, an enlightened being who deferred final liberation until all have found their way to salvation.

The Mahāyāna view of the Buddha and Buddha-nature opened the way for many forms of mind-cultivation. Esoteric and ritual sects meditated on mandalas or icons, visualizing the formless and qualityless Buddha as taking on various impermanent, concrete shapes for the sake of deluded beings. The Buddhas and Bodhisattvas which they visualized were no more real than their own egos, but through watching them arise and extinguish the ego-mind could realize the transient qualities of all things.[2] Philosophical schools used reason and dialectic to negate the realities of all things and all dualities, thus forcing the mind beyond its ordinary discursive views and frustrating it until only the innate enlightened mind remained.[3] Pure Land Buddhists visualized the paradise of Amitābha to stimulate their desire for salvation; the Pure Land was not a real or permanent paradise but an expedient means to detach the mind from its bondage to the so-called real world.[4] Other Buddhists meditated on one or more levels of the mind's sensory or ideational activity, thus checking the ordinary flux of thought and then mentally exploring the causes and conditions of that mental state until its illusory nature was understood.[5] Whatever the method, the goal of meditation was to break or redirect the ordinary flow of consciousness so that enlightenment could be manifested. But the above methods were only indirectly influential on Sung and Ming thought. By far the most prominent Buddhist influence at that time came from the Ch'an school.

Ch'an Buddhism, as we have seen, taught that the primary path to enlightenment was the one taken by the historical

Buddha—meditation. Ch'an Buddhists stripped meditation of what they considered to be frills; they did not allow inner visualization of Buddhas or paradises, nor did they focus on any of the activities of the ordinary mind. Ch'an meditation required "simply" laying down the illusory mind of the ego to awaken to the Buddha mind. It used thought to stop the flow of thoughts, concentrating all mental energies to cut off the normal flow of consciousness and to smash through normal rational and emotional modes until the Buddha mind was directly experienced. It allowed no object of meditation which could be comfortably contemplated, for this would be an extension of normal mental patterns. In order to facilitate the breakthrough, which amounted to a destruction of the ego, the master aided the students by literally shocking them out of their normal modes of thought. He might shout at students or strike them at moments of tension to make them drop the old ways of thinking, much as someone will drop an object if grabbed suddenly from behind. He might also shock them in the way he answered or refused to answer their queries. The following classic dialogue illustrates the point:

> A monk asked: "Who is the one who holds the sword in the state?"
> The Master said: "Ts'ao-shan" [i.e., myself].
> The monk said: "Whom do you intend to kill?"
> The Master said: "I shall kill all."
> The monk said: "Suppose you suddenly meet your parents. What will you do?"
> The Master said: "Why discriminate?"
> The monk said: "But there is yourself!"
> The Master said: "Who can do anything about me?"
> The monk said: "Why not kill yourself?"
> The Master said: "No place to start."[6]

In the Lin-chi school, the *kung-an* (J. *kōan*) device was used. The *kung-an* is a focus of meditation, a paradoxical formula pointing to the extrarational meaning of the one mind, the Buddha mind. By wrestling with the *kung-an*, which refuses to be a normal "mental object," students frustrate their ordinary modes of perception and thought until in exhaustion they achieve the state of no mind, no ego mind. At that point they realize that they are the Buddha, the enlightened one; beyond all dualities and rational discrimination, they have reached enlightenment and have seen the original face they had before they were conceived.[7]

During the Ming, as we have seen, Chu-hung popularized the combination of Ch'an meditation with the recitation of the Buddha's name from Pure Land Buddhism. He sought thereby to stem a growing decadence in the Ch'an school; the answers to *kung-an* were being published, resulting in many spurious enlightenments.[8] The recitation of the name was a meditative aid which focused and stabilized the mind, enabling monks and laymen alike to maintain meditative concentration in the midst of activity. It provided a concrete activity which made the earlier stages of meditation much more accessible to ordinary human beings.

Taoism

The primary goal of religious Taoism was to transcend the limits of mortality, to conquer death and attain life. This goal was shared by the Inner Alchemy school of Taoist meditation, but it was interpreted at different levels by different thinkers, some seeing the end of meditation as the physical and spiritual transformation of man into an immortal, a godlike being with an indestructible spiritual body infusing and illuminating the physical body. Others saw it as the transformation of man into a new spiritual state through the mind, a mind made new, reborn into its original state of unity with the Tao, a mind of pure luminosity which could light the entire cosmos. In its luminosity and voidness, empty of obstruction and open to all possibilities, it was coterminous and coexistent with the Tao.

Inner Alchemy meditation was a form of yoga, a disciplined method of physical and spiritual praxis leading to the destruction of the profane man and the rebirth of a new spiritualized man. In overall structure, the Inner Alchemy system of yogic transmutation had strong affinities with Indian and Tibetan yogas. In each, fundamental psychospiritual forces of the personality were manipulated through a complex, subtle physiology. As they moved, they cleansed and purified the centers and circuits of this subtle body, while they in turn were purified and reintegrated to release spiritual powers within the self. Despite the affinities, however, Inner Alchemy yoga was distinctively Chinese. It was based upon the Chinese metaphysics of yin and yang and the Five Phases, as contained in the Han commentaries to the *Book of Changes* and the texts of the Han alchemists. The model and language came from Chinese alchemy; Indian and Tibetan gods and mythologies had no place in the system.[9]

The transformation of the person in Inner Alchemy meditation was both physical and spiritual; desires and aberrant thoughts were conquered directly by a method of mind and body control, not by ethical cultivation. Ethics had its place; evil deeds were seen to arise from desires, and they could wipe out progress in meditation.[10] But spiritual progress was not measured by any external ethical transformation; the task of meditation was an inner rebirth based on a metaphysical model of the cosmic order. Inner Alchemy transformation was designed to counter the direction of the normal course of life, which was toward debilitation and death. In the Inner Alchemy view, humans were composed of two elements, *hsing* (human nature) and *ming* (life store). Nature is the source of human spiritual faculties (*shen*, spirit), while life store is the font of vitality (*ching*, vital essence). As they grow, people wrongly come to see themselves as set apart from the world and things. They want to get and to avoid; they love and they hate; they strive and withdraw. Over time the spiritual faculties are clouded over by desires, things, and sensory stimuli (activities of the mind), and the vital forces are wasted in sex, violent emotions, and desires, which cause the vital fluids (sexual fluids, sweat, saliva, moist breath) to drain away. When the spiritual faculties are dimmed and the life store exhausted, the result is death. Only by recovering the original *hsing* and *ming* can the process be reversed. The restoration of original *hsing* and *ming* in the microcosm of the self was parallel to the nondifferentiated state at the beginning of creation—that which antedated heaven. In the human microcosm this state represented the original self prior to impure thoughts; it was called the uncarved block or the infant in Lao

96 THE SYSTEM OF MIND-CULTIVATION

Tzu, and the sage or immortal embryo in Inner Alchemy. Through this re-creation the Taoist became physically and spiritually identified with the underlying cosmic unity of the Tao.

The process of transformation was elaborated in arcane terms and symbols. The internal yoga of Inner Alchemy dealt with mysteries which could not be learned for oneself. The language of alchemy screened the truth from all but the initiate who had learned it from an enlightened master. The path of meditation had its dangers; to overcome them one had to possess the secret knowledge of how to manipulate the powerful emotional, physical, and cosmic forces released.

The early stages of meditation involved a threefold effort: controlling thoughts to keep them from wandering after external temptations, controlling the breath in order to calm the emotions and the body, and controlling passions by means of sublimating sexual desires into heightened vitality. These efforts went against and attempted to conquer normal (profane) human reactions, thus reversing the direction of life.[11] They required a special posture to still the body, and intense concentration to master the flow of consciousness, the breathing cycle, and sexual impulses. This intense concentration focused and purified the mind; there was no room for extraneous or impure thoughts. The transmuted sexual essence with its life-producing properties became the basis of the elixir, the seed for the emergence of a new self. The controlled breath modulated and manipulated the functionings of the internal microcosm to refine the seed of the elixir with chemical techniques until the sage embryo was ready to emerge. In this system the body was a small-scale model of the universe in which all forces of nature were present, homologous to the cosmic laboratory.

The process of transmutation was modeled on the alchemical production of the elixir of life, which transmuted raw lead and mercury into a compound which captured the life-producing and life-sustaining properties of nature. After lead and mercury were gathered in their impure forms, they were separately refined in the laboratory through a process of repeated heatings and washings in a tripod, using drugs—herbal catalysts—to help wash away impurities. The regulation of the fires, the timing of heating and washing cycles and of the addition of catalysts, were all based on a knowledge of the creative processes of nature and of the movements of heavenly bodies in the cycle of Changes. The refined lead and mercury were then put together in the tripod and alchemically fused. This was the most difficult and mysterious stage of the process, for here the secrets of nature were "stolen" to reverse the movement from life to death. The fires were stopped at precisely the right moment after fusion, and the elixir was stored in a special place to give it time to "ripen." If removed prematurely, it would lose its life-giving qualities. Only someone with the secret knowledge of the workings of the cosmos could determine the right hour for the removal of the elixir, and only he could understand how to use it.

In the internal laboratory of the body, there were three main fields or points of concentration. The lower elixir field (*tan-t'ien*), about 1.3 Chinese inches below the navel, served throughout the process as the alchemical furnace. (A Chinese inch [*ts'un*] is slightly longer than a Western inch; 1.3 *ts'un* converts to roughly 1½ inches.) In the first stages of the process this field also served as the tripod, the locus into which effort was poured. Later the tripod was moved to the central elixir field, the yellow chamber (*huang-t'ing*), which corresponded roughly to the solar plexus. Finally, it was moved to the upper elixir field (*ni-wan*), located at a point between and behind the eyebrows. These three elixir fields were joined by a circuit to form the Center, in which all the psychospiritual forces were harmonized and reintegrated. The Center was the balance point, the inner core of psychic forces. Mental energies were drawn back into the Center and transmuted there. There was also a circuit running up the spine with various openings (or passes) ending in the brain, and another running down the front of the body back to the yellow chamber. Breath and vital forces were circulated through these channels in imitation of the movements of the heavenly bodies; the circulation was called the "revolutions of heaven." The circuits were linked to and controlled by the eyes, the main agency for directing and focusing attention.[12] The fields and circuits comprised a spiritual physiology which did not correspond precisely to any system of nerves or vessels locatable through medical observation. Yet the movement of heat and energy through this circuit transcended Inner Alchemy Taoism; it was attested to by adepts of many religions who subscribed to a similar mode of physical and mental discipline.[13] The elixir was refined in each of the three elixir fields in turn until it was ready to be "born" as the sage immortal.

The alchemical symbols of Taoist meditation were understood in light of chains of correspondences; terms in each chain were understood to be equivalent to and suggest each other.

Ching = sexual fluid (vital fluid)
     = vital essence (sublimated form)
     = Water (among the Five Phases)
     = kidney-orb (among the five organ orbs)[14]
     = *k'an* hexagram (in impure, postnatal state)
     = *k'un* hexagram (in pure prenatal state)
     = lead (an ingredient of the elixir)
     = earth (as opposed to heaven)
     = life store (*ming*)
Hsin = heart/mind (emotion, intellection, gate of the senses)
     = spirit (sublimated form)
     = Fire (among the Five Phases)
     = heart-orb (among the five organ orbs)
     = *li* hexagram (in impure, postnatal state)
     = *ch'ien* hexagram (in pure, prenatal state)
     = mercury (ingredient in the elixir)
     = heaven (as opposed to earth)
     = nature (*hsing*).

Underlying and permeating both these chains was *ch'i*, vital force,[15] the basic stuff and breath of the universe in which the human breath participates. The chain of correspondences gave the spiritual transmutation of the personality specific physiological correlates. At every point in the process the adept physically experienced the process of change.

The first phase of Inner Alchemy meditation, after learning to concentrate the mind and control the breath, was to subli-

THE SYSTEM OF MIND-CULTIVATION 99

mate and purify vital essence to be the first ingredient of the elixir. To do this, the adept checked the outward flow of vital force in the form of vital fluid (sexual fluids—semen in the male) and sublimated it into vital essence in the lower elixir field.[16] The accumulation of vital force in this field led to a sensation of heat and light, which were circulated with the breath through the inner circuits of the subtle physiology by means of directing and concentrating internal visualization by rolling the eyes. The circulation opened blocked passages in the body and sloughed off impurities in the form of tears, sweat, or gas. The body was gradually rendered pure and healthy. As the body and vital fluid were purified, the latter was transmuted into pure vital essence and stored in the yellow chamber (the central elixir field) from which it emitted the light of vitality. The adept continued internal circulation of vital force until he (or she) was able to lead it up to the openings in the channel leading up the back to the upper elixir field. There, by means of directing the gaze inward (a physical squint combined with inward-looking concentration), he shook loose the vital force of the brain, lifting the veil of obscurity from the light of spirit. This was known as the manifestation of the mysterious pass (*hsüan-kuan*), experienced in the form of a light appearing between the eyebrows; it appeared first in front of the adept, but through practice it could be drawn into the body to shine inwardly. This light represented the original countenance of the individual before he was conceived.

At this point the two lights, the light of vitality (transmuted vital fluid) and light of spirit (transmuted mind) have both emerged, but in their impure postnatal forms. In terms of alchemical symbolism, these two lights are lead and mercury, the two main ingredients of the elixir. Before the elixir could be produced, however, these two ingredients had to be further refined and then fused.

To prepare for the combination of the two ingredients (or lights) the adept further refined and mastered the light of spirit. He gradually learned to control its movements and its brightness, letting it out and gathering it in. Eventually he was able to direct it through the inner channels down to the yellow chamber where the light of vitality was stored, using internal vision to keep it there and swallowing saliva in a special way so as to nourish it. When the light moved or vibrated, he circulated it between the heart and kidney orbs, within the central region of the body, safely away from external bodily apertures through which it might escape, until it slipped into the inner cell of the lower elixir field, called the cavity of vitality (*ch'i-hsüeh*). This cavity served as a womb for the immortal or sage embryo. In this cavity the light of spirit (nature, *hsing*) and the light of vitality (life store) could copulate and thus recombine into their pure, prenatal forms, pure lead and mercury, pure nature and life store, *ch'ien* and *k'un*. When that copulation occured, the adept leaped out of his postnatal profane state into the prenatal, original essence of his being; the leap could transmute the human mind into the mind of the Tao. The copulation was also called the union of Fire and Water, and its completion was marked by stillness, in which all Five Phases of vital force in the body were reunited and balanced in the Center. The union of the two main elements was also a conception; the offspring was the sage embryo, the seed of the elixir, the new self. The conception was experienced as certain physiological sensations—humming, itching. They signaled that the fire should be extinguished so that the elixir could ripen within the caldron. At this point in Inner Alchemy, breathing was stopped to allow for the gestation of the fetus.

Gestation was accomplished by means of fetal breathing, the circulation of vital forces in the body on their own power with no conscious control of exhalation and inhalation. The fetal breath was "self-winding," circulating naturally on its own; the adept merely observed it. Fetal breathing represented a state of deep concentration or trance. If circulation faltered, it was controlled by eye movements, but it would normally go on by itself.

When the fetus was ready to emerge, the adept experienced a further sign, the appearance of a golden wheel of light containing a white wheel in its center. After the wheel appeared, the adept sought out a secluded spot in which, with the aid of friends, he gently moved the fetus up the channel in the spine to the top of the head from which it was born into the world. He now possessed a spiritual body to complement his physical one; the spiritual self could wander outside of him under his direction. Even then the process was not completed, for over against the sagely fetus appeared a demon which was formed from the remaining impurities in the self. This was the final obstacle and temptation, the last-ditch resistance of the profane self to spiritual transformation. The demon had to be conquered to strengthen the infant spiritual self. When the spiritual body became strong, it was drawn back in to sublimate and refine the body until the two selves were congruent. The final transcendence of the "body" and all bases of duality smashed space itself; nothing was left of the postnatal world. The old self was dead; the new spiritual self could take its place as master.

Among Inner Alchemy Taoists there were considerable disagreements as to the meaning of the process. Has the adept achieved physical immortality, spiritual immortality, or mystical union with the Tao? The language allowed for a variety of interpretations. Li Tao-ch'un, disciple of Inner Alchemy patriarch Po Yü-ch'an, once described thirteen vehicles or interpretations of Inner Alchemy. The three lowest vehicles were called the "depraved" path, and were considered by him to be outside the Tao. They interpreted alchemy in terms of sexual tantrism, refinement of the physical products of the body such as semen or menstrual blood, or the ingestion of some form of lead and/or mercury to gain eternal life.[17] The three middle vehicles were said to approach the Tao; they saw Inner Alchemy as a process of fasting; asceticism; imbibing dew, air, or sunlight; the worship of spirits; and manipulation of ritual formulas to gain spiritual powers and long life. The three upper vehicles, called "bypaths" of the Tao, practiced the correct meditative techniques, but they did not understand their cosmic or mystical basis; they saw the techniques as the sum of the process. Next, the three gradual vehicles represent increasingly profound interpretations of the process, leading to the highest "supreme single vehicle." They use different levels of alchemical symbols to see the process in increasingly cosmic or mystical terms. The spiritual attainments of meditation were conditioned by the adept's level of understanding. The different levels of symbols of interpretation also allowed a syncretist like Lin Chao-en to understand Inner Alchemy in terms of the symbols and religious language most consonant with his Confucian world view. Li Tao-ch'un's gradual and supreme vehicles suggested the basis by which this arcane and elaborate system could be translated by non-Taoist syncretists to accord with their religious views:

Gradual Vehicles:

The lower gradual vehicle takes body and mind as the tripod and furnace, vital essence and vital force as the drug, heart and kidney as Fire and Water, the five organ orbs as the Five Phases, liver and lung as lead and mercury, generative force as the true seed. The fire is controlled according to the progression of the seasons, and saliva is swallowed to irrigate and bathe it. The eyes, ears, and mouth are the three essential ingredients; the mysterious pass is the space between the kidneys and the navel; the combination of the Five Phases is the completion of the elixir. This is the method of the peaceful drug; there are over a hundred paths in it; if you can forget emotions, you can nurture life.

The middle vehicle takes *ch'ien* and *k'un* as the furnace and tripod, *li* and *k'an* as Fire and Water, the raven and hare [animals of the sun and moon] as the medicine. The generative force, spirit, two souls, and the will as the Five Phases, the body and mind as the dragon and tiger, vital force as the true seed. The fire is regulated according to the four seasons. One uses the Water *ch'i* in the body to irrigate and bathe the drug, keeping the inner realm in and the outer realm out to aid in the completion of the elixir. The Great Void, the palaces [centers of the mind], and the house of vitality are the three essential ingredients; the *ni-wan* pass in the head [i.e., the upper elixir field] is the mysterious pass. The combination of vital essence and spirit is the formation of the elixir. This is the middle path with several tens of branches; it is similar to the one below. If you follow it without neglect, you can attain long life and long vision.

The upper vehicle takes heaven and earth as the furnace and tripod; sun and moon as Fire and Water; yin and yang as the mechanism of change; lead, mercury, silver, sand, and earth as the Five Phases; nature and emotions as the dragon and tiger; thoughts as the true seed. One uses the mind to refine thoughts in order to control the fire; one stops the thoughts to nurture the fire. One nourishes the lights as the true aiding of the elixir, and takes conquering inner demons as the field of battle. Body, mind, and will are the three essential ingredients.

THE SYSTEM OF MIND-CULTIVATION 103

The mind of heaven is the mysterious pass. When the passions all return to human nature, that is the formation of the elixir. The harmonization of vital force is called bathing the elixir. These things lead to birth in a higher realm. This resembles the last two vehicles, but the object of application is different. It also has ten-odd branches. This is for talented adepts.

The Supreme Single Vehicle:

The supreme single vehicle is the matchless, absolute, wondrous Tao. It takes the Great Void as the tripod, the Great Ultimate as the furnace. Purity is the base of the elixir, and nonaction is the elixir's mother. Nature and life store are the lead and mercury; concentration and wisdom are Water and Fire; restraint of desires and anger is the intercourse of Fire and Water; the union of nature and feelings is the combining of Metal and Wood. Washing the mind to remove worries is bathing the elixir; maintaining sincerity and calming the will are firm completion. Precepts, concentration, and wisdom are the three essential ingredients. The Center is the mysterious pass. Enlightenment of the mind is fulfillment. Manifesting the nature is the formation of the elixir. The undifferentiated unity of the three originals [original nature, generative force, and vital force] is the sage embryo. The amalgamation of nature and life is the formation of the elixir. Having no body outside the self is releasing the embryo. Breaking through the emptiness is finishing up.[18]

The lowest gradual vehicle saw the process in terms of the physiological correlates of the internal microcosm; the second was dominated by the symbols and laws of change acting on earth; the third was dominated by the symbols of the movements of heavenly bodies. The supreme vehicle, however, was understood in terms of the highest metaphysical and cosmic symbols, the Great Void in which all exists and the Great Ultimate (*T'ai-chi*), the symbol of the unity behind all movements of the Tao. The supreme vehicle thus saw the new self as coexistent with reality itself; it was mystical in smashing the ordinary perception of reality as something "out there."

Neo-Confucianism

As we saw in our discussion of the Sung, Neo-Confucians elaborated a new spiritual ideal, the sage who would embody the full potential of the spiritual luminosity and vastness of mind and nature with which heaven endowed human beings. The realization of this ideal required a more profound understanding of the basis and process of self-cultivation.

Early Neo-Confucians sought to identify the basis of the religious identification of the self with the cosmos. Chang Tsai (1026–1077) posited *ch'i* (material force) as the stuff of reality, the one substance underlying the multiplicity of things. The *ch'i* of man unites him with all things in the universe as if they were his family. "Heaven is my father and earth is my mother, and even such a small creature as I finds an intimate place in their midst. Therefore that which extends throughout the universe I regard as my body and that which directs the universe I consider as my nature. All people are my brothers and sisters, and all things are my companions." [19] Chang Tsai envisioned an ethical mysticism in which the sage saw all men and things as intimately related to him through their common substance or *ch'i*. To achieve sagehood, one would have to purify and expand *ch'i*. Ch'eng I (1033–1107), on the other hand, saw the virtue of humanity or benevolence (*jen*) as the agent of the identification of man and the world: "The humane man regards Heaven and Earth and all things as one body. There is nothing which is not part of his self. Knowing that, where is the limit [of his humanity]?" [20] Thus he saw cultivation as the nurturing of *jen*.

The cultivation of sagehood required more than nurturing and expanding the core of human nature; it also meant holding in check those thoughts and feelings which obscured the moral mind and nature. Chou Tun-i (1017–1073) considered quiescence of mind the antidote for desires, unfettered emotions, and the distractions of external things. The unity and sincerity of the mind were harmed by agitation and reckless activity. In the state of quiescence sincerity of the mind could be restored; the sincere mind could make correct moral decisions. Therefore he taught taking quiescence as fundamental (*chu-ching*).[21] The Ch'eng brothers, although students of Chou Tun-i, felt that Chou's use of the term "quiescence" (*ching*) was dangerously close to the Buddhist view. Although Chou's quiescence was meant to be the basis of moral judgment and hence of moral action, the term itself failed to suggest an active aspect to self-cultivation. It could easily be misinterpreted. For the Neo-Confucians it was not enough to quiet and rectify the mind; inner virtue must manifest itself in outward demeanor and moral action. Thus the Ch'engs substituted for Chou Tun-i's *ching* (quiescence) another *ching* (reverence, or seriousness) as fundamental.[22] The inner state of reverence entailed attitudes of seriousness, caution, and sincerity which governed moral activity. It was an attitude of concentration and single-mindedness which sustained calm whether the mind was active or at rest. Seriousness in action required undivided attention, avoidance of distractions, and appropriate responses to every situation.[23]

Chu Hsi's synthesis of Sung Neo-Confucianism followed the Ch'eng brothers' adherence to seriousness. He taught the importance of the investigation of things (*ko-wu*), the investigation of the moral principles of external things and affairs through study and observation and the investigation of moral principles in one's own mind through ethical self-reflection. External investigation, or extension of knowledge, was not cut off from self-reflection (*hsing-ch'a*) or self-nurture (*han-yang*), since the principles of external things are the same as the principles in one's own mind. The moral principles (*li*) in the mind are equivalent to the heavenly endowed nature (*hsing*). When the mind acts in harmony with and manifests the nature, it is called the rectified mind, the mind of the Way. However, in most people a lifetime of dispositions and habit have obscured the moral nature; the loss of the inborn moral nature arises from people's differing physical endowments of material force (*ch'i*). When the mind acts in harmony with the physical endowment, it is called the mind of physical endowment (*ch'i-chih chih hsin*), or the human mind. This is the ordinary human mind, bound by emotions, bad habits, and external things. The purpose of self-cultivation was to transform the material human mind into the mind of the Way so that the moral principle of the original nature could be manifested.[24]

As an aid to study and self-reflection Chu Hsi and other teachers suggested that students, particularly beginning students, practice quiet sitting (*ching-tso*) to calm their minds and spirits. Quiet sitting was considered an aid to study, for if the spirit wandered there could be no concentration.[25] For the Neo-Confucians quiet sitting was not a form of meditation leading to enlightenment; it was simply one aspect of practice. Normally it was not practiced intensively, but was integrated into the daily routine of study and activity; often they sat for the length of time it took to burn a stick of incense. It was not practiced in any special place or under the direct supervision of a teacher; it was a personal act of calming and emptying the mind of distracted thoughts and emotions. There were no strict rules governing the methods of practice; body positions varied, and there were no rules for breath control or concentration techniques. There were no particular guidelines except to quiet the mind and concentrate on quiescence or seriousness. The calm and concentration thus achieved would aid the student in approaching affairs and perceiving their moral principles. Even for those practicing quiet sitting, ethical activity was still the ground on which sagehood was realized.

Although some of the Sung masters of Neo-Confucianism are said to have valued the practice of quiet sitting as part of the process of self-cultivation, none of them wrote about it extensively. In Chu Hsi's famous anthology of Neo-Confucian thought, *Reflections on Things at Hand*, the chapter "On Preserving One's Mind and Nourishing One's Nature" contains only the brief reference to quiet sitting.[26] The chapter focused instead on seriousness, quiescence, and the maintenance of a calm equilibrium in the midst of activity. However, the official anthology of orthodox Ch'eng-Chu school writings compiled under Ming government sponsorship in 1415[27] included several passages on quiet sitting in the section on self-cultivation (*ts'un-yang*). Chu Hsi had seen quiet sitting as a practice which *might* be helpful to certain students, but he did not view it as indispensable to self-cultivation. By the early Ming, however, followers of the Ch'eng-Chu school had come to place considerable emphasis on quiet sitting as part of the process of self-cultivation. In fact, the practice of quiet sitting became almost a criterion of orthodoxy in the Ming.[28]

Discussions of quiet sitting in the Ming anthology clearly distinguished it from Ch'an meditation practices. Chu Hsi wrote:

THE SYSTEM OF MIND-CULTIVATION 107

> Quiet sitting does not entail entering into a state of calmness where all thoughts are cut off, as in the case of Ch'an sitting in meditation. It is merely gathering in the mind and not letting any extraneous thoughts enter. Then the mind will be in a state of tranquillity and will naturally be concentrated. When there is some matter to attend to, one simply responds to that matter in an appropriate way, and then becomes tranquil once more.[29]

Chu Hsi understood quiet sitting as the maintenance of seriousness.

Ch'eng Hao advocated quiet sitting as an appropriate practice for those times when there were no other urgent tasks. "When there is nothing to put into practice, go and sit in meditation. For while sitting in meditation, we can cultivate our original mind and become calm to some degree. Although we are still not free from chasing after material things, when we come to an awakening, we can collect and concentrate our mind and then there will be a solution."[30] He viewed it as a form of mental preparation to hold the mind in readiness for an awakening.

Neo-Confucian quiet sitting did not lead to enlightenment, but it calmed the mind to prepare for the breakthrough in which one's relation to the principles of things became clear, and the principles would be able to manifest themselves.[31] Quiet sitting differed from Ch'an meditation, then, in the relative looseness about the techniques and conditions of sitting; in serving as an aid to rational and ethical thought instead of as a means to transcend it; and in functioning only as an aid to study and not as the direct path to enlightenment.

Philosophers of the Wang Yang-ming school rejected the idea that principle was equivalent to nature, an entitative state with no direct relationship to activity; they insisted that the mind, the active moral and intellectual faculty, was itself the seat of principle. Investigation of things was for them not a reflection on moral principles inherent in things and affairs, but rather the direct exercise of the moral faculty of the mind, innate good-knowing (*liang-chih*). Because of his identification of knowledge with action, Wang Yang-ming deemphasized the importance of quiet sitting. Self-reflection was not completely abandoned, but excessive self-reflection was seen as an obstacle to the active manifestation of the moral faculty.

Realizing moral knowledge in action was the way to understand it, not reflecting on it beforehand. For Wang Yang-ming himself the doctrine of innate good-knowing did not entail a rejection of study or self-reflection; it simply put them in their place, balancing them with the need to rely on one's moral faculties, not to use objective moral principles as an excuse to put off activating the sagely mind. Thus Neo-Confucians of the School of Mind sought active and dynamic means of cultivation, concrete ways to apply the innate sagely mind.

These then were the systems of mind-cultivation on which Lin Chao-en drew in his search for an accessible, practicable, and effective means of realizing and embodying the ideal of the sage.

MORALITY AND SELF-CULTIVATION

The essential task of self-cultivation taught by Lin Chao-en was to keep the mind securely within (literally in the "cavity" or "hollow" of the back; *ch'iang-tzu-li*) during all activity and repose. He took the doctrine of holding the mind within from a saying by Ch'eng I, "The mind must always be held within. If there is any crack on the outside, it will run away."[32] The mind as the faculty of sensory knowledge could be seduced by desire for external things and thus chase after them. However, the proper state of mind was to be "in the body," centered, in a state of equilibrium in which it could be the master of the emotive and intellectual faculties. The mind kept within, however, was not inert; through constant and sincere self-examination it remained alert and vigilant. It was always available, in readiness, not preoccupied with extraneous affairs or "out to lunch." Keeping the mind within was not a withdrawal from activity, but the basis for activity. Lin wrote,

> Scholars must have the mind within to be scholars. Farmers must have the mind within to be farmers. Artisans and merchants must have the mind within to be artisans and merchants. When you get to the point that all vision, all hearing, all speech, and all activity never fail to have

the mind within, then you are able to uphold the method of mind-cultivation of the Confucian school.[33]

Keeping the mind within was, like quiet sitting, a means of maintaining quiescence during all activities. Lin wrote,

> When responding to your tasks you must at every moment examine whether the mind is still as though in quiet sitting. . . .
> When responding to tasks, if you cannot avoid disturbing the mind and vital force, and if you cannot avoid indulging in sex, wealth, and frivolity, then your self-cultivation is not yet complete. You must thoroughly repent and discipline yourself. If you are able not to disturb the mind and vital force and not to indulge in sex, wealth, and frivolity, then you have found the way of self-cultivation and should redouble your efforts.
> In times of activity it is certainly easy to disturb the mind. In times of quiescence it is also easy to disturb the mind. When the mind is kept within, it is naturally undisturbed.
> When you practice self-cultivation in quiescence, the mind will be quiescent within. When you practice self-examination in activity, then the mind will be quiescent within.[34]

Lin Chao-en affirmed the Neo-Confucian view that the quiescence of quiet sitting was an equilibrium and alertness of mind which could serve as the basis of action. The sincerity of the centered mind was the basis of moral action. Constant self-examination heightened moral consciousness. "In serving my father can I truly be filial? Can I really keep the mind within? Can a single-minded thought of filiality truly emerge from the sincerity of my centered mind?"[35] Sincerity (*ch'eng*) was the integrity, unity, and harmony of the quiescent or reverent mind. In sincerity, there was no double-mindedness, and the mind embodied the harmony of the Mean (*chung*). Self-cultivation was centering the mind, maintaining its equilibrium. It did not require any special regimen or withdrawal from the world. On the contrary, self-cultivation should be part of all activities, waking and sleeping; even in danger, one should practice this attitude.[36] Lin warned his students against laxity, which would allow human weakness to damage the delicate moral balance of the mind. Caution and perseverance were essential to the correct practice of self-cultivation.

In the midst of activity and quiescence self-cultivation and self-examination truly cannot be abandoned even for a moment. If they are not, in quiescence the mind will be within, and the quiescence will not be abandoned for a moment. Is not [the power] of human feelings easily disregarded? It is because the [power of] human feelings is easily disregarded that I tell you students that you must strictly extend your self-cultivation every day in the midst of activity.[37]

In his view of mind-cultivation as based in moral action and self-reflection, Lin Chao-en was completely in accord with Neo-Confucian views of self-cultivation. He was also Confucian in his conviction that the cultivation of moral character, the sincere humane mind of the sage, was the beginning, middle, and end of spiritual transformation. Other benefits were merely secondary.

The nine stages of cultivation were not the first step in the curriculum of Lin's students. A disciple might study with Lin for years before learning the techniques of the nine stages,[38] but there was no delay in learning to make the vows to heaven. Before a student could receive any instruction from Lin Chao-en, he was required to declare in a vow to heaven his sincere intention to uphold the proper teachings of his own faith and the instructions of Lin Chao-en. As we have seen, Lin himself offered vows to heaven every morning and evening, and he urged his disciples to make them frequently. The vows were mainly ethical in content, declaring before heaven one's intention to avoid wrongdoing and to accomplish good works. Significantly, the vows were recorded at the end of Lin's essay on the nine stages, suggesting that he did not see them as something independent of the mind-cultivation process; they were a moral groundwork without which mind-cultivation would be pointless. They embodied the core of Lin's ethical teaching.

The vows to heaven were a commitment to religious and moral rectitude in thought and action. Confucians, Buddhists, and Taoists took parallel but separate initiation vows and further vows; in these Lin corrected the errors of the Three Teachings, as he would put it, by having students affirm the positive doctrines and values of their religion and eschew those which Lin felt to be misguided, those errors of

THE SYSTEM OF MIND-CULTIVATION   111

the Three Teachings which had disappointed and frustrated him during his search. These vows contained in simple form the standards of selectivity which Lin used in formulating his syncretic system. The vows for general use defined the religious responsibilities of members of the sect. Finally, the "further vows" contained a terse summary of Lin Chao-en's ethics, particularly social ethics. The vows enforced basic Confucian morality; they stressed proper conduct of social relationships and the importance of the family. Buddhist values, such as reverence for life, were not mentioned in the vows for general use. Lin's divergence from lay Buddhist values is seen in the fast of nonperversion. Buddhists and lay Buddhists saw abstention from meat as an act of reverence for life, and expression of compassion or humanity. However, Lin Chao-en saw abstention from meat simply as an act of moderation or discipline; excessive indulgence in meat was an immoderate or perverse desire which could harm the mind. In Lin's view, observing one meatless meal a day was sufficient to maintain one's discipline and moderation.

It is noteworthy that the vows, as the first step to sagehood, do not stop at rehearsing general moral principles (a good person should do A, B, and C); rather they anticipate and seek to avert moral errors which arise out of the religious, social, and occupational roles which comprise the lives of students (if I commit error X, Y, or Z, I am not a human being). The emphasis on sins and errors shows the vows to be a simple ritual form of self-examination, basic to rectifying the mind. Their specificity concerning the moral problems facing officials, merchants, wives, etc. is reminiscent of the pragmatic and concrete moral advice given in morality books for people in all walks of life.[39]

Vows to Heaven

Initiation Vows for Confucians:

I, the student so-and-so, having earnestly divined to choose an auspicious day, purified and washed myself and came with a ritual gift of introduction to receive instruction on the mind from the Master of the Three Teachings. Then for the first time I understood that the goodness within my nature is that of Confucius. Dare I not in fear and trembling carry out this practice morning and night? I vow with single-minded sincerity that my studies will not end until I have arrived at [the ideal of] Confucius. Further, dare I not observe the clear instructions and take the three bonds and five constant virtues as daily practice, taking filiality in my comings and goings as true conduct, practicing it within my home and carrying it out in the world, so that my studies will illumine the essence and be fit for application?

One must be clear about the distinction between rectitude and profit. One must be on guard against self-indulgence. One must be reproving of belligerent dispositions. One must be censorious of what are surely man's most serious and evil depravities—those concerning matters of continuing one's line, the three bonds, and the five constant virtues.[40]

If then I should destroy the three bonds and the five constant virtues; if I should be disloyal or unfilial; if I should fail to distinguish rectitude from profit; if I should not be on guard against self-indulgence; if I should be unreproving of belligerent dispositions or uncensorious of depravities—then I would be a sinner against Confucius. How could I establish myself in the space between heaven and earth? To this end I reverently present this petition, which I bring forward with fear and trembling.

Initiation Vows for Taoists:

I, the student so-and-so, having earnestly divined to choose an auspicious day, purified and washed myself and came with a ritual gift of introduction to receive instruction on the mind from the Master of the Three Teachings. Then I understood for the first time that the goodness within my nature is that of the Yellow Emperor[41] and Lao Tzu. Dare I not in fear and trembling carry out this practice morning and night? I vow with single-minded sincerity that my studies will not end until I have arrived at [the ideal of] the Yellow Emperor and Lao Tzu.

Further, dare I not observe the clear instructions, taking purity, clarity, loyalty, and filiality as the basis in order to observe the pure regulations of the Taoist school?[42] If I should be impure, unclear, disloyal, and unfilial, thereby destroying the pure regulations, then I would be a sinner against the Taoist school. How could I then establish myself in the space between heaven and earth?

From ancient times there has been death; how could anyone be able to live forever? I no longer dare to harbor a mind which covets life and thereby tread the path of Taoist heresies, becoming a disgrace to the names of the Yellow Emperor and Lao Tzu. If I should hear from Master Lin the Way which puts an end to such thoughts, I hope to return to Confucianism, to honor the continuance of my line and the teaching of the Sage. To this end I reverently present this petition, which I bring forward with fear and trembling.

THE SYSTEM OF MIND-CULTIVATION 113

Initiation Vows for Buddhists:

I, the student so-and-so, having earnestly divined to choose an auspicious day, purified and washed myself and came with a ritual gift of introduction to receive instruction on the mind from the Master of the Three Teachings. Then for the first time I understood that the goodness within my nature is that of Śākyamuni. Dare I not in fear and trembling carry out this practice morning and night? I vow with single-minded sincerity that my studies will not end until I have arrived at [the ideal of] Śākyamuni.

Further, dare I not observe the clear instructions, taking discipline, meditation, and wisdom as the basis, observing the pure regulations of the order? If I do not observe discipline, do not meditate, and do not obtain wisdom, then I destroy the pure regulations, and I am a sinner against the order. How could I then establish myself in the space between heaven and earth?

The four elements[43] have temporarily coalesced to form all things and the self, but in the end they will all return to nothingness. I no longer dare to harbor a mind which fears death, and thereby tread the path of Buddhist heresies, becoming a disgrace to Śākyamuni.

If I should hear from Master Lin the Way which puts an end to such thoughts, I hope to return to Confucianism, honoring the continuance of my line and the doctrine of the Sage. To this end I reverently present this petition, which I bring forward with fear and trembling.

Vows for General Use:

I vow that all the teachings on the mind which I have received will be diligently practiced, and that the clear instructions which I have been taught will be diligently observed. I vow with single-minded sincerity, truly as though the Lord on High were at hand, that I will no longer dare to go against this for the space of a meal or to leave this even for a moment.[44]

I vow to scrutinize my faults daily and to repent of them thoroughly. I have heard that all the activities and thoughts of sentient beings are sinful. I also am a sentient being, so how could all activities and thoughts of the course of my life not be sinful? Sometimes I commit wrongs in public and will be criticized by men in public. Sometimes I commit wrongs in private, and will be reprimanded by ghosts and spirits in private.

From this time forth, I vow that I will hate and correct all the wrongs I have done in days gone by; that I will set my mind on repentance; and that I will no longer dare to have the slightest trace of self-deceiving mind.

If I do not scrutinize my faults and repent, or if I repent of wrongs but have no regret afterward, then I have committed a sin against heaven. May heaven observe it.

I vow to honor and follow the tenets of the doctrine and to obey the laws of the world. Confucians should comport themselves as Confucians, Taoists as Taoists, and Buddhists as Buddhists. In the process of unifying ideas, I will not dare to force into a theory of equality those ideas which should be clearly distinguished, thereby foolishly mixing and muddling things and giving rise to disputes over right and wrong.

I vow that each year I will contribute a certain amount of silver, according to my means, to distribute to the unfortunate. I will privately aid them, not announcing it to others. However, I will begin with my relatives, since my first responsibility is to my own family.

I vow daily to observe a fast of nonperversion. (Commentary:) In a day one only fasts for one meal. If one takes morning as a fasting period, but in the morning someone holds a banquet, then one can fast at noon. If at noon there is another banquet, one can fast in the evening. There is no harm in eating the vegetables from a meat dish while fasting. If one observes the fast in this way, it is sufficient to serve as an act of discipline. If one disciplines the mind without lapse, then one's highest aspirations will become ever more effective. One can almost say that each day he observes the fast of nonperversion is a day he does not depart from the Way.

I vow that I will not dare privately to impart to others the doctrine of the mind which I have received; how much less would I dare to transmit it secretly for profit in money or gifts?

I vow to lecture on the *San-chiao kuei-ju chi*[45] and other collections for the benefit of others, and to print and distribute them to others according to my means. I further vow to support the bonds and virtues so that they will not topple, to return to Confucianism, taking Confucius as the Master, and to destroy the delusions of the Three Teachings.

Further Vows for Confucians:

I vow to respect the writings of the sages and to observe the sacrifices to the venerable ancestors. If one's family has not sacrificed to the ancestors or has not formerly had a shrine, I think that he should accordingly construct [a shrine or altar] in several layers, sufficient to display [the tablets] of the generations according to their ranks.[46]

I vow to let [my vital essence] flow in the spring and summer [of life] in order to shut it off [i.e., abstain from sexual activity] in the winter [of my life] to cultivate my original harmony.[47]

I vow to arouse greatly the true mind of the sage and worthy and not to stop until I have achieved it in truth. I will not revert to my former ways of mouthing words about Confucius while my actions betray his teachings, so that I become the laughingstock of the common run.

Supplemental Vows for Buddhists and Taoists:

I vow to return home this day [and every day] to attend to my livelihood so as to support my father and mother and care for my wife and

THE SYSTEM OF MIND-CULTIVATION   115

children. I will not revert to my former ways of betraying my parents to wander about, thus bringing upon myself the sin of unfiliality.

I vow to wear the cap and net [prescribed by law for scholars], thus respecting the writings of the state. I would not dare to use a turban, defying the statutes, and thereby casting myself outside of the influence of the kingly Way.

(Commentary:) Recently there has been someone of eminence living in the village who used to lecture on the doctrines of Confucius and Mencius, but he cast off the cap, got rid of the net, and wore a turban and religious garb, taking up the religious life and thereby following the errors of Buddhists and Taoists. I fear that he has not considered that the statutes on the net come from T'ai-tsu and the order for the cap from the imperial court. Instead he lightly abandoned them. How can that be called respecting the system of the kings and following the intentions of the Chou dynasty?

I vow that I will no longer associate myself with the doctrine of the "Way of Heaven"—transmigration without regard to distinctions of male and female, high or low station, or reincarnation—thereby profaning the rites, being disorderly, and not following social standards, destroying the school customs of the Buddhists.[48]

I vow to take the fasting of the mind as supreme. To abstain from wine and meats is the fasting of the mouth, but the mind has not necessarily been purified by that; therefore the fasting of the mind is supreme, and the fasting of the mouth is secondary.

Further Vows:

I, the disciple so-and-so, having received the doctrine of the mind, have diligently carried it out. I now further vow that from this time forth, if I act unrighteously, act against principle, consider evil [acts] as a possibility, bear to do harm, secretly harm goodness, secretly insult my ruler or parents, slander sages or worthies, insult morality, act rudely to my teacher, rebel against those whom I serve, use the language of wives and concubines, go against the instruction of my parents, disregard my duties to the souls of my ancestors, rebel against the orders of superiors, lightly disregard heaven's people, disturb the governing of the state, give rewards or punishments unjustly, indulge in excesses of indolence and pleasure, devise ways and means to reach beyond my allotted portion, become addicted to seizing things, harass and oppress orphans and widows, harm a child or destroy a fetus, squander the wealth of others, sow discord between relatives, use my authority to intimidate, allow my violence to wound others, not respond in gratitude for kindness, endanger others for my own safety, force those from good families into servitude, deceive and pounce upon the unwary, pry into people's private affairs, obscure others' good deeds, set aside the law to receive bribes, disparage the upright and slander the worthy, shift blame to others, harbor injurious thoughts, assist others in misdeeds, defame others under the cloak of rectitude, utter spells for myself or against others, delude people with witchcraft, hide a heart of poison under a face of compassion, assent with my mouth while dissenting in my heart, utter evil words, become overly reclusive, short the proper measures and scrimp on proper weights, mix falsity with truth, grasp at illegal profit—if I should commit any sin such as these, I am not a human being. From this time forth, dare I not be fearful, apprehensive, and self-reproving? Earnest in this, I reverently petition, bringing it forward with fear and trembling.[49]

The vows to heaven, as concrete commitments to moral and religious action, were one of the means by which the gradual spiritual transformation achieved through mind-cultivation was correlated at every point along the way with advances in moral character and behavior.

STILLING IN THE BACK

At the end of his spiritual search, Lin Chao-en had received the Confucian method of mind-cultivation from the enlightened master; the gist of that method was stilling in the back, based on the *ken* hexagram. The actual method of stilling in the back was delineated in the first of the nine stages of cultivation.

Lin summarized stage one: "The first is stilling in the back. Stop thoughts with thought in order to seek the mind."[50] Stilling in the back was a meditative regimen; mental concentration (thought) was used to stop the runaway flow of consciousness (thoughts). The goal of meditation was to seek the lost mind, as taught by Mencius.[51] This, in Lin's view, was the forgotten Confucian method of achieving sagely mind.[52] Thus stilling would seem to be straightforwardly Confucian. However, when Lin Chao-en went on to explain the theory of stilling in the back, he displayed an understanding of the *ken* hexagram which, as I will attempt to demonstrate in my analysis, was a unique fusion of Confucian and Taoist ideas.

Lin Tzu [Master Lin] said:
The character for back is composed of the characters for north and flesh; the back is thus the flesh of the north. The north is connected

THE SYSTEM OF MIND-CULTIVATION 117

with Water [among the Five Phases]. If we now make inferences from the Water of the back of the north, the mind, which is in the south, belongs to Fire. Fire is yang; being in the south, it resides in the front.[53] Water is yin; being in the north, it resides in the rear. Now if we wash the front-dwelling mind-Fire-south[54] with the rear-dwelling back-Water-north, this is the *Book of Changes'* "Wash the mind, move it back, and hide it in the secret place."[55] This is the method of mind-cultivation transmitted by the school of Confucius.

Hsi means to wash. The mind is connected with Fire; hiding it in the Water of the back is the meaning of washing it. *T'ui* means to move backwards. The mind resides in the front; hiding it in the rear, the back, is the meaning of moving it backwards.[56]

This puzzling interpretation was very much at odds with standard views of the hexagram *ken*.

The hexagram *ken* deals with the problems of movement and rest in relationship to tranquillity of mind. The judgment to the hexagram says,

> Keeping still. Stilling in the back
> So that he no longer clings to his body.
> Moving in the chamber,
> He does not see others.
> No blame.[57]

The commentary explains, "Keeping still means stopping," and "Stilling his stopping means stopping in his place."[58] It then further elucidates the principle of stopping:

> When it is time to stop, then stop.
> When it is time to move, then move.
> Thus movement and rest do not lose their proper times
> And their course becomes bright and clear.[59]

The image clarifies that the movements in question are those of the mind; "Thus the superior man does not permit his thoughts to go beyond their place."[60]

The commentaries on the first five lines of the hexagram deal with stilling in various parts of the body, and the sixth line is interpreted as dealing in a general way with "completion," that is, tranquillity achieved. This progressive stilling of parts of the body, seen in conjunction with the overall theme of tranquillity of mind, has suggested to some a yogic system.[61] Whether or not that was the original intention of the hexagram, Lin Chao-en exploited its meditative imagery in his interpretation.

Interpretations of *ken* among Sung Neo-Confucians can be divided into two classes: (1) those concerned with movement and stopping as moral issues, and (2) those concerned with tranquillity of mind.

The ethical interpretation related the idea of stopping at the proper place to knowing where to stop (*chih-chih*) and stopping at the highest good, from the *Great Learning*.[62] Ch'eng I discussed it in terms of a choice between compromising with others or standing firm: "If one cannot go or stop at the proper time but is absolutely rigid, he will be so firm and strong that in dealing with others he will be in conflict with them and offend them, and will be completely cut off from things."[63] Chu Hsi, commenting on the hexagram, interpreted the "proper place" as the moral duty appropriate to the role(s) of the individual. "To stop means to stop at the proper place, that is, the best place for one to abide, as humanity for the ruler and seriousness for the minister. 'Seeing not the person' means not to have oneself in view, and 'not seeing the people' means not to have others in view. In other words, have neither oneself nor others, but only moral principles, in view."[64] The moral man disciplined himself to act in an objectively appropriate way, not catering to the wishes or whims of himself or others.

Others interpreted *ken* in light of the problem of achieving tranquillity of mind. Ch'eng Hao interpreted the hexagram as a description of calming the nature by forgetting the distinction between internal and external:

> By calmness of nature we mean that one's nature is calm whether it is in a state of activity or in a state of tranquillity. One does not lean forward or backward to accommodate things, nor does he make any distinction between the internal and external. To regard things outside the self as external, and force oneself to conform to them, is to regard one's nature as divided into the internal and external. Furthermore, if one's nature is conceived to be following external things, then, while it

THE SYSTEM OF MIND-CULTIVATION 119

is outside, what is it that is within the self? . . . The *Book of Changes* says, "Stop in the back of a thing. See not the person. Walk in the hall and do not see the people in it." Mencius also said, "What I dislike in your wise men is their forced reasoning."[65] Instead of looking upon the internal as right and the external as wrong, it is better to forget the distinction. When such a distinction is forgotten, the state of quietness and peace is attained. Peace leads to calmness and calmness leads to enlightenment. When one is enlightened, how can the response to things become an impediment?[66]

The external things in this passage are objects or affairs; internal things are ideas and impulses. Ch'eng Hao continued, "But if in time of anger [for instance] one can immediately forget his anger and look at the right and wrong of the matter according to principle, he will see that external temptations need not be hated, and he has gone more than halfway toward the Way."[67]

Ch'eng I discussed *ken* in terms of the problem of achieving quiescence of mind in the face of desires:

> One cannot be at ease when he is resting [in moral principles] because he is stirred by desires. How can he rest when desires pull him forward? Therefore the principle of the hexagram *ken* is that one should "stop at the back." What can be seen is in front. To stop at the back is to put it where it cannot be seen. When one stops at the point where it cannot be seen, there will be no desires to disturb one's mind and one can be at rest.
> "See not the person" means not seeing oneself, that is, not being conscious of oneself. When one is no longer conscious of himself, he can be at rest. There is no way to do so if he cannot rid himself of self-consciousness.
> "Walk in the chamber and do not see the people in it." The space between the chamber and the porch is very near. But if one stops with his back to it, even what is nearest cannot be seen. This means that one is not lured into contact with external things. When he is free from such contact, internal desires will not arise. To rest in this way is to do so according to the proper principle of resting. In this kind of resting, "there will be no error."[68]

Unlike Ch'eng Hao, Ch'eng I saw external things as problematic because they give rise to desires. It was such an attitude that Ch'eng Hao was criticizing in his passage above, and Chu Hsi also found fault with it.[69] However, because Ch'eng

I saw external temptations as a serious problem, he interpreted "stopping in the back" as a means of not being lured into contact with external things.

In the early Ming the hexagram *ken* was the center of a controversy between Huang Wan (1480–1554), a critic of Wang Yang-ming,[70] and Wang Chi, one of Wang Yang-ming's disciples. Both men accorded a central place to *ken*. Huang Wan saw *ken* as the central teaching of the *Book of Changes:* "Of the subtle sayings of the *Book of Changes*, none is more essential than the stopping of *ken*. Of the essential doctrines of the *Book of History*, none is greater than holding to the Center. From these works, these doctrines have been handed down from sage to sage; all Ways come from this."[71] Likewise Wang Chi claimed, "In the three words 'stilling the back' Confucius suggested the true source from which the thousand sages established their destinies."[72] Like Huang Wan, Wang Chi associated *ken* with the doctrine of holding to the Center taught by Yao and Shun, the ancient sage patriarchs of the Confucian school.

However, although these two agreed in assigning *ken* a central position, their interpretations differed radically. Huang Wan followed Chu Hsi in applying the principle of *ken* to the moral nature; he understood "stopping in its place" as the key phrase. He said, "If you understand this foundation and can attain peace, then the substance will be established and the material force will be orderly; the material force being orderly, the functions of the mind will be executed."[73] In his interpretation, stopping had two aspects: (1) inner stopping, or resting in the substance of mind or moral nature, and (2) outer stopping, or resting in the back, stilling the functioning of the mind vis-à-vis external things. Once established, substance rested in its place always, for it was not to be unsettled by the movements of function. Outer stopping was governed by principles of the hexagram: "When it is time to stop, then stop. When it is time to go, then go." Stopping and going were determined by the virtues proper to one's role. "Once the substance is established, it can be applied to the relations between ruler and subject, father and son, state and individual, and none will fail to attain their proper place; this is to speak of stopping in terms of function."[74] Thus the establishment of the substance of moral nature was primary, and served as a basis for all moral activity.

Wang Chi's view of *ken* was based on a different view of human nature. He rejected the polarity of moral nature and material force, of substance and function, and insisted that the ideal of human perfection, the sage, was already present in the individual; it need only be manifested. It was therefore misleading to speak of establishing substance first. *Ken*, or stilling, meant to ground the functioning of mind in the natural life principle (*tzu-jan sheng-li*). Stilling the mind in the back was beneficial not because the back is unmoving, but because, since the five organs are connected to it, it governs all members of the body.[75] It is like the North Star in its place controlling the changes of the myriad things.[76] When the operations of the senses conform to this natural principle, the sagely mind will be manifested in and through function:

> When the eye is gazing at beauty, if you gaze at it as if with the back, then the eye will not be lured away by beauty, and the gazing will stop at perceiving brightness; when the ear is listening to sound, if you listen to it as though with the back, then the ear will not be lured away by sound, and the listening will stop at intelligence.[77]

That is to say, the functions of the mind need not be harmed by their contact with external things if the mind goes no further than its proper function. Wang Chi called this a "state of no thought," not the antithesis of thought, but rather a higher form of thought in accordance with natural principle. It was the state in which "one thinks, but it all proceeds from the natural, and there is no thought or contemplation apart from the natural. There is no room to insert the ego into the mind."[78] Thus for Wang Chi *ken* implied resting the mind in its own natural life principle so that the inherent sagely nature could be manifested in both substance and function.

While Lin Chao-en's full commentary on stilling in the back draws upon several Neo-Confucian interpretations, none of them suffices to explain his connection between stilling in the back and washing the Fire of the mind in the Water of the back.

The homologies of mind, Fire, and south and of Water and north (the back is a problem to which we will return presently) are present in Inner Alchemy. This would seem to suggest a Taoist genealogy for the identification of stilling in the back and the washing of the mind from the *Book of Changes*, but the connection of Lin's doctrine of stilling in the back to Taoist sources is more circuitous and complex than it at first appears.[79]

Yin Chen-jen in his *Hsing-ming shuang-hsiu wan-shen kuei-chih* had connected *ken* and washing the mind with the Sung Inner Alchemist Po Yü-ch'an:

> The passage "the sages, cleansing their minds (*hsi-hsin*) retired and laid them up in secrecy," as found in the *Book of Changes,* was the origin of the term "taking a bath," used by the immortals of the T'ang-Sung period, and of the '*Kên* the back' theory as proclaimed by many others in more recent times. The reasoning is the same. The heart [i.e., the mind, the same character as heart in Chinese], being Fire in its nature, is then to be enshrouded by Water sent down from the back; that is the meaning of "cleansing it." The heart is placed in front of the body, and it is directed to the back, which is opposite to the front; that is the meaning of "retirement." It is the natural course for beginners to subdue their minds. When the mind has been brought under control too rigidly, then one begins to be frivolous and unstable. There is a flame in the mind. Therefore, as a temporary measure, it is advisable to remove the mind of Fire from the south, and place it at the back, which is Water in the north. When Water and Fire become supplementary to each other, the confusion in thoughts will automatically cease. This is exactly what Po Yü-ch'an has said: "Cleansing the mind and removing one's worries from it is what is meant by taking a bath."[80]

Lin Chao-en himself cited the full context of Po Yü-ch'an's discussion of cleansing or washing the mind:

> To gather in the body and mind and to control and hide away the spirit and vital force is called "gathering the drugs." To have thought continue upon thought to form a single strip is called "intercourse." To wash the mind to remove one's worries is called "bathing." To coalesce the vital force and gather the thoughts together is called "forming the elixir."[81]

In Po Yü-ch'an's sequence, one gathered in the mind, achieved concentration, removed the cares of the mind, and then formed the elixir. Gathering in the mind and hiding the spirit were in a separate step in cultivation—"gathering drugs"—two steps before washing the mind. It would seem, then, that one did not wash the mind by gathering it in and hiding it (as Lin Chao-en and Yin Chen-jen had said), but by some other means. In Inner Alchemy, bathing (*mu-yü*) referred to the cleansing and purifying of spirit and vital essence at points in the front and rear channels during the inner circulation of vital breath. Po Yü-ch'an related bathing to mind-cultivation, but the details of the bathing differ from those of Lin and Yin Chen-jen; thus it would seem that Yin's *Hsing-ming kuei-chih* asserted the identification of "bathing" with the washing and stilling of the *Book of Changes*; it did not simply *record* an identification between these terms.

Po Yü-ch'an once made a suggestive comment about the *ken* hexagram: "Reading through the whole *Buddhāvataṃsaka-sūtra* is not so good as studying the hexagram *ken*."[82] He echoed an earlier statement by Chou Tun-i, "The entire *Buddhāvataṃsaka-sūtra* is contained in the *ken* hexagram."[83] Unfortunately, neither Po Yü-ch'an nor Chou Tun-i elaborated on their understanding of the application of the *ken* hexagram to the problems discussed in the sutra.

Po Yü-ch'an's disciple Li Tao-ch'un did elaborate on *ken* in relation to self-cultivation. However, Li discussed it not as a Taoist practice but as a Confucian practice parallel to Buddhist and Taoist techniques of meditation. According to Li, the Buddhists applied effort to keep thoughts from arising in order to manifest the Buddha-nature (*hsien-hsing*). Taoists cut off thoughts and dreams to achieve purity of mind with no desires, thus preserving the nature (*ts'un-hsing*). Confucians used the principle of *ken* to forget the self, external things, and the mind in order to calm and fully develop the nature (*ting-hsing; chin-hsing*).[84]

Li Tao-ch'un understood Ch'eng Hao's concept of forgetting the distinction of internal and external in Taoist terms as forgetting the self and things because he shared Ch'eng I's concern about desires arising from contacts with external

124 THE SYSTEM OF MIND-CULTIVATION

things. He carried the trend toward quiescence even further by advocating forgetting the mind (i.e., the thoughts) as well. Li Tao-ch'un may have reinterpreted the Confucian views in Taoist terms, but he did not relate them to the concept of washing the mind, as advocated by Lin Chao-en.

Indeed a perusal of the writings of Po Yü-ch'an, Li Tao-ch'un, and other Taoists whose doctrines have a special place of honor in Lin's writings on Taoism yielded no example of a link between *ken*, washing the mind, and self-cultivation.[85]

What, then, of the reference in Yin Chen-jen? The earliest edition of the *Hsing-ming kuei-chih* dates from the T'ien-ch'i period (1621–1628), although its preface is dated 1615.[86] The syncretic tone of the book suggests the possibility that the definition of stilling in the back and washing the mind in that text followed Lin Chao-en. The evidence for such an hypothesis is as follows.

First, the entries on stilling in the two texts are identical word for word (although my English translation of Lin's text differs slightly from Liu's translation of Yin's).[87] Thus it is improbable that the association of stilling in the back with washing the mind arose independently.

Second, Lin Chao-en's major essays on stilling in the back were written in 1579. Although the exact date of Lin's receiving the teaching on *ken* from the enlightened master is unclear, he was teaching his system of mind-cultivation by 1551, when he took his first disciples.[88] The exact date of the *Hsing-ming kuei-chih* is unknown, but if the earliest preface is 1615, it seems very likely that Lin was teaching stilling in the back well before Yin Chen-jen wrote his work. Indeed, Yin himself said that "others in more recent times" had taught stilling in the back. Those "others" may have been Lin and his followers.

Third, as we have seen, the hexagram *ken* had important connections with mind-cultivation among some Neo-Confucians. Four separate discussions of *ken* occur in the chapter "Preserving One's Mind and Nourishing One's Nature" of the *Reflections on Things at Hand*,[89] and yet another in the chapter on self-cultivation of the *Hsing-li ta-ch'üan* (Philosophy of nature and principle in its completeness).[90]

THE SYSTEM OF MIND-CULTIVATION 125

Finally, and most important, the use of the term stilling in the back required a departure from traditional Taoist chains of correspondences. As a Confucian syncretically integrating Taoist elements, Lin Chao-en had reason to be selective about the Taoist tradition. The identification of the mind (heart-orb), Fire, and south and of Water and north were common Inner Alchemy correspondences; but the north was normally identified with the kidney-orb, not with the back. This shift in the chain of correspondences identified the Taoist concept of balancing Fire and Water, the intermingling of the two lights of nature and vitality, with the Confucian symbols of stilling in the back. As Lin wrote to Yüan Tsung-tao, poet of the Hanlin Academy, "In carrying out stilling in the back, it is essential to have Water rise and Fire fall so that they are harmonized throughout the body."[91] The harmonization of Fire and Water was a Taoist term describing the intermingling of the lights of vitality and spirit. Lin's vision of the secret of mind-cultivation as stilling in the back built a bridge across the chasm between the doctrine of tranquillity of mind in the Neo-Confucian tradition and the techniques of attaining quiescence in Inner Alchemy.

Lin Chao-en was able to build this bridge by a tour de force which was a gain in terms of syncretic strategy but cost him something in terms of philosophical and linguistic rigor. He noted that the character for "back" was composed of the characters for "flesh" on the bottom and "north" on the top; therefore, he said, it *is* the flesh of the north. Hence it is also connected with the phase Water. Since the mind is connected with Fire, the meaning of stilling the mind in the back could be seen as the balancing of the Fire of the mind with the Water of the back. Water suggested the image of washing, and the *Book of Changes* said, "Wash the mind, move it back, and hide it in the secret place." Lin Chao-en took "move back" (*t'ui*), which is generally interpreted as the withdrawal of the sages, who are the subject of the sentence in the original passage,[92] (1) to apply to the mind: move *it* back; and (2) to indicate movement to the back, that is, the back as a part of the anatomy, the secret place within far removed from the sensory openings. By this means he defined "washing" as the hiding of the Fire of the mind in the Water of the back, linking the concept of washing the mind to the stilling of *ken*.

By skillfully identifying both the back and the kidneys as symbols of Water, yet retaining the distinction between the back as the area containing the passes of the internal circuits and the kidney-orb as the seat of Water and vitality, Lin Chao-en integrated the symbols of the *ken* hexagram with the language of cultivation of vital force in Inner Alchemy. This enabled him to use the rich storehouse of imagery and techniques of self-cultivation in Taoist yoga to expand and refine the Confucian doctrine of stilling the thoughts in order to preserve the moral mind from disturbances arising from outside. The reinterpretation of Taoist categories in the leap from back to kidneys facilitated the syncretic integration of the Three Teachings in the nine stages.

Lin achieved his integration by a skillful use of the two chains of correspondences which were discussed earlier in this chapter. To the mind-spirit-nature chain, he added the direction south and the front; to the vital fluid–vital essence–life store chain, he added the direction north and the back. He used one more chain which integrated Inner Alchemy and Confucian symbols.

Center = mind as ruler
   = centrality (harmony, the Mean, equilibrium)
   = Earth, the yellow center, the yellow chamber
   = the One, the a priori, the prenatal original unity
   = Great Ultimate
   = single *ch'i* underlying all multiplicity
   = single-mindedness (concentration, sincerity, the one thread)
   = universal truth of heavenly principle
   = spark of human mind; spark of spiritual light in men's minds; the seed of virtue
   = three elixir fields

The elements in this chain were seen as equivalent and interchangeable; they represented different ways of expressing the same reality.

In this last chain of correspondences, the fusion of Taoist and Confucian elements is clear. The spark of spiritual light

THE SYSTEM OF MIND-CULTIVATION   127

and the elixir fields were linked with the Confucian virtues of the Mean, sincerity, and humanity. Lin also interpreted the other two chains in a manner consonant with his Confucian outlook. Although he used a certain number of distinctively Inner Alchemist terms (revolutions of heaven, spark of spiritual light, gathering drugs, yellow chamber, elixir), he interpreted them as cosmic processes governed by the forces of the Changes. He avoided overt references to the alchemical laboratory procedures; never did he use such terms as tripod or caldron, furnace, lead and mercury, watching the fires, etc. In other words, he understood the alchemical process and imagery in terms of the highest two or three vehicles of interpretation described by Li Tao-ch'un in the section above on Inner Alchemy. He avoided and criticized literal interpretations of Taoist imagery. He once met a man named Ch'in who thought he understood the Taoist doctrine of holding to the Center (*shou-chung*). In response to Lin's questions he explained, "The space between the heart and kidneys is the Center. . . . The head has nine palaces; the *ni-wan* is the central palace. . . . The elixir field is 1.3 inches below the navel." However, he admitted that though he held to these centers, he had no results. Lin Chao-en blamed him for understanding these centers too literally: "The Way has no fixed substance; the Center has no fixed place. Since antiquity no one has been able to use secondary sensory experience to apprehend and glimpse this subtle and mysterious great Way."[93] The images and terms were not, in Lin's view, to be taken literally; they merely aided the human imagination in moving toward the ineffable Way.

Lin Chao-en was similarly careful in establishing his homology between the human microcosm and the external macrocosm. Again, he did not stress the symbolism of the alchemical laboratory. Since he saw the alchemical process as essentially cosmic, representing the forces and movements of the *Book of Changes,* his representation of the internal microcosm was also cosmic; within the human body was a little universe with mountains, rivers, etc.; it was a miniature of the world. Such a homology of the human body and the universe could be described completely by means of the triad of heaven, earth, and man described in the *Book of Changes*. Lin established this point in a commentary on the second of the nine stages:

> The *Book of Changes* says, "Change has no direction."[94] It also says, "The Changes encompass all ways in heaven and earth—this and nothing else."[95] The fact that it is without direction and that it encompasses all ways in heaven and earth makes it my Center. If it is my Center, it is my mind. Is it only the way of the Changes that is so? All things go up to the limit of what is covered by heaven and of what is supported by earth; what fills the space between them is all my Center. Being my Center, it is my mind.
>
> Looking at it from this point of view, the Center, or the mind, of heaven, earth, and man are all one. Which is the Center of heaven, the Center of earth, and the Center of man? Which is the mind of heaven, the mind of earth, and the mind of man? Therefore what is the Center is the mind, and what is the mind is the Center: it is only one.[96]

In other words, the processes of Change in heaven, earth, and man are identical, and they are all governed by the mind. Implicit in Lin's discussions was an understanding of the concrete Taoist discussion of the process of the changes in the internal microcosm; explicitly he discussed the cosmic forces of Change.

The relationship between the Inner Alchemy re-creation of the internal microcosm and the forces of Change in the cosmos can best be seen in the Diagram of the Great Ultimate (figure 1). This chart, made famous by Chou Tun-i, was a visual representation of the cosmic laws of Change, as understood by the Neo-Confucians. It was also a diagram of the Inner Alchemy process of re-creation, for, as we have seen, it originally derived from a Taoist source.

As a chart of the workings of Neo-Confucian cosmic law, the chart is read from top to bottom.[97] The first circle represents the Great Ultimate and the Ultimate of Nonbeing, the one principle from which all reality emerges. The second represents the balance of movement and rest, yin and yang, and all polar forces; it is the Mean before the emotions have arisen. When movement occurs, the polarities of yin and yang, *ch'ien* and *k'un* (heaven and earth), and the Five Phases interact according to their proper laws, leading to the produc-

THE SYSTEM OF MIND-CULTIVATION   129

Figure 1. Diagram of the Great Ultimate

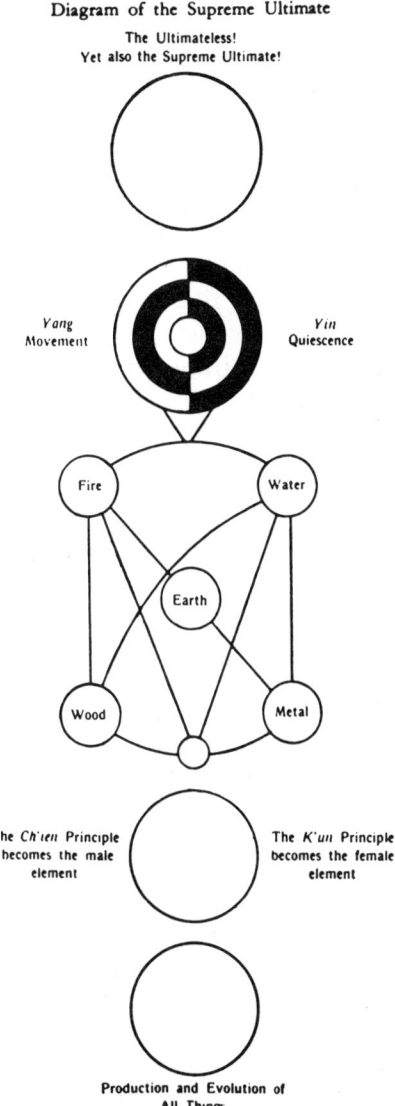

Reprinted from Fung Yu-lan, *A History of Chinese Philosophy*, Vol. II, *The Period of Classical Learning*, translated by Derk Bodde, 2d ed. (Princeton: Princeton University Press, 1961), p. 436, by permission of the publisher.

tion and evolution of all things. Thus, for the Neo-Confucians, the multiplicity of the world was not random or chaotic; it was all governed by rational principles which follow the cosmic laws governed by the one Great Ultimate.

As a chart of the internal process of re-creation (the reversal of profane life-draining movement to return to the beginning which antedates heaven), the chart is read from bottom to top, using the terminology of Inner Alchemy. The bottom circle represents the profusion of things in the world, and the next circle the multiplicity of thoughts and sensations which react to those things; multiplicity, with its destructive power, is produced by the interaction of opposites. These, then, are the forces which fragment the mind and vital essence. The center of the diagram with the Five Phases contains lines indicating the process of reintegration and centering. Wood (impure yin) is reintegrated into Water, and Metal (impure yang) is reintegrated into Fire. This represents the purification of lead and mercury, the two ingredients of the elixir. Lin Chao-en, as will be seen below, uses symbols from the Changes, saying that the trigrams *li* and *k'an* (impure yin and yang) are returned to *ch'ien* and *k'un* (pure yin and yang). Fire and Water (the lights of spirit and vitality, respectively) are combined in the small circle below, representing the lower elixir field. (The lines from Fire and Water to the unidentified circle, by the way, betray the Taoist origins of the chart; there is no necessary Neo-Confucian function for that small circle attached to Fire and Water.) When Fire and Water (the two lights) are united, the three elixir fields (the small circle at the bottom; the central circle labeled "Earth," equivalent to the yellow chamber; and the central point at the top linked to the next circle, representing the *ni-wan*) can be united to form the Center; they become functionally one. Thus all of the Five Phases (all of the diversifying, centrifugal forces in the self) are wedded to fertilize the sage embryo; the seed of the new self is depicted in the second circle from the top, representing the union of human nature and life store (*hsing* and *ming*). When the new self has matured and is ready to emerge, it embodies the One (the Great Ultimate), the not-yet-One (the Ultimate of Nonbeing, the Great Void), and goes beyond that

THE SYSTEM OF MIND-CULTIVATION   131

to undifferentiated Tao. The process of Change (devolution and creation), then, can be reversed to reintegrate the internal cosmos, to return to the pure and whole time at the beginning of creation, the original self.

In his nine stages, Lin used Buddhist and Taoist terms and techniques for Confucian ends. Although Buddhist and Taoist elements were divested of some of their content, his reinterpretation gave Confucian cultivation a new and more concrete form.

In stage one, stilling in the back was aided by the recitation of the phrase "Masters of the Three Teachings" (*San-chiao hsien-sheng*). This was an obvious imitation of Pure Land recitation of the name of Amitābha. As in Pure Land, the recitation was an aid to concentration for beginners. "It will be as though the reciters were standing in attendance on them [the masters]; they will not dare to be lax even for a moment."[98] According to Lin's instructions, students should begin by reciting orally, and then move the recitation into the back; when each thought is in the back, then the mind will be in the back. Focusing the mind in the back by reciting was based on the fact that in Chinese the word for recitation (*nien*) is also the word for thought. Whenever recitation is in the back, every thought (and hence the mind) is also in the back. Thus recitation of the names was an easy way to foster mental concentration and focus. Lin also wrote that recitation worked to disengage the mind from the temptations of the senses; when students were busy reciting, they would not be aware of other distractions. To make the practice even more Confucian, Lin used it as a metaphor for undistracted and concentrated study.

> Scholars take studying as their calling, so when the scholar reads the sentence "study and constantly practice it" it is just like reciting the phrase the Masters of the Three Teachings. Indeed, if the thought has entered the back, starting from this one sentence, a hundred, thousand, or ten thousand sentences will all likewise be in the back.[99]

The second stage was the revolutions of heaven. In the Inner Alchemy system, this represented the internal circulation of *ch'i* and heat through the channels of the inner microcosm. Lin, in his commentaries on stage two, did not discuss it in these terms, although in a letter to Yüan Tsung-tao he described the circulation of heat through these channels in overtly Taoist imagery.

> Now the elixir is connected with Fire; it cannot but be hot. When it is hottest, move it to the point 1.3 inches below the navel. After resting there a moment, move it back from the navel, raise it through the coccyx up to the *ni-wan* center, and down from the nose and mouth in a straight line to the point 1.3 inches below the navel.[100]

In commentaries to stage two, however, he discussed the revolutions of heaven in terms of the imagery of the *Book of Changes;* the theme of the stage was taking the Changes as the model in order to establish the Great Ultimate and the human Ultimate. The Great Ultimate in both Neo-Confucian and Taoist imagery was the One which is the source and governor of all multiplicity. In Confucian terms, it was also Principle, the unity of all principles, the standard of moral cosmic law. Thus there was not only a Great Ultimate, but a human Ultimate which represented a moral standard, a sort of "compass" which could be followed to keep all actions "on track." Thus the Great Ultimate was in human terms also the Mean, the equilibrium which balanced or centered all actions or feelings. Thus the revolutions of heaven were for Lin Chao-en not merely breath control and meditative discipline; they were a symbol for the first step of internal moral balance which would transform the mind and character in line with fundamental and innate moral principles.

The third stage was penetrating the passes. It was the stage associated with Lin's healing method, which will be discussed below. In alchemical terms, penetrating the passes was the movement of the light of vitality up the passes along the spine to dislodge the light of spirit in the *ni-wan* center of the brain. Lin Chao-en maintained his Confucian world view by deemphasizing the psychophysical experience of moving the light and heat through the passes, and discussing the movement instead in terms of removing from the mind the obscurities which result from sensory and emotional experience. Even healing, as we shall see, was essentially a matter of restoring the clarity of the mind.

The fourth stage said "Rest it in Earth and sincerely cultivate the seed of humanity in order to form the hidden elixir."[101] In alchemical terms, this corresponded to the nurturing of the light of vitality in the yellow chamber until the light of spirit could be drawn into that Center and wedded to vitality to form the sage embryo; it represented a gradual stilling and centering of the psychospiritual forces of the self. Lin's interpretation is distinctively Confucian. First, he saw the elixir not as the seed of an embryo, a new body, but rather as the spark of humanity (spiritual light) present in the original mind. Likewise, the fertilization and conception imagery were largely divested of their physiological imagery: "When the spark of spiritual light was originally in this Center, it was the first time heaven and earth gave birth to man."[102] As the place of man is between heaven and earth, so the mind of man is the product of a spark which appears between heaven and earth. Continuing his Confucian interpretation, he spoke not of gestation of an embryo, but of continuing the spark of humanity with goodness until it is fully formed,[103] based on a phrase from the *Book of Changes*. He also cited a Mencian discussion of the expansion of moral mind and nurture until it filled up the universe.[104] In this way he fused the Taoist imagery of re-creation of a new self with Confucian imagery of nurturing the moral mind and character.

The fifth stage described gathering from heaven and earth to collect the drugs. In alchemical terms, this meant both understanding the "drugs" or forces which would act as a catalyst for the "copulation" of the two ingredients and timing the catalytic action to facilitate the conception. It was a symbol for the mysterious leap from the profane postnatal state to the sacred beginning, the prenatal state. Although Lin used seed and gestation (continuation and expansion) imagery in his last stage, this one dealt with the leap to establish sagely mind. Since he did not take the conception and embryonic imagery literally, he felt free to rearrange the order; in his mind one first uncovered the spark or seed of the mind of humanity and then nurtured and expanded it until it was strong enough to restore the balance of the mind to its original sagely nature. The fertilization imagery in stage five was completely divested of its physiological aspects; he described it rather as the interaction of forces of the Changes recombining to move closer and closer back to the Great Ultimate. This will be discussed in more detail in the next chapter.

The sixth stage was that of Inner Alchemy gestation; for Lin it meant coalescing the spirit deep within until it was strong enough to be expanded beyond the self to the limits of the universe. Stages seven, eight, and nine followed what in Inner Alchemy would be the "birth" of the new self through the top of the head; in Lin's imagery it was expanding the mind of humanity or the sage to embody heaven and earth, to embody the Great Void, and to smash through the Void itself. Embodiment of heaven and earth was said to be release from death, but Lin vigorously argued that it was the mind alone which survived death. The Great Void was the Ultimate of Nonbeing, the empty *ch'i* from which the One, the Great Ultimate had emerged, and smashing through the Great Void went beyond all categories. Thus the top two stages represented a mysticism beyond all dualities. It was precisely such Buddhist descriptions of Nonbeing, emptiness, or voidness which the Neo-Confucians had criticized as undermining the moral foundations of Being. Yet Lin Chao-en managed to rescue these from this Buddhist "error" by identifying the voidness of the mind and the state beyond the Great Void with Confucian sincerity (*ch'eng*), a watchword for the state of mind in accord with the Mean, especially the Mean before any of the emotions had arisen. Hence, even in the highest reaches of his mystical vision, Lin Chao-en maintained the fundamentally moral character of the Confucian mind. Like Chang Tsai, his mysticism was ethical, and his sincerity was the basis of the unfailingly humane mind of the sage.

This has been a brief overview of the nine stages. The interplay of the Three Teachings and the utilization and reinterpretation of images will be discussed in more detail in the next chapter. The goal was Confucian, and Lin sought to explain and justify each stage in terms of Confucian moral cultivation; to do this, he had to depart from Neo-Confucian discussions of moral principle, investigation of things, and self-reflection, and instead focus even more closely than most

Neo-Confucians on images for internal tranquillity in the *Book of Changes*, Mencius, and the Mean.

He used Inner Alchemy techniques and imagery, always using the "higher" or more cosmically oriented interpretations of the process so that it could be explained in terms of the symbolism of the *Book of Changes*, which was a lingua franca of Taoism and Confucianism. He ignored the physical aids and controlling agents (using the eyes, retaining semen, etc.) of the Taoist system; he borrowed the mental praxis, but not the physical. He emphasized cultivation of spirit over life store, for he rejected the search for long life as a goal of cultivation. He saw the Taoist system as an aid for nurturing sagely mind.

The role of Buddhist ideas in the nine stages was complex. Lin made use of Buddhist techniques such as recitation of the name as an aid to mental concentration. His stress on mental effort as the sole guiding force of the yogic process is consistent with Ch'an; mind is the beginning, the middle, and the end of meditation. More importantly, Buddhism taught the realization of original nature in the highest stages of cultivation. Lin once described the ultimate principles taught by Buddhism: "There is outside of my body another body, which none has been able to maintain by rare methods; only when the void has been smashed can this realized body appear."[105] This larger body, like the *dharma*-body of the Buddha, was one with the universe; it represented ultimate spirituality. Lin described the stage of ultimate principles in various terms. In early stages one set the will on humanity; in middle stages, one applied humanity; in the stage of ultimate principles one's humanity accorded with heaven. In earlier stages one sought the lost mind (*ch'iu fang-hsin*); in the last stages one released (*fang*) the full power of the mind. In earlier stages one controlled thoughts by making them abide in their place to conquer the mind (*hsiang-fu ch'i hsin*); in the last stages there was no place to abide or be attached (*wu so chu*), only the absolute mind.[106] In the highest stage the mind expanded to become one with the absolute Void which contains the universe. Yet the description of the mind as beyond knowledge, will, and the Void was in tension with Confucian images also used to describe this stage: it represented the mind of Confucius able to follow his heart's will at seventy.[107]

Lin did not attempt to resolve fully the tension between the mystical language of Buddhism and the ethical language of Confucianism. He took seriously the ethical mysticism of the sagely mind forming one body with heaven and earth and all things; he turned to Taoism for a technique to aid in cultivating the mind's luminosity and to Buddhism to describe the cosmic mind. He assumed, however, that reality, even absolute reality, has a fundamentally moral structure and he ignored the issue of whether the mind is ultimately beyond good and evil.[108]

Because of his silence on the doctrines of his Ming contemporaries, it is difficult to place Lin Chao-en in the context of the Neo-Confucianism of his day, although it is clear that he belongs to the School of Mind.[109] His interpretation of stilling in the back has much in common with that of Wang Chi; both asserted a concept of stilling in the proper place which would allow the mind to take its place as the active ruler of the functions of body and spirit. On the other hand, Lin criticized the view that the sagely mind was already actually present in the self and need only be manifested; he felt there was need for a step-by-step method of cultivation. In this he showed affinities with the quietist school, which advocated effort at self-cultivation of the substance of the mind which would lead to the manifestation of substance in function. His affinity for this view may owe something to the fact that Lin visited Lo Hung-hsien, a major advocate of the quietist school, shortly before his decision to abandon examinations, and corresponded with him in later years.

Lin tried to reconcile these two views. He felt that through the moral will one could begin to exercise the sagely mind inherent within; thus one began self-cultivation with vows of ethical action. But such ethical behavior, while it illustrated the inherent seeds of sagely mind in all men, did not constitute the realization of the substance (*pen-t'i*) of the mind; that required self-cultivation to clear the mind of obscurities and to restore the original nature which existed prior to birth. Although from the start one's mind was the same mind as that of the Sages of the Three Teachings, its full spiritual transformation required considerable refinement and expansion through the method of the nine stages.

HEALING AND MIND-CULTIVATION

As we saw in the biography, the enlightened master told Lin Chao-en to use healing as a sign that his doctrine of mind-cultivation was powerful and effective. This was unheard of for a Confucian; Lin's acceptance of the role as healer and his understanding of the healing process further clarify his integration of the Three Teachings.

Healing was part of stage three of mind-cultivation: "The third is penetrating the passes; the brightness penetrates the limbs and apertures to refine the body."[110] Lin felt that illness arises when "The vital force is disorderly." Asked how the vital force becomes disorderly, he replied, "The spirit runs amok. When the spirit is calmed, the vital force will naturally follow its course. When the vital force naturally follows its course, illness will naturally be removed."[111] Blockage of the vital force was caused by the spirit's or mind's chasing after things, and could be removed by calming the spirit or by stilling the "waves" which the disordered spirit had caused.

Lin's student Ch'ih Ho-ch'un (dates unknown) explained that his master used the system of mind-cultivation to help heal the sickness of the mind and only secondarily that of the body: "Therefore is not the so-called sick mind what Mencius called the lost mind? Is not the method of mind-cultivation what Mencius called seeking the lost mind? . . . The sick body arises from the sick mind, and healing the body is based in healing the mind."[112]

The application of the revolutions of heaven or the circulation of vital force to move blocked vital force and cure illness was a Taoist technique intended originally to prolong life. Because Lin used this method he was labeled a Taoist by

138 THE SYSTEM OF MIND-CULTIVATION

many contemporaries. His student Liu Ching-pang (dates unknown) recorded,

> My teacher the Master of the Three Teachings taught along the southern coast the great doctrine of returning to the true principles of Confucius, and his method of healing was renowned as effective. At that time who did not label our master as one of the Taoist school? Our master did not dispute these charges. How could they know that he used this method as a minor test to be an aid in clarifying his Way?[113]

Because of such charges, Lin was concerned to clarify that his healing method was an outgrowth of moral self-cultivation. In response to a question about rectified and imbalanced vital force he replied:

> Doing good is yang; that is rectified vital force (*cheng-ch'i*). Doing evil is yin; that is imbalanced vital force (*pu-cheng-ch'i*). . . . If the human mind is not rectified and is thus yin, the constant [virtues] of the Way of man are lost. . . . If you purify the mind, turn to the Way, expel evil, and follow good, you thereby restore yang in your body; when the rectified vital force has been restored, will not the yin vital force be extinguished? When the rectified vital force is in the self, then will not depraved vital force be extinguished? The *chuan* says, "Evil spirits do not conquer virtue." This is the doctrine of "melting the imbalanced" of Master Chu Hsi.[114]

Some Taoists also saw healing as subordinate to and an outgrowth of the nurturing of a moral mind.[115] It was not from these that Lin sought to dissociate himself but rather from the search for long life or immortality as the goal of self-cultivation.

The most detailed example of Lin Chao-en's healing method is a cure for nasal catarrh:

> Now the lung-orb is like a canopy, and the heart-orb dwells below it. If the Fire in the heart-orb is [overly] bright, then the Metal in the lung-orb begins to boil. When the Metal of the lung-orb boils, nasal catarrh is formed.
>
> Let me now explain the method of curing it: The lung-orb has a tract, the root of which is below the left breast. One should apply the imagination to push it down to the feet[116] in order to purify the turbid yin of the Metal of the lung-orb. Again lead it upward with mental effort,

THE SYSTEM OF MIND-CULTIVATION 139

divide it, and lower the two streams into the Water of the right and left kidney-orbs. Again lead them by mental effort up to the neck; at the neck combine them and raise them to the crown of the head.

(Note:) The two kidney-orbs each have a root leading up to the neck, but there is only one root from the neck to the crown.

From the crown again apply mental effort to lower it to the lung-orb, and then from the lung-orb, again apply mental effort to lower it to the heart-orb.

(Note:) There is one root each leading from the crown to the lung-orb and from the lung-orb to the heart-orb.

From the heart-orb again use mental effort to divide it and lower the two to the right and left kidney-orbs. When the heart-orb has obtained the Water of the two kidney-orbs, how can the Fire of the heart-orb again flare up?

If in the course of a day and a night you perform this two or three times, each time comprising four or five of these cycles, then there will be no Fire to overcome the Metal, and no turbid yin [vital force] to soil the lung-orb.[117]

The first half of this procedure applied the mental effort of the concentrated mind to move the blocked vital force and remove its impurities. The turbid vital force represented the illness. Thus illness was used to expel illness—turbid vital force was used to refine and expel the illness of turbid vital force. In the second phase concentration and mental effort were directed back to the heart-orb (the mind) and the mind was stored in the Water of the kidney-orb to quench its Fires. This attacked the cause of the illness, the disturbance of the mind.

Many more cures were recorded in "Master Lin's Art of Healing" (*Lin-shih ch'üeh-ping kung-fu*).[118] The cures dealt with such problems as the following: ear ailments, toothache, acid stomach, dry mouth, retching, blood in the stool, spitting blood, various coughs, respiratory problems, stomach and intestinal gas, tenderness of the stomach, morning fever, general weakness, jaundice, hematoma, worms, palsy of the limbs, involuntary emission, sweating, constipation, urinary problems, diarrhea, hernia, burns, sunstroke and frostbite, cholera, skin ulcers, poisoning, piles, swollen glands, temporary derangement, corpulence, seven-day fever, infant illnesses, and women's problems with pregnancy, conception, labor, and menstruation.

The basic healing method involved the application of the first three of the nine stages. As a cure for chills Lin suggested: "Direct the thoughts to the back. First apply the secret method to put in motion the revolutions of heaven. When you become hot, apply Water and circulate it through the body."[119] This method suited illnesses involving cold, whereas the nasal catarrh case involved overheating the mind to affect the nasal passages.

Supplementary methods were also suggested, such as the following for intestinal gas:

> You must not be ruffled by annoyances, must be sparing of thoughts, and must cast off anger; then the vital force will not be blocked between the lung-orb and the diaphragm, and the Fire will naturally be dislodged and begin to circulate. If you lack appetite, you should send down the vital force and rest the mind in its place, and then the appetite will reappear. After the illness, if you drink too many hot fluids, the above method cannot be used. You can only purge it through urination or defecation. Or you can open the pores and sweat it out, which will alleviate the edema caused by fluid retention. In order to facilitate elimination, massage the area around the navel and the dorsal acupuncture point, then exhale the vital force through the mouth. Repeat twelve times.[120]

This cure used the supplementary aids of massage and expelling the illness through elimination or perspiration; these techniques also appeared in various other cures, along with swallowing accumulated saliva.

Both Lin's basic method and his supplementary techniques closely resemble those of Taoist Chang San-feng (dates unknown), some of whose writings appear in Lin's collected works.[121] According to Chang,

> The Way of preserving the body takes resting the mind and nurturing the kidneys as its bases. . . . If the kidneys are settled, then the Fire of the life store will not flare up, and if the mind is at peace, then the Fire of the spirit can shine down; spirit and vital force and vital essence can meet and coalesce, forming the fetal breath; then one can heal illness and extend one's years.[122]

Chang also discussed the types of illnesses:

THE SYSTEM OF MIND-CULTIVATION 141

> For illnesses of emptiness, it is fitting to visualize with the imagination and gather in. For illnesses involving fullness, it is fitting to use massage and leading of the obstructed mass. For illnesses of fever, it is fitting to spit out the old and take in the new, to exhale from the mouth and inhale through the nose to cool it. For illnesses of cold, it is fitting to preserve the vital force and hold it in the breath, and use the imagination to produce a Fire and warm it.[123]

Lin's cures followed similar principles, countering the direction of excess or imbalance.

Lin Chao-en gained considerable fame as a healer; not even his most vociferous critics denied the effectiveness of his cures. But how did they work? The recorded cures suggested something of the mechanism. Lin asserted that both the source of illness and its cure lay in the mind. To be sure, he did not develop a full theory of psychosomatic pain; in his view, illness arose from the disturbance of the mind by desires and emotions and was cured by the application of mental effort to control the forces of the body and to still the mind. In modern terms his cures seem to have attacked the psychological dimensions of illness.

First, this method was well suited to dealing with nervous disorders; the purpose of stilling in the back was to calm the mind. By stage three, the body had relaxed into a meditative state; the person was able to direct the mind to relax or control various parts of the body. The popularity of Hatha Yoga and other meditative techniques in the modern West as aids to relaxation and health immediately suggests the potential of Lin's method.

Second, while some traditional Chinese medical techniques seem in modern medical terms to function only because of the faith of the patient in the technique, the doctor, or the spiritual forces behind the charm or ritual,[124] Lin's cures directed the power of the mind to deal with the symptoms. That is, feverish patients concentrated to produce sweat, which would relieve the feeling of heat. If the throat was parched, the patient imagined dripping Water or saliva onto it and then swallowed the saliva to relieve the sensation of dryness. For blockage, the treatment was massage. Such treatments may only be palliative; they were not cures in the strict medical sense. But they produced a state which alleviated the discomfort; like our common "aspirin and bed rest," they made the patient more comfortable while the body healed itself.

Third, the method of alleviating symptoms was also applied psychologically; one applied mental effort to move blockages. Heaviness was floated by mental effort. Heat was washed by mental effort. A powerful psychosomatic aspect of illness is the patient's attitude toward his discomfort. If it is seized upon and worried about, it becomes even more acute. For this reason even modern doctors exude an air of authority and reassurance if they believe it will help a patient to cope with a problem. Lin's method calmed the mind and applied the mental effort of the patient to lessen the grip of discomfort.

Some of Lin's cures rested on the theory of correspondences involving the five organ orbs, the Five Phases, the five emotions, and so forth. A good case in point is the cure for nasal catarrh cited above. It is hard to imagine how the cure described could have any other function, in modern medical terms, than to assure the patient there was an explanation and cure for his ailment and to take his mind off the irritation in his nose. Whether that would lessen the volume of the catarrh I am not competent to judge.

Lin Chao-en's use of the nine stages to heal illness, besides identifying him with Taoism in the minds of many, put a strain on his Confucian self-identification, and he sought in a number of ways to reconcile healing with his Confucian world view. First, he inveighed strongly against Taoist views that the goal of the Way was health, long life, or immortality; he sought to disassociate himself from such "errors" associated with religious healing. Second, he explained his cures in terms of the Confucian cosmology of *ch'i* moving through the Five Phases of change in accordance with cosmic laws. Third, he linked the imbalance of *ch'i* in the internal microcosm to the moral activities of mind. The mind as ruler of the body is to maintain the balance of yin and yang and the Five Phases; but when the mind or spirit runs amok, distracted by things or emotions, the internal balance of *ch'i* is destroyed and illness ensues. Thus healing was an offshoot of mind-cultivation; until the mind was again the ordering agent in the body, its moral cultivation could not proceed. Healing was understood by Lin as a concrete form of balancing and stabilizing the mind.

CONCLUSION

Lin Chao-en's system of mind-cultivation was a complex fusion of Buddhist and Taoist images and techniques with a fundamentally Confucian goal and world view. At every stage along the way, Lin took great pains to reconcile Buddhist and Taoist elements, selectively reinterpreting them to accord with his Confucian views. If his self-identification and his internal sense of "orthodoxy" were so strongly Confucian, to what end did he borrow so heavily from the Taoist and Buddhist traditions? He wrote: "I took up the Way of sages and worthies determined to seek the means to realize it in myself [lit., my body], obtain it in my mind, and manifest it in my actions."[125] His system of mind-cultivation was designed to do just that.

The application of mind-cultivation to healing was a literal and direct way to realize the fruits of the Way in one's body. Disciples had concrete and physical proof, an undeniable sign, of their progress in mind-cultivation. They realized the power of their minds, and knew without a doubt that the sagely mind was innate within them. Healing was a sign which would cement their faith in and commitment to the process of self-transformation through moral cultivation. The concrete sign of healing satisfied the pragmatic nature of the Chinese; they had no use for subtle and complex speculations on abstruse issues. The elaborate system and complex imagery of the nine stages would have been rejected by many if there were not an early, visible sign of the efficacy of the system.

The yogic system of internal transformation and reintegration was a more gradual approach to the same goal. The internal microcosm was reordered and purged of a lifetime of impurities and obscurities. The mind was gradually purified, strengthened, and transformed or returned to its original state. The elaborate system of the nine stages would seem to us to boggle rather than clarify the mind. Remember, however, that students were taught one stage at a time under the personal supervision of an accomplished teacher. The advantage of the complex system was that it provided a step-by-step process in which the expansion of the sagely mind could be directly experienced. It began with relatively easy exercises, such as reciting the names of the Masters of the Three Teachings to achieve concentration by stilling the mind in the back. Each stage entailed a more difficult exercise of the luminous potential of the mind and its ability to order the cosmos. The disciple could feel and experience the fruits of mind-cultivation. In Lin's system the power of sagely mind was experienced virtually from stage one; the innate potential of sagely mind (good-knowing) was affirmed. However, followers were not expected to make a heroic and instantaneous leap into dynamic sagely action; the seeds of the sagely mind were slowly nurtured and expanded.

Finally, from beginning to end the Way was manifested in moral action. The vows to heaven established the commitment to moral action. At each step in the nine stages, specific moral virtues and capabilities were strengthened so that the internal transformation would have fruits in external activity.

Thus it was Lin's search for an accessible and concretely realizable Way that inspired the integration of the Three Teachings.

CHAPTER SIX

THE NINE STAGES

The nine stages of mind-cultivation were the core of Lin Chao-en's thought, and the finest example of his integration of the Three Teachings into a single Way. Because of the centrality of this system in the religious thought and practice of Lin Chao-en, the two most important essays on the nine stages will be translated in full and explicated in this chapter. "Selected Sayings on the Nine Stages" (*Chiu-hsü che-yen*), written in 1579, was a terse, even cryptic description of the nine stages followed by the vows to heaven, which were translated in the last chapter. "Direct Pointing to the Mind as Sage" (*Hsin-sheng chih-chih*), written in 1564 and published in 1578, elaborated on the process and its meaning. Unfortunately, it did not systematically follow the nine divisions. For the sake of clarity in explaining each stage, I have divided it according to topics and arranged it here as a commentary on the first essay.[1]

Even these two essays combined do not sufficiently clarify the process; they assume considerable familiarity with Lin's thought and with the technical language of Inner Alchemy. I will therefore draw on other writings of Lin Chao-en and Taoists as needed to elaborate specific points.

STAGE ONE

The first is stilling in the back. Stop thoughts with thought in order to seek the mind. ["Nine Stages," 1a]

Mental concentration (thought) was used to stop the runaway flow of the stream of consciousness (thoughts) in order to seek the mind. A reference to Mencius' "seeking the lost mind"[2] established the Confucian aim of stilling in the back.

> The *Book of Changes* says, "Stilling the back." The character for "back" is composed of [the characters for] north and flesh. North is the direction of Water, but the mind is connected with Fire. If one can take the Fire of the south and cultivate it in the Water of the north, this is what the *Book of Changes* said: "Wash the mind, move it back, and hide it in the secret place."[3] ["Nine Stages," 1a]
>
> *Hsi* means to wash. The mind is connected with Fire; hiding it in the Water of the back is the meaning of washing it. *T'ui* means to move backwards. The mind resides in the front; hiding it in the rear, the back, is the meaning of moving it backwards. ["Direct Pointing," 1b]

The fusion of Confucian and Taoist elements in Lin's interpretation was discussed in some detail in the section on stilling in the back in the last chapter. He departed from usual interpretations by developing the symbols of the hexagram in terms of their relationship to the phases of Fire and Water; in this way he was able to integrate stilling in the back with the balancing of the forces of Fire and Water in Inner Alchemy. However, he also departed from the traditional Taoist correspondences by relating Water to the back and not to the kidneys. In this way he was able to use the imagery of the *Book of Changes*, a revered Confucian classic, to establish a basis for the meditative process. He assimilated the active and step-by-step yogic transformation of Inner Alchemy to purify the mind and transform the self by translating the alchemical symbols into the symbols of the *Book of Changes*.

> Lin Tzu said, "The character for 'back' is composed of 'north' and 'flesh'; the back is thus the flesh of the north. The north is connected with the element Water. If we now make inferences from the Water of the back of the north, then the mind, which is in the south, belongs to

Fire. Fire is yang; being in the south, it resides in the front. Water is yin; being in the north, it resides in the rear. Now if we wash the front-dwelling mind-Fire-south with the rear-dwelling back-Water-north, this is the *Book of Changes*' 'Wash the mind, move it back, and hide it in the secret place.' This is the method of mind-cultivation transmitted by the school of Confucius." ["Direct Pointing," 1a]

The terms mind-Fire-south and back-Water-north have been hyphenated because their order does not seem to reflect the grammar of the situation. Literally, the passage reads "if we wash the south of the Fire of the mind," but it is not the south which is washed but the mind with its Fire; literally "with the north of the Water of the back," but it is not the north which washes it but the Water of the north. As noted earlier, these were two chains of corresponding or equivalent terms.

Lin Tzu said, "The five organ orbs are all connected to the back. When the mind is put in the Water of the back, the mind is pure and clean. When the mind is pure and clean, the five organ orbs are all pure and clean."

Someone asked, "When the mind-Fire-south is hidden in the back-Water-north, how is it that the Fire of the mind is not extinguished by the Water of the back?"

Lin Tzu said, "The ordinary fire and water of the world are functions of outward form, but the true Water and Fire within the body are functions of spirit. When water is predominant, fire is extinguished; when fire is predominant, water dries up. Such is the nature of ordinary fire and water. But as to hiding the mind-Fire-south in the back-Water-north, not only does the Water not dry up nor is the Fire extinguished, but also they interact and nourish each other. This is the working of the spirit." ["Direct Pointing," 1b]

Fire and Water in the body were functions of spirit working through vital force (*ch'i*). Originally there was but one vital force, which then divided into yin and yang and the Five Phases. The symbols Fire and Water were not to be understood in a literal or material way; the phases Fire and Water function as spiritual forces in the cosmic order; they do not behave like ordinary fire and water.

As in Wang Chi's interpretation, the back was the proper

place to still the mind because it was the pivot of the body, the point to which all the organs are connected.

> Let us now speak of it in terms of ordinary men; the spirit lodges in the eyes, but at night when one is sleeping soundly, it is hidden in the kidney-orb. This is also a meaning of the washing of the *Book of Changes*. When one gets up in the morning, is the spirit of the eyes not refreshed and clear? If it has not been stored in the kidney-orb at night, how can the spirit be clear?
> Let us now speak of it in terms of the Way of heaven; the sun is connected to heaven, and at night it sinks into the earth and is hidden in the sea. This is also a meaning of the washing of the *Book of Changes*. Now after the break of day, is the vital force of heaven not refreshed and clear? If it has not been in the sea at night, how can the vital force be clear?
> Now if in observing it in man it is like this, and in observing it in heaven it is like that, then the theory of stilling the back is essentially putting the front in the rear and the south in the north. What the *Book of Changes* teaches men can be called most subtle and profound. ["Direct Pointing," 2a–b]

The law of stilling described in the *Book of Changes* can be observed in the macrocosm of heaven and the microcosm of the human body; the Changes are the model for the triad of heaven, earth, and man. Lin had elaborated a similar view, although not related to *ken*, in his dialogues with his Taoist friend Cho Wan-ch'un. When Cho stated that the sun is the spirit of heaven, Lin explained, "Heaven's spirit is in the sun; man's spirit is in the mind. At night the sun is bathed in the sea; in sleep the mind is hidden in the kidney-orb."[4]

> Someone asked, "One nurtures the spirit of the sun in the Water of the sea, and one nurtures the spirit of the mind in the Water of the kidney-orb; these both can be grasped as fixed places. Coming to the back, can it not also be seen as a fixed place?"
> Lin Tzu replied, "Indeed, it cannot be seen as a fixed place. Sometimes in front, sometimes in the rear, sometimes above, sometimes below, spirit and illumination are within man."[5]
> (Note:) See the section of moving in the chamber for the subtle meaning of the Center having no fixed place; then you will understand it. ["Direct Pointing," 2b–3a]

If the sea was a fixed place (*ting-tsai*) in Lin's terms, then for him the term "place" implied not a point or position as on a grid but rather an area with definable boundaries, an inside and an outside. The back was not a fixed place; it was also referred to as "within" (*ch'iang-tzu-li*, lit. cavity). The back was seen as a region or hollow within the body, either between the organs or containing them. It was not a literal place to put the mind, but a symbol of internality, quiescence, and rest.

> Lin Tzu said, "The Fire of the mind is easily ignited. Among the successes, fame, riches, and honors and among the sounds, sights, smells, and tastes, when there are those that are pleasurable in that they accord with our desires, they immediately incite the mind to pleasure. This is the Fire of the mind being ignited so that the mind cannot rest at its place. When there are things that are maddening in that they oppose our desires, they immediately incite the mind to anger. This is also the Fire being ignited so that the mind cannot rest at its place. At first it will be fettered and wasted during the day; in the end even the still vital force of the night will not preserve it. Now when it comes to the point that the still vital force of the night will not preserve it, then how can we merely say that it is ignited? Rather, it has the strength of a prairie fire; I fear it cannot be put out." ["Direct Pointing," 3a]

The still vital force of the night is a reference to Mencius' *yeh-ch'i*.[6] Mencius wrote that night rest cuts off the external disturbing influences of the day, allowing the mind to return to its still, quiet, and innocently good state; for Lin Chao-en this was accomplished by storing the mind in the kidney-orb.

Although expressed in terms of Fire imagery, this view of stilling accorded with Confucian interpretations which stressed the maintenance of internal equilibrium in the face of external temptations. Stopping at the place meant to rest the mind within so that it would not be lured away by external things; in Lin's version one stilled the Fire of the mind which arose from desires caused by contact with externals.

Ken as a means of stilling thoughts was the second major theme of stage one.

> When it says "stop the thoughts with thought," it means to stop the depravity of outer[-directed] thoughts by means of the correctness of inner thought. However, the sage prizes the state of no thought. Even if the inward thought is correct, it is still thought. How could this be what Ch'eng Tzu called "forgetting both inner and outer"? This is to use error to leave error behind, to use an illusion to extinguish an

illusion. This is the method of mind-cultivation handed down by sages of old. Therefore the sequence of study is first to forget the outer; then one can forget the inner. ["Nine Stages," 1a–1b]

Lin followed Li Tao-ch'un's reinterpretation of Ch'eng's "forgetting."[7] He suggested recitation of the names as a simple means to stop the flow of thoughts.

> Lin Tzu said, "Beginning students should first recite the phrase 'Masters of the Three Teachings.' Confucius, Lao Tzu, and Śākyamuni are the Masters of the Three Teachings. Confucius' observing proper times, Lao Tzu's purity, and Śākyamuni's tranquil concentration are all expressions for our mind's original nature. Therefore if at all times and in all places one recites the phrase 'Masters of the Three Teachings,' it will be as if he were standing in attendance on them; he will not dare to be lax even for a moment. In reciting the 'Masters of the Three Teachings,' first recite from the mouth, then move it into the cavity of the back. After a time each thought will be only in the back. When each thought is only in the back, the mind is always in the back. Thought is the mind; thought arises from the mind, and there is nothing outside of the mind capable of thought." ["Direct Pointing," 3b]

The term *nien* meant both oral recitation and thought; thus when every recitation (*nien*) was in the back, every thought (*nien*) was in the back.

> Lin Tzu said, "The efficacy of stilling in the back is that it is a method of mind-cultivation which uses thought to stop thoughts. Thoughts that chase after external things are false and confused. Therefore I now redirect them to the inside." ["Direct Pointing," 4a]

Mencius taught that thoughts were false and confused (*wang*) when they were obscure or when they damaged the mind's function as the ruler of the body and the senses.[8] Elsewhere, Lin discussed the sources of falsity and confusion:

> The mind is originally empty. The mind is originally still and unmoving, and thus sincere. When it is excited, it becomes false and confused; it cannot remain empty. Therefore external excitation by sound, beauty, smell, and taste is falsity and confusion; internal excitation by arbitrary opinions, dogmatism, obstinacy, and egoism[9] is falsity and confusion. Master Chou [Tun-i] said, "The absence of falsehood and confusion is called sincerity."[10]

The sincere mind was free of confusion and empty like the original mind.

> Someone thought that thoughts which chase after external things are certainly false and confused; but are not thoughts redirected to the internal also false and confused?
> Lin Tzu said, "Anything involving 'having thoughts' is false and confused." ["Direct Pointing," 4a]

The mind which had thoughts had lost its original emptiness and was therefore false and confused. The true mind had no thought or contemplation (*ho-ssu ho-lü*), as taught by Wang Chi. This was the mind of the sage, in which no thoughts originate from the self; the mind accorded with the Way.[11]

> If they are all false and confused, then they are all wrong; why differentiate external and internal? Therefore, using thought to stop thoughts is to use an error to do away with an error. Using an error to do away with an error is to use barbarians to attack barbarians. Ch'eng Ming-tao [Ch'eng Hao] has said, "When external and internal are both forgotten, then a state of non-differentiation and peace is attained."[12] This is the ultimate principle of study. The *Book of History* says, "None of the Hua, Hsia, Man, and Mo barbarian tribes fail to obey."[13] This is the ultimate efficacy of government. But in the essentials of the beginning of study, one gives priority to forgetting the external. Only when the external has been forgotten can one speak of the efficacy of forgetting the internal; this is a doctrine of gradualness. ["Direct Pointing," 4a]

Lin Chao-en, like Li Tao-ch'un, reinterpreted Ch'eng Hao's statement to his own ends. He even misquoted it: the original statement says the mind will be quiet or clear (*ch'eng-jan*) and peaceful, while Lin used the term undifferentiated (*hun-jan*) and peaceful. His emendation was consistent with his reinterpretation. Ch'eng Hao did not advocate forgetting internal and external, but rather forgetting the distinction between internal and external. "Instead of looking upon the internal as right and the external as wrong, it is better to forget the distinction. When such a distinction is forgotten, the state of quietness and peace is attained."[14] Ch'eng's statement was directed against the tendency of Buddhists and Taoists to denigrate external affairs as less important than internal quiescence; in the Neo-Confucian view, external and internal were inseparable aspects of cultivation. Lin's reinterpretation, like Li Tao-ch'un's, suited a meditative discipline, first cutting off external distractions of the senses, and then transcending the internal flow of consciousness. However, he attempted to interpret external and internal excitation in Confucian terms—external being sensory knowledge and desires, but internal being not the flow of consciousness per se, but arbitrary dogmatism, obstinacy, and egoism; that is to say, moral problems emanating from an unregulated mind.[15]

> Lin Tzu said, "Perhaps the eye comes in contact with a thing, inciting our mind which loves beauty. But one need not incur blame from this beauty. If only one recites the 'Masters of the Three Teachings,' will not the mind obsessed with beauty forget the beauty? Perhaps the ear comes in contact with a thing, inciting our mind which loves sound. But one need not incur blame from this sound. If only one recites the 'Masters of the Three Teachings,' will not the sound-obsessed mind forget the sound?"
> Someone asked, "Is this not a fault of the mind?"
> Lin Tzu said, "If you censure the mind for this, do you not rather incite the mind? Now originally the self did not have this mind enamored of beauty and sound; it is only by seeing beauty and hearing sound that the self first comes to have this mind enamored of beauty and sound. Now if only one recites the 'Masters of the Three Teachings,' he will not be aware of the mind. When the sincerity of a single-minded thought is such that one is not even aware of the mind, how can it be aware of beauty and sound? Therefore it is said, 'One must engage in it without [the object of] rectifying the mind.' "[16] ["Direct Pointing," 4b–5a]

To censure the mind for being aroused by beauty or sound would accord with Huang Wan's view that the mind's substance should be still and its function should be regulated according to proper times. Inappropriate arousal, much less inappropriate action, was a fault. Lin's answer accorded with Wang Chi's interpretation that stilling meant stopping the mind at its proper function; there was no fault in arousal, only in chasing after external things.

Recitation of the names was explained as a means of concentration; if the thoughts were single-mindedly concentrated on reciting the names, the distracting forces of sensory knowledge could be ignored. This practice removed the mind's attention from sensory distractions; it did not seek to "conquer" each desire separately and was thus "without the object of rectifying the mind." The focus of the mind was simply moved inward, back to its proper place.

> Lin Tzu said, "Scholars take studying as their calling, so when the scholar reads the sentence 'study and constantly practice it'[17] it is just like reciting the phrase 'Masters of the Three Teachings.' Indeed, if the thought has entered the back, starting from this one sentence, a hundred, thousand, or ten thousand sentences will all likewise be in the back. Viewing it from this standpoint, each day I study is a day I carry on my endeavor; a year of study is a year of carrying on my endeavor. If I do not study but chase after external things, then I let the mind run away; I cannot carry on my endeavor." ["Direct Pointing," 5a–5b]

Scholars in traditional China recited the classics; thus study was a form of recitation. If study was pursued with concentration and a commitment to personal realization, it was a means of stilling the back.

> When one applies the same to scholarly exchanges, disputations of meanings, and social courtesies, only then can he apply his effort to it at all times and in all places. All sages and worthies since ancient times have minutely refined and achieved this Way from the three bonds, the five constant relationships and nowhere else. [A series of historical examples of sages and worthies exemplifying the three bonds and five constant relationships has been omitted.] . . . However, [today] the Way is not clear and regulated because scholars of this generation all fail to understand how to refine it. When one speaks to them about the Way, even eminent scholars say that nothing will do but to enter the mountains and practice quiescence. We today are bound by such vulgar [views]; how dare we so narrowly regard the scope of the Way? These depraved views of Taoist and Buddhist types have deeply misled the people. How can they know that to refine it with the three bonds, the five constant virtues, and with [one's proper social function as] a scholar, farmer, artisan, or merchant is the means by which one rubs out bad dispositions to effect a great aid in our self-cultivation? ["Direct Pointing," 5b–6a]

Although the theme of stage one was stilling or quiescence, Lin reconfirmed its intricate tie to concrete moral cultivation. Quiescence or enlightenment were not ends in themselves; the purpose of study, stilling, and mind-cultivation was to strengthen Confucian moral character. He did not want to fall into Buddhist or Taoist errors of putting spiritual aims above and beyond social values.

> People's greatest desires lie in wealth and sex; they are the hardest thing for them to abandon. When they dwell in the mountains, the wealth-obsessed mind is temporarily concealed; but if they think they have been able thereby to forget wealth, they are wrong. The sex-obsessed mind is temporarily concealed, but if they think that they have thereby been able to forget sex, they are wrong. Let us consider the meaning of entering the mountain to seek quiescence. The *ken* hexagram symbolizes the mountain; to put the mind in the mountain is the meaning of stilling in the back. But if one does not seek stilling in the mind, but seeks stilling in the mountains, how could it be right to say there is something to be gained in the mountains? Suppose one said that the mind could achieve quiescence and there were something to be gained in the mountain. However, it would merely be the gradual concealment [of desires]; when they reappear, you are right back where you started. Even more important are the great principles of human relations in the three bonds and the five constant relationships and the constant callings of scholar, farmer, artisan, and merchant. Can one turn from them, destroy and abandon them in order to seek the quiescent mind? Or can one not? ["Direct Pointing," 6a-6b]

Many Buddhists and Taoists withdrew to mountain temples to seek mental and spiritual tranquillity away from the distractions of the world. Lin argued, however, that true quiescence could not be achieved by withdrawing from the external stimuli of desire; such withdrawal only temporarily removed one from temptation; desires were concealed but not overcome. They would reappear to harm the mind at the first temptation. True quiescence was the equilibrium of mind in activity; it was the mind and not activity which was to be stilled. When the mind was in equilibrium desires could not ruffle it.

Lin Chao-en used a syncretic reformulation to "correct" the errors of some Buddhists and Taoists. The real meaning of withdrawal to the mountains had been lost. It was not withdrawal to a place away from the world. The mountain was the image of *ken*, stilling. Withdrawal to the mountains was a symbol for stilling the mind in the back. At the same time he offered the "correct" view of the Buddhist and Taoist prac-

THE NINE STAGES   155

tice; certain Ch'an and Taoist thinkers saw meditation as an attitude which should pervade all activity.[18]
An interlocutor asks about the Confucian meaning of enlightenment:

> "Confucius said, 'Hold fast and thereby preserve it.'[19] Now if it is already refined, what need is there to hold it fast?"
> Lin Tzu said, "The first thing is that one must hold it fast; hold it fast and then refine it."
> "Then what is it that is called 'holding it fast'?"
> "Take the analogy of an ordinary man holding a jade disk inside his garment; his every thought is on that disk. He only fears that a thief will be able to steal it. Therefore to hold it fast is to refine it." ["Direct Pointing," 8b]

The first stage of cultivation was to gather in the lost mind and hold it fast as though it were a treasure, keeping it in its proper place.

> Someone asked, "Today for the first time I have come to understand the stilling the back of the *Book of Changes,* but I am still confused about the phrase 'does not cling to the body.'[20] I venture to ask about it."
> Lin Tzu said, "This phrase speaks of it in terms of pure and single-minded effort. If I am only aware that there is my back and that I am stilling in my back, how can I be aware of what is outside the back and that there is this so-called body? One forgets it by 'not letting the thoughts go outside of their place.' If I am only aware that there is my chamber and that I am moving in the chamber, how can I be aware of what is outside the chamber and that there are so-called other people? One forgets them by 'not letting the thoughts go outside of their place.' This is the true meaning of 'not clinging'; is it not pure and single-minded observance?
> "In this way clinging is the opposite of losing. Have you really not heard of the determined scholar and the man of humanity?[21] The determined scholar and the man of humanity are only aware of their minds having this humanity; it comes to the point that they do not even cling to their lives, for because of this humanity they can lose their lives without regret. Or, they are only aware of their minds having this righteousness; it even comes to the point that they do not cling to their bodies, since for the sake of this righteouness, they can lose their bodies without regret. If one holds to it daily in this way, and refines it daily in this way, one can practice it not only at the court, but even in the midst of the three armies. One can practice it not only in

the midst of the three armies, but even while going into the midst of barbarians or when confronting danger.[22] Now where the body is, the mind is also; where the mind is, the thoughts are. If in every thought one does not forget [this practice], how can one cling to the body, much less be seized by external things?" ["Direct Pointing," 8b–9a]

By applying pure and single-minded concentration, you would "have neither oneself nor others, but only moral principles, in view," as taught by Chu Hsi.[23]

> Lin Tzu said, "The body of man has nine openings, and eight of them face south.[24] But the other is in the rear in order to pass impurities. Now the back contains none of these openings; it is like a wall. When one moves the mind back and hides it [there], how secret it is!" ["Direct Pointing," 10a]

The mind was stilled in the back because the back is deep within, secret, and far away from the distractions of the sense organs.

> The *pen-i* says, "If it stops where it should stop, then it will not move with the body."[25] If only it does not move with the body, one will be able not to cling to the body. Therefore, the true destination of the back fundamentally does not move with the body. It is like the North Star in the heavens, which also fundamentally does not revolve with the heavens.
> Someone asked about the true destination.
> Lin Tzu said, "It is the place where it is said Confucius and Yen Hui found their joy.[26] The *Book of Changes* says 'stop in its place.' The place [of contentment] is the place [where it stops]. To stop in its place is to abide in its place. Therefore, to abide in its place without moving is what makes heaven heaven; to stop in his place without moving is what makes man man." ["Direct Pointing," 10a]

They have stopped in the "place" which accorded with their true natures. Lin Chao-en said, "To wash the mind and move it back means to hide it in the nature."[27]

> Someone further asked, "The Way of the sage has no [fixed] place, so why does this say to stop in its place?"
> Lin Tzu said, "The North Star abides in its place, and heaven forgets about it. Stilled in the back, [the mind] rests in its place, and the sage forgets about it. Therefore, if there is a thought, there will be an attachment [to a thing], and consequently a place." ["Direct Pointing," 10b]

Lin contrasted resting something in its natural place and making it stop at some place. In the former no effort was needed; it could be forgotten. In the latter effort of thought gave rise to attachment. Wang Yang-ming applied a similar distinction to matters of liking and desire: "Not making a special effort to like or dislike does not mean not to like or dislike at all. . . . [It] merely means that one's likes and dislikes completely follow the Principle of Nature and that one does not go on to attach to that situation a bit of selfish thought."[28] Lin Chao-en applied this principle to mental concentration:

> Proceeding from thought to no thought is what Yao meant by "finding peace in your stopping";[29] one forgets about the place and is no longer aware of it. ["Direct Pointing," 10b]

Because it was the proper or natural place, it took no forced effort to remain there. At first thoughts were directed to the back, and then every thought came to be automatically in the back, and one could forget the back.

> The human body is very small; does it really have a North Star abiding in its place?
> Lin Tzu said, "The body of man is a microcosm; who does not know and believe that? Why then do you only doubt it in relation to the North Star? If we use the analogy of the North Star of the heavens, then the whole body would appear to cling to the North Star of the back in its functionings."
> "But then what is the meaning of 'not clinging' in stilling in the back?"
> Lin Tzu said, "The body certainly clings to stilling in the back in its functioning; the vital essence, spirit, life store, and arteries are thereby harmonized, and sight, hearing, restraint, and movement are thereby properly applied."
> "But stilling in the back is simply stopping at its place; what action does it perform?"
> "Have you not seen it in heaven? The whole body of heaven indeed clings to the North Star in its functionings; the sun, moon, and stars thereby illumine everything; the rain, wind, dew, and thunder thereby stimulate and enrich. However the North Star simply abides in its place and that is all; what action does it perform?" ["Direct Pointing," 10b–11a]

Like Wang Chi, Lin saw the back as the North Star which simply abides in its place, yet facilitates all functions. A commentator on the *Ts'an t'ung ch'i* also used this analogy in discussing the Great Ultimate. "Only if the emperor establishes the Ultimate can the people submit to the Ultimate. Only if the mind as ruler is able to be still and unmoving without willful activity and thereby maintain perfect uprightness can the members of the body obey it. It is like the North Star which abides in its place while the myriad stars grasp it."[30]

> Or one can see it in the millstone: When the millstone grinds things, does it not cling to the pivot in its functionings? But the pivot rests in its place and does not turn with the millstone. One can understand the Way of the North Star of heaven by observing the millstone. Therefore, when a gentleman begins study, he need only abide in his place like the North Star of the back.
> The yin line in the fourth position of the hexagram *ken* says, "Still the body." The image says, "Keeping the body still means to stop in the body."[31]
> Someone asked, "It says 'one does not cling to the body,' but it also says 'still the body.' How are these two 'bodies' different?"
> Lin Tzu said, "The 'body' of 'does not cling to the body' speaks in general terms of the human body; but is not the 'body' of 'still the body' the so-called Center of the body, which is within the back? Therefore, it is specifically referred to by the yin line in the fourth place. The stilling of the first position is in the toes, of the second in the calves, of the third in the hip, and of the fifth in the jaws, but the yin line in the fourth position is the line of the mind." ["Direct Pointing," 11a–11b]

In the progression of stilling through the parts of the body, "Still the body" was usually interpreted as stilling the trunk of the body,[32] but Lin asserted that it meant the cavity or inside of the body (*ch'iang-tzu-li*), which he identified with the back.

STAGE TWO

> The second is the revolutions of heaven: Imitate *ch'ien* and *k'un* in order to establish the Ultimate. ["Nine Stages," 1b]

When the mind was stilled in the back and every thought was in the back, the mind assumed its proper place as the ruler of the Center. In stage two, the mind began to function as that ruler. Like the Great Ultimate of the *Book of Changes*, it governed and united all proper movements and changes in the body without losing its stillness.

In early stages of cultivation the mind needed a conscious model for activity, namely heaven. Thus Lin cited the image of the hexagram *ch'ien* (heaven): "The movements of heaven are full of power. Thus the superior man makes himself strong and untiring."[33] He also drew heavily on the Great Treatise, chapter 10, which elaborated how the Changes allow men to model themselves on heaven and earth. Chapter 10 reads in part:

> The Changes, what do they do? The Changes disclose things, complete affairs, and encompass all ways on earth—this and nothing else. For this reason the holy sages used them to penetrate all wills on earth and

Figure 2. Some Hexagrams and Trigrams

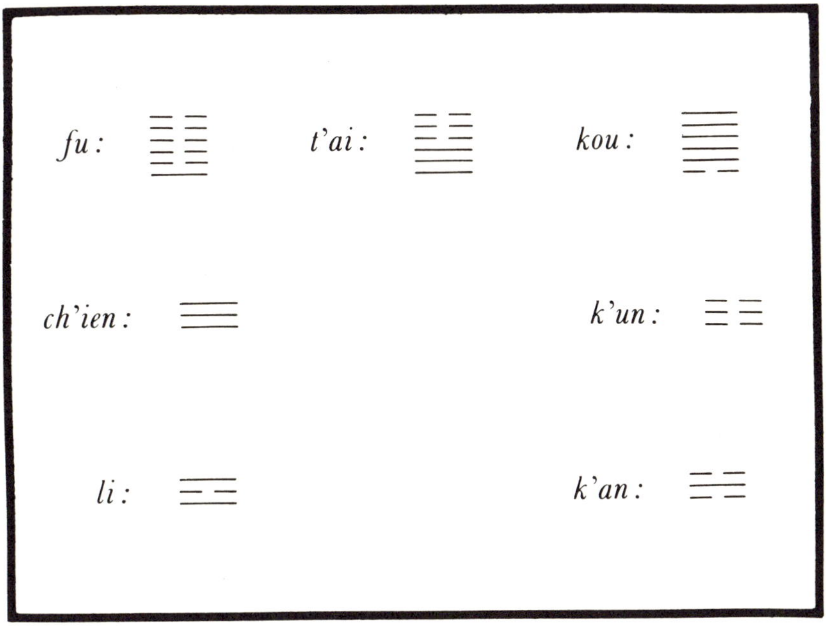

to determine all fields of action on earth, and to settle all doubts on earth. . . . In this way the holy sages purified their hearts, withdrew, and hid themselves in secret. They concerned themselves with good fortune and misfortune in common with other men. . . . Therefore they fathomed the tao of heaven and understood the situations of men. . . . Therefore there is in the Changes the Great Primal Beginning [i.e., the Great Ultimate]. This generates the two primary forces. The two primary forces generate the four images. The four images generate the eight trigrams. . . . Therefore: There are no greater images than heaven and earth. There is nothing that has more movement or greater cohesion than the four seasons. . . .[34]

Following this line of reasoning, Lin asserted that the human Ultimate was based on the same model as the imperial Ultimate and the Ultimate of heaven.[35] In the human body the forces of the hexagrams *ch'ien, k'un, li,* and *k'an* generated movements from the Great Ultimate just as they do in the cosmos.

> The mind forms the Great Ultimate and the revolutions of *ch'ien* and *k'un* revolve around it; this is the meaning of the "four seasons following their course."[36] Then my body is a microcosm of the universe. ["Nine Stages," 1b]
>
> Lin Tzu said, "*Ch'ien* and *k'un* are the gates of the Changes,[37] but the Great Ultimate is the Center, the mind. Let me discuss it in terms of the upper and lower trigrams together; the upper two lines [of the hexagram] are heaven, the lower two lines are earth, and the middle two lines are man.[38] Man is the Center of heaven and earth; he is the mind of heaven and earth. Again, let me discuss it in terms of the upper and lower trigrams separated; the Center of the upper trigram is the Center, the mind, and the Center of the lower trigram is also the Center, the mind. Even when the eight trigrams and the sixty-four hexagrams circle around it, the Center is still the Center, the mind.
>
> "The *Book of Changes* says, 'Change has no direction.'[39] It also says, 'The Changes encompass all ways in heaven and earth—this and nothing else.'[40] The fact that it is without direction and that it encompasses all ways in heaven and earth makes it my Center. If it is my Center, it is my mind. Is it only the way of the Changes that is so? All things go up to the limit of what is covered by heaven and down to the limit of what is supported by earth; what fills the space between them is all my Center. Being my Center, it is my mind.
>
> "Looking at it from this point of view, the Center, the mind, of heaven, earth, and man are all one. Which is the Center of heaven, the Center of earth, and the Center of man? Which is the mind of heaven,

the mind of earth, and the mind of man? Therefore what is the Center is the mind, and what is the mind is the Center: it is only one." ["Direct Pointing," 13b–14a]

The meaning of the passage turns on the multivalent meanings of the word *hsin*, which meant mind, center, or pivot. The mind was the ruler of the organism because it rested at the center, the pivot, of the organism; from its position as the Center it controlled the functionings which revolved around it and emanated from it. The word Center suggested not only that which is in the central position, but also the center of action, as in "nerve center." Conversely that which was the Center, the pivot, the ruling force of an "organism" could be seen as the mind of that organism; in this sense the ruler was the mind of the empire because all functions and principles of the empire emanated from him.

The same correspondence of "mind" and "center" was used to interpret the imagery of the *Book of Changes*. Trigrams and hexagrams (see figure 2) were divided into three sections representing the triad of heaven (upper), earth (lower), and man (middle). Man was in the center, in the position of pivot, mind, and ruler. Moreover to Lin the word "Center" implied not the exact middle, but rather all that is between the top (heaven) and the bottom (earth); man's position, the position of mind, filled the space between heaven and earth and encompassed all that is included therein—that is, it encompassed everything in the cosmos. From this position man acted as the mind, the ruler of the cosmos; he united heaven, earth, and man. Heaven, earth, and man each had a Center, a mind, an Ultimate, a pivot around which activity moved. However, since man occupied the central position, when the human mind was cultivated to extend to the minds of heaven and earth, it could unite with them and thus combine the three primal powers into one. The effectuation of such a union within the microcosm and the macrocosm was the task of self-cultivation.

Someone said, "Now you speak of the chamber and of moving in the chamber. I venture to ask the meaning of 'moving' in it."

162   THE NINE STAGES

> Lin Tzu said, "Moving means to move in it. It is the movement of the phrase 'the movement of heaven is full of power.'[41] In the movement of heaven, how great is the power in the revolutions of the sun! As to my body, which is a microcosm of the universe, the revolutions of heaven [in it] are full of power. The *Book of Changes* says, 'The movements of heaven are full of power. The gentleman strengthens himself without rest.'[42] If the Great Ultimate is established in the chamber in our body, then heaven extends to its outer reaches and 'goings and comings are endless.' "[43] ["Direct Pointing," 14b-15a]

Lin Chao-en associated the establishment of the Great Ultimate with the movements of heaven and the revolutions of heaven. The revolutions of heaven involved a system of circulation of vital forces through the channels in the body. Lin described stage two in a letter to Yüan Tsung-tao:

> Moving in the chamber is the revolutions of heaven; my body becomes a microcosm of the universe. In carrying out the revolutions of heaven, one must collect pure and clean vital force within the body's microcosm in order to nurture the spirit, and expel turbid vital force outside the body's microcosm in order to refine the body.[44]

The phrase "the movements of heaven are full of power" referred to the purification which resulted from the internal circulation of vital force.[45]

> The *ken* hexagram says, "When it is time to stop, then stop"; the Great Ultimate will be established in that. "When it is time to move then move"; the revolutions of heaven will move in that. ["Direct Pointing," 14b]

By stilling the mind in its place (the back, the pivot) one established the Great Ultimate, the centered mind. By modeling internal circulation of vital force on the laws of Change, the revolutions of heaven followed their proper course in the internal microcosm.

> Do we not also see it in the Great Treatise? The Great Treatise says, "Sun and moon alternate; thus light comes into existence."[46] It also says, "Cold and heat alternate; and thus the year completes itself." It also says, "Contraction and expansion act upon each other; thereby arises that which benefits." This is the method of mind-cultivation called moving in the chamber. ["Direct Pointing," 14b-15a]

THE NINE STAGES 163

The rising and falling circuits of the revolutions of heaven, described as yang and yin circuits, were seen as manifestations of the alternation of yang and yin movements in nature: sun and moon, heat and cold, expansion and contraction.

> Someone asked, "Moving in the chamber implies motion, so why do you also say, 'When the time comes to stop, then stop, and the Great Ultimate will be established in that'? How can moving in the chamber find its efficacy in stopping?"
> Lin Tzu said, "Stopping is the means by which one moves it [circulates vital force], for stopping means to still it [the mind] in the Center of the chamber, which is the one Great Ultimate of the body. Now motion, which circles outside the chamber, is heaven's revolutions within the body. Have you not seen it in heaven? What is encompassed by everything outside of earth all belongs to heaven. Therefore the North Star abiding in its place is the stopping of heaven. If we liken it [the North Star] to the Great Ultimate within our body, how could it not be the same? It is only that our body is small and that heaven and earth are vast. Heaven's motion has 365 degrees; if we compare it to the revolutions of heaven within the body, is it not the same? It is only that our body is small, but heaven and earth are vast."
> "The *Book of Changes* says, 'The thoughts of the gentleman do not go outside of their place.' I venture to ask the meaning of 'place'; is not the Center the place where it stops?"
> Lin Tzu said, "The Center of the back is the 'place.' The Center of the chamber is also the 'place.' Therefore when the thoughts do not go outside the Center of the back, one keeps them in place to preserve the mind. When the thoughts do not go outside the Center of the chamber, one keeps them in place to establish the Ultimate." ["Direct Pointing," 15b–16a]

Stilling the mind in the back was the means by which one established the Great Ultimate, the centered mind. The Great Ultimate was the pivot from which the mind governed the cosmic movements within the body.

> Lin Tzu said, "Human beings have a human Ultimate, and standing in the Center of the Way is establishing that they have an Ultimate. The nature is thereby carried to its end; the life store is thereby fully achieved. This [law of the Ultimate] is not only true for self-cultivation, for if one brings it forward and employs it in the realm, nothing can be outside of it. The emperor has an imperial Ultimate, and by standing in the Center of the realm, the emperor establishes his Ultimate. In this way the hundred offices are righted and the ten thousand peoples are

governed. But it is not only in the human Way that we observe this [law of the Ultimate], for even if we look for and examine it far off in the Way of heaven, there is nothing that can contradict it. Heaven has a heavenly Ultimate, and when the myriad stars circle around it, heaven establishes its having an Ultimate. From this the four seasons follow their course and the myriad things are born.[47] Now heaven indeed does not contradict this; how much less human beings![48] How much less the emperor going out to govern or the sage pursuing his studies! For this reason, the gentleman puts great store in establishing the Ultimate." ["Direct Pointing," 18b–19a]

The movements of heaven accorded naturally with the Ultimate, the moral order or pattern which reflected cosmic law. When people modeled themselves on this natural moral order, they moved in harmony with heaven. The full passage alluded to from the *ch'ien* hexagram expresses the idea succinctly:

> The great man accords in his character with heaven and earth; in his light, with the sun and moon; in his consistency, with the four seasons; in the good and evil fortune that he creates, with gods and spirits. When he acts in advance of heaven, heaven does not contradict him. When he follows heaven, he adapts himself to the time of heaven. If heaven itself does not resist him, how much less do men, gods, and spirits![49]
>
> Someone asked, "If the Way is one of nonaction, why do you always speak of establishing the Ultimate? Is this not close to clutching at it?
>
> Lin Tzu said, "Now even heaven has its Ultimate; does heaven also clutch at it? To take the analogy of planting a tree, when the root is secure, then what more is there to do? From it come branches, flowers, and fruit, and the unceasing life principle is naturally preserved in it. It certainly does not depend on any outside help to grow; indeed, how could one help it? This is like what I call establishing the Ultimate. Once the Ultimate is established, what further task is there? From it come the qualities of the worthy, the sage, and heaven; and the unstoppable true motive force [of the universe] is naturally preserved in it. It certainly does not depend on clutching; indeed, how could one clutch at it? Thus the planting of a tree lies in putting down a secure root, and study is rooted in establishing the Ultimate. This is something that [only the wise] man can share in the knowledge of; the Way is difficult to explain to ordinary men." ["Direct Pointing," 19a–19b]

Nonaction was activity in accord with the natural, while clutching implied willful, unnatural activity or effort.

STAGE THREE

The third is penetrating the passes; the brightness penetrates the limbs and apertures to refine the body. ["Nine Stages," 1b]

A master of Taoist meditation wrote that it took time to open the internal channel fully, but "as time passes, this moving heat will go up and down of itself and can, by the imagination, be spread to all parts of the body, reaching even to the nails and the ends of the hair, with the result that the whole body is warm and unusually comfortable."[50]

Lin wrote to Yüan Tsung-tao:

> Next [after stage two] there is the penetration of the passes. One thereby further extends it through the veins and tracts of the body, thus circulating the blocked vital forces. When the blocked vital forces have been dissipated, then the spirit is empty and the body is lively and healthy.[51]

Stage three refined the body; stilling in the back could be applied to cure illness.

> If one can understand how to penetrate the passes in order to refine the body, then the so-called seven apertures will penetrate each other and every aperture will be bright, rendering both body and spirit wondrous. How could this not lead to union with the absolute of the Tao? ["Nine Stages," 1b]

The seven apertures will be discussed in the commentary below.

> Someone asked, "Is not what the Taoists call refinement an error?"
> Lin Tzu said, "How could it be called an error? Now refinement means to refine something; the meaning of refinement is to heat metal with fire. A Taoist book says, 'Do not enter the mountain unless you have refined the returned elixir.'[52] Therefore to 'refine something' is to refine it with the three bonds, the five constant relationships, and the callings of scholar, farmer, artisan, and merchant." ["Direct Pointing," 7a]

The returned elixir (*huan-tan*) was an alchemical product repeatedly returned to the furnace for further refinement; Lin reinterpreted the term to suggest fine ethical refinement through constant practice.

> However, this refinement has four meanings: spiritual refinement, physical refinement, self refinement, and other refinement. Spiritual refinement is to hold fast to its preservation by refining the spirit. Physical refinement is to expel illness by refining the body. Self refinement is to refine the self with the self. Other refinement is to refine the self through others.
> Someone asked, "What is the meaning of self refinement?"
> Lin Tzu said, "This is what I call spiritual refinement and physical refinement." ["Direct Pointing," 7a]

That is, refinement of mind and body.

> "What is the meaning of other refinement?"
> Lin Tzu said, "This is what men of old called travail within and travail without."[53]
> "What is the meaning of physical refinement?"
> Lin Tzu said, "To expel sickness with sickness is like stopping the thoughts with thought; it is to avail oneself of the false to return to the true. The *Book of Rites* says, 'When purity and brightness are in the body, the will and vital force are spiritlike.'[54] Now if the body is unclear, it cannot be bright. If it is neither clear nor bright, the will and vital force will be stained in turn; how can they be spiritlike and have foreknowledge? The *Book of Changes* says, 'They were spiritlike and hence they knew the future.'[55] The Way of ultimate sincerity is purity and brightness in the body."
> Someone again asked about purity and brightness in the body. Lin Tzu said, "Man's body is made up of physical form and vital force, but it is not always able to maintain its purity. If the vital force is impure, then it is turbid. If the body is impure, then it is stained. Illness occurs when the turbidity of the vital force and the impurities of the body are sufficient to soil the seven apertures of the intelligence and make them ill." ["Direct Pointing," 7b]

The seven apertures of the mind of the sage corresponded to the functions of the seven sense openings in the head. Ordinary men also possessed the seven apertures, but theirs were obscured.[56] "The seven apertures are the means by which one opens his emptiness and passes vital force through it so that it circulates throughout the entire body."[57]

Being ill, [the body] is not clear and bright; it is not that of a sage. That is the cause. One recognizes that illness as illness in order to expel the illness.[58] Therefore it is said, "We recognize only the illness as ill; therefore he is not ill."

"But how is what the Taoists call refinement different from this?"

Lin Tzu said, "I do not know. But what I call the four meanings are what I myself practice; they are good methods for daily use. While there are four meanings, actually three of them essentially go back to one. What is that one? It is mind. The mind is the ruler of the Center. When the mind is the ruler of the Center, how could the spirit not be settled? How could the form not be pure? When the spirit is settled and the form is pure, that is like the Duke of Chou's inner travail and Confucius' outer travail; the Center will naturally be preserved in an unchaotic state. This is the essential principle of refinement." ["Direct Pointing," 8a]

Lin Chao-en agreed with the Taoists that refinement had both spiritual and physical aspects. However, he saw refinement of the mind and spirit as the basis and goal of all other forms of refinement; he was critical of those schools of Taoism which advocated dietary, gymnastic, sexual, or drug regimens as the primary mode of refinement. Inner and outer seem to be roughly equivalent to spiritual and physical refinement.

In another essay, Lin discussed in more detail the seven apertures of the sagely mind:

> An aperture is only its emptiness. If it is empty it can have shining intelligence; if it has shining intelligence it can attain wisdom. If one blocks this aperture with a material thing [by the mind attaching itself to the thing with a desire-ridden thought], the thing will be in the aperture. When the thing is in the aperture, it cannot be empty; not being empty it cannot be brightly intelligent; lacking bright intelligence, it cannot be conscious.[59]
>
> In my studies I have two doctrines of washing away sand to reveal the gold. There is washing away the sand of human desires in the mind to reveal the gold of the principle of nature so that the seven apertures open of themselves. There is washing away the sand of turbid vital force in the body in order to reveal the gold of pure vital force; in this case the seven apertures are also able to open.[60]

The apertures of the mind were blocked by material things when the mind was lured by things through the senses, but the blockage could be removed in two ways: (1) At the moral level of ridding the mind of desires, and thus its apertures of things; this was to attack the cause of the blockage. (2) At the physical level of removing the obstruction of turbid vital force which is blocked as a result of the desires; this is to attack the symptom. In Lin's view, the two levels reinforced each other.

STAGE FOUR

> The fourth is: Rest it in Earth and sincerely cultivate [the seed of] humanity in order to form the hidden elixir. ["Nine Stages," 2a]

"Rest it in Earth and sincerely cultivate the seed of humanity" was an allusion to a passage from the Great Treatise:

> Since in this way man comes to resemble heaven and earth, he is not in conflict with them. His wisdom embraces all things, and his tao brings order into the whole world; therefore he does not err. He is active everywhere, but he does not let himself be carried away. He rejoices in heaven and has knowledge of fate, therefore he is free of care. *He is content with his circumstances and genuine in his kindness,* therefore he can practice love.[61]

The phrase in italics, which in Chinese is the same phrase as Lin's, is the source of the allusion. The original passage concerned the ethical benefits of the sage's emulation of heaven and earth, and the translator has rendered it in light of the commentaries, which elaborate the ethical implications. Lin Chao-en substantially reinterpreted the phrase in terms of the symbolism of Taoist yoga, but the ethical dimensions suggested by the Great Treatise were not lost, for Lin interpreted the Taoist system in ethical terms. Earth was the phase of the Center. Thus "resting it in the Earth" is another way of resting it in the Center, the base of moral equilibrium. To rest in the Center is to move inward, to reverse the centrifugal and dissipating forces and return to the stable core and source of Being, deep within. The commentaries explored the meaning of the Center in the system of homologies between the macrocosm and the microcosm.

The zenith of heaven is 84,000 li from the nadir of earth. Thus there is a central place between heaven and earth at 42,000 li from each. If we regard the human body as a microcosm, the heart and navel are 8.4 Chinese inches apart, and there is a central place between the heaven and earth of the body 4.2 inches from each. What is it that we call the Earth? East is Wood; west is Metal; south is Fire; north is Water; and the center is Earth. If we can rest the spark of humanity in our mind in the Earth-center and thereby sincerely nurture it, then Water and Fire will be combined and the hidden elixir will be formed. ["Nine Stages," 2b]

Lin Tzu said, "The head of man is the K'un-lun mountains; the four limbs are the four seas; and the belly is the Middle Kingdom. If the belly is the Middle Kingdom, then in the north is Mount Heng, in the south is Mount Heng, in the east is Mount T'ai, and in the west is Mount Hua. The center of the belly is the middle of the Middle Kingdom with Mount Sung towering in the center.[62] In ancient times the Lo district, because it was considered the center of heaven and earth, was called the Earth-center." ["Direct Pointing," 12a]

The geography of the internal microcosm was elaborated to establish a Center in the body equivalent to the center of earth. The K'un-lun Mountains stretched across North and much of Western China; they were the source of many rivers. Hence the homology to the head, from which all arteries emanated in the subtle physiology. Five sacred mountains established the five directions. Mount Sung of the Lo district in Honan was known as the center of heaven and earth because three generations of rulers reigned from there.[63] Thus the center of the Middle Kingdom, as the Center of the body, was the position of the ruler, the mind.

The *Book of Changes* says, "Ch'ien is the head; k'un is the belly."[64] It also says, "He seeks the right place and abides in the body."[65] The body is also the belly, and k'un is connected with Earth. It also says, "He moves in the chamber."[66] The chamber is the Earth of k'un. Have you not seen it in heaven and earth? From the zenith of heaven to the nadir of earth is altogether 84,000 li; in the body's microcosm the distance between the heart and navel is 8.4 inches. The space between the heart and navel is the space between heaven and earth, so the center of the Center is the Center of the chamber. ["Direct Pointing," 12a]

The *Book of Changes* associated the hexagram *k'un* (earth) with the belly, the Center of the body; thus belly and *k'un* are associated with Earth. Lin identified the chamber of "moving in the chamber" with the Earth of *k'un*, the belly, equidistant between heart and navel. The chamber of *ken* was identified with the yellow chamber, the middle elixir field of Inner Alchemy.

> When the spark of spiritual light was originally in this Center, it was the first time heaven and earth gave birth to man. ["Direct Pointing," 12b]

Fertilization was the second major theme of this stage. The spark of spiritual light established in the Center was like the sperm entering the womb to fertilize an egg, thus giving birth to man. As the *Hsing-ming kuei-chih* expressed it, at conception "a drop of original yang vital force falls into the place that establishes the life store."[67] In terms of the *Book of Changes*, the three lines of a trigram were a symbol for procreation, birth—the emergence of three from two. The central line of a trigram was the position of man, while the top and bottom lines represent heaven and earth. Before man, there was only heaven and earth, father and mother; man emerged when a spark of spiritual light, a vital essence, was established in the space between the two. The fertilization of Inner Alchemy was not to create a new life (a forward movement), but rather to move backward to the cosmic origins of the self, to the very beginning. Then the self would be made new.

> Can we not also see it in the egg? The yellow in the Center is the Earth-center; it is like the space between heaven and earth. The *Book of Changes* says, "Yellow and in the Center."[68] This is also the meaning of the Center's being yellow. In the yellow Center of the egg there is a spot which is the Great Ultimate of the egg. ["Direct Pointing," 12b]

The symbol of the egg established yellow as the color of the Center (Earth) where fertilization occurred. The identification of yellow and the Center came from the commentary to *k'un*; it further strengthened the association of Center, earth, Earth, belly, and so forth. Further the *k'un* commentary used the term "center" in the sense of "being centered"; it described

THE NINE STAGES 171

the sage as yellow (the color of moderation) and in equilibrium, or centered.[69]

> Therefore as the Center of heaven and earth is called the Earth-center, so is the Center in my body called the Earth-center; as the center of the egg is called the yellow Center, so is the Center of my body the yellow Center.
> Has this yellow Center no fixed place?
> Lin Tzu said, "Indeed, it has no fixed place. Using the analogy of the womb: there are deep and shallow wombs; there are floating and sinking wombs. The yellow Center is the same: there are yellow Centers in the top and in the bottom, in the front and in the rear."
> Someone asked, "Does the space between heaven and earth, being the Center of heaven and earth, also have no fixed place?"
> Lin Tzu said, "It also has no fixed place. Let me now discuss it in terms of the six lines of the hexagram. When the single yang line appears in the first place, we have the hexagram *fu* [see figure 2, p. 159] and the space between heaven and earth seems to be below earth. When the first three places are yang, we have the hexagram *t'ai*, and the space between heaven and earth appears to be above earth. ["Direct Pointing," 12b–13a]

This pictographic interpretation of these hexagrams took the broken lines to represent sky or air, and the solid lines to represent solid earth. Thus in *fu* it appeared that ground level was below earth in the sense that the sky extended down into the first two lines which were the "earth lines" of the hexagram. Similarly in *t'ai* the earth went up into the position of man and the ground lines thus appeared to be above the "earth positions" of the hexagram. The yang and yin symbolism was reversed for the sake of visual clarity; strictly speaking yang solid lines should have represented heaven or sky, and yin broken lines should have represented earth.

> Concerning the meaning of the world "space between" (*chien*), it is an error to insist that it means the centermost place of the earth. The spiritual transformations of heaven and earth have no [fixed] place or form; they certainly cannot be grasped or reckoned. They are like the seed of a fruit which sends new life out through its point, and the heart of the lotus seed penetrates deep within it. How much more when the egg obtains its yang! It may be the centermost part of the yellow, or above or below, or in front, or in the rear; such is the case when there is no fixed place. Viewing it in this way, as to the meaning of "space be-

tween," must one arrive at the centermost point between heaven and earth before one can call it the "space between"? ["Direct Pointing," 13a]

Lin continually emphasized that the back, the Center, and the yellow chamber were not fixed places. Students were not to take the spatial images literally, seeing the transformation as primarily physical. Nor were they to spend effort to force the mind and concentration into a rigid preconceived mold. The "space between" allowed considerable latitude, particularly for beginning students.

Someone asked, "Does not the method of mind-cultivation called moving in the chamber entail some concrete method of endeavor which can be put into words? I ask you, sir, to clarify it by instructing me."

Lin Tzu said, "Let me now try to discuss its method. One should first rest the mind of the Five Phases in the mind of the Center, thus forming the Earth-center, and thereby sincerely nurture it. When the Five Phases and yin and yang forces in the body come naturally to follow the true cosmic cycle of increase and decrease, then mind, body, nature, and life store can be united. It contracts, expands, goes, and comes; it is truly like the alternation of the sun and moon and the alternation of cold and heat. It is like the natural course of the evolutions of heaven. It is also the microcosm within my body. It has a will at first, but in the end it has no will." ["Direct Pointing," 15a]

In this passage Lin explained the process of yogic reintegration using the symbols of the *Book of Changes*. The natural cycle of cosmic increase and decrease (cosmic breathing) was imitated until the forces of the internal microcosm were back "on track," and followed that cycle without conscious effort (will). Then mind and life store would be united. The inner microcosm would recover its internal balance. "Cosmic cycle of increase and decrease" is a somewhat free translation of *hsiao-hsi chen-chi*. *Hsiao-hsi* is the seasonal cycle of the increase and decrease of yin and yang forces as they fill and empty the universe, a kind of cosmic breath. *Chen-chi* is the motive power, the secret force or spring of the universe.

The Inner Alchemy explanation of the same process clarified how it was achieved in actual meditative practice. The cycle of increase and decrease referred to the circulation of vital forces in the body by means of breath control. In stage three the student circulated blood and breath through the internal revolutions of heaven by means of mental effort and breath control. However, in this stage the ascents and descents (cosmic increases and decreases) of vital forces in the internal circuit were no longer directed by will or mental effort; the revolutions naturally followed the proper course as defined by the model of the workings of heaven. This was called the greater revolutions of heaven or fetal breathing. The adept stopped "winding the wheel" which controlled the revolutions after the embryo was conceived. Mind, body, nature, and life store were the aspects of the self which united in order to conceive the sage embryo; they were symbolized by the yin and yang, the lights of spirit and vitality, the trigrams *li* and *k'an*, and Fire and Water.

> Lin Tzu said, "When yin and yang [combine] and the spark of goodness falls into the chamber, it develops into the nature. In the wondrous union of this yin and yang is formed the unfathomable spirit. It is like husband and wife uniting so that a spark of goodness falls into the womb; it develops into a person. This wondrous union of husband and wife forms the unknowable Tao. When a person has been formed through this wondrous union, this child can again beget a child, and they beget and beget without end. Now when the nature has been formed through this wondrous union, it becomes sagely, spiritlike, cultured, and martial, and undergoes endless transformations." ["Direct Pointing," 16a–16b]

As yin and yang unite to create all things and husband and wife unite to produce the next generation, so the union of internal yin and yang forces formed the embryo of the nature, established by a spark of goodness; this nature matured into a sagely being with all the sagely virtues.

> Lin Tzu said, "Before man is born, he does not yet have nature and life store; he has not yet received this spark of spiritual light. At the very beginning of life, heaven endows him with a nature. He thereupon receives the spark of spiritual light, which is continued by goodness until the nature is complete.[70] The *Book of Changes* calls this one spark of spiritual light the Great Ultimate; in that case, the nature and life store have not yet divided. When the Great Ultimate divides into yin

and yang, nature and life store are differentiated. The nature lodges in the physical mind and its name is spirit. The life store lodges in the navel and the kidney-orb, and its names are vital force and vital essence." ["Direct Pointing," 16b–17a]

The spark of spiritual light (*i-tien ling-kuang*) was a technical Inner Alchemy term for the circle of light which appeared in the mysterious pass when the adept was able to shake loose the mental obscurities of spirit. It was experienced as a circle of light between the eyes, but it could be internalized and nurtured to become a strong and pure light. This light has been defined as follows:

> It is something possessed by all men, in every individual. This ray is so vast it can fill the entire universe; it is so small it can be hidden in a grain of rice. It is true yin.[71] When this spark cannot become a great ray, it is because it is obstructed by the seven passions and the six desires, so that it cannot pierce through them. The method of the immortals is to couple it with true yang, as adding oil to a fire to make it burn brightly, so that it can shine so brightly that there is no space left for the seven passions and the six desires. This is like the clouds dispersing to let through the rays of the sun; with no clouds for ten thousand li, the red sun occupying the empty heavens, its rays will naturally illumine the three thousand worlds.[72]

The spiritual light was a symbol of the luminosity of consciousness nourished in meditation. Lin identified the light with the heavenly endowed nature of the *Doctrine of the Mean*.[73] He also interpreted it to mean the Tao, or the mind of Tao, based on a passage in the *Book of Changes:* "The union of one yin and one yang is Tao. Continued with goodness, it becomes the nature. The humane man discovers it and calls it humanity. The wise man discovers it and calls it wise. The people use it daily and are not aware of it."[74] The result of the union of yin and yang was the seed of moral nature. He further identified it with the Great Ultimate, the united prenatal Tao, the source of all change and the principle underlying all moral principles. By identifying the spark of spiritual light with heavenly endowed nature, the mind of Tao, the Great Ultimate, and the One, Lin endowed the spark of spiritual light with clear ethical significance.

In the *Book of Changes* the Great Ultimate produced the trigrams; the One divided into the two forms (broken and unbroken); the two divided into four emblems (four combinations of broken and unbroken lines); and the four divided into the eight trigrams (the permutations of combinations of three broken and unbroken lines).[75]

In Inner Alchemy the production of trigrams symbolized the devolution of integral unity into harmful multiplicity. The one Tao, the Great Ultimate, divided into the two forms—yin and yang. The substances of yin and yang correspond to the two primary trigrams, *ch'ien* and *k'un*, which in turn correspond to nature and life store in their pure forms, their original unity. However, as the person reacts to external phenomena, the mind (an aspect of nature) chases after external things, and the vital essence (an aspect of life store) drains away in its unsublimated form as semen or female sexual fluids as a result of physical desires. These movements of mind and of vital essence rend apart the original unity of nature and life store; they are pulled in separate directions in their pursuit of externals. In this postnatal, fragmented state, the nature lodges in the physical mind and life store in the navel and kidney-orb. But that is not all. The sundering of the union of nature and life store changes them; their substances are no longer pure. Pure nature is represented by the trigram *ch'ien*, three unbroken lines (see figure 2 on p. 159). Pure life store is represented by the trigram *k'un*, three broken lines. After their fragmentation their inner core is damaged. The function of nature in the movement and activity of mind and spirit is represented by trigram *li;* the function of life store in the activities of vital essence and vital fluid is represented by *k'an* (figure 2).[76] The symbolism is visible in the structure of the trigrams; their inner lines have been damaged in their sundering. *Li* and *k'an*, postnatal or impure nature and life store, must be reunited before the lines can be restored and *ch'ien* and *k'un*, pure or prenatal nature and life store, will be restored. Thus this theory of separation both symbolizes the loss of primal wholeness and the symbolic base from which that wholeness may be restored.

Lin Tzu said, "When nature becomes spirit, it lodges in the physical mind. The spirit is connected with the phase Fire; when it encounters a thing it burns. How can it not be lured away by things? In this case, even when the vital force is purified in the night, the spirit is still in the physical mind. Day after day the person is transformed [by things] into things; how could this merely constitute being lured away by them? Therefore, first gather in the lost mind and still it in the back in order to establish the foundation. After that, return the spirit to the nature and the vital force to the life store, and then reunite them into one; this is called going from yin and yang to the Great Ultimate. If you do not understand stilling in the back, then you do not understand preserving the mind. If you do not understand preserving the mind, then you do not understand establishing the foundation. If the foundation is not established, how can the spirit not run wild? When the spirit has run wild, how can the vital force not disperse? When the vital force has dispersed, how can one return the yin and yang to the Great Ultimate, thereby restoring the one spark of spiritual light?" ["Direct Pointing," 17a–17b]

Moving from *li* and *k'an* to *ch'ien* and *k'un* and thence to the Great Ultimate was a cosmic model for moving from spirit and vital force back to nature and life store and hence to the original sagely mind.

Mencius said, "The gentleman draws [his bow], but does not discharge [the arrow]."[77] It seems that the so-called "restraining the self with propriety"[78] is the means by which Mencius draws the bow. To restrain with propriety is to "return to propriety."[79] To restrain it with propriety is to "stand in the Center of the Way."[80] The Center of the Way is the Center of Yao and Shun [the doctrine of the Mean taught by the sages], and to stand is to "sincerely hold fast to it."[81] Confucius' "standing firm at thirty"[82] and Mencius' "first stand fast in the greater part"[83] are both this "standing." But how can one say "stand in the center of the Way" and also say "sincerely hold fast to it"? Now what "knowledge attains" is this Center, and what "humanity preserves" is this Center.[84] What one knows, loves, and delights in[85] is that one knows this Center, and loves and delights in it. When it is completely formed, it is nature; to "complete the nature and preserve it always"[86] means to preserve this Center. ["Direct Pointing," 18a]

The Great Ultimate was the pivot, the mind, the Center; it was also the Mean, perfect harmony with propriety and moral virtues.

THE NINE STAGES   177

Lin Tzu said, "The *Book of Changes* speaks of the one spark of spiritual light saying, 'As a continuer, it is goodness.'[87] Mencius also called it goodness, saying, 'What commands our liking [in people] is called goodness.'[88] He also called it the 'incipient sign' [of goodness], saying, 'That by which humans differ from the lower animals is merely an incipient sign [of goodness].'[89] Now that which commands our liking is as subtle as this incipient sign; it is this incipient sign of goodness, endowed at birth, which we possess by virtue of our nature. Then what is the meaning of 'possessing it in the self is called true humanity'?[90] Now when heaven gives birth to humans, even though we say that the nature possesses this incipient sign of goodness, the common folk use this incipient sign of goodness every day without realizing that it is that which commands our liking which the nature always has.[91] Although they have it, it seems that they do not, and they are not able to say that 'we truly have it in us.' If we are able to understand that this goodness which commands our liking is something which we inherently possess and which we use every day, and if we rest it in the Earth of our body and sincerely nurture it, how could this goodness not be something that we are filled with?[92] When Mencius called this true [humanity], he went from that to 'filling it up,' and he went from that to 'brightness displayed.'[93] The abundance amassed over time is achieved stage by stage. However, when he says 'filled up' why does he also say 'brightness displayed'? Is it not that he realizes that this goodness which commands our liking originally comes from the Great Void? It is most spiritual, most sagely, most spiritlike, and most bright. Emperor Yao took this goodness and extended it in order to extend his light to the outer limits of the four directions, to heaven above and to earth below.[94] King Wen took this goodness and extended it in order to light the four directions and to manifest it in the lands of the West.[95] The Duke of Chou took this goodness and extended it in order to illumine heaven above and earth below, and to apply it diligently to the four directions.[96] The display of brightness is certainly as great as this, but at the beginning it is only the incipient sign." ["Direct Pointing," 19b–20a]

A passage from Mencius provided a Confucian version of the nurturing and expansion of the spark of spiritual light to become coextensive with the universe. Lin interpreted the spark of spiritual light as the seed of heavenly endowed nature. In this passage Mencius posited a seed of virtue in humans, an incipient sign which separated them from the animals; he also described an almost mystical expansion of that virtue. The passage reads,

A man who commands our liking is what is called a good man. He whose goodness is part of himself is what is called a real man. He whose goodness has been filled up is what is called a beautiful man. He whose completed goodness is brightly displayed is what is called a great man. When this great man exercises a transforming influence, he is what is called a sage. When the sage is beyond our knowledge he is called a spirit man.[97]

The sage kings expanded this goodness to its full extent and transformed the world. Lin wrote, "When nature has been formed through this wondrous union, it becomes sagely, spiritlike, cultured, martial, and undergoes endless transformations";[98] he interpreted the spiritual transformations of Taoist yoga as the Confucian ethical and mystical expansions and transformation of the sagely mind.

> Confucius said, "How could I dare to rank myself with the sage or the humane man?"[99]
> Someone asked, "What is meant by sageliness and humanity?"
> Lin Tzu said, "The unfathomable spiritlike brightness of the mind is called sageliness, and the unceasing life will of the mind is called humanity. The word 'mind' in these sentences is the mind of the Center, not the mind [heart-orb] of the Five Phases. The sage becomes spiritual by gaining this mind; humanity arises through this aspect of mind. Humanity of the centered mind is what I call the one spark of spiritual light. Mencius said, 'Humanity is the human mind.'[100] Now in the loyal subject and the filial son, the one spark of the sincere mind (*tan-hsin*) is bright and undarkened; this is indeed one spark of spiritual light. In this way, this humanity originally rested in the mind of the Center, having been endowed at birth. The sage who rests his humanity in this mind of the Center thus does no more than to restore his humanity to the mind of the Center and keep it resting there. Thus this sageliness and this humanity are both based in the nature. Yang Shih [1053–1135] said, 'In human nature there is no space to add a single thing.'[101] If there is a thing there, then of course it is not spiritlike and bright, so how could one become sagely? It is of course without the life will, so how could it achieve humanity? This is why the *Great Learning* put great stock in 'ridding the mind of things in order to advance knowledge.' "[102] ["Direct Pointing," 22a–22b]

Sageliness was spiritlike brightness, the radiance or illumination of the mind of the sage and of the spiritual light of the immortal. Unceasing life will was humanity (*jen*), the most fundamental of Confucian virtues and the seed of virtue in the mind.[103] It also meant the seed of the embryo which would mature into the realized man. Lin identified the seed of virtue and of the embryo with the spark of spiritual light; if nurtured they would expand until the vast and spiritual mind of the sage was manifested. The spark of sincere mind (*tan-hsin*) also literally meant elixir—mind; the elixir was for Lin fundamentally moral. Nurturing the elixir in the Center was the same as holding to the Mean.

> Recently there was a man named Ch'in who was a Confucian, but revered the doctrines of Lao Tzu. When he first heard the doctrine of holding to the Center (*shou-chung*)[104] [from a Taoist], he asked Lin Tzu about it.
> Lin Tzu said, "In what place is the Center?"
> The man replied, "The space between the heart and the kidneys is the Center."
> Lin Tzu said, "Have you held to it?"
> He replied, "I have held to it, but I have not yet seen any good results."
> Several years later he made a further inquiry about holding to the *ni-wan* aperture [upper elixir field].
> Lin Tzu said, "In what place is the *ni-wan*?"
> The man replied, "The head has nine palaces; the *ni-wan* is the central palace."
> Lin Tzu said, "Have you held to it?"
> The man replied, "I have held to it, but I have not yet seen any good results."
> Several years later he made a further inquiry about holding to the elixir field.
> Lin Tzu said, "In what place is the elixir field?"
> The other replied, "It is 1.3 inches below the navel."
> Lin Tzu said, "Have you held to it?"
> The other replied, "I have held to it, but I have not yet seen any good results." Mr. Ch'in said, "Is what the men [who taught these three doctrines] transmitted to people all wrong?"
> Lin Tzu said, "Though you held to them, how can you achieve any results? Now these three men all wanted to catch a glimpse of Lao Tzu's great Tao by means of hearsay. Can one, then, relying on secondary sensory experience, apprehend and have knowledge of the great Tao of Lao Tzu? Now this so-called Center, which is the space between the heart and the kidneys, the *ni-wan*, which is the Center of the nine palaces, and the elixir field, which is 1.3 inches below the navel, are all printed in Taoist books and can be examined there. So why did you depend upon these three men first to understand and discuss them?"

"In what way can it be done?"

Lin Tzu said, "The Way has no fixed substance; the Center has no fixed place. Since antiquity no one has been able to use the secondary sensory experience to apprehend and glimpse this subtle and mysterious great Way, but in direct transmission from mouth to mouth and from mind to mind, the true motive force of the universe is naturally preserved in it. Even if one has the wisdom of Yen Yüan or Jan Niu,[105] how can he know it except by transmission from a master? How much more so those whose wisdom does not equal Yen Yüan's or Jan Niu's!

"Now we need not discuss further the so-called Way of the Taoist types, but I venture to express some doubts about the so-called Confucianism of the Confucian types. They say 'rectify the mind,'[106] but they do not examine it in themselves to find out how to rectify it. They say 'do not rectify the mind,'[107] but they do not examine it in themselves to find out how their own minds do not depend on rectification. They say 'make the will sincere'[108] but they do not examine it in themselves to find out how to make their own wills sincere. They say 'have no will'[109] but they do not examine it in themselves to find out how their own wills do not depend on being made sincere. As to all the similarities and differences of various terms and appellations, they only rely on taking a few [disjointed] words from the classics in order each to establish his own school and then carry their search into remote corners to create a wealth of clichés. How could such studies have something to be gained in one's own mind and to be embodied in one's self?" ["Direct Pointing," 23a–25a]

Mr. Ch'in failed to see any results in his practice because he and his teachers had taken their alchemical symbols too literally; they understood the Centers of Taoist yoga purely as foci of yogic effort. They had forgotten that the alchemical language and the yogic symbols were meant to point beyond to a transcendent Way. Characteristically, Lin used Taoist language to criticize Taoist errors; virtually every Taoist teacher stressed the transcendent Way which must be transmitted directly from mind to mind. All taught that the secrets of Taoist meditation lay in understanding the esoteric meaning of the alchemical language. However, Lin had his own interpretation of that secret meaning, and his interpretation had a Confucian cast. Mr. Ch'in had failed, according to Lin, because he had not perceived the fundamentally ethical character of the Tao. For Lin the Centers of Taoist meditation were also symbols of the Center, the Mean, the equilibrium and harmony of the sagely mind and nature. Mr. Ch'in failed to understand the fundamentally ethical nature of the task. Lin also criticized Confucians of his day for not examining it in themselves to find out how to achieve their doctrines of mind and will. They were wrong in believing that their so-called knowledge (disjointed words from the classics) would be translated into practice without serious self-reflection.

STAGE FIVE

The fifth: Gather from heaven and earth to collect the drugs. ["Nine Stages," 2b]

In the previous stage *li* and *k'an* (postnatal spirit and life store) where balanced, manifesting the spark of spiritual light. In Inner Alchemy this was directing the light of sublimated vitality to the *ni-wan*, where with concentration, it lifted the veil of obscurity and manifested the light of spirit (the mysterious pass). The spark was then led to the Center where it began the series of transformations leading it back to the Great Ultimate. In stage five *li* and *k'an*, postnatal yin and yang, spirit and life store, united to reestablish *ch'ien* and *k'un*, prenatal yin and yang, spirit and life store. This union constituted a leap back from the profane to the sacred. The two main ingredients of the elixir (lead and mercury) have been refined and put into the caldron, but the chemical reaction required the catalytic effect of certain substances (drugs) from nature inserted at precisely the right moment. The reaction was a mysterious and spiritual transformation, a leap to another dimension of reality.

Between the *hai* and *tzu* points a single yang appearing in heaven and earth brings the hexagram *fu* [figure 2, p. 159]. The same is true in the body's microcosm. Between the *ssu* and *wu* points, a single yin appearing in heaven and earth brings the hexagram *kou*. The same is true in the body's microcosm. ["Nine Stages," 2b]

Hai, tzu, ssu, and *wu* are four of the twelve earthly branches in the Han system of correspondences. The internal revolutions of heaven were modeled on the movements of heavenly bodies as they are seen in the sequence of the Changes; the internal circuit of the revolution was divided into sections labeled by the twelve earthly branches.[110] After the winter solstice yang reappears, symbolized by *fu*. After the summer solstice yin reappears, symbolized by *kou*. Likewise in the internal microcosm when the vital forces pass from the twelfth point in the circuit to the first (at the base of the penis, or the clitoris?), yang appears; when they pass from the fifth to the sixth point, yin appears. At one level this was related to conservation of the vital essence. *Fu* was the point in cultivation when the penis erected, and *kou* was the point where it is contracted without ejaculation.[111] At another level it indicated the functions of the two halves of the internal circuit of revolutions. Yang vital forces were purified during the ascent in the channel running up the back; yin forces were purified during the descent in the forward channel.[112] The erection of the penis was the manifest sign of the movement of yang, the raw material needed to spiritualize the body, to strengthen the seed of the embryo. Yang was not only semen, but heat, light, fire, the spiritual or expansive life force.

> Thus between *hai* and *tzu*, even if we gather the yang from within our body, we thereby also gather the yang appearing in heaven and earth. When we have gathered the yang in heaven and earth, will not the yang of heaven and earth all return to our body? Between the *ssu* and *wu* hours, even if we gather the yin from our body, we thereby also gather the yin appearing in heaven and earth. When we have gathered the yin appearing in heaven and earth, will not the yin of heaven and earth all return to our body?
>
> Someone objected, "But heaven and earth are far off; I venture to ask the method of gathering them."
>
> Lin Tzu said, "Heaven and earth are not far off; their yin and yang vital forces constantly flow in and out of our body. Our body is not near; its yin and yang vital forces constantly form connections with heaven and earth. Therefore although heaven and earth are extremely broad and vast, one can nonetheless gather them from the body and have something left over." ["Nine Stages," 2b–3a]

The exchange of the inner lines of *li* and *k'an* was carefully timed to accord with the movements of the cosmos. *Li* could take the yang line from *k'an* only at the point between *hai* and

THE NINE STAGES   183

tzu, when the single yang line first appeared and contained within it all yang potential of the cycle. This restored *ch'ien* to its pure form. Conversely *k'an* could take the yin line from *li* only between the *ssu* and *wu* points when the yin line first appeared and contained in it all potential yin growth. One Taoist work explained it as follows: "To take from the lead means to use the filling action of vital force in the center of *k'an* to fill in the empty spirit in the center of *li* and to take the true yin at the center of *li* and return it to transform the fullness at the center of *k'an* into emptiness."[113] Vital force (*ch'i*) fills up the universe, giving material form to things. The function of spirit is that of being empty and penetrating, illuminating and dispersing. The Great Ultimate or primal unity was a balance of these two; to achieve the Great Ultimate one must restore the nature of being empty to that which fills and the nature of filling up to that which is empty. The fragmenting forces of polarity can be reversed to integrate the microcosm. Stage five does not seem to have a direct moral equivalent, but it was preparation for the stabilization and expansion of sagely mind.

STAGE SIX

> The sixth: Coalesce the spirit in the cavity of vital force. ["Nine Stages," 3a]

In stage six this newly realized substance of the moral mind was placed in the center of the Center, the pivot within the pivot of the functioning life principle, so that it could rule without even the slightest adjustment.

> The space between the two kidneys is called the cavity of vital force; it is the aperture within the aperture. It is mysterious and more mysterious. Lao Tzu said, "The gate of the mysterious female is called the root of heaven and earth."[114]
> If one is able to take what is coalesced in the space between the heart and the navel and lower and hide it in the cavity of vital force, then one sends it back to the caldron of Earth, firmly sealing it there to wait until the true yang elixir comes from outside. But the spirit is the elixir,

and moving the elixir into the Earth caldron is to coalesce the spirit in the cavity of vital force. ["Nine Stages," 3a-3b]

The cavity of vital force was the inner cell of the lower elixir field, and the "womb" in which the immortal or sagely fetus developed. The Taoists described the cultivation of the spiritual fetus:

> The method consists at the start of collecting the spirit to drive it into the cavity of vitality [under the navel] so that vitality will envelop spirit, until when utter stillness prevails both will gather and unite into a whole which will slip into that cavity where it will remain in an unperturbed state called the immortal [Tao] fetus. This fetus is not a real one having form and shape; for it is an incorporeal manifestation of the union of spirit with vitality.[115]

In Inner Alchemy the union of prenatal spirit and vital essence to conceive the fetus was experienced as stillness. The elixir, the fetus, was sealed in the Earth caldron to allow gestation. During gestation one continued to sublimate yang sexual fluids into vital essence; the resultant vitality nurtured the fetus until the physical signs indicated immanent birth. This may be the meaning of Lin's yang elixir which comes from outside. Yang meant manifest as opposed to hidden; yang coming from outside would mean that the elixir manifested itself. Since the elixir was humanity, the appearance of the yang elixir would be the external manifestation of the sagely mind in the countenance and in action.

STAGE SEVEN

> The seventh says: Free yourself from birth and death by embodying heaven and earth. ["Nine Stages," 3b]

The manifest sagely mind expanded to embody heaven and earth. Chu Hsi once described the expansion of moral principle until there is nothing outside of it:

> The operation of the principle of the mind penetrates all as blood circulates and reaches the entire body. If there is a single thing not yet en-

tered, the reaching is not yet complete, and there are things not yet embraced. This shows that the mind still excludes something. For selfishness separates and obstructs, and consequently one and others stand in opposition. This being the case, even those dearest to us may be excluded. Therefore the mind that leaves something outside is not capable of uniting itself with the mind of Heaven.[116]

Lin Chao-en did not believe the mind was united with heaven and earth by embracing one thing and then another; he opposed Chu Hsi's doctrine of the investigation of things. Rather, he advocated attuning the mind gradually to the principle of nature inherent within the self until the sagely mind was released to expand and unite with the mind of heaven and earth. Lin suggests in more detail than his fellow Neo-Confucians the stages of the mystical expansion of sagely mind.

> Now heaven and earth are very vast. If we say "embody heaven and earth," how could it be other than to take the vastness of heaven and earth as my own body? My vital force is the vital force of heaven and earth. Therefore I can first use my own vital force as vital force, and then use the vital force of heaven and earth as my vital force. When I use the vital force of heaven and earth as my vital force, then my vital force can permeate the vital force of heaven and earth and circulate with it. In this case, in the Center of the vastness of heaven and earth something will naturally coalesce which conjoins with my elixir. Only after that can it be called the yang elixir. ["Nine Stages," 3b–4a]

Lin Chao-en explained the mechanism of embodying heaven and earth as unification of their vital forces. This was consonant with the Taoist theory of breathing in the *Hsing-ming kuei-chih*.[117] It also had Confucian dimensions. Mencius taught that the vast vital force, if nourished by uprightness, would fill up all in heaven and earth.[118] Although it may be incorrect to interpret Mencius' phrase as having mystical overtones,[119] later Neo-Confucian commentators such as Lin understood it in that way. One's substance expanded to fill the universe.

What transcended birth and death in this stage was the mind. Lin wrote,

The sage considers death to be a matter of returning; he does not consider death to be the end of thought. Therefore, what dies is the body, and what does not die is the mind. Mencius said, "Neither early death nor long life causes double-mindedness."[120] That is the sage's Way of immortality. The myriad things are all potential obstructions; the sage does no more than unite his vital force with their vital forces to form one body with them. How can he maintain an isolated existence in the world?[121]

For the sage, what does not die is the mind; what achieves long life is humanity. The mind and humanity are one. When we speak of them from the point of view of their united substance, we call them mind; when we speak of them in terms of the principle, we call them humanity.[122]

The linking of humanity with mind and hence with long life recalls Ch'eng I's statement that the humanity of the sage's mind forms one substance with all things. Forming one substance with them, it is coexistent with them, and thus transcends life and death.

Nature and life store were not bound by physical form:

What dies in men is their body, but the nature and life store have never been extinguished. This is the subtlety of nature and life store; they penetrate day and night, past and present, and have not birth or death. But people of the world do not understand nature and life store; they often take them to be the body. Therefore, there are those who take the body to be nature and life store; there are those who consider spirit and vital force to be nature and life store; and there are those who take nature and life store to be nature and life store, but can forget them both; only then can one call it being of one body with the Great Void.[123]

STAGE EIGHT

The eighth says: Transcend heaven and earth to embody the Great Void. ["Nine Stages," 4a]

The embodiment of heaven and earth attained the One, the whole of ordinary reality, the Great Ultimate. But the Great Ultimate was not the highest reality. In the "Diagram of the Great Ultimate Explained," Chou Tun-i wrote, "The Five

Phases are the one yin and yang; the yin and yang are the one Great Ultimate; and the Great Ultimate is fundamentally the Ultimate of Nonbeing."[124] As the Taoists had taught, even the totality of all that exists was not the final reality, for it did not include that from which Being sprang: what is constantly changing and producing new realities out of what is not yet. Nonbeing, what is not-yet-Being, encompasses the larger potentials of reality and is closer to the origins.[125] Lin Chao-en identified the Great Void with the Ultimate of Nonbeing, the true beginning.

> Now the Great Void is perfect empty vastness. When we say "embody the Great Void," how could it be other than to take the empty vastness of the Great Void as my own body? Now my void is the same as the void of the Great Void. Therefore I can first take my own void as my void, and then later I can take the void of the Great Void as my void. When I can take the void of the Great Void as my void, then I unite my void with the void of the Great Void, forming one substance. When I have accomplished this, then in the Center of the empty vastness of the Great Void something will naturally coalesce which conjoins with my elixir. Only after that can I name it the *sha-li* ray.[126] ["Nine Stages," 4a–4b]

The filling movement of vital force was appropriate for embodying the material world of heaven and earth. In this stage, however, one strove to embody the Great Void, empty vastness. The void or emptiness within was the spirit or sagely mind, pure luminosity unobstructed by things. The spark of spiritual light, the luminosity of the unobstructed mind, was expanded to illumine and "embody" the Great Void from which all Being springs.

> Lin Tzu said, "In the seed of a fruit, there is a kernel which is its Great Ultimate; it embraces the two [principles of yin and yang]: it is one yin and one yang. The *Book of Changes* says, 'There is in the Changes a Great Ultimate. This generates the two primary forces.'[127] Therefore the two forces of the Changes transform and generate, but the Great Ultimate is one and spiritlike, and the Ultimate of Nonbeing is the not-yet-One and antedates heaven. What antedates heaven is the Great Void. The brightness of spirit illuminates through this, and Change proceeds from this; the wondrous functioning of the one spark of spiritual light is as vast as this." ["Direct Pointing," 17b]

The Great Void was the Ultimate of Nonbeing, that which existed before the unity of heaven and earth. It was the not-yet-One. The spark of spiritual light was the original countenance of the person before the union of nature and life store; hence it was the light of pure spirit which could penetrate to the Great Void, the primal state.

> Lin Tzu said, "Now the Great Void exists as heaven, exists as earth, and exists as the sun. As to the Great Void of the sage, his vital force is also the vital force of heaven, and his physical form is also the form of earth. His spark of spiritual light is also the sun of heaven and earth. Therefore, the rays of the sun reach everywhere within heaven and earth, so how could the shining of my spark of spiritual light be different from that of the sun? However, where there is spirit there is vital force; the vital force of heaven circulates everywhere within heaven and earth. How could the filling action of my vast rectified vital force [128] be different from that of heaven? The spirit originally had no spirit; the vital force originally had no vital force. The vast voidness of the Great Void is that there is absolutely nothing within heaven and earth or outside heaven and earth that is not the Great Void. How could the empty vastness of my Great Void be different from the [cosmic] Great Void?" ["Direct Pointing," 21b–22a]

The vital force of the sage filled the world as the air filled it; the spiritual light of the sage illumined the world as the sun illumined it. The voidness of spirit united with the cosmic Great Void, the very source of Being. A patriarch of Inner Alchemy defined the embodiment of the Great Void in virtually identical terms: "Refining the void means to unite the void of the yang spirit [within us] with the void of the Great Void, fusing them until they are congruent; this makes the self become one substance with the Great Void and circulate with heaven and earth."[129]

> Someone asked, "The Great Void is empty; are heaven and earth also empty?"
> Lin Tzu said, "Heaven and earth are also empty."
> "But heaven and earth have form and vital force; how can they be empty?"
> Lin Tzu said, "Heaven and earth have form and vital force, and yet do not have form and vital force; in that, they are empty."
> He asked again, "Is the sage also empty?"
> Lin Tzu said, "The sage is also empty."

"But the sage has mind and body; how can he be empty?"

Lin Tzu said, "The sage has mind and body, and yet does not have mind and body; in that, he is empty."

"Now if it has form and vital force, how can it also not have form and vital force?"

Lin Tzu said, "To have and yet not have form and vital force is to forget form and to forget vital force."

"If one has mind and body, how can he also not have mind and body?"

Lin Tzu said, "To have and yet not have mind and body is to forget the mind and to forget the body."

Lin Tzu said, "Form and vital force are petty aspects of heaven and earth, but what makes heaven and earth great goes beyond form and vital force; it is not something form and vital force can limit. Mind and body are petty aspects of the sage, but what makes the sage great goes beyond mind and body; it is not something mind and body can limit. Therefore, how empty is the Great Void! And yet the Great Void is not aware that vital force and form fill up the Great Void. How empty are heaven and earth! Heaven and earth are not aware that the myriad kinds fill up the space between heaven and earth. How empty is the sage! The sage is not aware of the myriad things ranged before him. Therefore the Great Void, heaven and earth, and the sage are one; it is only that heaven and earth both have and do not have vital force and form, and that the sage both has and does not have mind and body. In this way, the means by which they cover and support, by which they shine and alternate, by which they contract and expand, by which they flow through life and transformations, are all the wondrous functioning of the Great Void, are all the wondrous functioning of heaven and earth, are all the wondrous functioning of the sage. They are one and the same in their emptiness, and they are one and the same in their wondrous functioning. I therefore say that the Great Void, heaven and earth, and the sage are one." ["Direct Pointing," 25a-26b]

The virtue of the Great Void was that it was "not aware" of things.[130] This empty mind had no care. In a commentary on the *Analects* Lin wrote, "The state before joy, anger, grief, and happiness appear is the stage of unity of substance with the Great Void. After their appearance, if they are properly regulated, this is unity with the functions of heaven and earth."[131] He also explained it in terms of the mind as a mirror which could receive and reflect reality: "The mirror of the mind is the Great Void. The mirror of the mind of Confucius is the Great Void. The mirror of the mind of Confucius is not different from that of men; the Great Void of the mirror of the mind of Confucius is not different from that of men."[132] The inner voidness was the original and universal substance of sagely mind.

STAGE NINE

> The ninth says: Break up the Void in order to realize the ultimate principles. ["Nine Stages," 4b]

The image of breaking up the Great Void as the final stage of contemplation came from the Inner Alchemy tradition. "The training should continue no matter how long it takes until the four elements (that make up the body) scatter, and space pulversizes leaving no traces behind; this is the golden immortal sage of the indestructible diamond-body."[133] Lin did not speak of the diamond-body; for him it was the final leap beyond subject-object consciousness. The student was not even aware of the Great Void of Nonbeing from which Being emerges. This state of mind beyond all distinctions, beyond emptiness and non-emptiness, shows strong Buddhist influence. It was analogous to the realization of the unconditioned Buddha mind. The Great Void is even beyond Nonbeing. In Chinese thought Nonbeing surrounded Being and defined the boundaries between Being and what-is-not-yet or what-is-no-longer. In other words Nonbeing is the "other side" of Being; the two exist in mutual dependence. The Great Void, however, was empty; there is no "other side" of the Great Void. It is so vast and so empty as to be beyond distinctions; there is no "other" and no "negation" of the Great Void. This is the beginning of the not-yet-One, that which precedes and encompasses both Nonbeing and Being. Hence Lin spoke of the ultimate principles as Buddhist; the Buddhists developed and elaborated this doctrine of unconditioned, absolute mind.

> This is the perfection [of the nine stages]; nothing more can be added. What thought or contemplation is there?[134] There is no will or action.[135] How can there be a "principle"? Why then do we insist on saying "principle"? How can there be "realization"? Why then do we

insist on saying "realization"? We cannot even speak the single word "ultimate." We depend on the words "principle" and "realization" in order to clarify it. Therefore simply by taking the vastness of heaven and earth as my body, embodying their body, I have not yet done it. By taking the empty vastness of the Great Void as my body, embodying heaven and earth, I have not yet reached the perfection [of the nine stages]. Thus I must arrive at emptiness and break it up; then it is empty and moreover forgotten. How much more would I forget heaven and earth? How much more would I forget the body? When one arrives at this place, if you seek the three masters, not even they are there.[136] ["Nine Stages," 4b]

The *Doctrine of the Mean* says, "Brightness arising from sincerity is called the nature. Sincerity arising from brightness is called instruction."[137] What is it that we call sincerity? "The still and unmoving"[138] is sincerity. What is it that we call brightness? The illustrious with no darkness is brightness. When the spiritual light naturally appears in the still and unmoving Center, that is brightness arising from sincerity. When the illustrious and undarkened spirit is one with the original nature so that there is nothing that can be grasped, that is sincerity arising from brightness. Therefore when there is sincerity there is no further task; when there is brightness one achieves sincerity through self-examination. ["Direct Pointing," 20b–21a]

Although immediately above Lin identified the state of breaking up the Void as unconditioned mind beyond all dualities and words, he integrated that doctrine with the still and unmoving sincere mind of Neo-Confucianism. The first appearance of the spiritual light in the self was the *Doctrine of the Mean's* "brightness arising from sincerity," with sincerity understood as the mind concentrating on the One, the Mean. When the light of spirit, the humanity of sagely mind, was fully expanded, the clarity of the mind could support sincerity. The mature moral mind could immediately perceive and follow moral principles while effortlessly maintaining its centrality. That was sincerity arising from brightness. Although in the highest stage of self-cultivation the mind was unconditioned, it did not transcend the distinctions of morality. Even the absolute reality beyond the Great Void had moral dimensions and the absolute Tao was the normative basis of action. Here Lin revealed his deep-seated Confucianism.

Lin Tzu said, "The Great Ultimate is the One; it is the spark of spiritual light; it is brightness. The Ultimate of Nonbeing is the not-yet-One; it is the state before the spark of spiritual light; it is sincerity. I have used the analogy of a rock: it is still and cold, so how could it possess what we call fire? But if you strike the rock, a spark of true fire arises within it. When the incipient fire takes on form, it passes from faggot to faggot, and it is unceasingly bright. When the faggot has been exhausted, where is the fire then? In this way, when it has returned to its still, unmoving original nature, the nature is sincere. Therefore the spark of spiritual light is the incipient sign of sincerity and brightness; its illustriousness and brightness are like the shining of the sun and moon in that sincerity and brightness are endless." ["Direct Pointing," 21a]

Sincerity, or concentration on the One, was the beginning of effort. In the ordinary postnatal world, sincerity (concentration) was the effort of cultivation which led to the appearance of the spark of spiritual light; this was conscious sincerity, an effort of mind and will. Such sincerity gave rise to the spark of spiritual light as striking a rock produces a spark of fire. This light was nurtured and expanded through the various phases of self-cultivation until at the end it returned to stillness, the still and unmoving state of ultimate sincerity in the prenatal or sagely mind. Ultimate sincerity was also concentrated on the One, but not by an act of will; its quiescence, its adherence to the One or the Center, was the natural result of a mind beyond distraction.

> The *Doctrine of the Mean* says, "The state before pleasure, anger, sorrow, and joy have appeared is called the centrality [or equilibrium] of the Center."[139]
>
> Someone asked, "The mind of the sage certainly possesses this equilibrium of the Center, but does the mind of an ordinary man also possess it?"
>
> Lin Tzu said, "This is the mind of an infant, the mind of no thought or contemplation. How could ordinary men not have the mind of an infant? It is only that ordinary men do not have the means to extend it to its utmost. It may appear to be preserved or appear to be destroyed; thus they cannot in all cases be regulated by the Center. If it is moved by good, then it will be good; if it is moved by evil, then it will be evil. Because their Center has no ruler, it is affected by things."
>
> Someone asked about the principle of extending it to the utmost.
>
> Lin Tzu said, "Extending it to the utmost means first to extend it to the Center, then to sincerely hold it fast."[140] ["Direct Pointing," 23a]

All humans have the Center, but because of the distraction of things, their minds have ceased to rule the Center and instead chase after things. The task of cultivation was to reestablish the mind as the ruler of the Center, and then to hold it fast in the state of ultimate sincerity. Ultimate sincerity (*ch'eng*), undistracted and undivided sagely mind, was the basis of all virtues—humanity, compassion, wisdom, faithfulness, etc. Sincerity was the Mean, the balanced and centered mind, fully reintegrated and whole.

> The *Book of Changes* says, "Whatever goes beyond this indeed transcends all knowledge."[141] If the incipient springs of this are not in the self, transformation cannot be effected. I cannot understand what is taught today by those who teach, and what is studied by those who are instructed by others. Those who teach men say, "Your original nature is originally empty, and the visual forms before you are all your wondrous functioning; how then could it also depend upon practice, verification, and discussion?" Those who are instructed by others say, "My original nature is empty and the circumstances before me are all my wondrous functioning; how then could it also depend upon practice, verification, and discussion?"
> The *Doctrine of the Mean* says, "Journey afar starts from the near, and a climb to the heights starts from low ground."[142] Does this unexcelled virtue [of the Great Void] seem far off? Its far reaches are boundless; one gazes into the distance and cannot see them. How much less can we follow them? Does it seem elevated? At the peak of its loftiness, there is nothing higher. We look up, but cannot see it. How much less could we be able to climb to it? I think that with this unexcelled virtue, there is no way for me to apply my mind and extend my strength; therefore I rather hold to the teaching of starting from the near and from the low so that I may be able thereby gradually to restore the original nature. "Study below in order to penetrate above."[143]
> Someone asked, "If the original nature is empty, do you regard it as having something that cannot be gotten from study?"
> Lin Tzu said, "I certainly do not depend on study to attain it."
> "Now you say 'do not depend on study to attain it,' so why do you complain that 'there is no way to apply my mind and extend my effort'?"
> Lin Tzu said, "Before I was born, I was indeed empty; but having received [something], now I must forget it. Those who hear of this all laugh [because it seems so simple]. In sum, I naturally possess it; I naturally restore it. What difficulty is there? However, this is [also] Confucius' time when he did not transgress what is right[144] and the place of ultimate principle. If one is not the most ultimately sagely and

spiritlike person in the world, how could he have anything to do with this [fully realized sagely mind]? Then do not today's scholars neglect this too early in pursuing their studies?" ["Direct Pointing," 26b–27b]

Lin concludes his discussion of the system of self-cultivation by reiterating his criticism of the false views of contemporary Neo-Confucians. In his criticism of contemporary teachers, Lin explained why, unlike his contemporaries in the School of Mind, he felt the need for this elaborate and gradual method of mind-cultivation. Although he agreed that the sagely mind in its empty vastness was innate in all persons, they had in the course of living "received something" which obscured their original mind. It required effort and cultivation to remove obscurities and restore the original mind. Moreover, the transformation could not be accomplished in one dramatic leap; one had to start from the bottom and at the beginning and gradually penetrate to the higher reaches. Lin's nine stages of mind-cultivation offered an accessible, gradual, and effective means to restore and realize the original nature and full potential of the mind.

CHAPTER SEVEN

THE TRUE TRANSMISSION OF THE THREE TEACHINGS

Lin Chao-en's nine stages of stilling in the back were, as we have seen, a complex integration of elements of the Three Teachings; his practicable sagely Way was fundamentally syncretic. Yet Lin Chao-en was hardly "soft" on what he considered to be the errors of the Three Teachings. His syncretism, although central to his thought, was highly selective. Syncretic unity did not mean that Confucianism, Taoism, and Buddhism were the same, but that there was a correct transmission of the Three Teachings which came from the same source and led to the same goal.

In the first chapter of this book, I argued that selectivity is essential to the dynamic of syncretism. This chapter will explore the syncretic selectivity of Lin Chao-en in order to show the function of syncretism in the evolution of his religious thought, and its limitations in light of his internal or "gut" orthodoxy. It will also explore how the personal syncretic integration was translated into pedagogy as Lin sought to convey his religious vision to others.

THE EARLY YEARS: CONFUCIAN SYNCRETISM

Lin Chao-en's religious search grew out of disillusionment with the spiritual vacuity of what teachers of Confucianism,

Taoism, and Buddhism had to offer. Finally, as we saw in the biography, he met the enlightened master, who revealed to him the long-lost Confucian doctrine of stilling in the back, the key to sagely mind. In the early years following his meeting with the enlightened master, his syncretism had a strikingly Confucian tone. His self-identification and internal orthodoxy were Confucian; he went to great lengths to reconfirm his orthodoxy by defining the boundaries beyond which he had not gone. He sometimes sounded almost anti-Buddhist and anti-Taoist.

When he recounted receiving the Confucian method of mind-cultivation from the enlightened master, he did not feature its debt to other traditions. Nor did he claim (as he did in later writings) that the methods taught by the other schools were essentially the same. It was important to his sense of internal orthodoxy that this was a Confucian answer to a Confucian problem. If he had borrowed from other traditions, it was only to aid in achieving a Confucian goal.

The regulations and curriculum of his early school were immaculately Confucian, even though at that time he was already healing and teaching the method of stilling in the back.[1] Likewise, the earliest collection of his sayings (*Lin Tzu; Master Lin*)[2] depicted him as the defender of the true transmission of Confucius against the intellectualizing extremes of the Sung Neo-Confucians. He defended Buddhism and Taoism against detractors who regarded them as unworthy of study, but he did not discuss or develop their ideas. In the *Lin Tzu*, his syncretism was even more conservative than that of many of his Ming contemporaries.

The early Lin Chao-en was very concerned about the dangers which he felt organized Buddhism and Taoism posed to the Confucian order. He approved of laws supervising members of religious orders, limiting temple lands and rental incomes, and specifying the legal circumstances of ordination. However, in Lin's mind, the greatest threat of Buddhism and Taoism was their neglect of familial virtues in their vow of celibacy. He wrote,

> ... The greatness of mind, nature, and human relationships in the original teachings of the two masters [of Buddhism and Taoism] were

truly no different from the truths of Confucianism. But when the teachings of the two masters were lost in transmission, and Buddhists and Taoists came to honor the "fatherless" doctrine,[3] neglecting human relationships, then for the first time they began to differ from Confucianism.[4]

The neglect of family and the failure to produce descendants were, in Mencius' eyes, the lowest form of unfiliality.[5] Lin Chao-en believed that monastic celibacy offended against the most profound moral laws, indeed the natural laws of the universe.

In his concern, he drafted a petition to the emperor, calling for "the clarification of human relationships in order to exalt the teachings of Confucianism."[6] He praised Ming laws which prohibited eldest or only sons from entering orders lest they endanger the continuance of their line. He noted that the Ming code required observance of family laws: "All Buddhist and Taoist priests and nuns must pay obeisance to their parents, sacrifice to their ancestors, and observe mourning according to their family rank, as all people do. If they disobey, they will be given a hundred blows and defrocked."[7] However, he thought that these measures did not go far enough. He asked that all monks and nuns except a few "wizened eccentrics" be required to marry and produce offspring, faithfully observing all Confucian family rituals. They could live apart from the temple, and go in to perform rites, teach, and practice. In addition to their tradition's scriptures, they should lecture on the *Classic of Filial Piety* and the *Analects*.[8] Such measures would insure the flourishing of "human relationships" and the familial values of Confucianism. In another work, he suggested marrying the monks of his home P'u-t'ien to local prostitutes.[9] Strange bedfellows!

Lin's proposal that monks and nuns should marry was in direct conflict with Ming Law, which stipulated: "Any Taoist priest or Buddhist monk who takes a wife or concubine will receive eighty blows and be defrocked. The woman's family will bear equal culpability."[10] The law, which conflicts with Chinese stress on the continuance of the family line, was presumably an attempt to avoid a population boom of little Buddhists and Taoists. Lin sought in his petition to ease this fear by requiring that any descendants of these "holy" mar riages could only become monks and nuns by going througl the regular ordination procedures; if they did not do so the) would be registered as scholars, farmers, artisans, or merchants, depending on the original backgrounds of their families.[11] Although the Japanese came to allow ordained Buddhists to marry and establish hereditary priesthoods, this was never acceptable to the Chinese.

Lin Chao-en's attacks on celibacy demonstrated his vigilance against Buddhist and Taoist errors and his firm commitment to Confucian values. He proved that as a syncretist he could turn to these two traditions without in any way compromising his Confucian orthodoxy; thus he sought to free himself to accept what was correct in these two traditions.

MASTER OF
THE THREE TEACHINGS

Lin Chao-en's narrowly Confucian syncretism was a product of "boundary anxiety"; he was trying very hard to demonstrate that his ideas were within the boundaries of Confucian orthodoxy.[12] Later events in his life helped him to redefine his Confucian identity, and thus paved the way for a more radical syncretism.

During Lin Chao-en's involvement in the burial and comfort of the victims of pirate raids, he gradually assumed the role of religious teacher, ministering to the spiritual needs of his countrymen. He and his disciples began to proselytize actively to an audience which went far beyond students preparing for examinations. As he assumed the role of religious teacher, Lin Chao-en's leanings toward other traditions were brought into the open. He transcended the narrowly defined mold of a Confucian teacher for which, since he lacked a degree, his qualifications were questionable. Further, his syncretic adaptation of Taoist and Buddhist methods in the nine stages stretched his brand of Confucian cultivation well beyond the boundaries of ordinary Neo-Confucian practice. In his own mind his method was Confucian, and in many ways it represented current Neo-Confucian ideas. However, because of its bold syncretism, it did not fit comfortably into any established school. It was at least eccentric and singular; it was perhaps "heretical."

Through his involvement in philanthropy and ministry to the souls of the dead, Lin expanded the role of teacher in a religious direction. He did not abandon his Confucian convictions and commitments; he simply redefined and tempered them to his new role. Because of his broader vision and broader audience, he affirmed the Three Teachings as three embodiments of the one Way, bringing them together in his school. He attempted to integrate the doctrines of the Three Teachings so that all people could be included in a single Way.

As Lin assumed his new role, there was a subtle but discernible shift in his writings on syncretism, visible in *Hsia-yü* (Sayings on *hsia*), written in 1565, after the pirate raids.[13] This essay gave nearly equal time to each of the Three Teachings, ranging over a wide variety of doctrines. Each of the Three Teachings, rightly understood, was a legitimate expression of the correct understanding of the mind; the Way was not the monopoly of one school. Lin demonstrated how the doctrines of the Three Teachings illumined each other. When asked about the Buddha, he interpreted Buddhahood in Neo-Confucian terms: "When the mind is preserved, that is seriousness; when the mind is preserved, that is Buddhahood."[14] Although his self-identification was still fundamentally Confucian, he was more relaxed about affirming the positive contributions of the other traditions. He even came to acknowledge that his discovery of stilling in the back in the meeting with the enlightened master had been fundamentally syncretic. In retrospect it no longer had such a strictly Confucian meaning. He wrote in his later years,

> From my youth I was able to study for the civil service examinations in the hope of achieving some lofty position and gaining some glory in this world. But when I was almost thirty I suddenly had an awakening. I abandoned examination studies and followed the Confucian lectures [in the academies], but all that I saw in them were petty details on matters of limited scope and the lowness of scholarly irrelevancies. I felt

that the principles imparted by Confucius were not such as this. Then I abandoned the study of the Confucian school and followed the Buddhists and Taoists. But all that I saw was that they were sunk in the practices of sitting like dried logs and playing with empty notions and in the arts of conserving vitality and stopping up vital force. I also felt that the Ways of Śākyamuni and Lao Tzu were not such as this. So again I gave up the heterodox path and spurred my mind down the correct road, establishing my determination with zeal. My original sincerity became increasingly fervent. I was fortunate to hear the principles of integrating the Three Teachings, which I believed with all my heart.[15]

He also wrote to Lo Hung-hsien, whom he had visited just before abandoning examination studies, "Now I have rejected [the heterodox paths of my earlier days] and have been fortunate to hear the principles of integrating the Three Teachings, which penetrate and combine the forces of the one thread of Confucius, Lao Tzu's obtaining the one, and Śākyamuni's returning to the one."[16] The one referred to is the Center, the mind, cultivated in the nine stages of stilling in the back.[17]

As a syncretic teacher and an advocate of the integration of the Three Teachings as an ideal, Lin Chao-en tried to define for his students the boundaries of the correct understanding of the Way; he identified the errors and the distorted doctrines in each of the Three Teachings and rectified or reinterpreted them to accord with the true Way. To do this he reexamined the intellectual and religious heritage of China, rectifying errors and identifying the "true transmission" in each of the schools. He also devised pedagogical methods to correct errors and recover true understanding.

SYNCRETIC SELECTIVITY

Lin Chao-en's intellectual reexamination of the Chinese intellectual heritage in light of his syncretic vision was recorded in the *San-chiao hui-pien* (Joint chronicle of the Three Teachings).

The *Joint Chronicle of the Three Teachings* begins with [the creator] P'an-ku and extends to the Yüan [1260–1368] dynasty, bringing together and chronicling the Three Teachings in order to point directly to the errors of their followers and to integrate them with the Confucianism of Confucius.[18]

However, in addition to exposing errors he also identified thinkers who defended or revived the true doctrines, and those who understood the unity of the Three Teachings. His syncretic purpose is suggested by the fact that he ended his collection with a famous syncretic essay by Liu Mi (dates unknown), called *San-chiao p'ing-hsin lun* (Viewing the Three Teachings with a balanced mind). Lin commented,

> The *P'ing-hsin lun* said, "The Confucians established a teaching based on uprightness (*cheng*); the Taoists established a teaching based on honor (*tsun*); the Buddhists established a doctrine based on the great (*ta*)."[19] In my view, there is no uprightness without honor, and no honor without greatness.
>
> The *Yüan-tao p'ien* of Emperor Hsiao of the Sung [r. 1163–1189] said, "Govern the mind with Buddhism; govern the body with Taoism; govern the world with Confucianism."[20] In my view there can be no governing of the world without a basis in governing the self, and there can be no governing of the self without a basis in governing the mind. It is like Li Shih-ch'ien's [dates and biographical details unknown] saying, "Buddhism is the sun; Taoism is the moon; Confucianism is the five stars."[21] It is like Chang Shang-ying's [1043–1121] saying, "Confucianism treats the skin; Taoism treats the blood and veins; Buddhism treats the marrow."[22]
>
> Indeed, how well these men knew that the Ways of the Three Teachings return to one! In recent times there have been some opinionated eccentrics who claim that in the space of a single day one is a Buddhist insofar as one is able to be still and calm, one is a Taoist insofar as one is able to abide in emptiness and nothingness, and that one is a Confucian insofar as he is able to manage affairs. That is not to combine the Three Teachings into one! One is always a Buddhist, always a Taoist, and always a Confucian. In my view when the Way of the Three Teachings is undifferentiated within the self, there is no place it reaches that is not Confucian, no place it reaches that is not Taoist, and no place it reaches that is not Buddhist. If one can be still and calm, then one can abide in emptiness and nothingness; if one can dwell in emptiness and nothingness, then one can manage affairs.[23]

The *Joint Chronicle* is the most detailed record of Lin Chao-en's selective reinterpretation of Chinese religious thought. It is also the most comprehensive record of Lin's knowledge of Chinese religious thought and history; it defines the sources in tradition from which he drew his own thought.

According to the *Joint Chronicle*, the true transmission of Buddhism was the Ch'an line of patriarchs. Lin's hero was the Sixth Patriarch, Hui-neng, because of his reduction of the entire Buddhist tradition to aspects of the enlightened mind of the universal Buddha-nature. Hui-neng gave Buddhist support to Lin's belief that celibacy and monasticism were not essential to Buddhism. He said,

> If one wishes to practice it is all right to do so as a layman; you do not have to be in a temple. If you are able to practice as a layman, you will approach the good mind of the man of the East. If you are in a temple but do not practice, you will approach the evil mind of the man of the West. Only if the mind is pure is it the Western land of self-nature.[24]

Hui-neng not only laid a basis for lay Buddhist practice; he also defined the Western Land or Pure Land as a state of mind attained in meditation. "As the *Ching-ming ching* has said, 'The straightforward mind is the place of practice; the straightforward mind is the Pure Land.' "[25] Hui-neng gave Lin Chao-en Buddhist support for seeing all of Buddhism as a method of mind-cultivation.

Lin Chao-en also praised Buddhists who integrated Buddhism with Confucian values. He cited, for instance, Fo T'u-teng (fl. 4th cent.), who in 329 argued that the Buddhist injunction against killing living things did not prohibit a ruler from using capital punishment.[26] He was critical of magical uses of Buddhism, such as the recitation of scriptures to avoid calamities.

In the *Joint Chronicle* true Taoism entailed a correct understanding of the interrelationship of mind and vital force, nature and life store. Lin acclaimed the classic to which Inner Alchemy Taoists had turned: "The words of the *Ts'an t'ung ch'i* [Homology of the Triad] were truly able to break through all the confusions of antiquity."[27] He traced in considerable detail the rise of the Inner Alchemy school, particularly those thinkers who represented syncretic and reformist tendencies.[28]

His Taoist hero was the Yellow Emperor, who not only transmitted the Way but was one of the sage-founders of civilization. He represented for Lin the original Taoist teaching, lost and misunderstood by later Taoists, of concern for society and social values.

The true Way was lost when the difficult teachings of Lao Tzu and Chuang Tzu were misunderstood by those who "merely fabricated elegant deceptions based on their writings,"[29] particularly the Neo-Taoists of the period of disunion. Most Neo-Confucians would have considered Inner Alchemy writings far more open to dangerous misinterpretation than the writings of Lao Tzu and Chuang Tzu. Lin Chao-en was one Confucian who turned to meditative Taoism rather than philosophical Taoism as the mainstream of Taoist tradition. He held Lao Tzu's classic the *Tao-te ching* in special veneration, for he wrote a commentary to it and cited it extensively throughout his corpus. However, he did not turn to the writings of later Taoist philosophers. It was in the contemporary meditative Taoism of Inner Alchemy that he found affinities with Neo-Confucian thought.[30]

In the *Joint Chronicle*, Lin traced the line of early Confucian thought and then the rise of Neo-Confucianism in some detail. He gave special attention to Shao Yung (1011–1077),[31] and Chou Tun-i, who pioneered Neo-Confucian cosmological speculations, with some debt to the Taoists. He praised Chou Tun-i for establishing the relationship between cosmological principles and moral cultivation of sincerity[32] and Li T'ung (1088–1158), Chu Hsi's teacher, for emphasizing quiescence.[33] These two had laid the foundation of Neo-Confucian mind-cultivation. Chu Hsi, the architect of the school, was acclaimed as a thinker but especially as a man of integrity who had to face unjust slander because of his attempt to revive the Way.[34] However, intellectually Lin favored Lu Hsiang-shan, the progenitor of the School of Mind, for emphasizing spontaneous mind and honoring moral nature. Although his discussion of Confucianism did not extend into the Ming, Lin clearly identified himself with the roots of the Ming School of Mind, except that his interests in the cultivation of quiescence and in cosmological speculations were more marked than many of his contemporaries.[35]

The *Joint Chronicle* demonstrates that while Lin was aware of the richness of the religious heritage, he selected as the true transmission those strains of thought which illumined the theory and cultivation of the mind. The collection also provides information about the breadth of Lin's knowledge. Not surprisingly, he was most well-read in the Confucian tradition, both in the classics and in the Sung thinkers. His knowledge of Taoism is broad and varied, although he does not seem to be well-versed in ritual texts. Buddhism was by far the weakest leg of the tripod of the Three Teachings; his knowledge seems to be limited to major texts of the Ch'an tradition and extremely influential scriptures. Despite these limitations, Lin's syncretic vision was not limited to a few books or ideas; he had gleaned from the broad Chinese tradition a true transmission of the Three Teachings, reaching back to the sage-founders and coming up to his times.

THE ART OF TEACHING SYNCRETISM

In the *Joint Chronicle*, Lin Chao-en used his principles of syncretic selectivity to correct misconceptions and identify the core of truth in Confucianism, Buddhism, and Taoism. This gave him the basis on which to build a curriculum to teach the Way to others. He was enough of a teacher, however, to realize that he could not simply share his personal understanding of the truth of the sagely Way and expect others to believe it. That is why he used healing to confirm the authority and effectiveness of his method of mind-cultivation. He also realized that since the true transmission of each of the Three Teachings had been lost, misconceptions and errors abounded in the minds of the people. As a teacher, he attempted to identify and correct those errors, not attacking or insulting people's beliefs as a sectarian might,[36] but providing a means for reinterpretation of those beliefs in light of the core of truth contained within them. These were the methods of a religious teacher, whose aim was to lead people back to the correct Way. They were not meant to be philosophical arguments reflecting on truth. The pedagogical methods devised by Lin showed his concern to provide all those able to consider embracing his broad integration of the Three Teachings a means of transition from past errors to the higher truths of the sagely Way.

His writings exhibit five pedagogical methods used to establish the proper understanding of syncretic selectivity: (1) using barbarians to defeat barbarians; (2) three languages for one Way; (3) correspondences; (4) radical redefinition; and (5) remythologization.

Using barbarians to defeat barbarians was a famous stratagem in Chinese history, playing barbarian tribes off against themselves or each other. Lin Chao-en realized that persuasion was much more powerful if it called on authorities which people already accepted. Thus whenever possible he used Buddhist sources to correct the errors of Buddhism, and likewise for Taoism and Confucianism. He used such a strategy, for instance, in his arguments against monasticism and celibacy. He argued that since the founders of Buddhism and Taoism (Śākyamuni, the Yellow Emperor, and Lao Tzu) had married and produced children, there could be no conflict between marital relations and the attainment of the Way. Further, eminent figures of both traditions in later Chinese history had established families without harming their spiritual natures. Kumārajīva (344–413), the great translator of Buddhist texts, had two sons, and the position of Heavenly Master was hereditary in the Chang family.[37] His argument was, to be sure, a bit forced: (1) Śākyamuni had left his home and family in order to seek enlightenment; (2) the historical evidence for the lines of Yellow Emperor and Lao Tzu was highly suspect; and (3) Kumārajīva was forced to marry by his well-meaning imperial patron.[38] More convincing, perhaps, were Lin's frequent references to the *Vimalakīrti-sūtra*, which established the basis for lay Buddhist practice. If his arguments were not entirely convincing in a philosophical sense, Lin Chao-en attempted to show that sources within Budhism and Taoism could be cited to prove that celibacy and monasticism were not essential to attaining the spiritual fruits of those traditions. There was then a basis for reconciling the teachings of Buddhism and Taoism with Confucian social and familial values.

Three languages, one Way. Lin Chao-en believed that the true Way of sagely mind could be expressed in the language of each of the Three Teachings. It was not the monopoly of one tradition. Thus he not only wrote commentaries on the classics of each of the Three Teachings, but essays and collections were sometimes composed in a tripartite division, with one section for each religion, citing the sources and using the language of that tradition. The most extensive work using this structure was a collection on the correct understanding of mind and human nature. There were three works in two *chüan* each, briefly citing a broad range of thinkers with Lin's comments. The works were entitled, respectively, "Excerpts of the Central Essentials for Followers of Confucius," "Excerpts on the Great Way of the School of the Mysterious [Tao]," and "Excerpts on the Fundamental Principle of the Emptiness of Self-nature."[39]

A shorter work in three divisions was *Pen-t'i chiao* (Instructions on original nature), containing brief formulations of the meaning of human nature in each of the Three Teachings. In the Confucian section, the original nature was said to be beyond ordinary knowledge and yet the embodiment of virtues. "In Confucius' statement, 'Do I have knowledge of it?' what he had no knowledge of [because it was beyond ordinary knowledge] was original nature."[40] "What is still and unmoving in original nature is sincerity; what is spiritlike and boundless in original nature is sageliness."[41] In the section on Taoism, original nature was discussed in terms of primal undifferentiated vital force and of the elixir. "The single vital force which antedates heaven, the undifferentiated original quintessential vitality, is the original nature. . . . What transforms by means of original nature is the spirit elixir. What remains indestructible over ages by means of this original nature is the golden elixir."[42] In the Buddhist section the original nature was seen as the mind, which is the source of all illusory things and yet is completely untouched by the qualities of illusory existence. "The original nature gives rise to the myriad things; the original nature gives rise to wisdom. . . . Externally the original nature is free from all marks of existence. Internally the original nature leaves behind all the appearances of emptiness."[43] The original nature, the Buddha mind, is never lost, even in the midst of the world of saṃsāra. The languages used in each of the sections was quite distinctive; yet in the mind of Lin Chao-en, they all expressed the same truth.

Correspondences. The establishment of chains of correspondence to integrate and reconcile diverse elements in one Way went back at least to the Han dynasty. It was similar to the *ko-i* method used by early Buddhists to reconcile their religion with Chinese thought. It also was used to establish homologies between various microcosms of the macrocosm and between various levels of symbology in Inner Alchemy Taoism. Lin Chao-en used this well-established syncretic method to demonstrate the common ground and shared themes of the Three Teachings. This was a pedagogical rather than an analytical device; only rarely did Lin Chao-en explain the meaning of the correspondences or how they enhanced the original concepts. They were meant to be suggestive and to build bridges between traditions.

For instance, he suggested that the Three Teachings had corresponding doctrines of inner stillness and equilibrium in Buddhist tranquil concentration (*chi-ting*), Taoist purity and stillness (*ch'ing-ching*), and Confucian timeliness of action (*shih-chung*).[44] Each of these described a state in which inner quiescence was the basis for appropriate action.

There were corresponding doctrines for maintaining the internal equilibrium in the Confucian holding fast to the Center (*chih-chung*), Taoist preserving the Center (*shou-chung*), and Buddhist emptying the Center (*k'ung-chung*).[45] In Lin's mind, these were different terms for the same process in mind-cultivation.

Each of the Three Teachings had a doctrine for conquering and purifying the mind. The Buddhists called it conquering the mind (*hsiang-fu ch'i hsin*); the Taoists called it emptying the mind and filling the belly (*hsü-hsin shih-fu*); the Confucians called it washing the mind and hiding it (*hsi-hsin t'ui-ts'ang*).[46]

Redefinition. Selective reinterpretation of borrowed elements was part of the dynamic of syncretism. However, as a syncretic teacher Lin not only redefined terms which he had integrated into his personal vision; he also redefined terms and symbols which were in the belief systems of his followers in order to integrate as much as possible from the Three Teachings into his unified Way. He attempted to show that the "real meaning" of these ideas was consistent with the correct understanding of the Three Teachings. The reinterpretations were often reductionistic, forcing a rich concept or symbol into a simpler mold. However, he sought to explain and defend his "correct" interpretation and to justify it whenever possible with authorities from the tradition the concept came out of.

He redefined elixir (*tan*) as the seed of humanity (*jen*) or original good nature. When properly nurtured this seed would grow into the mind of the sage.

The P'eng-lai islands, the legendary abode of the immortals for which emperors had searched in vain, were merely the true destination or goal within the internal microcosm; what gained deathlessness there was the mind. Immortality was not to be sought either externally or in the body, but the sagely mind was coterminous with creation.[47]

The vegetarian diet or fasting (*chai*) of the Buddhists was really meant to be a fast or calming of the mind (*chai-hsin*), as taught by the Taoist Lieh Tzu.[48] Lin did not oppose abstention from meat as a spiritual discipline, but felt that it should be practiced in moderation and not seen as an end in itself; even Amitābha Buddha had eaten from a meat stew.[49]

Remythologization. Lin Chao-en retold and explained the meaning of parables (*yü-yen*), by which he meant more or less what today we call myth. Parables were stories told in the language of religious symbolism, the real meaning of which lay in a truth to which the symbols pointed. He repudiated literal or mistaken interpretations of these stories and explained their real meaning.

For instance, he reinterpreted birth legends surrounding heroes or sage kings, claiming that they merely represented attempts to point to the spiritual virtues or qualities of the sage.

They say that [the sage] Fu-hsi's mother conceived when she trod on the footprint of a giant, and something moved within her mind. This is only men of later generations spiritualizing the story because they considered the virtue (*te*) of Fu-hsi as something which could harmonize with heaven above and earth below. Therefore they particularly spiritualized the story. Śākyamuni's birth from his mother's right ribs and the story of Lao Tzu's birth from his mother's left armpit are the same sort of strange tale. As to the birth of Confucius, [they say that] two dragons surrounded the house, five stars descended into the courtyard, divine maidens held up fragrant mists in the sky, and an auspicious unicorn spit up a jade tablet in his village. Are these worthy of belief?[50]

Lin Chao-en betrayed a rationalist Confucian bent in his readiness to attack "superstition." But elsewhere he treats the symbols in the stories as significant in their own right, although not to be understood literally. For instance he remarked that the reputed birth of Lao Tzu at eighty-one years of age used the number eighty-one because it was nine times nine, suggesting that Lao Tzu was endowed with supreme yang vital force. Nine was the number symbolizing strong yang in the *Book of Changes*.[51]

A famous Chinese myth was that of Archer Yi who shot down nine of ten suns which appeared in the sky and were rapidly desiccating the land. Lin Chao-en interpreted this myth as a parable of yang run wild, unbalancing the Five Phases.[52] In Lin Chao-en's system yang represented Fire and the mind; when the fire of the mind was fueled by its chasing after external things, it could burn out of control and upset the internal microcosm.

Even the story of Bodhidharma sitting facing the wall for nine years to seek enlightenment was remythologized to fit into Lin Chao-en's system. In Ch'an, the story had served to underscore the profound commitment required of the seeker of truth in Ch'an. However, Lin wrote,

As to sitting facing the wall, it indeed has a special meaning; it refers to washing the mind, moving it back and hiding it in the secret place in order to nurture the spirit and restore the still original nature. This is like seeing nothing while facing the wall. Therefore we say, "When his mind is like a wall, he can enter the Way." The number of nine years symbolizes the nine of yang, and so means to obtain yang.[53]

Finally, he interpreted T'ao Ch'ien's (365–427) renowned tale of the Peach Blossom Spring as a quest for original mind.[54] In the tale, a fisherman one day lost his way and found himself in a lovely peach grove. At the far end of the grove was a spring which emerged from a small opening in a mountain. He went through the opening, which was at first extremely narrow, but suddenly opened onto a spacious plain, which turned out to be inhabited by people leading a simple life. They told him they had fled the disorders of the Ch'in dynasty (221–209 B.C.E.) and had been cut off from outsiders since that time; they knew nothing of China since the Ch'in. They wined and dined their guest, asking from him news of the world. When he came out he told local officials, but they were unable to find the way back to the spring. Eventually people stopped looking for it.

According to Lin Chao-en, this story should be taken as an elaborate allegory. The fact that the protagonist was a fisherman symbolizes the liveliness of the mind; when one's mind attains the free and easy nature of the fish, one has achieved self-realization (*tzu-te*). The very narrow opening in the mountain represents the narrow space within the self where one stills the mind, the opening serving as a symbol for that inner space. The sudden opening onto a spacious plain suggests the immeasurable vastness of the cultivated mind. The fact that people had fled the disorders of the Ch'in to go to a cut-off place refers to leaving behind the vulgar confusions and disorders which beset the mind to still it in the inner space. Cutting off contact with the outside world represents the fact that the far reaches of the mind cannot be spoken of to outsiders and ordinary men. The inability of the officials to find the way back symbolizes the impure mind which loses the Way. Finally, the fact that people gave up trying to find the place is suggestive of the fact that the doctrine of mind was lost for so long that people neglected even to seek it.[55]

Lin Chao-en's remythologization operated on the same syncretic principles as the rest of his syncretic thought; it reinterprets the religious symbols and the language in terms of Lin's understanding of the doctrine of mind.

In his five methods for teaching syncretism, Lin showed respect for all Three Teachings as valid vehicles of the Truth. The specifically syncretic writings—particularly in the modes of redefinition and remythologization—were marked by conceptual simplicity and reductionism. They were also almost popular in content, since they dealt with well-known myths and tales. All this tends to suggest a more popular, less scholarly audience for such writings.

There was in fact a dichotomy in Lin's writings between relatively philosophical and scholarly writings which were loaded with allusions and scholarly citations and other essays which were more simple, repetitive, and parallelistic in style. The scholarly literature was represented, for example, by commentaries on the Four Books, essays on the teachings of the sages, or by any of his relatively speculative works.[56] Simpler works were represented, for example, by the parables and an essay reinterpreting the errors of the Three Teachings. For instance, "The Parable of Silk and Silver" told in simple terms how local people during the pirate raids hid their gold and valuables and used silver scraps and silk as a means of exchange that would not be worth looting. Lin suggested that the sagely mind is like the silk and silver scraps, a treasure which we possess and use daily without realizing its potential value.[57]

Another essay in an almost popular style cast a simple discussion of Inner Alchemy concepts as a dialogue between Master Thus-void (*Erh-hsü-tzu*) and Mr. Undifferentiated Void (*Hun-hsü-shih*). The text is so highly repetitive, going through the same formula again and again with different key words, that it seems to have been designed for recitation as a learning and/or liturgical device.[58]

Lin Chao-en also devised a simplified system of Changes, described in "The Tetragrams of the Three Bonds." The tetragram was determined by casting three coins twice to obtain two duograms. Getting all heads was Heaven (*ch'ien*); all tails was Earth (*k'un*); one head was the Sun; one tail was the Moon. From the combinations of duograms sixteen tetragrams could be derived. The symbolism of the system was extremely simple. Heaven was lord, father, and husband.

Earth was subject, mother, and wife. Sun was lord, male, and husband. Moon was minister, female, and wife. The commentaries were also extremely simple, dealing solely with ethical issues related to the three bonds.[59]

Some of Lin's writings used pictographic symbols to illustrate concepts. The most interesting (see figure 3) represented the elixir (*tan*) as the visual symbol for the one spot or seed of humanity (*jen*) in the Center, represented by a circle. Developing the seed through the continuous cultivation of the one thread of Confucius transformed the seed of the elixir into the Center (*chung*), the spiritual equilibrium before the emotions have appeared.[60] Such symbolic visualizations were pedagogical devices which illustrated the process and transformation of cultivation in simple, visual terms for those who were not able easily to grasp the cosmological theory of the nine stages.

The clearest example of Lin's popular writings was "Plain

Figure 3. Pictographic Illustrations of Sagely Transformation

The elixir (*tan*):	丹
The one spot or seed of humanity:	·
The Center:	◯ or ☐
Tan as the seed in the Center:	⊡
The one thread of Confucius:	ǀ
The developed Center (*chung*):	中

and Simple Explanations" (*I-chieh li-yü*), a summary of Lin's basic teachings in semivernacular Chinese. The preface states that the essay was published to "provide those with minimal literacy (*shao wen-tz'u che*) a simple explanation of the Way."[61] Thus it is clear that Lin intended to reach a broader, more popular audience, although there is insufficient information to establish how popular an audience his writings actually reached. Lin and his disciples taught along the roads and drew crowds which included the poor.[62] Lin Chao-en taught that the Way should be simple and accessible to all. When asked what could be called the Way, he replied, "What is simple and easy to understand, what can be understood by ignorant men and women, can be called the Way. What is simple and easy to do, what can be done by ignorant men and women, is called the Way. What can be practiced above by the Son of Heaven and below by the common people is called the Way."[63]

Lin Chao-en had, as we have seen, a strong sense of religious calling. The nature of some of the syncretic writings strongly suggests that he in fact sought to teach all men, less educated people as well as his own students, and designed some of his teachings to be understandable to all. The broad and open Way required a broad and open doctrine.

THE RELATIONSHIP OF THE THREE TEACHINGS

The Three Teachings had to be integrated actively, for their transmissions had been lost and errors abounded. Lin Chao-en could not condone any facile affirmation of their unity which ignored the hard work of rectifying errors to return to the true Way.

> Someone asked, "Are the Three Teachings identical?"
> Lin Tzu said, "I do not know."
> "But you have said that the Three Teachings combine into one (*san-chiao ho-i*), so why do you now say that you do not know?"
> Lin Tzu said, "The meaning of the words 'combine into one' is not what we mean by 'identical.' I often lament that men of today are

rarely able to understand the meanings of words. If one does not understand the meanings of words and yet wishes to clarify the writings of the former sages, will there not be a difficulty?"
"Then what is the meaning of the words 'combine into one'?"
Lin Tzu said, " 'Combining into one' means to unite them and make them one. How could it mean to make them identical? If combining into one were the same as identical, one could use the word 'one' and that would do. Would it not be redundant also to use the word 'combine'? Therefore to combine and make them one means to combine Confucian, Taoist, and Buddhist types and unite them with the Confucianism of Confucius."[64]

Moreover, if Lin Chao-en's campaigns against the social errors of Buddhism and Taoism could be taken to suggest Confucian predominance in the syncretism of Lin Chao-en, he himself argued against such a view. He reminded his disciples that he was advocating a return of *all three* teachings to true Confucianism, and that Confucians as well as Buddhists and Taoists were in need of reform.

Someone asked, "Now those who study Confucianism are Confucianists. Why do you say to unite Confucians with the Confucianism of Confucius?"
Lin Tzu said, "What the world calls Confucianism is not what Confucius called Confucianism."
"But the Buddhists and Taoists do not marry or produce children. How could their teaching not differ from the Confucianism of Confucius?"
Lin Tzu said, "Lao Tzu did not fail to marry and beget children. The idea of Taoist celibacy began with Sung Yi-tsu [?] and is not the teaching of Lao Tzu. As for the Buddhists, some do not marry and have children, but others do. Essentially the Buddha is the mind. The teaching of Śākyamuni certainly does not only involve celibacy. This is why I wish to unite the Confucians, Buddhists, and Taoists and combine and unite them with the Confucianism of Confucius."[65]

Lin decried the decline of Confucian learning into pedantic and sterile scholarship. Learning, like social relationships, was an integral part of moral cultivation. Fragmentary and trivial scholarship neglected the fundamental moral values of mind and nature, and thus obscured the Way, as did the Taoist and Buddhist neglect of human relationships. Thus the Confucians, like the Buddhists and Taoists, had lost sight of the fundamentals and had to return to the Confucianism of Confucius.

The essential unity of the Three Teachings could not be realized until errors were corrected and the true core of transmission understood. Likewise, although all men possess the seeds of sagely mind, they must leave behind the errors of chasing after external things and develop their sagely potential. Thus Lin taught a gradual, step-by-step method of cultivation. He said, "I think that with this transcendent virtue there is no way for me to apply my mind and extend my strength; therefore I hold to the teaching of starting from the near and from the low so that I may thereby gradually restore the original nature. 'Study below in order to penetrate above.' "[66] The near and the low were the Way that could be followed (k'o-shih-yu chih tao),[67] namely simple ethical practice. Because Confucianism taught the importance of virtuous practice, it was the near and low point from which practice began.

> The operations of heaven are without sound or smell;[68] this is the unmanifested mysterious virtue. How can one speak of it in words? But the order of studying it must begin with virtuous practice. Virtuous practice means the manifesting of virtue in practice; it is the Way which people may be made to follow, and it is what Confucius used to teach men. Therefore in the ranks of the sage's school Yen and Min are counted first;[69] is this not because they took virtuous conduct as the most important?
>
> As to nature and the heavenly Way, we called them life store and humanity, but this is the so-called unknowable;[70] [Confucius] rarely spoke of it.[71] If one is not above average in talent, he is not suited to hear it.
>
> What Confucius taught to men was what [the sages] Yao, Shun, Yü, T'ang, Wen, and Wu used to govern the realm. It is greatly concerned with the ordinary daily life of the people; they cannot be without it for a single day. Therefore if ordinary men are without this, they have no means to enjoy happiness or to utilize profit. If sages and wise men are without this, they cannot aspire to sagehood or heaven. This is the greatness of Confucius' teaching, and throughout all generations in the world, people are all my brothers; not one of them is not among those whom Confucius cares for.
>
> Now the teachings of Buddhism and Taoism are both the epitome of subtlety, and they specialize on the Way for worthies and the wise.

Therefore Lao Tzu speaks of the Great Ultimate and Śākyamuni of the Ultimate of Nonbeing, which is the Great Void. Lao Tzu speaks of the One, and Śākyamuni of the not-yet-One, which is the Great Void. If one does not precede them with what Confucius taught, how can he find a gate for entering into the so-called epitome of subtlety? . . . Therefore the studies of students ought to take Confucius' teaching as prior.[72]

Lin divided the nine stages of mind-cultivation into three sections: Confucianism establishes the basis (*li-pen*); Taoism enters the gate (*ju-men*); and Buddhism makes principles ultimate (*chi-tse*).[73] Confucianism was the fundamental starting point; Taoism and Buddhism built on that basis. However, Lin Chao-en denied that the three divisions were to be seen as a compartmentalization of the Way; in actuality all Three Teachings participate in the entire process.

> Those who are Confucians say, "I am a Confucian"; those who are Taoists say, "I am a Taoist"; those who are Buddhists say, "I am a Buddhist." Thus the teachings are divided into three. But it is my intention to bring them together in order to reunite them in the basic unity of the Way of Confucius, Lao Tzu, and Śākyamuni. I have used the words "that which can be followed" in order that the basis may be established; that is how one teaches its beginning. I have used the words "that which is knowable" in order that the gate may be entered; that is how I teach its middle; not only does saying entering the gate teach its middle, but moreover making principles ultimate can teach its end. The teachings of Confucius, Lao Tzu, and Śākyamuni all have the beginning, middle, and end, and they all have no beginning, middle, and end.[74]

The Way is one, and each of the Three Teachings embodies the Way.

> If you do not understand why the teachings of Confucius, Lao Tzu, and Śākyamuni are three, then you have no means of recognizing their oneness, that insofar as they comprise the quintessence of the Way they are one and undifferentiated.
> If you do not know why the Ways of Confucius, Lao Tzu, and Śākyamuni are one, then you have not the means to unite the three and achieve the greatness of the teachings.
> Now if you know the one and unite the three, then separately they are not three and united they are not one—that is greatness! That is quintessence![75]

At the level of the fundamental starting point, Confucianism is prior because it teaches simple virtues for all to follow which, though simple, underlie and pervade the Way. However, in terms of the ultimate understanding of mind and nature, the Three Teachings teach one truth.

Lin Chao-en saw the Way as all-encompassing, leaving nothing in heaven and earth outside of its purview. Even Buddhists and Taoists must belong to this Way, since they belong to the human race. In a commentary to the famous passage "All men within the four seas are brothers,"[76] Lin remarked:

> The Western Inscription says, "All people are my brothers and sisters."[77] Therefore if one takes physical parents as parents, then those who are born of the same parents are my brothers. If one takes heaven and earth as one's parents, then all who are born of heaven and earth are also my brothers. Now as for Buddhists and Taoists, can they live outside of heaven and earth? If they cannot live outside of heaven and earth, what are they if they are not people of my mother's womb, if they are not my brothers?[78]

Lin Chao-en called this single Way, the unity before the Three Teachings were differentiated, *hsia*. He said, "What is *hsia* is great, and the Great Ultimate is within it. The Great Ultimate gives rise to yin and yang, but the yin and yang are united in *hsia*. The yin and yang give rise to the Five Phases, but the Five Phases are united in *hsia*."[79] He also said, "The principles of what antedated heaven are all provided in *hsia*."[80]

> What makes Confucianism Confucianism, what makes Taoism Taoism, what makes Buddhism Buddhism, and what makes the most wondrous of Confucianism, Buddhism, and Taoism most wondrous is all exhausted in *hsia*. Heaven obtains *hsia* to become pure, earth obtains *hsia* to become settled, and man obtains *hsia* to become sagely.[81]

Thus *hsia* was the single unity which underlies all things and gives them their true identity, like the Tao of Lao Tzu. Because it is the unity underlying all phenomena, "The great awakening always returns to the single *hsia*."[82]

Hsia, then, is the original, primal unity through which the sage forms one body with all things. The ultimate unity of the Three Teachings was based in the mystical expansion of the sagely mind. The relationship between the syncretic ideal and the all-embracing vastness of the sagely mind is discussed in an essay called "The Unlimited Meeting of the Three Teachings" (San-chiao wu-che ta-hui). The title comes from the Buddhist term Wu-che ta-hui or Pañca (varsikā) pariṣad, an assembly held every five years for communal confession, penance, and forgiveness.[83]

When asked about the unlimited meeting, Lin responded that his intention in teaching was to effect a reconciliation of the Three Teachings, including rich and poor, young and old, wise and ignorant, worthy and unworthy, and men of all four callings. He wished "to make Confucians follow Confucius, to make Taoists follow Lao Tzu, to make Buddhists follow Śākyamuni, but not to call them Confucians, Taoists and Buddhists; to combine them into one, so that undifferentiated they will return to the primordial beginning."[84] Lin lamented that his intention had been misunderstood; he had not been able to fulfill his mission to effect an "unlimited meeting" of the Three Teachings.

The interlocutor suggested that one way to avoid "startling" people would be to base the "meeting" solely on Confucianism, which taught virtues vast enough to encompass heaven and earth. To this Lin replied, "Your words are excellent, but if you insist on saying Confucians, then it is not broad and vast; then such a meeting is not unlimited. Such indeed one-sidedly rests in the one corner of the Confucian school. Could you still say that you modeled yourself on the vastness of heaven?"[85]

The virtue of heaven was vast enough to encompass all men, all things, even the ghosts and spirits of the mountains and rivers. The dharma-body of the Buddhists also encompassed the entire universe, and the vital force of the Taoists was one with the cosmos. Thus the vast, rectified sagely mind encompassed all within heaven and earth, and there was no room for divisions into schools and sects.

On the other hand, the meeting and reconciliation should include the manifest aspects of the religions as well as the mind; the oneness of the Three Teachings should not merely rest in the ultimate realization of sagely mind, but should be reflected also in doctrine.

> If there are manifest aspects but no mind, the gentleman calls it doctrine only. In that case what can serve as the wonders of application? If there is mind but no manifest aspects, the gentleman calls this goodness only.[86] What can he do in order to manifest the form of the doctrine? When both are simultaneously present, mutual aid and mutual completion are effected.[87]

The Three Teachings are one because their Way is the same; this Way is the moral law of the universe. No school, man, beast, or thing can remain outside of its purview. The sagely mind of the Three Teachings is one. The ultimate reconciliation and integration of the Three Teachings comes from the original mind which is beyond manifest aspects and beyond the ordinary knowledge of words. This mind is in a state of mystic unity, forming one body with all men, things, heaven, and earth. Doctrines can only describe the knowable Way which has manifest aspects, but the true Way lies beyond that. While emphasizing the need for a simple, knowable, followable Way, Lin Chao-en did not reduce sagehood (or Buddhahood, or the state of the Realized Man) to those simple terms. In its ultimate reaches, the mind embraces all things and all truths. At that point there can no longer be any distinction or priority among the Three Teachings; they are one because they lead back to the Grat Ultimate and beyond it to the undifferentiated unity of *hsia*.

CHAPTER VIII

THE LEGACY OF LIN CHAO-EN

THE RELIGIOUS ORGANIZATION

The life of Lin Chao-en was shaped by his calling to be a religious teacher. He sought to teach all people, regardless of their religious or social backgrounds, the means by which to realize the sagely mind within themselves. To that end, he established a religious organization which embraced Confucians, Buddhists, Taoists, and scholars, farmers, artisans, and merchants. Ho Ch'iao-yüan (chin-shih, 1586), in a biography of Lin Chao-en, confirmed that Lin's students included rustics and merchants as well as officials and scholars. He commented, "For those ignorant people who were not easily able to enter, he first attracted them with methods of moving in the chamber, the nine stages, healing, and stilling, causing them gradually to give rise to the mind of the Way and leave behind their outer-directed thoughts."[1] Huang Tsung-hsi (1610–1695), in his biography of Lin, noted that Lin had several thousand disciples from all religions, in part because he had "unusual arts for aiding the people, so that in times of crisis disciples flocked to him."[2] Thus two eminent outside observers of the cult attested to the popular appeal of Lin's methods of making the Way accessible to ordinary people.

The Three Teachings cult was a proselytizing religion. Lin Chao-en and his disciples practiced healing in order to gain and affirm the faith of new converts. They preached along the roads and in the cities,[3] and published collections of Lin's writings to aid in the dissemination of his ideas. They established branches in towns and in Chin-ling (modern Nanking).[4] Lin supervised the teaching work of his disciples and punished those who used the cult for their own profit.[5] The disciples, for their part, took vows to distribute and lecture on Lin's writings, thus carrying on his work.

Aside from the nine stages of mind-cultivation and the vows to heaven, there are only the most meager hints about forms of study, ritual, and practice in the religious organization. The early regulations gave a detailed program for Confucian studies but this must have been modified somewhat to accommodate the entry of Buddhists, Taoists, merchants, and artisans. The posted regulations established separate wings for each group, and enjoined them from mixing with other groups. This certainly suggests that there were separate curricula according to the religious and social backgrounds of students. There may also have been common assemblies and common rituals.[6] Lin designed a ritual costume called the three bonds and five constants gown.[7] He wrote a set of hymns, complete with instructions for chanting.[8] Some of his writings were so formulaic and repetitive that they may have been designed for some responsive reading, or perhaps as a simple form of study for those who could not read well.[9] Moreover, the vows to heaven served the ritual function of confession and confirmation of commitment, either privately or communally.

The lack of information about cult ritual may be due in part to Lin's status as a commoner. He was not a scholar-official, yet he had set himself up as a teacher. He was not insensitive to his ambivalent status as a teacher who was still officially a student.[10] He adopted healing to verify the authority of his teaching in the eyes of prospective disciples; yet such authority was essentially religious, and had weight only in the eyes of nonscholars. In his writings and in his vows to heaven he did everything possible to affirm the "orthodoxy" and uprightness of his actions as a teacher, being especially careful to maintain his financial honesty. Finally, his published and disseminated writings excluded works which might be misunderstood as "heretical" or dangerous by Confucian scholar-officials. It was only after his reputation as teacher and philanthropist was established during the pirate raids that he felt somewhat freer to share his religious views and practices; even so, his most sensitive writings were not published until just after his death.

Despite all of these precautions, there was some concern among scholar-officials about the strange ideas and practices advocated by Lin Chao-en. Kuan Chih-tao of the T'ai-chou school met Lin, read his works, and found both man and writings wanting:

> I met him once some thirty years ago in Pai-sha; his appearance was very ordinary. Later I perused his writings. Generally he had not succeeded in penetrating to the foundations of the Sages of the Three Teachings, but instead had seized upon their influence to formulate a doctrine, urgently wishing to publish his name in his time. This is indeed a lure which entices the reckless and the false![11]

Although he accused Lin Chao-en of seeking a name through his teaching, Kuan elsewhere praised Lin's ethical conduct. The crux of his complaint seems to have been that Lin did not correctly understand the philosophical basis of the unity of the Three Teachings. Kuan Chih-tao's syncretism was more markedly Confucian than Lin's. He was no doubt offended by the Taoist and Buddhist influence in Lin's system of self-cultivation, feeling that it did not put sufficient emphasis on purely moral cultivation. Despite his criticism, Kuan Chih-tao grudgingly classed Lin as an offshoot of his own T'ai-chou school.

Hsieh Chao-che (1567–1624) never met Lin Chao-en, but he was a contemporary Fukienese. As a youth of thirteen or fourteen he read the writings of Lin Chao-en; even at that time he felt there were problems and he wrote an essay in refutation. Later, as an adult, he witnessed the practices of the cult and found his earlier criticism entirely justified.[12]

Huang Tsung-hsi was disturbed by Lin's involvement in

Taoist Inner Alchemy, attributing his "death by insanity" to the evil results of such practices.[13]

It was probably on the basis of such criticism that Lin Chao-en and Li Chih came to be known long after Lin's death as the two heretics of Fukien.[14] In addition to this epithet, there is questionable evidence linking Lin's name with the publication of a book by Li Chih.[15] However, there is no evidence that the two men met or corresponded. Given the differences in their social views and personal styles, they would hardly have been compatible. Each would have been profoundly insulted to find himself linked with the other.

Those who knew Lin well defended him against detractors, claiming that they misunderstood his practices. Ch'i Chikuang (1528–1587), the commander responsible for finally subduing the pirates in P'u-t'ien, was cured by Lin of a serious illness. He was so impressed by Lin that he returned to study with him whenever he had free time.[16] He defended Lin against those who suspected that he taught strange arts seeking physical immortality, saying that Lin taught the sage's understanding of long life as knowledge of the true meaning of death.[17]

GROWTH OF THE CULT

Lin Chao-en chose, or his disciples ascribed to him, a religious mode of death. He retired from active teaching and withdrew into spiritual contemplation, increasingly assuming the characteristics of the holy man oblivious to the outside world. His disciples recorded that he passed away in a state of mystical trance and that his body regained its youthful appearance at death—a clear sign that death was not a defeat, but rather a passage to another spiritual abode. They eulogized him as a deity or semideity who appears in the world to save men and then returns to union with the cosmos to assist in the work of ongoing creation. Lin's transition to the status of deity or semideity took place immediately upon his death, for the seed of this development had been ripening as the cult and Lin's fame had spread.

Immediately after his death Three Teachings Shrines (*Sanchiao tz'u*) sprang up over the entire region. There was a flurry of publication activity, including the *Collected Works of Master Lin* in 1608 and the *Chronological Biography of Master Lin* in 1610, only twelve years after his death. In 1600 the cult published the "scriptures" of Lin Chao-en, containing the secret oral transmission of his teachings. Because of their esoteric nature they had not been published with earlier collections. However, near the end of his life, Lin ordered a disciple to edit and publish them, fearing they might otherwise be lost.[18]

After Lin's death the disciples set up a lecture hall and incense burner (for devotions), and convened assemblies on the first and fifteenth of the month. In his early school regulations, Lin had set aside those days for students to have an outing together in imitation of the disciples of Confucius.[19] Now, however, the function was overtly religious, like worship services at Buddhist temples and religious societies, which were often held on the first and fifteenth.

Hsieh Chao-che charged that Lin's disciples used talismans, ritual documents, and arts to overcome and conquer ghosts in the manner of the White Lotus sect. Some disciples used the healing method for their own profit and became little better than shamans.[20] If this is true, the practices of the cult quickly departed from the instructions of Lin Chao-en, who had nothing but scorn for such practices.[21] Hsieh's charges are not corroborated by other evidence, nor are they consonant with what is known of the cult as it exists today. His report may not be entirely accurate, or it may not represent the mainstream of the cult.

The only other information on the early cult is contained in the writings of two men who became Masters (*fu-tzu*) to carry on Lin's teaching after his death. Lin Chih-ching and Lu Wen-hui (dates unknown for either) represent a second-generation understanding of Lin Chao-en's teachings. Both are included as Masters in the present-day pantheon of the Three-in-One cult.[22]

Lin Chih-ching's name did not appear in Lin Chao-en's collected works, but he established a Three Teachings Shrine in 1590 at Yüeh-hsiu.[23] He wrote in his *Ming-hsia chi* (Collection on illumining *hsia*) that he heard the essentials of the Way from the Master of the Three-in-One Doctrine (*san-i chiao-chu*), also identified as Master Lin, Hsia-wu-ni. Lin Chih-ching studied with Lin Chao-en for some time before receiving the secret oral transmission; after that, he waited on the Master for years while studying the advanced secret teachings.[24]

In the *Ming-hsia chi* Lin Chih-ching (Master Chen-ming) is depicted as a teacher in his own right carrying on the line of Lin Chao-en. His disciple, Ch'en Su-k'un (dates and biography unclear) wrote, "I venture to say that since there are the Three Ni's [i.e., the Sages of the Three Teachings] there must also be Hsia-wu-ni [Lin Chao-en]; that since there is the *Fen-nei* collection [of Lin Chao-en], there must also be the *Ming-hsia chi*."[25] In other words, Lin Chao-en was essential to the transmission of the Three Teachings, and Lin Chih-ching and his writings were essential to carrying on the teachings of Lin Chao-en.

In the *Ming-hsia chi*, Lin Chih-ching commented on statements and teachings of Lin Chao-en. The major themes of the collection, roughly in order of emphasis, were as follows: (1) The cosmological foundation of Lin Chao-en's thought, consisting of an interplay of Inner Alchemy thought and the metaphysics of the *Book of Changes;* the cosmology was extensively related to self-cultivation by stilling in the back. (2) The relationship of the Three Teachings, and Lin Chao-en's position as the transmitter and reviver of the correct Way of the Three Teachings. (3) The Confucian teachings of Lin Chao-en. (4) The healing method.[26]

There was a discernible, though slight, shift in emphasis from Lin Chao-en's thought; Lin Chih-ching gave slightly more weight to Taoist aspects, pursuing certain elements of Taoist theory beyond the discussions in Lin Chao-en's known writings. For instance, he discussed at length the *hun* and *p'o* souls and their relationships to the cosmology,[27] although these were never discussed by Lin Chao-en.

The *Ming-hsia chi* continued the divinization of Lin Chao-en. In it Lin Chao-en was described as one who embraces the sun in the void and, coterminous with heaven and earth, shines down to illumine and save all generations, as Confucius was a sun in the Spring and Autumn period.[28] Like the divine sages, his birth and life were marked by auspicious signs. Lin Chih-ching claimed that Lin Chao-en once told him, "I am the great Master of Dharma . . . , Śākyamuni and I stand shoulder to shoulder."[29] In fact, he was seen as greater than the sages of the Three Teachings: "The Master of our doctrine combined the teachings of the Three Masters and reunited them in the true Confucianism of Confucius; he saw and gathered together the completion of the sages—is he not even greater than they?"[30]

Certain religious concepts appeared in Lin Chih-ching's thought, albeit briefly and in passing, which had no place in the religious world view of Lin Chao-en. The most striking examples were a quotation from the Queen Mother of the West (Hsi-wang-mu) and a reference to the powers of Yüan-shih T'ien-tsun.[31] These two deities did not appear in Lin Chao-en's known writings; if they had it is virtually certain that they would have been reinterpreted to fit into his "correct" interpretation of the Three Teachings.

Lu Wen-hui, known to his followers as Master Hsing-ju, wrote a collection called *Chung-i hsü-yen chi* (Empty words on the Center and the one), with prefaces ranging from 1597 to 1599.[32] Lu Wen-hui was present at the death of Lin Chao-en.[33] He established a Three Teachings Shrine at Yao Island in the Han River in 1602.[34] According to his disciples, Lu waited on Lin Chao-en in his last years, and was ordered by him to compile a collection of his works and to publish the Hsia-wu-ni scriptures (secret teachings of Lin Chao-en, Master Hsia-wu-ni), which had until then been oral secret teachings. They felt this was tantamount to having received the robe and bowl, the traditional signs of the transmission of the doctrine among Ch'an patriarchs.[35] Thus his disciples saw him as the second patriarch of the Three-in-One doctrine, the true successor to Lin Chao-en. However, the Hsia-wu-ni scriptures that are included in the *Collected Works* bear other names as recorders and publishers. Furthermore, those scriptures, the body of oral transmission, were not included in Lu

Wen-hui's collection, at least in its present form. There are simply some explanatory charts, and Lu's own writings, expanding many of Lin Chao-en's concepts.[36] Since Lin Chih-ching's disciples also saw him as the successor of Lin Chao-en, it seems that there were several successors and at least the germs of a rivalry among them.

Lu Wen-hui was a thinker and teacher in his own right. His collection of Lin Chao-en's writings was rearranged so that mutually illuminating essays were grouped together. The brief essays in his own collection were lucid expansions of Lin's thought, particularly the Inner Alchemy theory behind self-cultivation. He elaborated the unity of the Three Teachings, claiming that the sageliness of Confucius, the mystery (*hsüan*) of Lao Tzu, and the meditation (*ch'an*) of the Buddha were not limited to their respective schools; each of them also encompassed the truth of the other two sages. He also wrote that the *hsia* nature is the greatness which includes the three bonds, five constant virtues, the four callings, and the Three Teachings in the Center and the one.[37]

His writings, however, were not simply comments on Lin Chao-en's thought. Lu Wen-hui was particularly interested in explicating the appearance and nurturing of the spiritual light (*ling-kuang*). He traced its appearance at successive points in the meditative process: first above the navel; then between the eyes; then at the crown of the head; in the chest; in the soles of the feet; in the eyes, ears, mouth, and nose; and finally radiating from all the pores of the body.[38] Lu also developed an interesting Taoist correlation for the concept of washing the mind, moving it back, and hiding it in the secret place. He cited the *T'ai-hsüan ching:* "Hiding in the deep abyss, floating free, one preserves the Center."[39] Lu explained that the deep abyss was equivalent to the true destination, or secret place; floating free was effortless concentration like Mencius' neither forgetting nor helping; and that hiding and preserving the Center is the same as washing the mind and hiding it.[40] Like Lin Chih-ching, he described Lin Chao-en, under his divinized name of Hsia-wu-ni, as the equal, if not the superior, of the Sages of the Three Teachings.[41]

Lin Chih-ching and Lu Wen-hui set themselves up as teachers, spread the doctrine of Lin Chao-en, and began to put their own imprint upon it. Even as early as this, the thought of Lin Chao-en was rendered even more hospitable to elements from the Inner Alchemy tradition and, in a limited way, to certain supernatural elements of all traditions.

A QUESTION OF INFLUENCE

After Lin Chih-ching and Lu Wen-hui, the history of the Three Teachings cult is lost until modern times, except for one lead provided by Huang Tsung-hsi. He wrote that Chu Fang-tan and Ch'eng Yün-chang "ornamented the extraneous arts of Lin Chao-en, but obliterated him to establish themselves."[42] The identity of Chu Fang-tan is unclear, but Ch'eng Yün-chang was Ch'eng Chih (1602–1651), of the nineteenth-century T'ai-ku sect.[43] Some alleged that the T'ai-ku sect was an offshoot of the tradition of Lin San-chiao, who combined Ch'an and Taoism with the school of Wang Yang-ming, or, more precisely, the Yao-chiang branch of the school, which included Lo Hung-hsien.[44] Ch'eng Chih carried on this teaching, "ornamenting the extraneous arts of Lin Chao-en, but departing from the starting point."[45] After Ch'eng's death his disciples each taught their own version of his doctrine. Among those disciples was Chou T'ai-ku (dates unknown), founder of the T'ai-ku sect. Ch'eng Chih also had some connection with a sect called the *Ta-ch'eng chiao* (Teaching of the great vehicle) and that the T'ai-ku school was sometimes called the *Ta-ch'eng chiao* (Teaching of the great completion) to capitalize on the similarities in the names (the two *ch'eng*'s are homophones).

Ch'eng Chih's writings on the Three Teachings yield no evidence on direct contact between Ch'eng and Lin and no similarity in either doctrinal content or social views.[46] The one possible link was the appearance of the doctrines of stilling in the back, and washing the mind, moving it back, and hiding it in the secret place.[47] However, a simple reference to stilling in the back and washing the mind is not sufficient to establish the influence of Lin Chao-en, since these terms appeared in a number of Confucian and Taoist texts of the period, with a variety of interpretations.[48] There is as yet no firm evidence to confirm or deny connection between Lin Chao-en and Ch'eng Chih.

One argument for keeping the case open may be found in an examination of the T'ai-ku school itself. A careful reading of secondary documents and modern scholarship on this cult suggested that, although there is no evidence of direct contact, there were at least intriguing doctrinal affinities between this school and the thought of Lin Chao-en.[49]

These doctrinal affinities may be measured against seven central themes or categories in the thought of Lin Chao-en.

(1) Interest in cosmology based on a combination of a certain strain of Inner Alchemy Taoist thought and Neo-Confucian themes from the Four Books and the metaphysics of the *Book of Changes*. The cosmology described the structure of Being and creation, and at the same time served as a basis for practice by virtue of the identity of the human microcosm and the natural and ontological macrocosms.

(2) The *ken-pei* system of mind-cultivation, relating the themes of the hexagram *ken* in the *Book of Changes* with Inner Alchemy meditation and the Confucian themes of self-cultivation of sagely mind.

(3) The use of healing as a verification of mind-cultivation.

(4) The integration of the Three Teachings, combining elements of all three and interpreting each in terms of the others.

(5) *Hsia* as the all-embracing greatness underlying the Way and the unity of the Three Teachings.

(6) The primacy of moral cultivation with the goal of attaining the sagely mind inherent in all men.

(7) Confucian rationalism rejecting reliance on supernatural deities, rites, or charms.

The thought of the T'ai-ku school, as described in modern scholarship, showed some affinity with every one of the seven categories.

(1) *Cosmology*. Like Lin Chao-en, the cosmology of the T'ai-ku school was based on the "Explanation of the Diagram

of the Great Ultimate" of Chou Tun-i. Both used the *Tao-te ching* and the *Homology of the Triad* as major sources for interpreting the cosmology.⁵⁰ Like Lin they used symbols, such as a circle for emptiness, with variations on it to represent the various states through which man and the cosmos pass.⁵¹

(2) *Self-cultivation*. Like Lin Chao-en, the T'ai-ku school saw self-cultivation as a process of restoring original good nature through (a) holding fast to the Center (*chih-chung*); (b) following the steps of self-cultivation prescribed in the *Great Learning* and the *Mean* as interpreted by Neo-Confucians; and (c) stilling in the back, interpreted as a means of returning to the centrality before the emotions have appeared by keeping the thoughts in their place.⁵² This closely parallels the Confucian language used by Lin to describe the *ken-pei* system. The problem is whether they also understood it in Inner Alchemy terms. Although modern studies did not include any Inner Alchemy language in the section on self-cultivation, the section on cosmology discussed the interaction of the forces of trigrams *ch'ien* and *k'un*, *li* and *k'an* in much the same way that Lin did.

(3) *Healing*. The biography of Chou T'ai-ku states that he occasionally healed illness as part of his teaching, but does not describe his method.⁵³

(4) *The Three Teachings*. T'ai-ku criticisms of Buddhists and Taoists were similar to those of Lin Chao-en. They criticized Taoists for exhausting themselves in the search for long life, and the Buddhists for following a practice which was too demanding and gave none but the exceptional hope for self-fulfillment; it was Confucianism which offered the greatest hope of saving men.⁵⁴ Lin also praised Confucianism because it was the simple Way that could be followed by all. Further, the T'ai-ku doctrine of cultivation and enlightenment seems to have been a synthesis of all Three Teachings. Li Ching-feng (1801?–1887), founder of the Southern Branch of the T'ai-ku sect, used doctrines of all Three Teachings in his poems.⁵⁵ The doctrine of enlightenment showed influence of Taoist traditions of cultivation of nature and life store according to the systems of the *Ts'an t'ung ch'i*,⁵⁶ which was also central to Inner Alchemy.

(5) *Hsia*. Chou T'ai-ku said, "Men of Chou followed Chou [1122–255 B.C.E.]; men of Yin followed Yin [trad. 1766–1122 B.C.E.]; but the Way follows Hsia [trad. 2205–1766 B.C.E.]."[57] Hsia represented the Way in its earliest form, its original and true form. Further research is needed to determine whether other writings of the T'ai-ku school developed this concept into something resembling Lin Chao-en's concept of the all-encompassing primordial *hsia*.

(6) *Sagely mind*. The T'ai-ku sect saw all men as good and endowed with the capacity for sagehood.[58] The purpose of cultivation was to realize sagely nature as bright virtue or the virtuous nature.[59] Moreover, Chou T'ai-ku was an offshoot of the School of Mind; he taught a version of Wang Yang-ming's innate good-knowing *(liang-chih)*.[60] All of this coincides nicely with the teaching of Lin Chao-en.

(7) *Confucian rationalism*. The major thinkers of the T'ai-ku sect were Confucian rationalists. The secretiveness of the cult led to widespread misunderstanding about their teachings.[61]

The affinities described above do not establish that Lin Chao-en influenced this sect, but the similarities are intriguing. There were also differences, notably the lack of an articulated theory of the unity of the Three Teachings and the social thought of the T'ai-ku school, which was distinctively different from that of Lin Chao-en.[62] These differences may reflect the greatly different historical circumstances in which Lin's cult and the T'ai-ku school arose. Although the matter requires further research, the affinities suggest that the thought of Lin Chao-en, or thought in the same general tradition, spread beyond the confines of Lin Chao-en's Three-in-One doctrine.[63]

MODERN REMNANTS

Although there is no direct evidence, the cult of Lin Chao-en seems to have continued to spread and flourish in southeast China. In 1744, in response to a petition denouncing the heretical views and potential subversive threat of Three Teachings cults in South China, the Ch'ing government legally proscribed such cults.⁶⁴ The petition did not mention Lin Chao-en's Three-in-One doctrine by name, but it would have been included under the prohibition. Despite that prohibition, the cult is alive and well today among overseas Chinese in Singapore and Kuala Lumpur. It now serves as an ethnic, or more precisely a dialect association for Fukienese, particularly people from Hsing-hua county, which includes P'u-t'ien.⁶⁵ Given the heavy Fukienese migration to Taiwan in the century after the death of Lin Chao-en, it would not be surprising to find the cult extant there, although to my knowledge no one has yet reported it.⁶⁶ The Japanese invasion of 1939 occasioned a revival of the cult in Fukien and the reprinting of the biography of Lin Chao-en; the sponsor of the reprint cited Lin's heroic deeds against the Japanese pirates of his day.⁶⁷ Stone inscriptions from the Singapore temples show that the members there also saw the cult of the Three Teachings as a center of resistance against the Japanese; they held redemption festivals and other ceremonies frequently during the five years of Japanese occupation. At the end of the war they built a grotto and established periodic festivals to commemorate its founding.⁶⁸ For a 1954 redemption festival the sect gathered contributions from believers and other supporters, trained masters in the scriptures of the Three Teachings, and assembled actors for religious dramas.⁶⁹

No one has done an exhaustive study of the modern cult. The available evidence suggests both continuities and discontinuities with what is known of the teaching of Lin Chao-en. First, the cult is still centered around Lin Chao-en under the name Hsia-wu-ni. In the early twentieth century, it was customary for followers of Lin Chao-en to gather at his grave for memorial services; a photograph dating from the twenties or thirties commemorates such a gathering.⁷⁰ Every temple of the cult has an image or painting of Lin Chao-en. He is flanked, most commonly, by Cho Wan-ch'un, his Taoist friend of the period of search, and by Chang San-feng, a Taoist whose writings are included in the *Collected Works of Master Lin*.⁷¹ Chang San-feng is said to have visited Lin in 1581 and discussed with him the secrets of the Way.⁷² Lin evidently met one of the apparitions of Chang San-feng or another Taoist who was using his name; the historical Chang San-feng seems to have died in the early years of the Ming (fourteenth century), but his appearances were reported time and again through the early centuries of the dynasty.[73]

The concept of the unity of the Three Teachings is still venerated; images in the temples very often include the Sages of the Three Teachings. One temple inscription refers to "sitting to participate in the wondrous mind verified in meditation of the nine stages," suggesting that the meditative regimen of the nine stages is still a part of practice at some level.[74]

Finally, the writings preserved in the temples suggest considerable intellectual continuity, if they are indeed studied by members of the cult.[75] Contemporary temples possess two sets of Lu Wen-hui's collection of Lin's writings,[76] one of the four major collections of Lin's works. This set contains virtually all of the major writings of Lin Chao-en included in other collections. Also preserved is a copy of the *Ming-hsia chi* collection of Lin Chih-ching. Thus the second generation Masters have left their stamp on the present-day cult, for in these temples the thought of Lin Chao-en is preserved, studied, and interpreted through their collections. The temples also contain one full set and at least three partial sets of the twelve "scriptures" of Lin Chao-en, independent of those which are included in the larger collections. Although these works largely dropped out of the published and circulated collected writings, they were preserved in temples as the esoteric teachings of the cult. Since even these far-flung temples in Southeast Asia contain the important writings of Lin Chao-en, his thought seems to have retained its place as the basis of the cult, although it is not yet known how extensively and by whom his writings were actually studied.

On the other hand, there are evidences of discontinuities—new elements introduced into the cult, or new emphases. For instance, one stone inscription suggests that some of the priests are known as Master Immortal (*hsien-shih*),[77] a term unknown in the early writings of the sect. Second, the pantheon includes a slightly broader range of deities than Lin Chao-en would have sanctioned. Besides Lin Chao-en, the Sages of the Three Teachings, Cho Wan-ch'un, Chang San-feng, and six eminent disciples of the cult, the pantheon includes Maitreya Buddha, the guardians of Buddhist temples Chia-lan and Wei-t'o, and Ho Hsin-yin (1517–1579), an unorthodox Neo-Confucian roughly contemporary with Lin Chao-en.[78] There is some justification for the inclusion of Maitreya Buddha, given the fact that a "scripture" on Maitreya is attributed to Lin Chao-en.[79] The inclusion of the two guardian deities and of Ho Hsin-yin does not represent a particularly startling departure or a marked popularization of the cult, given the absence of such extremely popular deities as Kuan-yin, Kuan-kung, the Yellow Emperor, the Jade Emperor, and Sheng-mu, who is particularly popular in the area along the Fukien coast and Taiwan.[80] The inclusion of one or more of these latter deities would have been a much surer sign of popularization; the pantheon is remarkable for its consistency with the past, despite the inclusion of three figures who cannot be accounted for in early writings.

The inclusion of Ho Hsin-yin is a mystery. Ho visited Lin Chao-en during the years 1561–1562. However, while Lin's biographers record that Ho praised Lin's thought highly,[81] Ho Hsin-yin's collected works record that he left feeling they had very little in common.[82]

Ho Hsin-yin sought to alleviate the tensions between traditional Confucian views of social morality and the rapidly changing structure of Ming society. He saw the family system, in particular, as an obstacle to broader loyalties and cooperation. Therefore Ho emphasized friendship and teacher-student relations (which he saw as an extension of friendship relations) and elevated the broader clan structure over the residential family unit. Although he failed as a reformer, he attempted a reassessment of Confucian values in terms of the needs of his day.

Lin, on the other hand, followed the traditional Confucian teachings about human relationships to the letter with unquestioning faith. He felt the conflict between his status as a scholar and the fact that he was neither serving in the government nor studying for the examinations. He urged the registered students among his followers to pursue examination studies, although he himself had chosen not to. He was at pains to prove that his personal choice did not entail a renunciation of Confucian social values; hence those values become an unquestioned theme in his philosophy. Despite the considerable differences in their social thought, both Ho and Lin sought to make the teachings of Confucianism more accessible to people in general. They both felt that Confucianism should answer the needs of all the people, and tried, albeit in different ways, to achieve that end. Perhaps that shared commitment explains the cult's veneration of Ho Hsin-yin.

Many questions about the present cult remain unanswered. What is the curriculum of study? Has there been a direct line of transmission unbroken since the sixteenth century? Is the priesthood of Masters now hereditary, or how is it chosen? What sort of ritual life is followed? Do all believers practice the meditative regimen of the nine stages? Has the healing method survived? Is there still an attempt to include adherents of all Three Teachings? What festivals are observed? Is the teaching still predominantly Confucian? Are the petitions to heaven still offered by believers, or by the Masters of the cult? What distinctions in practice and study are there between lay followers and those who aspire to become Masters? Is it exclusively a Hsing-hua dialect association, or are people who do not speak the dialect welcomed into the cult on some basis? The answers await further research.

CONCLUSIONS

Although Lin Chao-en did not become a figure of national stature in his own time or after his death, his teaching is still alive. He may have influenced other Three Teachings religions of the seventeenth and nineteenth centuries. Although not a major figure, he represented currents and concerns of religious thought which had enduring appeal for some segments of society.

Lin Chao-en's life and thought reflect several important currents in early and mid-Ming thought: the openness to syncreticism; the strong affirmation of the universality of sagehood; the call for a return to the basic teachings of Confucius and Mencius; the vital concern with action, interpreted in Lin's case as the realizing and living of the sagely ideal. The rapid social change and the intellectual climate of the time led Neo-Confucians to experiment, question, and seek new styles. Lin's style was to affirm within Confucianism the levels of spirituality which rendered it hospitable to Taoist and Buddhist forms of spiritual cultivation, while at the same time affirming, and bringing Taoists and Buddhists to affirm, the basic social and ethical values of Confucianism. He was above all representative of the intensely felt spirituality among Ming thinkers; he developed more than any thinker studied to date the religious dimensions of Neo-Confucianism.

Lin Chao-en was not an intellectual giant or a strikingly creative thinker; he drew upon ideas already prevalent in the School of Mind and in Buddhist and Taoist circles. His contribution was the remolding of borrowed ideas into a syncretic religious teaching, understandable and followable for himself and others, with a well-defined system of study and practice.

His own youthful search for a concrete way to embody the truths he was studying and realize in himself the mind of the sage opened him to the lessons and methods of Confucianism, Buddhism, and Taoism. The nine stages of stilling in the back showed him the Way, which combined the Confucian moral cultivation of the seeds of sagely mind with Buddhist and Taoist methods of concentration and self-transformation. The nine stages were a gradual method of cultivation starting with very easy exercises and moving step by step to the ultimate reaches of sagehood. Since his own search had been for an accessible and concrete method for realizing sagely mind, as a teacher he was concerned that people of all religious and social backgrounds should have access to the Way. Thus he taught the Way in the language of all Three Teachings and painstakingly "corrected the errors" of the Three Teachings, reinterpreting popular beliefs and "misconceptions" to be consistent with his understanding of the Way of sagely mind. Although his interpretations were sometimes forced, they were designed to move students gradually into a new plane of religious thought and belief. His commitment to making the Way accessible to all was also manifested in his simple and semivernacular writings for those who lacked extensive formal education. Lin Chao-en was not only a syncretic thinker, combining ideas of the Three Teachings to form his personal philosophy; he was also a syncretic teacher. By integrating the Three Teachings, he meant not only to integrate the ideas and doctrines, but also to combine believers in the Three Teachings into a single Way.

Lin Chao-en's thought was a synthesis of the Three Teachings. So was his understanding of sagehood. For him, as for all Confucians, the sage represented a dual model: the sagely ruler who devoted himself to public service and the aid of the people, and the transmitter of the Way who could rectify the minds of the people. As a Confucian, Lin felt the call to public service. As a youth he had petitioned the government concerning strategies for self-defense during the pirate raids and for the reform of Buddhism and Taoism. He was active in public service from famine relief to the burial of corpses during the pirate raids. However, his decision not to take examinations and become an official marked the end of his chances for traditional public service. He never suggested that his decision resulted from his disillusionment with the corruption and political pressures of his day, although many of his contemporaries spurned official service for those reasons.[83] Although he wrote on Confucian themes such as ancestral sacrifices, rituals, and the well-field system, he never discussed political issues.

Instead, over the course of his life he increasingly identified himself with the other side of the sagely ideal, the teacher of men. His early school emulated the style of Confucius, and he expressed in his vows to heaven his serious commitment to his role as teacher. However, he was not simply a teacher of the classics, one who prepared his students for examinations; he was also a religious teacher, a converter and savior of men. He believed that he was called to revive the true transmission of the Way, lost since the times of Mencius. His disciples believed he was the equal of the Sages of the Three Teachings.

> At times he is in the world, a Master with form and countenance who draws the eight trigrams, achieves Nirvāṇa, and elucidates the Three Teachings. At other times he is outside the world, a Master without form or countenance, who encloses heaven and covers earth, who penetrates mountains and rivers, who rises and sets with the sun and moon.[84]

To his disciples he was in Confucian terms the sage who forms one body with heaven and earth and all things through his mind of humanity. He also resembled the Bodhisattva, the enlightened being who chose through compassion to take on human form in this world to save sinners, or the Taoist immortal or realized man who could appear in various avatars to revive the lost Way. His death was depicted as a religious "passing away," confirming his embodiment of spiritual truth. He was both a teacher and a religious teacher.

Lin Chao-en developed the religious potential of Neo-Confucianism through his syncretic openness to ideas and practices from Buddhism and Taoism. He adopted healing techniques, meditative disciplines, alchemical interpretations of the *Book of Changes,* and mystical speculations. However, in his own mind, he was still a Confucian teaching the Confucian Way. Thus he not only adopted the ideas and practices of the two religions; he also adapted them to his Confucian world view. Even in this most radical Chinese syncretist, the principles of selectivity and the tenacious affirmation of the "home" tradition are clearly visible. The case of Lin Chao-en helps to illustrate dynamics of syncretism in the history of religion.

APPENDIX A

Sources for the Study of Lin Chao-en

Chronological Survey of Secondary Research
Lin Chao-en's name came to the attention of scholars early in this century. The *Lin-tzu ch'üan-chi* (Collected works of Master Lin) was listed as part of a gallery of sources on the Three Teachings by Ashikaga Enjutsu, "Sō igo ni okeru sankyō chōwa no kōgai to sono sankō shomoku" (An outline of the blending of the Three Teachings from the Sung on, with a list of sources), *Tōyō tetsugaku* 16, no. 3 (1909):54–58. Koyanagi Shigeta briefly reviewed the contents of the *Lin-tzu ch'üan-chi* stored in the Gakushūin in Tokyo in "Minmatsu no sankyō kankei" (Relations of the Three Teachings in the late Ming), in *Takase hakushi kanreki kinen shinagaku ronsō* (Volume commemorating the sixtieth birthday of Professor Takase) (Tokyo: Kōbundō, 1928), pp. 349–70. Shigematsu Shunshō briefly discussed Lin Chao-en as a syncretist, based on an early Ch'ing account of his career, in "Shina sankyōshi jō no jakan no mondai" (Some problems in the history of the Three Teachings in China) *Shien* 21 (1939):125–53. Kubota Ryōon published a composite view of Lin's career based on Ming and early Ch'ing secondary accounts in *Shina judōbutsu kōshōshi* (History of interactions of Confucianism, Taoism, and Buddhism in China) (Tokyo: Daitō, 1943), pp. 322–23. Yang Shu-liang published a brief chronological biography based on the *Lin-tzu pen-hsing shih-lu* (True record of the activities of Master Lin) entitled "Hsia-wu-ni-shih tao-t'ung chung-i san-chiao tu-shih ta-tsung-shih chuan-lüeh" (Brief biography of Hsia-wu-ni, savior and master of the line of the Center and the one of the Three Teachings), in *Fu-chien wen-hua* 3 (1935):41–44.

Mano Senryū published the first study which explored Lin Chao-en's ideas on the basis of his own writings. He placed Lin in the context of larger syncretic trends in the Ming and discussed his ties to the school of Wang Yang-ming and his use of Buddhist and Taoist ideas. "Mindai ni okeru sankyō shisō; toku ni Rin Chōon o chūsin to shite" (Three Teachings thought in the Ming dynasty, with special reference to Lin Chao-en), *Tōyōshi kenkyū* 12 (1952):18–34. Sakai Tadao wrote a valuable study of Lin Chao-en's life and social views. He was the first to mention, if briefly, Lin's system of mind-cultivation and its relation to healing. He also reviewed arguments about Lin's influence on later religious cults. *Chūgoku zensho no kenkyū* (Researches in Chinese morality books) (Tokyo: Kokusho kankōkai, 1960), pp. 263–84. Mano Senryū published in a second article laying important groundwork for research on Lin Chao-en. He included a detailed biography based on the *Lin-tzu nien-p'u* (Chronological biography of Master Lin) and information on Lin and his clan in gazetteers. He also reviewed the contents of several sets of the *Lin-tzu ch'üan-chi*. "Rin Chōon to sono chosaku ni tsuite" (On Lin Chao-en and his writings), in *Shimizu hakushi tsuitō kinen Mindaishi ronsō* (Collection of articles on Ming history in commemoration of Professor Shimizu) (Tokyo: Daian, 1962), pp. 421–59. Professor Mano has recently published another study on Lin Chao-en, with new information on Lin's relatives, extant writings, and the publication and teaching activities in the cult. This study is contained in Professor Mano's *Mindai bunkashi kenkyū* (Studies on Ming cultural history) (Kyoto: Dōhōsha, 1979), pp. 433–503. We look forward to further research on Lin Chao-en from this Japanese scholar.

The first study in English was published by Liu Ts'un-yan. It is important because Liu was the first to explore Lin Chao-en's relationship to the Taoist tradition. Although he sometimes overstates the case for Taoist influence on Lin, he defines essential questions and areas of investigation, and provides many valuable research leads. "Lin Chao-en: The Master of the Three Teachings," *T'oung Pao* 53 (1967):253–78. Wolfgang Franke published two fascinating articles on the modern remnants of the cult in Southeast Asia. The first reported on temples of the cult in Singapore, providing pictures of the temples and the pantheon and translations of a stone inscription bearing information on the cult in the twentieth century. "Some Remarks on the 'Three-in-One Doctrine' and its Manifestations in Singapore and Malaysia," *Oriens Extremus* 19 (1972):121–30. The second article reviewed biographical information on Lin Chao-en, including full translations of several Ming and early Ch'ing accounts of Lin and his cult. "Some Remarks on Lin Chao-en (1517–1598)," Oriens Extremus 20 (1973):161–74. Finally, Lienche Tu Fang wrote a biography of Lin based on Yang Shu-liang and Ming and Ch'ing sources, for the Dictionary of Ming Biography, 1368–1644, 2 vols., eds. L. Carrington Goodrich and Chaoying Fang (New York: Columbia University Press, 1976).

While the studies described here are a beginning, they barely scratched the surface. Much work remains to be done.

Biographical Sources

The most important sources for the study of the life of Lin Chao-en come from within his cult. His cousin and disciple Lin Chao-k'o edited the *Lin-tzu nien-p'u* (Chronological biography of Master Lin) in 1610. It is preserved in the Hōsa Bunko, Nagoya, Japan. Although clearly a partisan source, this biography is based very closely on information found in the letters and personal documents of Lin Chao-en. It represents the perceptions of those closest to him during his lifetime; it is far from outright hagiography. This source is also very rich in information about the publishing, teaching activities, and spread of the cult. The *Lin-tzu pen-hsing shih-lu* (True record of the activities of Master Lin), 2 *ch.*, is preserved, incomplete, in the 1631 ed. of *Lin-tzu ch'üan-chi*, Gest Memorial Library (L:28; see appendix E) and in a 1939 reedition of a 1655 original, ed. Lu Wen-hui and Ch'en Chung-yü (reported in Franke, "Lin Chao-en," p. 162). Only the first *chüan* contains biographical materials, and it has a 1599 preface by Chang Hung-tu. This account is less rich in verifiable factual details than the *Lin-tzu nien-p'u*; it relies more on anecdotes about Lin's life from the mouths of disciples and relatives. It is an excellent supplement to the *nien-p'u*, since it includes very different information.

Although they are less rich in detail, a few Ming and Ch'ing sources contain biographical information on Lin Chao-en. First, there are biographies in local histories: *Min shu* (Book of Fukien), ed. Ho Ch'iao-yüan (1630), 129.20b–21b, under eminent commoners; *Fu-chien t'ung-chih* (Gazetteer of Fukien), ed. Ch'en I (Fukien: Cheng-fu chiao-yü-t'ang, 1938; reprint of Ming ed.), sec. 47 on Taoists, 14a; *Hsing-hua P'u-t'ien hsien-chih* (Gazetteer of P'u-t'ien, Hsing-hua) by Wang Ta-ching, reed. Liao Pi-ch'i (1879 supplement of 1758 ed.), 34.7b, under auspicious events. These and other gazetteers contain further information on Lin's clan, his friends and disciples, his grave, and his donations for repair of temples of various religions. However, they add little to biographical information in sources within the cult.

Accounts of Lin Chao-en were also found in Ming and early Ch'ing sources. Hsieh Chao-che wrote an account based on eyewitness observation of the cult and examination of Lin's writings. Although a fellow Fukienese, he is quite critical and classes Lin along with millenarian Buddhist cults. Unfortunately, he does not give much evidence to verify his charges. *Wu tsa tsu* (Five miscellaneous sacrificial plates), 16 *ch.* (Japanese ed., 1789, originally pub. 1616 in China), 8.44a ff. Ho Ch'iao-yüan wrote a positive and reasonably knowledgeable account of Lin and his thought, the latter based on *San-chiao wu-che ta-hui* (Unlimited meeting of the Three Teachings, I:18; see appendix C), although that work is not mentioned by name. He also wrote a biography of Lin's friend Cho Wan-ch'un. *Ming-shan tsang* (Storehouse of the mountain of names), 20 vols. (1640 ed., written 1586), *pen-shih chi* sec. 8a–9a. Huang Tsung-hsi wrote the most detailed biography of Lin Chao-en outside the cult; he seems to have studied one of the cult's biographies. He did not include his biography in the *Ming-ju hsüeh-an* (Anthology of Ming Neo-Confucians), because he did not consider him an "orthodox" Neo-Confucian; in fact, he seems to have been quite concerned about Lin's dabbling in Inner Alchemy. *Lin san-chiao chuan* (Biography of Lin San-chiao) in *Nan-lei wen-an* (Critical comments on literature by Huang Nan-lei) (1680 pref.), 9.1a–2b. There are some other sources, but they add little that is new.

Biographical information on Lin Chao-en may also be gleaned from his writings, particularly in letters and personal documents included in published collections of his works.

The Writings of Lin Chao-en

In the course of his life Lin Chao-en produced a considerable volume of written material. In addition, his sayings were recorded by disciples, submitted to him for approval, and then published as dialogues. The *Lin-tzu nien-p'u* records that during his life and after his death Lin's disciples repeatedly gathered these works, edited them, and published them in a series of collections. This was for them an act of religious merit, since as part of their training they took a vow before heaven to publish and distribute Lin's writings (*Chiu-hsü che-yen*, Selected sayings on the nine stages, XVI:1.9b). Because publishing was an act of merit, the collections often include prefaces and colophons by disciples recording the circumstances of their work. These have added to our knowledge of the evolution of Lin Chao-en's thought.

SOURCES FOR STUDY OF LIN CHAO-EN 243

There is extant one collection published during Lin's lifetime, the *Lin-tzu sheng-hsüeh t'ung-tsung san-chiao kuei-ju chi* (Collection of Master Lin's doctrine of the sages uniting the schools of the Three Teachings under true Confucianism), 4 *ch.*, compiled in 1567 by order of Lin Chao-en, with prefaces dated 1569 and 1570. The collection is preserved in the Sonkeikaku Bunko, Tokyo. A table of contents to this collection is provided in appendix B.

There are also three large collections published in the years after Lin's death. The best-known is the *Lin-tzu ch'üan-chi* (Collected works of Master Lin), edited by Wang Chen-kang, with a 1606 preface by Lin Chao-k'o. There are eleven sets of this collection in Japan: Gakushūin in Tokyo, 32 vols.; four sets in the Naikaku Bunko, Tokyo, in 40, 40, 39, and 20 vols.; Sonkeikaku Bunko, Tokyo, in 20 vols.; Hōsa Bunko, Nagoya, in 20 vols.; Jinbun Kakgaku Kenkyūjo, Kyoto, 24 vols.; Kyoto Furitsu Toshokan, 40 vols.; Kyoto University Library; Kyushu University Library, Fukuoka. I have seen and compared all but the first, which has been described in detail by Mano Senryū ("Rin Chōon," pp. 442–47), and the last two. In Mano Senryū's latest volume, he also reported a set in the Harvard Yenching Library (*Mindai bunkashi kenkyū*, p. 455), which I have not yet seen. An annotated table of contents to this collection is provided in appendix C. Aside from minor details (pages out of order, etc.), there are almost no differences between the sets. The exceptions—two or more editions of the voluminous commentaries on the Four Books (V:2–VIII:2), two editions of *Hsien-hsing p'ien* (On manifesting the nature, XVIII:1), and two versions of *San-i chiao-chu Hsia-wu-ni pen-t'i ching* (Sutra on the original nature of Hsia-wu-ni, Lord of the Three-in-One, XX:8)—only serve to highlight the consistency among the various sets of this enormous collection, which totals nearly 1500 leaves.

A second posthumous collection is the *San-chiao cheng-tsung t'ung-lun* (Discussions on the combination of correct principles of the Three Teachings), 107 *chüan*, edited by Lu Wen-hui in 1597. This collection was proscribed by the Ch'ing government (Franke, "Lin Chao-en," p. 171). The collection is preserved in the collection of rare books brought from Peking, now in the National Central Library of Taiwan, and on microfilm in the Library of Congress microfilm series of Rare Books of the National Library of Peking, reels 1038–39. Meno Senryū has established that these two extant copies, while generally the same, are not identical (*Mindai bunkashi kenkyū*, p. 466 and n. 79). There is much overlap between this and the "collected works," but all writings have been recarved and reordered. Eleven works of the *Ch'üan-chi* do not appear in this collection, and this collection contains thirteen works not contained in the two collections discussed above. The collection also includes the writings of Lu Wen-hui, representing the thought of the second-generation teachers of the sect. A table of contents to the collection is provided in appendix D.

There is a second edition of the *Lin-tzu ch'üan-chi*, published around 1631, in 48 vols., preserved in the Gest Memorial Library, Princeton University. An annotated table of contents is provided in appendix E. This collection differs considerably from the 1606 edition. Nearly half the 1606 collection is missing from this edition, which consists mainly of commentaries, personal documents, and major scholarly works. All works have been considerably reedited, and the entire collection has been recarved. There are some interesting new titles, including a collection of essays from Lin's student days (*Lin-tzu ch'üan-chi wen-lüeh*, Selections of writings from Lin Tzu's collected works, L:18), letters to Lin from scholars (*Shih cha*, Ten letters, L:17), and the *Lin-tzu pen-hsing shih-lu* (L:28). It also contains within it another collection: *Fen-nei chi* (Collection on the world as my family), L:22, 12 *ch*. (pref. 1627). The *Lin-tzu nien-p'u* recorded a 64 *chüan* version of that work, which seems to be lost. The *Fen-nei chi* is also reported in the Academia Sinica of Peking (*Pei-ching jen-wen yen-chiu-so tsang shu-mu* [Peking: Pei-ching jen-wen yen-chiu-so, 1938], p. 376).

Full collections of Lin Chao-en's works are preserved in only a few libraries. Catalogues of famous collections also include a number of titles of single works by Lin. Most common are his commentaries to Taoist and Buddhist works, a set of essays on the essentials of the mind according to the Three Teachings (XV:3–8), and the *San-chiao hui-pien* (Joint chronicle of the Three Teachings, XI:1–XII:6).

Finally, there is an interesting supplementary source on Lin Chao-en, the novel by P'an Ching-jo, *San-chiao k'ai-mi kuei-cheng yen-i* (Romance of the Three Teachings exposing delusions and returning to the truth), written around 1615. It is preserved only in the Tenri University Library. According to Sawada Mizuho, the novel was a biting satire of the teachings of Lin Chao-en, and his disciples attempted to destroy the work ("Sankyō shisō to heiwa shōsetsu" [Colloquial novels and Three Teachings thought], *Biburia* 16 [1960]:37–39). I am presently studying this novel, and my impression differs from Sawada; although in the first chapters it appeared to be a satire, the disciples of Lin Chao-en straightened themselves out and set out to expose delusions and correct errors of people in all walks of life.

Lost Works

Some writings of Lin Chao-en appear to be no longer extant. The *Lin-tzu fu-ch'u chi* (Master Lin's collection of returning to the beginning) was edited shortly after Lin's death (*Lin-tzu nien-p'u*, 60a–b). The preface to this collection heads the 1606 *Lin-tzu ch'üan-chi*, but the contents of the present *ch'üan-chi* differ considerably from the listed contents of the *fu-ch'u chi*.

Of the twelve scriptures of Lin Chao-en (*Lin-tzu nien-p'u*, 62a–b), only one is preserved in an extant collection (XVIII:9–11), and partial sets are preserved in temples reported by Franke in a personal communication.

The *Lin-tzu nien-p'u* also reported a second, nameless collection which was distributed to temples (62b–63b). It contains titles not by Lin Chao-en, such as the *Book of the Jade Pivot* (*Yü-shu ching*, TT. 25) and the *Recorded Sayings of Lu Hsiang-shan* (*Hsiang-shan yü-lu*). No record of such a collection appears in any library catalogue I have examined to date.

APPENDIX B

Lin-tzu sheng-hsüeh t'ung-tsung san-chiao kuei-ju chi

(Collection of Master Lin's doctrine of the sages uniting the schools of the Three Teachings under true Confucianism). Preserved in the Sonkeikaku Bunko. *Chronological Biography* (*Lin-tzu nien-p'u*, 42b) records that it was compiled in 1567; prefaces date from 1569 and 1570.

CONVENTIONS:
1. The four *chüan* of the collection are denoted by A, B, C, and D.
2. Each title within the *chüan* will be numbered consecutively in roman numbers: A:I, A:II, etc.
3. Pages are numbered consecutively within the *chüan*, not under separate titles. Pages of a particular work will be designated in the form: A:I. 1a–1b.

All references to Lin Chao-en's writings in this book that follow the form described above are to this collection. Cross-referencing of titles listed in other collections is provided in appendix F.

A:I. 1a–1b   *Hsin-sheng tzu-hsü* (Author's preface to the *Hsin-sheng* collection).
A:II. 1b–2b   *Hsin-sheng hsiao-hsü* (Small preface to the *Hsin-sheng* collection).
A:III. 3a–b   *Hsin-sheng mu-lu* (Table of contents to the *Hsin-sheng* collection).
A:IV. 4a–30a *Hsin-sheng chiao-yen* (Instructions on the mind as sage). Dated 1575 in *Chron. Biog.*

A:V.31a–40b	*Hsin-ching chih-mi* (Pointing to delusions with the parable of the mind as a mirror). Dated 1568, *Chron. Biog.*
A:VI.40a–62b	*Ch'iao-yang chiao-yen* (Instructions to disciples in Ch'iao-yang). 1572 pref.
B:I.1a–21b	*Shu-sheng* (On the study of the sages). Dated 1566, *Chron. Biog.*
B:II.22a–53b	*Tsung-K'ung ta-yü* (Replies to questions on following Confucius).
C:I.1a–9b	*Yü-chang ta-yü* (Replies to students in Yü-chang). Dated 1573, *Chron. Biog.*
C:II.20a–52b	*Yü-chang hsü-yü* (Further replies to Yü-chang). Afterword, 1573.
C:III.53a–74b	*San-shan shih-yen* (Collected sayings on the three mountains). Dated 1567, *Chron. Biog.*
D:I.1a–13b	*Liu Po-tzu p'ien* (On disciple Liu Po-tzu).
D:II.14a–20b	*Ts'un-hsing kuei-t'iao* (Regulations for preserving the mind and self-examination). Dated 1567, *Chron. Biog.*
D:III.21a–30b	*Chu-tai li chi t'u-shuo* (Explanations with diagrams, setting out the generations' tablets for ancestral rites and sacrifices). Dated 1558, *Chron. Biog.*
D:IV.31a–37a	*Ko-hsüeh chieh* (Interpretation of the study of song). 1565 colophon; 1566 postface.
D:V.38a–41b	*Tiao-ku wen-wu li she t'u-shuo* (Explanation with diagrams in consideration of the ancient archery rite and drinking ceremony).
D:VI.42a–51b	*Ch'ung-li t'ang* (Hall in honor of ritual). Dated 1554, *Chron. Biog.*
D:VII.52a–57b	*Ming-ching t'ang* (Hall for expounding classics). Dated 1554, *Chron. Biog.*
D:VIII.58a–62b	*Ch'ang-ming chiao* (Teachings on the always illumined). 1561 colophon.
D:IX.63a–64b	*I chiao* (Instructions on the *Book of Changes*).
D:X.65a–67a	*Lin-tzu sheng-hsüeh t'ung-tsung tsung-hsü* (General preface to the collection). 1570.
D:XI.68a–69a	*Sheng-hsüeh t'ung-tsung hsü* (Preface to the collection). 1569.

APPENDIX C

Lin-tzu ch'üan-chi

(Collected works of Master Lin). Preserved in several sets in the Naikaku Bunko and other libraries. Ed., 1606. Some sets are bound in forty volumes, but this table follows the Naikaku Bunko twenty-volume set, which is complete and available on microfilm. There are only minor discrepancies between sets.

CONVENTIONS:

1. Each of the twenty volumes will be numbered consecutively in roman numerals.
2. All independently paginated units within each volume (even brief prefaces or afterwords) will be numbered consecutively in arabic numerals: I:1, I:2, etc.
3. The total number of pages for each work is provided, to aid readers in scanning volumes to locate a particular title.

All references in the book which use the form described above are to this collection. Cross-references to the same titles in other collections are provided in appendix F.

I:1	*Lin-tzu ts'un-ch'u tsung-chi hsü* (Preface to Master Lin's collection on preserving the beginning). 3 pp. 1606.
I:2	*Ts'un-ch'u chi hsü* (Preface to the *Ts'un-ch'u* collection). 3 pp.
I:3	*Ch'ang-tao ta-chih* (Principles of expounding the Way). 2 pp.
I:4	*Yüan-tsung t'u-shuo* (Explanation and diagram of the original school). 2 pp. Dated 1565, *Chron. Biog.*

I:5	*San-chiao ching lüeh* (Excerpts from the classics of the Three Teachings). 5 pp. Dated 1588, *Chron. Biog.*
I:6	*Shuo hsia* (Discussions on *hsia*). 3 pp. Dated 1567, *Chron. Biog.*
I:7–8	*Hsin-ching chih-mi* (Pointing to delusions with the parable of the mind as mirror). (7) 2 pp. (8) 9 pp.
I:9	*Ch'ang-ming chiao* (Teachings on the always illumined). 6 pp.
I:10	*Pen-t'i chiao* (Instructions on the original nature). 6 pp. Dated 1565, *Chron. Biog.*
I:11–12	*Ssu-yin yü* (Parable of silk and silver). (11) Foreword, 2 pp. (12) Text, 5 pp. 1577 colophon.
I:13	*Ch'i-ch'iao ta-wen* (Answers to questions on the seven apertures). 7 pp. Dated 1577, *Chron. Biog.* Published 1581.
I:14	*Ho-ssu ho-lü chieh* (Interpretation of no-thought and no-deliberation). 5 pp. Dated 1567, *Chron. Biog.*
I:15	*Hsing-ming ta-yü* (Replies on human nature and life store). 8 pp. 1581 colophon.
I:16	*Hsin-shen hsing-ming t'u* (Diagram of mind, body, nature, and life store). 7 pp. Dated 1562, *Chron. Biog.*
I:17	*Hsin-sheng t'u-shuo* (Explanation of the diagram of the mind as sage). 7 pp.
I:18	*San-chiao wu-che ta-hui* (The unlimited meeting of the Three Teachings). 8 pp.
I:19	*Fen-nei chi fen-che pien-lan tzu-hsü* (Author's preface to selected readings from the *Fen-nei* collection). 16 pp. Collection 1583, *Chron. Biog.*
I:20	*Hsin-sheng chiao-yen* (Instructions on the mind as sage). 24 pp.
I:21	*Yü jen p'ien* (On humaneness and human desires). 12 pp. Dated 1583, *Chron. Biog.*
II:1–3	*Hsin-sheng chih-chih* (Direct pointing to the mind as sage). (1) Foreword, 2 pp. (2) Text, 35 pp. (3) Colophons, 8 pp., 1567. Dated 1564, *Chron. Biog.*
II:4–5	*Hsin pen-hsü p'ien* (On the mind's original voidness). (4) Foreword, 1 p. (5) Text, 35 pp. Dated 1575, *Chron. Biog.*
II:6	*Hsin pen-hsü chih-chih* (Direct pointing to the mind's original voidness). 5 pp. Dated 1575, *Chron. Biog.*
II:7	*Wu-sheng fen-che pien-lan* (Selected readings on no-birth). 2 pp.

II:8–10	*Wu-sheng p'ien* (On no-birth) (8) *ch.* 1, 24 pp. (9) *ch.* 2, 27 pp. (10) colophons, 2 pp. Dated 1586, *Chron. Biog.*
III:1–2	*Hsien-yen* (The a priori abundant). (1) Foreword, 2 pp. (2) Text, 45 pp. Dated 1575, *Chron. Biog.*
III:3–5	*Yüan-shen shih-i* (The true meaning of original spirit). (3) Preface, 5 pp. (4) Foreword, 3 pp., 1584. (5) Text, 14 pp., 1584.
III:6	*Meng-chung-jen* (Man within a dream). 10 pp. 1583.
III:7	*Fo p'u-sa i* (The meaning of Buddha and Bodhisattva). 5 pp.
III:8	*Chen-wo ch'ang-yen* (Good words on the true self). 4 pp.
III:9	*Sung-chang* (Hymns). 9 pp.
IV:1	*Ch'üan-shih* (The conditional and the absolute). 9 pp.
IV:2	*Yü-yen* (Parables). 16 pp.
IV:3	*P'o-mi* (Breaking down delusions). 27 pp.
IV:4	*Ch'ih-chai pien-huo* (Discussion of doubts about fasting). 5 pp.
IV:5	*Nien-ching pien-huo* (Discussion of doubts about reciting sutras). 5 pp.
IV:6–7	*Hsing-hsin shih* (Poems of the awakened mind). (6) Preface, 2 pp. (7) text, 23 pp. Dated 1559, *Chron. Biog.*
IV:8–9	*Hsing-hsin shih che-chu* (Notes on selected poems of the awakened mind). (8) Text, 30 pp. 1560. (9) Colophon, 2 pp., 1562.
IV:10	*Lien-chü* (Couplets. 14 pp. Dated 1567, *Chron. Biog.*
V:1	*Lu t'an* (Discussing the deer). 2 pp.
V:2–VI:4	*Ssu-shu piao-che cheng-i* (Correct interpretation of the Four Books, by topic). V: (2), 40 pp., (3) 37 pp. VI: (1), 30 pp., (2) 31 pp., (3) 27 pp., (4) 37 pp. 1577 and 1592 editions, *Chron. Biog.* Varies slightly from set to set.
VII:1–VIII:2	*Ssu-shu piao-che cheng-i hsü* Correct interpretation of the Four Books, by topic, continued) VII: (1), preface, 7 pp., (2) 33 pp., (3) 31 pp., (4) 13 pp., (5) 35 pp. VIII: (1), 34 pp., (2) 42 pp. 1586, *Chron. Biog.*
IX:1–8	*Tao-te ching shih-lüeh* (Brief interpretation of the *Tao-te ching*). (1) Preface, 3 pp. (2) *ch.* 1, 23 pp. (3) *ch.* 2, 24 pp. (4) *ch.* 3, 20 pp. (5) *ch.* 4, 25 pp. (6) *ch.* 5, 22 pp. (7) *ch.* 6, 28 pp. (8) Colophons. 1588.
X:1–5	*Chin-kang ching t'ung-lun* (Discussion of the Diamond Sutra). (1) Foreword, 3 pp., (2) *ch.* 1, 15 pp., (3) *ch.* 2, 15

LIN-TZU CH'ÜAN-CHI 251

	pp., (4) *ch.* 3, 15 pp., (5) *ch.* 4, 23 pp. Dated 1580, *Chron. Biog.*
X:6–7	*Hsin ching shih-lüeh* (Brief interpretation of the Heart Sutra). (6) Preface, 3 pp. (7) Text, 19 pp. Dated 1580, *Chron. Biog.*
X:8	*Hsin ching kai-lun* (General discussion of the Heart Sutra). 25 pp.
X:9	*Fu hsin ching shih-lun chiu-cheng hsiao-chien* (Brief abridgement of the correct interpretation of the Heart Sutra). 2 pp.
X:10–11	*Ch'ang-ch'ing-ching ching shih-lüeh* (Brief interpretation of the Book of Constant Purity and Quiescence). (10) Preface, 4 pp. (11) Text, 11 pp. Dated 1581, *Chron. Biog.*
X:12	*Erh-ching shih-lüeh hsiao-pa* (Colophon to the brief interpretation of the two scriptures). 2 pp. 1582.
XI:1–XII:6	*San-chiao hui-pien yao-lüeh* (Joint chronicle of the Three Teachings). XI:(1) Foreword, 4 pp., (2) Preface, 2 pp., (3) *ch.* 1, 29 pp., (4) *ch.* 2, 46 pp., (5) *ch.* 3, 38 pp., (6) *ch.* 4, 46 pp. XII: (1) *ch.* 5, 24 pp., (2) *ch.* 6, 28 pp., (3) *ch.* 7, 29 pp., (4) *ch.* 8, 30 pp., (5) *ch.* 9, 31 pp., Postface, 1563. (6) Preface, 1563. Dated 1562, *Chron. Biog.*
XIII:1–4	*Chiu-kao* (Manuscripts). (1) *ch.* 1, 17 pp., (2) 17 pp., (3) 17 pp., (4) postfaces, 3 pp. Dated 1554, *Chron. Biog.*
XIV:1–7	*Hsü-kao* (Manuscripts, continued). (1) *ch.* 1, 20 pp. (2) 14 pp. (3) 19 pp. (4) 15 pp. (5) 19 pp. (6) 15 pp. (7) 14 pp.
XV:1	*Yü-chang ta-yü* (Replies to students in Yü-chang). 19 pp.
XV:2	*Yü-chang hsü-yü* (Further replies to Yü-chang). 31 pp.
XV:3–4	*Fen-che tsung-K'ung hsin-yao* (Excerpts from Essentials of the mind for followers of Confucius). (3) *ch.* 1, 12 pp., (4) *ch.* 2, 12 pp. Dated 1565, *Chron. Biog.*
XV:5–6	*Fen-che hsüan-tsung ta-tao* (Excerpts from The great Way of the followers of Taoism). (5) *ch.* 1, 12 pp., (6) *ch.* 2, 12 pp. Dated 1565, *Chron. Biog.*
XV:7–8	*Fen-che hsing-k'ung tsung-chih* (Excerpts from Principles of the emptiness of self-nature). (7) *ch.* 1, 12 pp., (8) *ch.* 2, 12 pp. Dated 1565, *Chron. Biog.*
XVI:1	*Chiu-hsü che-yen* (Selected sayings on the nine stages). 19 pp. Dated 1579, *Chron. Biog.*
XVI:2	*Hsüeh-tao yao-shen hsün-shih chu-sheng* (Instructions to students: What is necessary in studying the Way?). 3 pp.

252　APPENDIX C

XVI:3　　　*Shu-t'ien-kao* (Manuscripts of vows to heaven). 38 pp.
XVI:4　　　*Wu ch'ieh-pu-k'o shih-chieh chu-sheng* (Admonitions to students on the five absolute prohibitions). 2 pp.
XVI:5–6　　*Lin Tzu* (Master Lin). (5) Preface, 1 p. (6) Text, 40 pp. 1553.
XVI:7　　　*Hsia-yü* (Savings on *hsia*). 26 pp. Dated 1565, Chron. Biog.
XVII:1　　 *Ming-ching t'ang* (Hall for expounding classics). 6 pp.
XVII:2　　 *Li-pen* (Establishing the basis). 12 pp.
XVII:3　　 *Ju-ching* (Confucian classics). 16 pp.
XVII:4　　 *Ko-hsüeh chieh* (Interpretation for the study of song). 4 pp.
XVII:5　　 *Shih-wen lang-t'an* (Discussion of extravagance in poetry and prose). 13 pp. 1564.
XVII:6　　 *Hsin-nan p'ien* (On difficulties in belief). 6 pp.
XVII:7–8　 *Ts'un-hsing kuei-t'iao* (Regulations for preserving the mind and self-examination). (7) Foreword, 3 pp. (8) Text, 6 pp.
XVII:9　　 *Ch'ung-li t'ang* (Hall in honor of ritual). 11 pp.
XVII:10　 *Chu-tai li chi t'u-shuo* (Explanation with diagrams, setting out the generations' tablets for ancestral rites and sacrifices). 15 pp.
XVII:11　 *Tiao-ku wen-wu li she t'u-shuo* (Explanation with diagrams in consideration of the ancient archery rite and drinking ceremony). 4 pp.
XVII:12　 *Ching-t'ien* (The well-field). 5 pp.
XVII:13　 *Liu mei t'iao ta* (Replies on six items for improvement). 8 pp. Dated 1556, Chron. Biog.
XVII:14　 *Tao-ho yü-t'an* (Vague discussions on controlling the river [of life force]). Dated 1577, Chron. Biog.
XVII:15　 *San-kang kua* (Tetragrams of the three bonds). 6 pp.
XVIII:1　 *Hsien-hsing p'ien* (On manifesting the nature). 16 pp.
XVIII:2　 *T'an-ching hsün-shih* (Instructions on the Platform Sutra). 9 pp.
XVIII:3　 *Chiao-wai pieh-ch'uan* (Separate transmission outside the teachings). 19 pp., 1580–1581.
XVIII:4　 *Hsing-ming jen-tan* (The elixir and human nature, life store and humaneness). 9 pp.
XVIII:5　 *Hsü shih chen-hsin* (You must know the true mind). 15 pp.
XVIII:6　 *Ch'ang-tao p'ien* (On the absolute Way). 13 pp.
XVIII:7–11　*San-chiao tao-t'ung chung-i ching* (Scripture on the one

	in the Center in the line of the Three Teachings). (7) Prefaces, 4 pp. (8) Colophon, 1 p. (9) *ch.* 1, 11 pp. (10) *ch.* 2, 12 pp., (11) *ch.* 3, 10 pp. Taught in 1584; published in 1600.
XIX: 1–4	*Hsia i* (Hsia is one). (1) Introduction. (2) Foreword, 3 pp. (3) *ch.* 1, 46 pp. (4) *ch.* 2, 43 pp.
XX: 1–5	*Wu-yen lu* (Record of the dialogues). (1) Foreword, 3 pp. (2) *ch.* 1, 12 pp., (3) *ch.* 2, 12 pp., (4) *ch.* 3, 11 pp. (5) Colophon, 2 pp.
XX:6	*San-feng hsien-sheng hsüan ko hsüan t'an* (Songs and talks on the mysterious Way by Master Chang San-feng). 10 pp. 1581.
XX:7	*San-i chiao-chu shuo Mi-le tsun-fo pao-ching* (Precious sutra honoring Maitreya Buddha preached by the Lord of the Three-in-One). 3 pp.
XX:8	*San-i chiao-chu Hsia-wu-ni pen-t'i ching* (Sutra on original nature by Hsia-wu-ni, Lord of the Three-in-One). 2 pp. Published 1600.

APPENDIX D

San-chiao cheng-tsung t'ung-lun

(Discussions on the combination of correct principles of the Three Teachings) 1597 edition. Preserved in the Library of Congress, Peking Library Rare Book Microfilm Series, reels 1038–39.

CONVENTIONS:
1. All titles from this collection are indicated by the letter "S."
2. Numbers of titles follow the order of the table of contents on the microfilm; if a title does not appear in the table of contents, it will be numbered by the preceding title, followed by "a": S:a, S:29a, etc.
3. Titles which appeared in appendices B and C will merely be noted, with a cross-reference to the full listing in the earlier appendix.
4. Colophons and prefaces, even if paginated independently, will be listed under the main entry, since they do not have separate titles in the table of contents.

All references to writings of Lin Chao-en in this book which are preceded by "S" are to this collection. For complete cross-listings, see appendix F.

S:a   *San-chiao cheng-tsung t'ung-lun tzu-hsü* (Author's preface to this collection). 1597.
S:1   *San-chiao ho-i ta-chih* (The meaning of uniting the Three Teachings). 39 pp. 1584 colophon.
S:2   *Yüan-tsung t'u.* See I:4.

S:3   *Ch'ang-tao ta-chih.* See I:3, although this version is larger.
S:4   *Yüan-shen shih-i.* See III:4–5.
S:5   *Meng-chung-jen.* See III:6. 1597 preface.
S:6   *Fo p'u-sa i.* See III:7.
S:7   *Hsien-hsing p'ien.* See XVIII:1.
S:8   *Ch'ang-tao p'ien.* See XVIII:6.
S:9   *Hsia-yü fu-hsü.* See XVI:7. Includes a supplement and 1600 preface.
S:10 *Hsin-ching chih-mi.* See A:V and I:7–8.
S:11 *Pen-t'i chiao.* See I:10.
S:12 *Ch'ang-ming chiao.* See D:VIII and I:9.
S:13 *Yüan-chiao* (Instructions on the original). 10 pp.
S:14 *Lin Tzu.* See XVI:5–6.
S:15 *Tsung-K'ung t'ang* (Hall for honoring Confucius). 17 pp.
S:16 *Yü jen p'ien.* See I:21.
S:17 *Ming-ching t'ang.* See D:VII and XVII:1.
S:18 *Shih-wen lang-t'an.* See XVII:5. Includes some appendices.
S:19 *Ko-hsüeh chieh.* See D:IV and XVII:4.
S:20 *Tiao-ku wen-wu li she t'u-shuo.* See D:V and XVII:11.
S:21 *Chu-tai li chi.* See D:III and XVII:10.
S:22 *Ch'ung-li t'ang.* See D:VI and XVII:9.
S:23 *Tao Shih jen-lun shu-kao* (Draft petition on Taoists and Buddhists and human relationships). 12 pp. 1597.
S:24 *Liu mei t'iao ta.* See XVII:13.
S:25 *Ching-t'ien.* See XVII:12.
S:26 *Tao-ho yü-t'an.* See XVII:14.
S:27 *San-kang kua.* See XVII:15.
S:28 *Chiu-hsü che-yen.* See XVI:1. Somewhat shorter version.
S:29 *Shu-t'ien wen-kao.* See XVI:3.
S:29a *Ch'ang-tao shu-ch'i t'iao-ta* (Replies on items concerning vows to heaven and teaching the Way). 3 pp.
S:30 *Hsin-sheng chih-chih.* See II:1–2.
S:31 *Hsin-sheng chiao-yen.* See A:IV and I:20.
S:32 *Hsien-yen.* See III:1–2.
S:33 *Ts'un-hsing kuei-t'iao.* See D:II and XVII:7–8.
S:34 *Ch'i-ch'iao ta-wen.* See I:13.
S:35 *Ch'u-hsüeh p'ien* (On the beginning of study). 17 pp.
S:36 *Chiao-wai pieh-ch'uan.* See XVIII:3. Recorded 1622.
S:36a *Ho-ssu ho-lü chieh.* See I:14.
S:37 *Hsin ching shih-lüeh.* See X:6–7.
S:38 *Hsin ching kai-lun.* See X:8.
S:39 *Ch'ang-ch'ing ching.* See X:10–11.

S:40 Chin-kang ching kai-lun. See X:1–5, although titles differ.
S:41 Ssu-yin yü. See I:12.
S:42 Hsin-sheng t'u-shuo. See I:17.
S:43 Hsin-shen hsing-ming t'u-shuo. See I:16.
S:44 Hsing-ming ta-yü. See I:15.
S:45 Hsin yao (The mind and the hexagrams). 12 pp.
S:46 T'ien jen i-ch'i (The single vital force of heaven and man). 9 pp.
S:47 San-chiao wu-che ta-hui. See I:18.
S:48 Chen-wo ch'ang-yen. See III:8.
S:49 Tao yeh cheng-i p'ien (The way and the callings are one). 16 pp.
S:50 Tu-shih (Saving the world). 9 pp.
S:51 Shan-jen (Man of the mountains). 12 pp. 1578.
S:51a Tzu-shu Ssu-yin yü chüan-tuan. Foreword to S:41; see I:11.
S:52 San-chiao hui-pien yao-lüeh. See XI:2–XII:2. Ch. 7–9 are missing.
S:53 Yü-chang ta-wen. See C:I and XV:1. Variant title.
S:54 Yü-chang hsü-yü. See C:II and XV:2.
S:55–62 Ssu-shu cheng-i. A slightly altered version of VII:2–VIII:2.
S:56a San-chiao hui-pien tzu-hsü. Preface to S:52. See XII:6.
S:91 Tao-te ching shih-lüeh. See IX:1–5. The last two chüan are missing. Listed as 91 in the table of contents, but appears after 62 on the microfilm.
S:63 Chung-i hsü-yen (Introduction to the Center and the one). Writings of Lu Wen-hui. Prefaces 1598 and 1599.
S:64 Hsing-ling shih (Poems on the spiritual luminosity of human nature). 34 pp. 1600 pref.
S:65 Tao-t'ung lun (Discussions of correct transmission). 6 pp. Prefaces 1597 and 1598.
S:66 San-feng hsien-sheng. See XX:6.
S:67 Wu-yen lu. See XX:1–5. Foreword, 1600.
S:68 Cheng-tsung yao lu (Record of essentials of the correct Way). 7 pp.
S:69 Fei san-chiao (What is not the Three Teachings). 8 pp.
S:70 Shih ch'u-shih fa (The method of leaving the world while in the world). 8 pp.
S:71 Li-pen p'ien. See XVII:2.
S:72 I-chieh li-yü (Plain and simple explanations). 14 pp.
S:73 Hsin-nan p'ien. See XVII:6.
S:74 Wu-sheng p'ien. See II:8–10. A shortened version.

S:75	*Fen-che sheng-hsüeh hsin-yao.* Same as XV:3–4, although titles differ.
S:76	*Tsung-hsüan ta-tao.* See XV:5–6. Variant title.
S:77	*Hsing-k'ung tsung-chih.* See XV:7–8.
S:78	*Hsing-hsin shih.* See IV:7. 1604 preface.
S:79	*Hsing-hsin shih che-chu.* See IV:8.
S:80	*Lien-chü.* See IV:10.
S:81	*Chiu-kao.* See XIII:1–3. This is only 22 pp., considerably shortened.
S:82	*Hsü-kao.* See XIV:1–7; this is considerably shortened to 37 pp.
S:83	*Hsin pen-hsü p'ien.* See II:5.
S:84	*Hsin pen-hsü chih-chih.* See II:6.
S:85	*Hsü shih chen-hsin.* See XVIII:5. This version is shorter.
S:86	*Ch'üan-shih.* See IV:1.
S:87	*P'o-mi.* See IV:3.
S:88	*Yü-yen.* See IV:2.
S:89	*Ch'ih-chai pien-huo.* See IV:4.
S:90	*Nien-ching pien-huo.* See IV:5.
S:91	(Appears here before S:63.)

APPENDIX E

Lin-tzu ch'üan-chi

(Collected works of Master Lin) Colophon, 1631. Preserved in Gest Memorial Library, Princeton University. Bound in 48 volumes, but the binding is arbitrary and often breaks in the middle of a work.

CONVENTIONS:
1. All titles from this collection will be indicated by the letter "L."
2. Each title will be numbered consecutively in arabic numerals: L:1, L:2.
3. When titles have appeared in earlier appendices, the reader will be referred to an earlier entry. Only new information will be given in this appendix.

All references in the book preceded by "L" are from this collection. Full cross-listing of titles is provided in appendix F. The page format of this edition differs from the 1606 edition (appendix C); the reader cannot rely on page references to the other edition when using this set.

L:1 *Lu t'an*. See V:1. (Same page format.)
L:2 *Tsung-mu* (General table of contents).
L:3 *Ssu-shu cheng-i (tsuan)*. See V:2–VI:4. Kyoto Daigaku Jinbun Kagaku Kenkyūjo contains this work in its 1606 *ch'üan-chi*. General discussion and six *chüan* of line-by-line commentaries.
L:4 *Tao-te ching shih-lüeh*. See IX:1–8.
L:5 *Ch'ang-ch'ing-ching ching shih-lüeh*. See X:10–11.
L:6 *Hsin ching shih-lüeh*. See X:6–7.

LIN-TZU CH'ÜAN-CHI 259

L:7 *Chin-kang ching t'ung-lun.* See X:1–5. Foreword, 1584.
L:8 *San-chiao yüan-pien.* See XI:1–XII:6, although titles differ. 1588 preface.
L:9 *Hsien-yen.* See III:2.
L:10 *San-chiao ching lüeh.* See I:5.
L:11 *Ju-ching.* See XVII:3. 1567 colophon; 1574 commentary.
L:12 *Hsing-hsin shih che-chu.* See IV:8.
L:13 *Hsing-hsin shih chüeh-chü.* See IV:7. Order is different. Variant title. 1559 colophon.
L:14 *(Lin-tzu) Lien-chü.* See IV:10.
L:15 *Chiu-kao.* See XIII:1–4.
L:16 *Hsü-kao.* See XIV:1–7.
L:17 *(Shu)-t'ien wen-kao* (Manuscripts of vows to heaven). 2 *ch.* Some overlap with XVI:3. 1561 colophon.
L:18 *Lin-tzu ch'üan-chi wen-lüeh* (Selections of the writings from Lin Tzu's collected works).
L:19 *Shu Liu Tseng erh-sheng chu-shih yü* (Reply to students Liu and Tseng). 4 *ch.* 1565.
L:20 *Ho-i ta-yao* (Essentials of integration). 1571.
L:21 *(Hsing-ling) Sung-chang.* See III:9.
L:22 *Fen-nei chi* (Collection on the world as my family). 12 *ch.* Preface 1627.
L:23 *Hsin-sheng chih-chih.* See II:1–3.
L:24 *San-chiao tao-t'ung chung-i ching.* See XVIII:9–11. 1631 preface.
L:25 *Wu-yen lu.* 2 *ch.* See XX:2–3, XX:5. 1626 preface.
L:26 *Cho hsiao-hsien shih* (Poems of Cho, the little immortal). See XX:4. Colophon 1612.
L:27 *Shih cha* (Ten letters). 1599.
L:28 *Hsing shih* (True record of actions of Master Lin). 38 pp.

APPENDIX F

Alphabetical List of Titles

Following is an alphabetical listing of the romanized titles of writings of Lin Chao-en included in the four collections studied for this book.

CONVENTIONS:
1. Entries of the form A:I, B:IV, etc., are from *Lin-tzu sheng-hsüeh t'ung-tsung san-chiao kuei-ju chi,* listed in appendix B.
2. Entries of the form I:1, II:7, X:10–12, etc., are from the 1606 *Lin-tzu ch'üan-chi,* listed in appendix C.
3. Entries of the form S:1, S:29a, etc., are from the *San-chiao cheng-tsung t'ung-lun,* listed in appendix D.
4. Entries of the form L:1, L:22, etc., are from the 1631 *Lin-tzu ch'üan-chi,* listed in appendix E.

Ch'ang-ch'ing-ching ching shih-lüeh, X:10–11, S:39, L:5.
Ch'ang-ming chiao, D:VIII, I:9, S:12.
Ch'ang-tao p'ien, XVIII:6, S:8.
Ch'ang-tao shu-ch'i t'iao-ta, S:29a.
Ch'ang-tao ta-chih, I:3, S:3.
Chen-wo ch'ang-yen, III:8, S:48.
Cheng-tsung yao lu, S:68.
Ch'i-ch'iao ta-wen, I:13, S:34.
Chiao-wai pieh-ch'uan, XVIII:3, S:36.
Ch'iao-yang chiao-yen, A:VI.
Ch'ih-chai pien-huo, IV:4, S:89.
Chin-kang ching kai-lun, S:40; same as the next entry.

LIST OF TITLES   261

Chin-kang ching t'ung-lun, X:1–5, L:7.
Ching-t'ien, XVII:12, S:25.
Chiu-hsü che-yen, XVI:1, S:28.
Chiu-kao, XIII:1–4, S:81, L:15.
Cho hsiao-hsien shih, L:26. Same as *Wu-yen lu*, ch. 3.
Chu-tai li chi t'u-shuo, D:III, XVII:10, S:21.
Ch'u-hsüeh p'ien, S:35.
Ch'üan-shih, IV:1, S:86.
Chung-i hsü-yen, S:63.
Ch'ung-li t'ang, D:VI, XVII:9, S:22.
Fei san-chiao, S:69.
Fen-che hsing-k'ung tsung-chih, XV:7–8, S:77.
Fen-che hsüan-tsung ta-tao, XV:5–6, S:76.
Fen-che sheng-hsüeh hsin-yao, S:75; same as the next entry.
Fen-che tsung-K'ung hsin-yao, XV:3–4, S:75.
Fen-nei chi, L:22.
Fen-nei chi fen-che pien-lan tzu-hsü, I:19.
Fo p'u-sa i, III:7, S:6.
Fu hsin ching shih-lun chiu-cheng hsiao-chien, X:9.
Ho-i ta-yao, L:20.
Ho-ssu ho-lü chieh, I:14, S:36a.
Hsia i, XIX:1–4.
Hsia-wu-ni pen-t'i ching, XX:8.
Hsia-yü (fu-hsü), XVI:7, S:9.
Hsien-hsing p'ien, XVIII:1, S:7.
Hsien-yen, III:1–2, S:32, L:9.
Hsin-ching chih-mi, A:V, I:7–8, S:10.
Hsin ching kai-lun, X:8, S:38.
Hsin ching shih-lüeh, X:6–7, S:37, L:6.
Hsin-nan p'ien, XVII:6, S:73.
Hsin pen-hsü chih-chih, II:6, S:84.
Hsin pen-hsü p'ien, II:5, S:83.
Hsin-shen hsing-ming t'u(-shuo), I:16, S:43.
Hsin-sheng chiao-yen, A:IV, I:20, S:31.
Hsin-sheng chih-chih, II:1–3, S:30, L:23.
Hsin-sheng t'u-shuo, I:17, S:42.
Hsin-sheng tzu-hsü, . . . *hsiao-hsü*, . . . *mu-lu*, A:I–III.
Hsin yao, S:45.
Hsing-hsin shih (chüeh-chü), IV:7, S:78, L:13.
Hsing-hsin shih che-chu, IV:8, S:79, L:12.
(Fen-che) Hsing-k'ung tsung-chih, XV:7–8, S:77.
Hsing-ling shih, S:64.

Hsing-ming jen-tan, XVIII:4.
Hsing-ming ta-yü, I:15, S:44.
Hsing shih, L:28.
Hsü-kao, XIV:1–7, S:82, L:16.
Hsü shih chen-hsin, XVIII:5, S:85.
(*Fen-che*) *Hsüan-tsung ta-tao*, XV:5–6, S:76.
Hsüeh-tao yao shen hsün-shih chu-sheng, XVI:2.
I chiao, D:IX.
I-chieh li-yü, S:72.
Ju-ching, XVII:3, L:11.
Ko-hsüeh chieh, D:IV, XVII:4, S:19.
Li-pen (*p'ien*), XVII:2, S:71.
Lien-chü, IV:10, S:80, L:14.
Lin Tzu, XVI:5–6, S:14.
Lin-tzu ch'üan-chi wen-lüeh, L:18.
Lin-tzu sheng-hsüeh t'ung-tsung tsung-hsü, D:X.
Liu mei t'iao ta, XVII:13, S:24.
Liu Po-tzu p'ien, D:I.
Lu t'an, V:1, L:1.
Meng-chung-jen, III:6, S:5.
Mi-le tsun-fo pao-ching, XX:7.
Ming-ching t'ang, D:VII, XVII:1, S:17.
Nien-ching pien-huo, IV:5, S:90.
Pen-t'i chiao, I:10, S:11.
P'o-mi, IV:3, S:87.
San-chiao cheng-tsung t'ung-lun tzu-hsü, S:a.
San-chiao ching lüeh, I:5, L:10.
San-chiao ho-i ta-chih, S:1.
San-chiao hui-pien yao-lüeh, XI:1–XII:6, S:52, S:56a, L:8.
San-chiao tao-t'ung chung-i ching, XVIII:7–11, L:24.
San-chiao wu-che ta-hui, I:18, S:47.
San-chiao yüan-pien, L:8, same as *San-chiao hui-pien*.
San-feng hsien-sheng (*hsüan ko hsüan t'an*), XX:6, S:66.
San-i chiao-chu Hsia-wu-ni pen-t'i ching, XX:8.
San-i chiao-chu shuo Mi-le tsun-fo pao-ching, XX:7.
San-kang kua, XVII:15, S:27.
Shan-jen, S:51.
Sheng-hsüeh t'ung-tsung hsü, D:XI.
Shih cha, L:27.
Shih ch'u-shih fa, S:70.
Shih-wen lang-t'an, XVII:5, S:18.
Shu Liu Tseng erh-sheng chu-shih yü, L:19.

Shu-sheng, B:I.
Shu-t'ien wen-kao, XVI:3, S:29, L:17.
Shuo hsia, I:6.
Ssu-shu cheng-i (*tsuan*), V:2–VI:4, L:3.
Ssu-shu cheng-i hsü, VII:1–VIII:2, S:55–62.
Ssu-yin yü, I:12, S:41.
Sung-chang, III:9, L:21.
T'an-ching hsün-shih, XVIII:2.
Tao-ho yü-t'an, XVII:14, S:26.
Tao Shih jen-lun shu-kao, S:23.
Tao-te ching shih-lüeh, IX:1–8, S:91, L:4.
Tao-t'ung lun, S:65.
Tao yeh cheng-i p'ien, S:49.
Tiao-ku wen-wu li she t'u-shuo, D:V, XVII:11, S:20.
T'ien jen i-ch'i, S:46.
Ts'un-ch'u chi hsü, I:2.
(*Lin-tzu*) *Ts'un-ch'u tsung-chi hsü*, I:1.
Ts'un-hsing kuei-t'iao, D:II, XVII:7–8, S:33.
(*Fen-che*) *Tsung-hsüan ta-tao*, XV:5–6, S:76.
Tsung-K'ung t'ang, S:15.
Tu-shih, S:50.
Tzu-shu Ssu-yin yü chüan-tuan, I:11, S:51a.
Wu ch'ieh-pu-k'o shih-chieh chu-sheng, XVI:4.
Wu-sheng fen-che pien-lan, II:7.
Wu-sheng p'ien, II:8–10, S:74.
Wu-yen lu, XX:1–5, S:67, L:25.
Yü-chang hsü-yü, C:II, XV:2, S:54.
Yü-chang ta-wen (or: *ta-yü*), C:I, XV:1, S:53.
Yü jen p'ien, I:21, S:16.
Yü-yen, IV:2, S:88.
Yüan-chiao, S:13.
Yüan-shen shih-i, III:3–5, S:4.
Yüan-tsung t'u (*shuo*), I:4, S:2.

ABBREVIATIONS AND CONVENTIONS

Conventions used to indicate standard editions of Chinese works:

SPPY *Ssu-pu pei-yao* (Shanghai: Chung-hua shu-chü, 1927–1935)
SPTK *Ssu-pu ts'ung-k'an* (Shanghai: Commercial Press, 1922)
TSCC *Ts'ung-shu chi-ch'eng* (Shanghai: Commercial Press, 1932)

Conventions used to refer to works from the Buddhist and Taoist canons:

T *Taishō shinshū daizōkyō* (Tokyo, 1914–1922)
The *Harvard Yenching Index* gives both a serial number for each work and a volume under which it may be found in the canon. Page references will be cited with the *volume* number. References to works as a whole without specific pagination will give volume and serial numbers.

TT *Tao Tsang* (1963 and 1923 reeditions of the Ming edition)
The *Harvard Yenching Index* provides the *ts'e* number(s) for each work, which are printed on the back of the boxes. The beginning of each *ts'e* lists all works contained in order. Page references for single-*chüan* works will immediately follow the TT. number; for multi-*chüan* works, the TT. number will be followed by *chüan* and page numbers.

Conventions used to refer to writings of Lin Chao-en:

A:I, B:I, C:III, etc. are from the *Lin-tzu sheng-hsüeh t'ung-tsung san-chiao kuei-ju chi*. See appendix B.
I:1, IV:8, XII:3, etc. refer to the 1606 *Lin-tzu ch'üan-chi*. See appendix C.
S:1, S:29a, etc., refer to *San-chiao cheng-tsung t'ung-lun*. See appendix D.
L:1, L:22, etc., refer to the 1631 *Lin-tzu ch'üan-chi*. See appendix E.

NOTES

PREFACE
1. Gerardus Van der Leeuw, *Religion in Essence and Manifestation: A Study in Phenomenology*, trans. J. E. Turner (New York: Macmillan, 1938), p. 610.

I. THE PROBLEM WITH SYNCRETISM
1. William E. Soothill, *Three Religions of China: Lectures Delivered at Oxford* (London: Oxford University Press, H. Milford, 1923), p. 13.
2. *The Christian Message in a Non-Christian World*, with a foreword by His Grace the Archbishop of New York (London: Edinburgh House, for the International Missionary Council, 1938), p. 201.
3. Hajime Nakamura, *The Ways of Thinking of Eastern Peoples: India, China, Tibet, Japan*, revised English translation, ed. Philip B. Wiener (Honolulu: East-West Center Press, 1964), pp. 290–94; citation from p. 293. Henri Maspero, *Les Religions Chinoises* (Paris: Presses Universitaire de France, 1967), pp. 111–38. Ch'ing-k'un (C. K.) Yang, *Religion in Chinese Society: A Study of Contemporary Social Functions of Religion and Some of Their Historical Factors* (Berkeley: University of California Press, 1961), p. 25 and pp. 123–26. For a critique of general theories about Chinese syncretism and a discussion of the syncretic point of view, see Wing-tsit Chan, *Religious Trends in Modern China*, The Haskell Lectures at the University of Chicago, 1950 (New York: Columbia University Press, 1953), pp. 178–83.
4. See, for instance, Soothill, *Three Religions*, pp. 11–12.
5. Chu Hsi, T. (Tzu) Yüan-hui, posthumous title, Wen-kung; b. Fukien. *Sung shih* (History of Sung) (Wu-chou: T'ung-wen shu-chü, 1903), 419.1a. For a biographical sketch in English, see Wing-tsit Chan, trans. and annotator, *Reflections on Things at Hand: The Neo-Confucian Anthology compiled*

by *Chu Hsi and Lü Tsu-ch'ien* (New York: Columbia University Press, 1967), xxxvi–xxxix.

6. See Liu Ts'un-yan, "Taoist Self-Cultivation in Ming Thought," in Wm. Theodore de Bary and the Conference on Ming Thought, *Self and Society in Ming Thought* (New York: Columbia University Press, 1970), p. 312 and n. 52. Also see Sakai Tadao, "Shushi to dōkyō" (Chu Hsi and Taoism) in *Shushigaku nyūmon* (Introduction to Chu Hsi studies), Shushigaku taikei, no. 1, ed. Abe Yoshio (Tokyo: Meitoku shuppansha, 1974), pp. 411–26, esp. 413–23. Chu Hsi's *Chou-i ts'an t'ung ch'i chu* (Notes to the Homology of the triad of the Chou *Changes*), 3 *chüan*, is found in TT. 623. The *Yin-fu ching k'ao-i* (Researches on the book of spirit charms) is in the *Chu-tzu i-shu* (Surviving works of Master Chu), 25 *ch.* in 12 vols. (Taipei: I-wen yin-shu kuan, 1969; based on K'ang-hsi [1662–1722], ed. of Pao-kao t'ang), last item. *T'iao-hsi chen* (Exhortations on breath control) is contained in *Chu-tzu wenchi* (Collected literary works of Master Chu) (SPPY ed.), 85.6a. As Nathan Sivin has noted in his stimulating article, it is not at all clear that breath control or the writings of Han alchemists, such as the *Chou-i ts'an t'ung ch'i*, can be labeled "Taoist" in any meaningful sense. It cannot be demonstrated that persons associated with these were Taoist, nor that the ideas originated among Taoists. On the other hand, it is true that Sung intelligentsia associated breath control and alchemy with "superstitious" Taoism, and hence it is significant that Chu Hsi, the great defender of Confucianism against Buddhist and Taoist excesses, studied these so-called "Taoist" works. See Nathan Sivin, "On the word 'Taoist' as a Source of Perplexity: With Special Reference to the Relations of Science and Religion in Traditional China," *History of Religions* 17 (Feb.-May 1978): 303–30, esp. 318–28.

7. *Encyclopedia of Religion and Ethics* (1913–27), s.v. "Syncretism." Some modern studies have transcended this view to explore syncretism in a more positive way. See, for instance, Sven Hartman, ed., *Syncretism*, based on papers read at the Symposium on Cultural Contact, Meeting of Religions, Syncretism, held at Åbo on Sept. 8–10, 1966, included in Scripta Instituti Donneriani Aboensis (Stockholm: Almqvist and Wiksell, 1976). However, the view of syncretism as "at the expense of truth" has prevailed in the work of such an eminent scholar as Richard Gombrich, whose view will be discussed in this chapter (see n. 8). Moreover, as we shall see later in the chapter, Robert Baird denies the meaningfulness of the category for religious studies, claiming that if real harmony between religions was achieved *without inconsistencies* (italics mine), the word "synthesis" would be more suitable than "syncretism." Baird, *Category Formation and the History of Religions*, Religion and Reason, no. 1 (The Hague: Mouton, 1971), pp. 142–52.

8. Richard Gombrich, *Precept and Practice: Traditional Buddhism in the Rural Highlands of Ceylon* (Oxford, Eng.: Clarendon Press, 1971), pp. 45–50.
9. *Encyclopedia of Religion and Ethics*, s.v. "Syncretism."
10. Baird, *Category Formation*, pp. 142–52.
11. Ibid., p. 145.

12. Intention is not meant to suggest private psychological motivations to which the researcher has no access. By "intention" I mean the meaning and significance of syncretism, the function it has in the life and thought of the syncretist, and its aims and goals, insofar as these may be deduced from the statements, ideas, and practices of the syncretist.

13. Helmer Ringgren, "The Problem with Syncretism," in Hartman, ed., *Syncretism*, pp. 1–9.

14. Frederick J. Streng, *Understanding Religious Life*, The Religious Life of Man Series, 2d ed. (Enrico, Cal.: Dickenson, 1976), pp. 1–9.

15. Carl Gustav Diehl, "Replacement or Substitution in the Meeting of Religions," in Hartman, ed., *Syncretism*, pp. 149–59.

16. Gerardus Van der Leeuw, *Religion in Essence and Manifestation: A Study in Phenomenology*, trans. J. E. Turner (New York: Macmillan, 1938), p. 610.

17. Syncretists differ widely in the sophistication of their conceptualization of borrowed elements, and sometimes they seriously impoverish the meaning of the ideas they borrow. Scholars will make judgments as to whether an instance of syncretism has enriched the tradition or introduced more problems than it solved. However, such judgments must be made in light of a full understanding of the problems which the syncretist sought to solve; the religious as well as the philosophical meaning of syncretism must be understood before the "success" of syncretism may be adequately evaluated. By "misunderstanding" or "impoverishing" an idea or practice, the syncretist might ingeniously alleviate a spiritual problem which he or she faces.

II. SYNCRETISM AND SECTARIANISM IN EARLY CHINA

1. For a broad historical outline, the reader is referred to classics by Asian scholars: Tokiwa Daijō, *Shina ni okeru bukkyō to jukyō, dōkyō* (Buddhism, Confucianism, and Taoism in China), Tōyō bunko ronsō, no. 13 (Tokyo: Tōyō bunko, 1930); Kubota Ryōon, *Shina judōbutsu kōshōshi* (The history of interactions of Chinese Confucianism, Taoism, and Buddhism) (Tokyo: Daitō, 1943). Also worthy of note, although they are not comprehensive histories of all three teachings, are: Yoshioka Yoshitoyo, *Dōkyō to bukkyō* (Taoism and Buddhism), 2 vols. and cont. (Tokyo: Toshima shobō, 1959, 1970, resp.); Araki Kengo, *Bukkyō to jukyō* (Buddhism and Confucianism) (Kyoto: Heirakuji shoten, 1972); Jao Tsung-i, "San-chiao lun yü Sung Chin hsüeh-shu" (The Three Teachings theory and scholarship in the Sung and Chin), *Tung-hsi wen-hua* 11 (May 1968):24–32.

2. *Analects* 7:1. Translation follows Wing-tsit Chan, trans. and comp., *A Source Book in Chinese Philosophy* (Princeton: Princeton University Press, 1963), p. 31.

3. Herbert Fingarette has proposed a suggestive explanation of the at-

traction and significance of *li* for Confucius. *Confucius—the Secular as Sacred* (New York: Harper and Row, 1972), esp. pp. 1–17.

4. Michel Strickmann of the University of California at Berkeley contends that Taoism as a tradition does not properly begin until the Han dynasty. There is merit to this view, particularly in terms of defining a *religious* tradition. In Han Taoism patterns emerged of ritual and meditation, of revelation and authority, and of religious praxis which evolved through the centuries. However, Lao Tzu (and to a lesser extent Chuang Tzu) remained important patriarchs within Taoism. Moreover, they were the Taoists through which outsiders (Confucians and Buddhists) were most often introduced to the tradition. Lao Tzu and Chuang Tzu, then, both belonged to the tradition and stood apart from it as Taoist thinkers for the non-Taoists. Interpretations of these two differ markedly, depending in part on whether they are seen in the light of evolving Taoist religious thought or in light of more general Chinese thought.

5. Even the name Lao Tzu tells us little, since it merely means "old master." Eiichi Kimura has attempted to reconcile the diverse and conflicting legends to deduce the sort of person Lao Tzu may have been. "A New Study on Lao Tzu," *Philosophical Studies in Japan* 1 (1959):85–104.

6. See Burton Watson, trans., *Chuang Tzu: Basic Writings* (New York: Columbia University Press, 1964), introduction, pp. 1–3.

7. Although it has been traditionally thought of as a Taoist term, Herrlee G. Creel has argued that its origins were Legalist. "On the Origin of *Wu-wei*," in *What is Taoism? and Other Studies in Chinese Cultural History* (Chicago: University of Chicago Press, 1970), originally published in *Symposium in Honor of Dr. Li Chi on his Seventieth Birthday* (Taipei: Ch'ing-hua hsüeh-pao she, 1965), part 1, pp. 48–78.

8. Dim Cheuk (D.C.) Lau, trans., *Lao Tzu, Tao te ching* (Middlesex, Eng. and Baltimore, Md.: Penguin Books, 1963), chap. 37, p. 96.

9. *Analects* 15:4; translation adapted from Chan, *Source Book*, p. 43.

10. See Fingarette, *Confucius—the Secular as Sacred*, pp. 1–17.

11. The traditional Chinese tendency to see all reality as one whole led them to stress the similarities rather than the differences between two things or ideas. In general, Western thought seeks to define each thing *over against* others so as to establish its distinctive identity. The tendency in Chinese thought is to relate each thing to others, identifying the rich suggestivity and relatedness of the thing. Thus they are much more tolerant of ideas which are partly true, or true in one sense. It is not that they do not recognize what is untrue, but that they tend to focus on the aspects which are true.

12. "Five Phases" (*wu hsing*) is often translated Five Agents or Five Elements. I am following Nathan Sivin and Manfred Porkert, who argue that these are not elements (material constituents of reality) but phases in the evolution of vital force (*ch'i*), each phase governed by certain forces and associations. See Manfred Porkert, *The Theoretical Foundations of Chinese Medicine: Systems of Correspondence* (Cambridge: MIT Press, 1974), introduction.

II. SYNCRETISM AND SECTARIANISM 269

13. For a fuller discussion of Han correspondences, see Fung Yu-lan, *A History of Chinese Philosophy*, 2 vols., trans. Derk Bodde (Princeton: Princeton University Press, 1952–53), 1:379–99, 2:1–32.

14. The *Ts'an t'ung ch'i* was traditionally attributed to Wei Po-yang, but may in fact have been the work of several compilers. There is a less than adequate English translation by Lu-ch'iang Wu, "An ancient Chinese treatise on alchemy, entitled Ts'an t'ung ch'i, written by Wei Po-yang about 142 A.D., now translated into English by Lu-ch'iang Wu, with introduction and notes by Tenney L. Davis," *Isis* n.s. 18 (1932):210–89. There is a new Japanese translation by Honda Wataru which I have not yet seen.

15. From Chih-i's commentary to *Jen-wang ching* (Sutra on the benevolent ruler), *Hsü Tsang-ching* (Continuation of the Tripitaka) I.40.4.376a–b; translation is adapted to fit the conventions of this book from Kenneth K. S. Ch'en, *The Chinese Transformation of Buddhism* (Princeton: Princeton University Press, 1973), p. 57. To distinguish the Five Phases from the ordinary materials which share the same name, I capitalize them. The phase Wood represents a phase in the evolution of vital force governed by wood-like attributes; it has nothing to do with wood per se.

16. Mou Tzu, *Li-huo lun* (Discussion of doubts) in *P'ing-chin-kuan ts'ung-shu* (Collections of the P'ing-chin hall) (1884 pref.) 1.15a–b; cited from Erik Zürcher, *The Buddhist Conquest of China: The Spread and Adaptation of Buddhism in Early Medieval China*, 2 vols. (Leiden: E. J. Brill, 1959), p. 13. The *Li-huo lun* was translated by Paul Pelliot, "Meou Tse ou les Doutes Levés," *T'oung Pao* 19 (1920):255–433; excerpts were translated into English in Wing-tsit Chan et al., comps., *The Great Asian Religions: An Anthology* (New York: Macmillan, 1969), pp. 182–84.

17. For a fuller discussion of the assimilation of Buddhism in China, see Zürcher, *Buddhist Conquest*, and Ch'en, *Transformation of Buddhism*.

18. On the *hua-hu* controversy, see Zürcher, *Buddhist Conquest*, pp. 290–320; Wang Wei-ch'eng, "Lao Tzu hua-hu shuo k'ao-cheng" (Researches on the theory of Lao Tzu converting the barbarians) *Kuo-hsüeh chi-k'an* 4, no. 2 (1934):1–222; Joseph Thiel, "Der Streit der Buddhisten und Taoisten zur Mongolenzeit," *Monumenta Serica* 20 (1961):1–81; T'ang Yung-t'ung, *Hsi-yü, Han-Wei liang-Chin Nan-pei ch'ao fo-chiao shih* (History of Buddhism in Han, Wei, the two Chins, and the North-South dynasties) 2 vols. (Taipei: Sheng-wu yin-shu-kuan, 1965; rpt. of Shanghai, 1938 ed.), 1:42–44, 75–81.

19. *Kuang hung-ming chi* (Broad collection of the expansion of enlightenment) 30 *ch.*, ed. Tao-hsüan, T.52.136–43. Both Kubota (*Kōshōshi*, p. 152) and Wang Wei-ch'eng ("Hua-hu shuo," p. 37) verify that the author of this essay lived during the Northern Chou, but I have been unable to identify a Tao-an of that period.

20. His method was called *p'an-chiao* (classification of doctrines). See Kenneth K. S. Ch'en, *Buddhism in China: A Historical Survey* (Princeton: Princeton University Press, 1964), pp. 303–13. Biography of Chih-i in *Hsü Kao-seng chuan* (Continued biographies of eminent monks), 30 *ch.*, ed. Tao-hsüan, T.50.562c–68a.

21. Tokiwa, *Shina ni okeru*, pp. 643–45.

22. Shigematsu Shunshō discusses a group of farcical Three Teachings dramas and gives the text of one which has been preserved. "Shina sankyōshi jō no jakan no mondai" (Certain problems regarding the history of the Three Teachings in China) *Shien* 21 (1939):138, 155.

23. Shigematsu, "Jakan no mondai," p. 134. Po Chü-i, T. Lo-t'ien, H. (Hao) Yüan-pai, was a native of Hsin-chen, Honan. *T'ang shu* (History of T'ang) (Shanghai: K'ai-ming shu-tien, 1935), 3511.4. For a biographical sketch in English, see Arthur Waley, *The Life and Times of Po Chü-i, 722–846 A.D.* (London: Allen and Unwin, 1951). Po was renowned as a poet and essayist. Jonathan Winthrop Haeger has argued that the Three Teachings debates had degenerated into ridicule and amusement; given this situation, he continues, Sung syncretism had to be diachronic, returning to older ideas, rather than synchronic. "The Intellectual Context of Neo-Confucian Syncretism," *Journal of Asian Studies* 31 (1972):499–513. Such an argument fails to appreciate the way in which the atmosphere of competition in the T'ang had stimulated mutual knowledge and influence among the Three Teachings.

24. Shigematsu, "Jakan no mondai," p. 151.

25. *Ch'ang-li hsien-sheng chi* (Collected works of Han Yü) 40 *ch.*, ed. Li Han (SPPY ed.) 39.3a–5b, translated in Wm. Theodore de Bary et al., *Sources of Chinese Tradition*, 2 vol. paperback ed. (New York: Columbia University Press, 1964) 1:372–74. Han Yü, T. T'ui-chih, H. Ch'ang-li, was from Ch'ang-li in present-day Ling-yüan county of Chihli. Han Yü was a superb prose stylist and one of the forerunners of the Neo-Confucian movement. See *T'ang shu*, 160.3496.2.

26. *Yüan-jen lun* (On the original nature of man) T.45.708a; cited from Wm. Theodore de Bary et al., *The Buddhist Tradition in India, China, and Japan* (New York: Modern Library, 1969), p. 181. For a biography of Tsung-mi, see *Sung Kao-seng chuan* (Sung biographies of eminent monks), T.50.741c–43a.

III. THE HEYDAY OF SYNCRETISM

1. Shigematsu Shunshō, "Shina sankyōshi jō no jakan no mondai" (Certain problems regarding the history of the Three Teachings in China) *Shien* 21 (1939):125–52.

2. See, for instance, Kenneth K. S. Ch'en, *Buddhism in China: A Historical Survey* (Princeton: Princeton University Press, 1964), whose section on Sung and post-Sung Buddhism is entitled "Decline." Yü Chün-fang (Kristin Greenblatt) has argued against this view, seeing the lay Buddhist movement as a positive development in its own right. "Yün-ch'i Chu-hung: The Career of a Ming Buddhist Monk" (Ph.D. diss., Columbia University, 1973), published as *The Renewal of Buddhism in China* (New York: Columbia University Press, 1980).

3. On Pure Land Buddhism and Amitābha's vow, see Wm. Theodore de

III. THE HEYDAY OF SYNCRETISM 271

Bary et al., *Sources of Chinese Tradition*, 2 vol. paperback ed. (New York: Columbia University Press, 1964), 1:334–46.

4. Yü Chün-fang, "Yün-ch'i Chu-hung," pp. 79–80, 123.

5. Philip B. Yampolsky, *The Platform Sutra of the Sixth Patriarch: The Text of the Tun-huang Manuscript with Translation, Introduction, and Notes* (New York: Columbia University Press, 1967), pp. 158–59. Hui-neng was a native of Hsin-hsing, southwest of Canton. See *Kao-seng chuan* (Biographies of eminent monks), ed. Hui-chiao, T.50.8.754–55; *Ching-te ch'uan-teng lu* (Record of the transmission of the lamp), comp. Tao-yüan of the Sung (SPTK ed.), 5.3a–5b.

6. Wang An-shih, T. Chieh-fu, from Fu-chou, Lin-ch'üan. See *Sung shih* (History of Sung) (Wu-chou: T'ung-wen shu-chü, 1903), 327.1a.

7. For a fuller discussion, see Wing-tsit Chan, "Chu Hsi's Completion of Neo-Confucianism," in Françoise Aubin, ed., *Études Song in memoriam Étienne Balazs*, ser. 3, no. 1 (The Hague: Mouton, 1973), pp. 59–90.

8. On the balance between the inner and outer aspects of self-cultivation see Benjamin Schwartz, "Some Polarities in Confucian Thought," in David S. Nivison and Authur F. Wright, eds., *Confucianism in Action* (Stanford: Stanford University Press, 1959), pp. 50–62. On the tension between quietism and activism, see Wm. Theodore de Bary, "Introduction," in *Self and Society in Ming Thought* (New York: Columbia University Press, 1970), pp. 15–19.

9. See Wm. Theodore de Bary, "Neo-Confucian Cultivation and the Seventeenth-Century 'Enlightenment,' " in idem and the Conference on Seventeenth-Century Chinese Thought, *The Unfolding of Neo-Confucianism* (New York: Columbia University Press, 1975), pp. 160–62.

10. He was "centered" in the sense that one centers clay on a potter's wheel: hence in equilibrium, balanced, in harmony. The Mean, which carries all the above connotations, is the focus of *The Doctrine of the Mean* (*Chung-yung*), one of the Confucian Four Books. *Wei-fa chih chung* is from *The Mean*, 1. See James Legge, *The Four Books: Confucian Analects, The Great Learning, The Doctrine of the Mean, and the Works of Mencius* (New York: Paragon, 1966; unaltered reprint of Shanghai, 1923 ed.), p. 351. For a modern study of this Confucian classic, see Tu Wei-ming, *Centrality and Commonality: An Essay on Chung-yung*, Monograph 3 of the Society for Asian and Comparative Philosophy (Honolulu: University Press of Hawaii, 1976).

11. On the Diagram of the Great Ultimate and its Neo-Confucian commentary, see Fung Yu-lan, *A History of Chinese Philosophy*, 2 vols., trans. Derk Bodde (Princeton: Princeton University Press, 1952–53), 2:434–51. The diagram and its place in the system of mind-cultivation of Lin Chao-en will be discussed in chapter five.

12. Ch'en T'uan, (fl. 956–984), a forerunner of Inner Alchemy Taoism, is credited as being a major figure in the transmission of the diagram to Chou Tun-i (1017–1073). See Tokiwa Daijō, *Shina ni okeru bukkyō to jukyō, dokyō* (Buddhism, Confucianism, and Taoism in China), Tōyō bunko ronsō, no. 13 (Tokyo: Tōyō bunko, 1930), pp. 664–65, and Fung Yu-lan, *Chinese*

Philosophy, 2:440–41. As shall be discussed in chapter five, the internal evidence of the chart supports the theory of its Taoist origins.

13. *Chin-ssu lu*, 14 *ch.*, ed. Chang Po-hsing (SPPY ed.), 13.2b; cited from Ch'eng I, *I-shu* (Surviving works) (SPPY ed.), 2A.9b. Translation adapted from Wing-tsit Chan, trans. and annotator, *Reflections on Things at Hand: The Neo-Confucian Anthology Compiled by Chu Hsi and Lü Tsu-ch'ien* (New York: Columbia University Press, 1967), p. 283. (Hereafter referred to as Chan, *Reflections*).

14. Julia Ching, "The Goose Lake Monastery Debate," *Journal of Chinese Philosophy* 1 (1974):161–78, esp. pp. 170–71. Lu Hsiang-shan, T. Chiu-yüan, was a native of Chin-ch'i, in present-day Kiangsi. *Sung shih*, 434.9b. For an account of his life, see Siu-chi Huang, *Lu Hsiang-shan, a Twelfth Century Chinese Idealist Philosopher* (New Haven: American Oriental Society, 1944), pp. 12–17.

15. The thesis of the Confucian and loyalist origins of the founders of Inner Alchemy has been advanced by Ch'en Yüan, "Nan-Sung ch'u Ho-pei hsin tao-chiao k'ao" (Researches on the new Taoism in Hopei in the early Southern Sung), *Fu-jen ta-hsüeh ts'ung-shu* 8 (1941), entire issue.

A word may be useful at this point concerning in what sense the new Taoism is new and in what sense it is Taoism. Many of the practices and ideas which came to form the core of Inner Alchemy had long roots in the Chinese past. In the T'ang and early Sung these elements were beginning to coalesce. For instance, the Diagram of the Great Ultimate may be traced backward from Ch'en T'uan, who lived in the early Sung, into the T'ang. However, the "founders" of Inner Alchemy fused these elements into a more systematic doctrine and praxis, establishing schools and transmissions. In addition, unless further research discredits Ch'en Yüan's hypothesis, these "founders" (given their Confucian educations) disassociated themselves from what they considered to be the errors of some Taoists and sought to establish the true Way. As we shall see below, many of the ritual and theistic elements which they sought to exclude were later reincorporated. Were they Taoist? The issue is particularly complex in terms of the forerunners of the tradition, such as Ch'en T'uan. If Ch'en was an initiated Taoist, I am unaware of it. Perhaps precisely because of the "loose" connections these figures had with formal Taoism, interaction between men like Ch'en and Chou Tun-i was possible. On the other hand, although the founders and their disciples were not initiated in liturgical Taoism, they established a tradition which is Taoist in some senses: (1) they identified themselves as Taoists; (2) they revered Lao Tzu and the *Tao-te ching* as sources of authority; and (3) they saw themselves as the true transmission of the Way. Then again, their rejection of certain "Taoist excesses" gave them a broader basis for dialogue with Confucians and Buddhists.

In terms of the present study, Inner Alchemy is also Taoist in the sense that Lin Chao-en viewed this school as the correct transmission of the Taoist way. To be more precise, he saw *certain* transmissions within the Inner Alchemy school as the revival of the Way of Lao Tzu.

III. THE HEYDAY OF SYNCRETISM 273

On Wang Che, H. Ch'ung-yang, see Ch'en Yüan, "Hsin tao-chiao k'ao," pp. 11–17; Tokiwa, Shina ni okeru, pp. 679–83; Kubota Ryōon, Shina judōbutsu kōshōshi (The history of interactions of Chinese Confucianism, Taoism, and Buddhism) (Tokyo: Daitō, 1943), pp. 267–69 (hereafter referred to as Kubota, Kōshōshi). Biography in Chin-lien chen-tsung hsien-yüan hsiang-chuan (Biographies of immortals in the true school of the golden lotus), by Liu T'ien-su and Hsieh Hsi-ch'an (Yüan dynasty), TT.76.5.18a.

16. The oral secret (k'ou-chüeh) was the mechanism of transmission in Taoism; the master would teach certain esoteric truths only to those disciples who he felt were ready to carry on his line. These teachings did not always remain secret, however, for long strings of "oral transmissions," pithy statements of doctrine attributed to famous teachers, were included in Ming Taoist works. See, for instance, Yin Chen-jen, Hsing-ming shuang-hsiu wan-shen kuei-chih (Revealed doctrine of the dual cultivation of nature and life store taught by the myriad spirits), 4 ch. (1615 preface), 2.11a–16a. The same term was also used in Buddhism. Lü Tung-pin, personal name Yen, was said to be from Tung-p'ing county, Shensi. For a biography, see Chin-lien chen-tsung hsien-yüan hsiang-chuan, TT.76.5.15a, and Li-shih chen-hsien t'i-tao t'ung-chien (General mirror of true immortals who embodied the Way throughout the generations), 53 ch., by Chao Tao-i of the Yüan, TT.139–48.45.1a.

17. He recommended the Hsiao-ching (Classic of filial piety), the Tao-te ching of Lao Tzu, and the Ch'ang-ch'ing-ching ching (Book of constant purity and quiescence), TT.341. Kubota, Kōshōshi, pp. 268–69.

18. Ko Hung, T. Chih-ch'uan, from Tan-yang, near modern Nanking. For a translation of his autobiography, see James R. Ware, trans., Alchemy, Medicine, and Religion in the China of A.D. 320: The Nei P'ien of Ko Hung (Pao-p'u tzu) (Cambridge: MIT Press, 1966), pp. 6–21. T'ao Hung-ching, T. T'ung-ming, was from Mo-ling in present-day Kiangsu. Liang shu (Book of Liang) (Shanghai: K'ai-ming shu-tien, 1935), 51.1835.3.

19. Over the course of time the Inner Alchemy school began to reincorporate elements from the ritual tradition, particularly during the Yüan dynasty when the Mongol rulers were interested in rites and magic. See Ch'en Yüan, "Hsin tao-chiao k'ao," pp. 34–63. During the Ming, Inner Alchemy Taoism was absorbed by the Cheng-i (correct and single) sect. See Tokiwa, Shina ni okeru, pp. 700–8. The relation between Inner Alchemy and earlier strains of ritual Taoism deserves much more detailed research.

20. See Yoshioka Yoshitoyo, Eisei e no negai (The search for long life), Sekai no shūkyō, no. 9 (Kyoto: Tankōkai, 1970), p. 162. Po Yü-ch'an, H. Hai-ch'iung, original name Ko Ch'ang-keng, was from Min-ch'ing county, Fukien. See Li-shih chen-hsien t'i-tao t'ung-chien, TT.139–48.49.16b ff.

21. See, for example, Hai-ch'iung Po Chen-jen yü-lu (The recorded sayings of Realized Man Po Hai-ch'iung), 4 ch., ed. Hsieh Hsien-tao, TT.1016.3.5a, 3.12b–13a.

22. Hsiao T'ien-shih, Tao-chia yang-sheng-hsüeh kai-yao (Essentials of

274   III. THE HEYDAY OF SYNCRETISM

Taoist theories of nurturing life), 2d ed. (Taipei: Tzu-yu ch'u-pan-she, 1971), pp. 128–30.

23. *Chiao-wai ming-yen*, in *Chung-ho chi* (Collection on equilibrium and harmony), 6 *ch.*, ed. Ts'ai Chih-i, TT. 118–19.6.23b.

24. Production (*tsao*); transformation (*hua*). *Tsao-hua* as a compound for creation goes back to *Chuang Tzu*, 6. These terms are used in a technical sense in this essay. *Tsao* is movement from Nonbeing to Being, roughly equivalent to Buddhist *sheng* (arising). *Hua* is movement from Being to Nonbeing, roughly equivalent to Buddhist *mieh* (extinction). Explained by Li Tao-ch'un, *Chiao-wai ming-yen*, *Chung-ho chi* 6.12b. The citation is from 6.23b.

25. T'ien-t'ai Buddhists taught insight in contemplation (*kuan*) and concentration in stopping thoughts (*chih*). For a fuller discussion, see Fung Yu-lan, *Chinese Philosophy*, 2:368–86, and Lu K'uan-yü, *The Secrets of Chinese Meditation: Self-cultivation by Mind Control as taught in the Ch'an, Mahāyāna, and Taoist Schools in China* (London: Rider, 1964), pp. 109–62.

26. Dust of mental objects (*fa-ch'en*; Sanskrit, *guṇa*): the qualities of objects which give rise to defilements of the mind.

27. The double obstructions of things (*shih*) and their principles (*li*) was discussed in *Yüan-chüeh ching* (Sutra of original enlightenment), T. 17.916b. See also Mochizuki Shinkō, *Mochizuki bukkyō daijiten* (The Mochizuki dictionary of Buddhism), 10 vols. (Tokyo: Sekai shoten kankō, 1958–63).

28. "Wisdom of judgment" (*chüeh-tuan*) refers to judgments about things and their principles, a true understanding of the causation of things.

29. *Chiao-wai ming-yen*, *Chung-ho chi*, 6.23b–24b.

30. The process of yogic transmutation in Inner Alchemy will be discussed more fully in chapter five.

31. "Wisdom sword" (*hui-chien*) is the firm and decisive mind unseduced by objects, the centered and ruled will undeluded by objects. It is able to cut off passions and vexations and to chase away evil spirits. Fire talismans had ritual functions in sectarian Taoism; they were used to drive off evil spirits. Here they are used to dissipate desires. The six desires arise from birth, death, eye, ear, mouth, and nose.

32. *Chiao-wai ming-yen*, *Chung-ho chi*, 6.24b–25a.

33. See *Chuang Tzu*, 6, 14, and 19, translated in Burton Watson, trans., *The Complete Works of Chuang Tzu* (New York: Columbia University Press, 1968), pp. 90–91, 155, 205–7, respectively.

34. Ch'eng Hao, T. Po-ch'un, H. Ming-tao, from Honan. *Sung shih*, 427.4b; *I-Lo yüan-yüan lu* (Record of the origins of the school of the two Ch'engs) by Chu Hsi (Cheng-i t'ang ed.), 2.1a. For a brief English biography, see Chan, *Reflections*, xxix–xxx.

35. *Ming-tao wen-chi* (Collected literary works of Ch'eng Hao), 59 *ch.* (SPPY ed.), 3.1a–1b, translated in Chan, *Reflections*, p. 41.

36. "Settled" (*ting*) of the *Great Learning:* "The object of pursuit is determined." See Legge, *Four Books*, p. 309. Because Li Tao-ch'un interpreted the word as a mental state allowing one to forget things, I have rendered it as "settled."

III. THE HEYDAY OF SYNCRETISM 275

37. *I ching,* Judgment to the *ken* hexagram. See Richard Wilhelm, trans., *The I Ching or Book of Changes,* trans. into English by Cary F. Baynes, corrected 3d ed. with a foreword by C.G. Jung and preface by Hellmut Wilhelm, Bollingen Series, 19 (Princeton: Princeton University Press, 1968), pp. 652–53. (Hereafter referred to as Wilhelm/Baynes, *I ching.*)

38. *Chiao-wai ming-yen, Chung-ho chi,* 6.25a–25b.

39. This is the argument put forward by Araki Kengo, "Confucianism and Buddhism in the Late Ming," in de Bary, *Unfolding,* pp. 40–41. Araki is discussing Sung principle from the standpoint of Ming Neo-Confucians of the School of Mind; Sung principle was not quite as immutable as he suggests, but Ming Neo-Confucians (and perhaps Sung Buddhists and Taoists) seem to have understood it to be so.

40. From the *Yü-chih wen-chi* (Collection of imperial compositions), included in *Chin-ling fan-ch'a chih* (Record of temples in Nanking), ed. Ko Yin-liang (Nanking: photoreproduction of Seng-lü k'an-pen, 1936; originally published by the Nanking Central Buddhist Registry in 1627), ch. 1. The essay is quite obscure and does not lend itself to coherent translation. I have relied on Sakai Tadao's interpretation in his *Chūgoku zensho no kenkyū* (Researches on Chinese morality books) (Tokyo: Kokusho kankōkai, 1960), pp. 227–33. Sakai, in turn, has relied on annotations by the Ming scholar Yang Ch'i-yüan, who will be discussed in the text, below.

41. Sakai, *Zensho,* p. 230. The three bonds and five constant virtues (*san-kang wu-ch'ang*) were basic social virtues of Confucianism. The three bonds were the relationships between ruler and subject, parent and child, husband and wife. The five constant virtues were humanity, righteousness, decorum (ritual propriety), wisdom, and trustworthiness. These go back to the earliest Confucian teachings, and the phrase *san-kang wu-ch'ang* goes back at least to the Confucian Tung Chung-shu in the former Han dynasty. See Wing-tsit Chan, trans. and comp., *A Source Book in Chinese Philosophy* (Princeton: Princeton University Press, 1963), p. 277.

42. See Mano Senryū, "Mindai ni okeru sankyō shisō; toku ni Rin Chōon o chūshin to shite" (Three Teachings thought in the Ming dynasty, with special reference to Lin Chao-en) *Tōyōshi kenkyū* 12 (1952):19; Shimizu Taiji, "Mindai ni okeru shūkyō yūgō to kōkakaku" (Ledgers of merit and demerit and religious syncretism in the Ming), *Shichō* 6 (1936):29–55; Ryūchi Kiyoshi, "Mindai no sōkan" (The monk-officials of the Ming), *Shina bukkyōshi gaku* 4, no. 3 (1940):35–46, and Sakai, *Zensho,* pp. 38–57, 228–29.

43. Sakai, *Zensho,* pp. 228–31.

44. Jan Jakob M. de Groot discussed in detail how official concerns over security, threats to social values, and the threat of withdrawal of moneys from the tax base were used as pretexts for the control and persecution of religious groups. *Sectarianism and Religious Persecution in China: A Page in the History of Religions,* 2 vols. (Amsterdam: J. Miller, 1903–4). Daniel L. Overmyer has reviewed not only how this attitude affected government policy but how much it affected what was written about religions. See *Folk Buddhist Religion: Dissenting Sects in Late Traditional China* (Cambridge: Har-

vard University Press, 1976). Yang Ch'i-ch'iao has written an article on the tension between the imperial family's involvement with religious practices and the interests of the state, and on the laws which sought to protect the latter. "Ming-tai chu-ti chih ch'ung-shang fang-shu chi ch'i ying-hsiang" (The veneration of Ming emperors for magicians and their influence), in *Ming-tai tsung-chiao* (Ming religion), Ming-shih lun-ts'ung, no. 10 (Taipei: Hsüeh-sheng shu-chü, 1963), pp. 203–97.

45. Wang Yang-ming, personal name Shou-jen, T. Po-an, native of Yü-yao in Chekiang. *Ming shih* (History of Ming) (Taipei: I-wen yin-shu-kuan, 1961), 195.1a; *Ming-ju hsüeh-an* (Anthology of Neo-Confucians of the Ming) 62 *ch.*, ed. Huang Tsung-hsi (SPPY ed.), 10.3a–4b. For biographical sketches in English, see Wing-tsit Chan, trans. and annotator, *Instructions for Practical Living and Other Neo-Confucian Writings by Wang Yang-ming* (New York: Columbia University Press, 1963), xxi–xxix; Frederich Goodrich Henke, *The Philosophy of Wang Yang-ming* (London: Open Court Press, 1916), pp. 3–44. There are two recent books on Wang Yang-ming: Julia Ching, *To Acquire Wisdom: The Way of Wang Yang-ming* (New York: Columbia University Press, 1976), and Tu Wei-ming, *Neo-Confucian Thought in Action: Wang Yang-ming's Youth (1472–1509)* (Berkeley: University of California Press, 1976).

46. Araki, "Confucianism and Buddhism," pp. 45–46. On innate good-knowing, see *Ch'uan-hsi lu*, pt. 2, sec. 161 and pt. 3, sec. 311–12, translated in Chan, *Instructions for Practical Living*, pp. 140–41 and 238–39. Also see T'ang Chun-i, "The Development of the Concept of Moral Mind from Wang Yang-ming to Wang Chi," in de Bary, *Self and Society*, pp. 93–120, esp. pp. 100–8.

47. Translation follows Araki, "Confucianism and Buddhism," p. 44. Araki cites the *Wang Wen-ch'eng kung ch'üan-shu* (Collected works of Wang Yang-ming), 38 *ch.* (Hong Kong: Kuang-chih shu-chü, 1959), 31.603, the *Shan-tung hsiang-shih-lu* (True account of the localities of Shantung). However, the edition he cites is unavailable in American university libraries, and in consulting a Ming edition edited by Hsü Ai (Ming, n.d.), I was unable to locate the citation either in *ch.* 31 or in the preface to the *Shan-tung hsiang-shih-lu*, which appeared in a different *chüan*. In fact a scan of the collection did not yield this saying by Wang Yang-ming. It must be that there are two different versions of this collection.

48. On the left-wing T'ai-chou school, see Okada Takehiko, "Wang Chi and the Rise of Existentialism," in de Bary, *Self and Society*, pp. 121–44.

49. Araki Kengo, *Mindai shisō kenkyū* (Researches on Ming thought) (Tokyo: Sōbunsha, 1972), p. 280. Wang Ken, H. Hsin-chai, was from T'ai-chou, Kiangsu. See also Wm. Theodore de Bary, "Individualism and Humanitarianism in Late Ming Thought," in idem, *Self and Society*, pp. 157–71, esp. pp. 159–62; and biography by Julia Ching in *Dictionary of Ming Biography, 1368–1644*, 2 vols., ed. L. Carrington Goodrich and Chaoying Fang (New York: Columbia University Press, 1976).

50. *Wang Lung-hsi ch'üan-chi* (Collected works of Wang Lung-hsi), 3 vols. (Taipei: Hua-wen shu-chü, 1970; facsimile of 1882 ed.), 1.18b. Trans-

III. THE HEYDAY OF SYNCRETISM 277

lation adapted from Araki, "Confucianism and Buddhism," p. 46. Wang Chi, T. Ju-ching, H. Lung-hsi, was from Shan-yen, Chekiang. *Ming shih*, 283.12a–15a; *Ming-ju hsüeh-an*, 12.22b; biography by Julia Ching in *Dictionary of Ming Biography*.

51. *Tung-yüeh cheng-hsüeh lu* (Record of advances of studies in Eastern Kwangtung), 16 *ch*. in 2 vols., Ming-jen wen-chi ts'ung-k'an, 25 (Taipei: Wen-hai ch'u-pan-she, 1970), 7.23a–b. See also Sakai, *Zensho*, pp. 246–47.

52. *Yang Fu-so ch'üan-chi* (Collected works of Yang Ch'i-yüan), 14 vols., Chao Hou ed. (1599 ed.), *Tung-jih chi* (Record of eastern days), 10; cited from Araki, "Confucianism and Buddhism," p. 47. Yang Ch'i-yüan, T. Chen-fu, H. Fu-so, was from Kuei-sheng, now in Hui-yang county, Kwangtung. *Ming-ju hsüeh-an*, 34.22a; biography by Julia Ching and Huang P'ei, *Dictionary of Ming Biography*.

53. *Ch'in-ting Ssu-k'u ch'üan-shu tsung-mu* (General guide to the collected works of the four storehouses), ed. Chi Yün (Ch'ien-lung [1736–1795] ed.) 132.4a–b. See also Sakai, *Zensho*, p. 239. Yang calls himself *pi-ch'iu*.

54. *Pai Su-chai lei-chi* (Categorized collection of Pai Su-chai), 22 *ch*., Chung-kuo wen-hsüeh chen-pen ts'ung-shu series (Shanghai: Shanghai tsa-chih kung-ssu, 1935), 17.1; translation cited from Araki, "Confucianism and Buddhism," p. 53. Yüan Tsung-tao, T. Po-hsiu, was from Kung-an, Hopei. *Ming shih*, 288.12b; discussed in C. N. Tay's biography of Yüan Hung-tao, *Dictionary of Ming Biography*.

55. Chiao Hung, T. Jo-hou, H. Tan-yüan, from Chiang-ning, near modern Nanking. *Ming shih*, 288.7b; *Ming-ju hsüeh-an*, 35.8b. See Edward T. Ch'ien, "Chiao Hung and the Revolt against Ch'eng-Chu Orthodoxy," in de Bary, *Unfolding*, pp. 272–303.

56. Reference to *Tao-te ching*, I and IV; see Dim Cheuk (D. C.) Lau, trans., *Lao Tzu, Tao te ching* (Middlesex, Eng. and Baltimore, Md.: Penguin Books, 1963), pp. 57 and 60. See also *Chiao-shih pi-ch'eng* (The vehicle of Mr. Chiao's pen), 6 *ch*. (Shanghai: Sheng-wu yin-shu-kuan, 1935; original ed. 1606), 4.103, and Edward Ch'ien, "Chiao Hung," pp. 279–80, 282–83.

57. *Chiao-shih pi-ch'eng hsü*, 2.171; Ch'ien, "Chiao Hung," p. 285.

58. Li Chih, original name Lin Tsai-chih, T. Hung-fu, Ssu-chai, H. Cho-wu, Wen-ling, from Ch'üan-chou, Fukien. Jung Chao-tsu, *Li Chih nien-p'u* (Chronological biography of Li Chih) (Peking: Sheng-huo tu-shu hsin-chih san-kuang shu-chü, 1957); biography by K. C. Hsiao in *Dictionary of Ming Biography*. See also de Bary, "Individualism and Humanitarianism," pp. 188–225, and Shimada Kenji, *Chūgoku ni okeru kindai shii no zasetsu* (The frustration of thinking in recent China) (Tokyo: Chikuma shobō, 1970), pp. 161–229.

59. Like other Confucians, Li Chih referred to Ming T'ai-tsu's use of this statement in support of syncretic attitudes; the statement, "There are not two Ways under heaven" comes from *Hsün Tzu*, 21; compare Burton Watson, *Hsün Tzu, Basic Writings* (New York: Columbia University Press, 1963), p. 121. *San-chiao p'in* (Classifications of the Three Teachings) (Ming ed.), preface, 1a–2a.

60. *Hsü Fen-shu* (A book to burn, continued) (Peking: Chung-hua shu-

chü, 1959), 2.77; translation cited from de Bary, "Individualism and Humanitarianism," p. 211.

61. *San-chiao p'in*, 67a-b.
62. Kuan Chih-tao, T. Teng-chih, H. Tung-ming, from Lou-chen, in present-day Wu county, Kiangsu. *Kuan-kung hsing-chuang* (Activities and appearances of Master Kuan) in *Mu-chai ch'u-hsüeh chi* (Collection of Mu-chai's beginning of studies) 110 *ch.*, by Ch'ien Ch'ien-i (SPTK ed.; 1643 original), 49.1; *Kuan-kung mu-chih ming* (Grave inscription of Master Kuan) in Chiao Hung, ed., *Kuo-ch'ao hsien-cheng lu* (Record of distinguished officials presented at court) 120 *ch.* (1616 ed.), 99.164a–167b.
63. Araki, "Confucianism and Buddhism," p. 49. See also Araki, *Mindai shisō*, p. 280.
64. Hu Chü-jen, T. Shu-hsin, H. Chin-chai, from Yü-kan, in Kiangsi. *Ming shih*, 282.1b; *Ming-ju hsüeh-an*, 2.1a–2a; biography by Julia Ching in *Dictionary of Ming Biography*. Anne Meller Ch'ien of Columbia University is completing a dissertation on Hu Chü-jen.

Ch'en Hsien-chang, T. Kung-fu, H. Pai-sha, from Hsin-hui county, Kwangtung. *Ming shih*, 283.1b; *Ming-ju hsüeh-an*, 5.2a–3b; Ho Ch'iao-yüan, ed. *Ming-shan tsang* (Storehouse of the mountain of names), 20 vols. (1640 ed.), 79.15; biography by Huang P'ei and Julia Ching in *Dictionary of Ming Biography*.

65. Sakai, *Zensho*, pp. 273–75. Chan Ling, 1498 *chin-shih*; held office of instructor in Cheng-chou, Honan and Lü-chou, Szechuan. His name does not appear in indices to Ming biographical sources or gazetteers.
66. For Wang Yang-ming's letter to Lo Ch'in-shun, see Chan, *Instructions for Practical Living*, pp. 157–65. Lo's letter to Wang was translated by Irene Bloom, "Notes on Knowledge Painfully Acquired: A Translation and Analysis of the *K'un-chih chi* of Lo Ch'in-shun" (Ph.D. diss., Columbia University, 1976). Lo Ch'in-shun, T. Ch'ung-sheng, H. Cheng-an, was from T'ai-ho, Kiangsi. *Ming shih*, 282.15b; *Ming-ju hsüeh-an*, 47.1a; biography by Tu Ching-i in *Dictionary of Ming Biography*.
67. *Hsing-ming shuang-hsiu wan-shen kuei-chih*, preface, 1b. The identity of Yin Chen-jen, or True Man Yin, is unclear; for a discussion of the problem, see Sakai, *Zensho*, p. 290.

We do not know whether Yin Chen-jen was initiated as a Taoist or a member of any Taoist organization. However, his work shows him to be well versed in the techniques of Inner Alchemy meditation and in various ritual and magical practices associated with members of Taoist sects. We may then assume that he represents at least one strain of contemporary Taoism.

68. *Hsing-ming kuei-chih*, 2.2a–2b; I have been unable to locate the source of "Only a man who can recognize men who have not died can escape death."
69. Sakai, *Zensho*, pp. 350–51. Yüan Huang, T. K'un-i, H. Liao-fan, from Wu-chiang, Kiangsu. *Tz'u Shang-pao shao-ch'ing Yüan kung chuan* (Biography of Master Yüan presented to the Shang-pao and Shao-ch'ing) in *Yü-an*

hsiao-chi (The small collection of the hut of the ignorant one), 15 *ch.*, ed. Chu Ho-ling (K'ang-hsi [1662–1722] ed.), 15.13a; biography by Lienche Tu Fang in *Dictionary of Ming Biography*. There is an excellent chapter on Yüan Huang's life and thought in Sakai, *Zensho*, on which I have relied extensively. Pages 318–55.

Please note that I have termed Yüan Huang's contribution Taoistic rather than Taoist. Theories of moral retribution as part of Taoist practice stem from some of the Han sects and the practices of the "Internal Hygiene" school in the period of disunion. See Yoshioka Yoshitoyo, *Eisei e no negai* (The Search for Long Life), Sekai no shūkyō, no. 9 (Kyoto: Tankōkai, 1970), and Holmes Welch, *Taoism: The Parting of the Way*, rev. ed. (Boston: Beacon Press, 1957), pp. 105–12. Moreover, as Sakai has noted, many of the earliest texts were associated with Taoists. However, the ideas of moral retribution were also grounded in the popular tradition and were seen very early to be compatible with all Three Teachings. In the Ming, however, the practice of keeping accounts of good and bad deeds and making vows about moral aspirations became much more current among Confucian intellectuals. Yüan Huang, with his origins on the fringes of that class, seems to have been a key figure in transforming these practices into forms acceptable to Confucians.

70. See Sakai, *Zensho*, chapter one.
71. Ibid., p. 343. Sakai gives examples of some of these interpretations.
72. See de Bary, "Individualism and Humanitarianism," p. 176.
73. For a discussion of the importance of this scripture during the Ming, see Pei-yi Wu, "The Spiritual Autobiography of Te-ch'ing," in de Bary, *Unfolding*, pp. 79–89.
74. Wu, "Te-ch'ing," pp. 67–80; see also Kubota, *Kōshōshi*, pp. 317–22. Te-ch'ing, T. Ch'eng-yin, H. Han-shan, was born in Ch'üan-chiao, near modern Nanking. *Ming-shih chi-shih pen-mo* (Critical account of historical events of the Ming), 80 *ch.*, by Ku Ying-t'ai (1658 ed.), *ch.* 67; *Han-shan ta-shih nien-p'u su-chu* (Taipei: Chan-shan-mei ch'u-pan-she, 1967); biography by Pei-yi Wu in *Dictionary of Ming Biography*. See also Sung-peng Hsu, *A Buddhist Leader in Ming China: The Life and Thought of Han-shan Te-ch'ing* (University Park: Pennsylvania State University Press, 1979).
75. Kubota, *Kōshōshi*, pp. 317–21.
76. Araki, "Confucianism and Buddhism," p. 58. On Ta-hui Tsung-kao, see *Hsin-hsü Kao-seng chuan* (New and continued Biographies of eminent monks), ed. Yü Ch'ien (Taipei: Liu-li ching-fang, 1923), 12.11b–13a.
77. Araki, "Confucianism and Buddhism," p. 60. Ta-kuan, personal religious name Chen-k'o, H. Tz'u-po, native of Wu-chiang, Kiangsu. In *Ming-chi* (Record of Ming) (SPPY ed.), 45.19b.
78. Araki, *Mindai shisō*, pp. 282–84. Chu-hung, T. Fo-hui, H. Yün-ch'i, born in Jen-ho, near Hangchow. *Yün-ch'i fa-hui* (Collection of teachings of Chu-hung) (1897 ed.), 28.30b, 55a; 34.2b, 11a, 23a; *Fu-hsü Kao-seng chuan* (Addenda to Biographies of eminent monks) (1621 ed.), 5.55a; biography by Yü Chün-fang in *Dictionary of Ming Biography*.

280   III. THE HEYDAY OF SYNCRETISM

79. Leon Hurvitz, "Chu-hung's One Mind of Pure Land and Ch'an Buddhism," in de Bary, *Self and Society*, p. 453.
80. *Chu-ch'uang sui-pi fu erh-pi san-pi* (Miscellaneous notes from the bamboo window, with addenda) (Taipei: Chung-kuo fo-chiao wen-hua kuan, 1972; reprint of Chin-ling k'o-chin-ch'u, 1897 edition) *erh-pi*, 21a; see Hurvitz, "Chu-hung's One Mind," p. 475.
81. Hurvitz, "Chu-hung's One Mind," p. 473; Araki, *Mindai shisō*, p. 284.
82. *Yün-ch'i fa-hui, Chieh-shu wen-pien* (Questions about the commentary on the precepts), 5.1b. Kristin Yü Greenblatt (Yü Chün-fang) "Chu-hung and Lay Buddhism in the Late Ming," de Bary, *Unfolding*, pp. 99–100, 115.
83. Yü, "Chu-hung," p. 127.
84. Ibid., p. 95. Yü Chün-fang discusses these issues at more length in her dissertation (Columbia, 1973; see above, n. 2).
85. Liu Ts'un-yan, "Lin Chao-en: Master of the Three Teachings," *T'oung Pao* 53 (1967):260–61.

IV. BIOGRAPHY OF LIN CHAO-EN

1. Appendix A lists and discusses biographical sources, secondary scholarship, and available writings of Lin Chao-en.

Lin Wan-jen never held office. For a biographical sketch, see Lin Chao-k'o, ed., *Lin-tzu nien-p'u* (Chronological biography of Master Lin) (1610), 1b (hereafter referred to as *Chronological Biography*); *Lin-tzu pen-hsing shih-lu* (True record of the activities of Master Lin) (1600 pref., although some material is dated later), 1.2a (hereafter referred to as *True Record*).

2. *Ch'ung-tsuan Fu-chien t'ung-chih* (Revised Fukien gazetteer) 278 *ch.*, reedited by Ch'en Shou-ch'i from the Cheng-i shu-yüan MS (1868 ed.), 55.31a, said to be cited from *Pa-ming t'ung-chih* (Eight gazetteers of Fukien).

3. *Ch'ung-tsuan Fu-chien t'ung-chih*, 55.31b. See also James B. Parsons, "The Ming Dynasty Bureaucracy," in *Chinese Government in Ming Times: Seven Studies*, ed. Charles O. Hucker (New York: Columbia University Press, 1969), p. 207.

4. On Lin Fu, see *Huang-ming ying-shih ming-ch'en pei-k'ao lu* (Record of researches on officials granted posthumous titles in the Ming), 8 *ch.*, ed. Lin Chih-sheng (late Ming), 7.29a; *Hsing-hua P'u-t'ien hsien-chih* (Gazetteer of P'u-t'ien, Hsing-hua), 36 *ch.*, ed. Wang Ta-ching; new ed. Liao Pi-ch'i (1879 ed. based on 1758 ed.), 17.53b; *Hsing-hua fu-chih* (Hsing-hua gazetteer), 26 *ch.*, ed. Lü I-ching and K'ang Ta-ho (1575 pref.), 13.26b; *Ch'ung-tsuan Fu-chien t'ung-chih*, 199.43 ff.; *Kuo-ch'ao hsien-cheng lu* (Record of distinguished officials presented at court), 120 *ch.*, ed. Chiao Hung (1594 pref.), 58.42a–44b.

5. In order to be consistent with entries in biographical sources, all ages will follow the Chinese system, in which a child is one year at birth and one additional year older each New Year. Thus at six Chinese years, Lin was four or five by Western reckoning.

IV. BIOGRAPHY OF LIN CHAO-EN 281

6. *True Record*, 1.11a. Representative selections of set essay forms are included in *Lin-tzu ch'üan-chi wen-lüeh* (Selections of the writings from Lin Tzu's collected works), L:18 (see appendix E).
7. *True Record*, 1.2b.
8. For Lin Wan-ch'ao's biography, see *Ch'ung-tsuan Fu-chien t'ung-chih*, 199.46a; *Hsing-hua fu-chih*, 18.26b; *Hsing-hua P'u-t'ien hsien-chih*, 22.16a; *Kuo-ch'ao hsien-cheng lu*, 87.83a–84a.
9. The funerary inscription is preserved in *Kuo-ch'ao hsien-cheng lu*, 87.83a–84a. Lo Hung-hsien, T. Ta-fa, H. Nien-an, was from Chi-shui in Chi-an, Kiangsi. See *Ming shih* (History of Ming) (Taipei: I-wen yin-shukuan, 1961), 283.16a; *Ming-ju hsüeh-an* (Anthology of Neo-Confucians of the Ming), 62 *ch*., ed. Huang Tsung-hsi (SPPY ed.), 18.1; *Lo hsien-sheng chuan* (Biography of Master Lo) in *Keng T'ien-t'ai hsien-sheng wen-chi* (Collected literary works of Keng Ting-hsiang), 20 *ch*., Ming-jen wen-chi ts'ung-k'an, 20 (Taipei: Wen-hai ch'u-pan-she, 1970; based on 1598 ed.), 14.29; biography of Lo Hung-hsien by Stanley Y. C. Huang in *Dictionary of Ming Biography, 1368–1644*, 2 vols., ed. L. Carrington Goodrich and Chaoying Fang (New York: Columbia University Press, 1976).
10. Indirect reference to wheelwright P'ien's denigration of the classics as the dregs of the ancients in *Chuang Tzu*, 13; see Burton Watson, trans., *The Complete Works of Chuang Tzu* (New York: Columbia University Press, 1968), pp. 152–53.
11. *Ch'iao-yang chiao-yen* (Instructions to disciples in Ch'iao-yang), A:VI.58b–59a (see appendix B).
12. On the movement to establish academies in the Ming, see John T. Meskill, "Academies and Politics in the Ming Dynasty," in Hucker, *Chinese Government in Ming Times*, pp. 149–74.
13. See Jung Chao-tsu, *Ming-tai ssu-hsiang shih* (History of Ming thought) (Taipei: K'ai-ming shu-tien, 1962), pp. 139–41.
    Lienche Tu Fang, in her biography of Lin Chao-en in the *Dictionary of Ming Biography*, suggests that his decision to forgo studies occurred at about the time when, after his father's death, he canceled the remainder of debts owed to the family. Certainly this action was symptomatic of his new direction and religious commitment, but it does not explain his motivation, except that it is somehow connected with the father's demise. My analysis of motivation is meant to supplement Fang's. Certainly the fact that Lin Chao-en continued to correspond with Lo Hung-hsien in order to articulate his religious commitment suggests that Lo may have directly or indirectly influenced Lin's decision.
14. The ninefold refined elixir was originally one of the most powerful elixirs of long life. In Inner Alchemy, the nine stages of refinement were understood in terms of self-cultivation, and the elixir was understood as the seed of the true self within. See Hsiao T'ien-shih, *Tao-chia yang-sheng-hsüeh kai-yao* (Essentials of Taoist theories of nurturing life), 2d ed. (Taipei: Tzu-yu ch'u-pan-she, 1971), pp. 64–72.
15. *Chronological Biography*, 7a–b. *Chin-tzu* is a pun on *chin-shih*, the most advanced degree in the government examination system.

16. For Cho Wan-ch'un's biography, see *Ming-shan tsang* (Storehouse of the mountain of names), 20 vols., by Ho Ch'iao-yüan (1640 ed.), *fang-wai* sec. 1.15a–16a; *P'u-feng ch'ing-lai chi* (Collection of pure music in P'u-t'ien style), 60 *ch.*, ed. Chang Wang-ch'en (1722 pref.), 48.2a–3a; *Min shu* (Book of Fukien), 154 *ch.*, ed. Ho Ch'iao-yüan (1630),138.14b–15b; *Hang-chou fu-chih* (Hangchow gazetteer), 100 *ch.*, ed. Ch'en Shan (1686 ed.), 35.7a; *Wu-yen lu chüan-tuan* (Foreword to Record of the dialogues), XX:1.1a–4a (see appendix C); *Wu-yen lu pa* (Colophon to same), XX:5.1a–2b.

17. *Wu-yen lu chüan-tuan*, XX:1.1a–1b. One Chinese pint (*sheng*) equals 31.6 cubic inches; 10 *sheng* equals one Chinese peck (*tou*).

18. *Wu-yen lu*, XX:4.1b.

19. *Wu-yen lu chüan-tuan*, XX:1.2b.

20. See Anna Seidel, "A Taoist Immortal of the Ming Dynasty: Chang San-feng," in Wm. Theodore de Bary and the Conference on Ming Thought, *Self and Society in Ming Thought* (New York: Columbia University Press, 1970), pp. 483–531. Such Taoist eccentrics were not always Taoists in the strict sense of being initiated, or belonging to some Taoist organization. This "type" was a social label. However, Cho Wan-ch'un does seem to be versed in the ideas of the Inner Alchemy system, although it is by no means clear that he was a teacher or even a particularly skilled adept. On the problem of the definition of Taoist, see Nathan Sivin, "On the Word 'Taoist' as a Source of Perplexity: With Special Reference to the Relations of Science and Religion in Traditional China," in *History of Religions* 17 (Feb.–May 1978):303–30.

21. *Hsin-sheng chih-chih* (Direct pointing to the mind as sage), II:2.27b–29a.

22. De Bary, "Introduction," *Self and Society*, pp. 8–13.

23. Root of heaven and earth (*t'ien-ti chih ken*) from Lao Tzu, *Tao-te ching*, IV: see Arthur Waley, trans., *The Way and its Power: A Study of the Tao Te Ching and its Place in Chinese Thought* (New York: Grove Press, 1958), p. 149.

24. *Hsin-sheng chih-chih*, II:2.29b. The technical terms are from the lexicon of the alchemical tradition. The adept of Inner Alchemy had to master the secret meanings of these terms in order properly to understand the process of cultivation.

25. The intellectual revival of Buddhism in the Ming was discussed in the last chapter.

26. *Hsin-sheng chih-chih*, II:2.32b–33a.

27. Unfortunately this date is unclear; we do not know "within ten years" of what. The calling was certainly before (and probably shortly before) 1551 when Lin took up his role as teacher. (See below.)

28. The five classics include the *I ching* (Book of changes), *Shu ching* (Book of history), *Shih ching* (Book of odes), *Li chi* (Book of rites), and *Ch'un-ch'iu* (Spring and autumn annals). The Four Books are the *Ta-hsüeh* (Great learning), *Chung-yung* (Doctrine of the Mean), *Lun-yü* (Analects of Confucius), and *Meng-tzu* (Mencius). Chu Hsi began the designation of the

IV. BIOGRAPHY OF LIN CHAO-EN 283

Four Books, singling them out as the starting point for Confucian studies. The first two were originally included in the *Book of Rites*. Because these are well-known classics, I will refer to them throughout the book by their translated titles, although the reference numbers to the Chinese text will also be given.

29. "Fullness of body" and "plumpness of countenance" are allusions. The first is from *Great Learning*, 1: "Riches adorn a house, and virtue adorns the person. The mind is expanded and the body is at ease [lit., full or plump]. Therefore, the superior man must make his thoughts sincere." See James Legge, *The Four Books: Confucian Analects, The Great Learning, The Doctrine of the Mean, and The Works of Mencius* (New York: Paragon, 1966; unaltered reprint of Shanghai, 1923 ed.), p. 325. The second is to *Mencius* 7A:21: "What belongs by his nature to the superior man are benevolence, righteousness, propriety, and knowledge. These are rooted in his heart; their growth and manifestation are a mild harmony [or: plumpness] appearing in the countenance, a rich fullness in the back, and the character imparted to the four limbs." Legge, *Four Books*, pp. 949–50. Plumpness was a sign of health and prosperity in Chinese culture.

30. *K'un* hexagram. "When the gentleman is yellow and centered, he makes his influence felt in the outer world through reason." Translation adapted from Richard Wilhelm, trans., *The I Ching or Book of Changes*, trans. into English by Cary F. Baynes, corrected 3d ed. with foreword by C. G. Jung and preface by Hellmut Wilhelm, Bollingen Series, 19 (Princeton: Princeton University Press, 1967), p. 395. (Hereafter referred to as Wilhelm/Baynes, *I ching*.)

31. An allusion to *Mencius* 2A:2; see Legge, *Four Books*, p. 528.

32. *Hsin-sheng chih-chih*, II:2.33a–b. Medicine (*i*) and will (*i*) pun in Chinese; Lin builds the identification on the basis of that pun.

33. See appendix A.

34. *True Record*, 1.1b.

35. Morohashi Tetsuji, ed., *Daikanwa jiten* (Comprehensive Chinese-Japanese dictionary) (Tokyo: Daishūkan shoten, 1955–1960), 13805.245, traces the term back to Wang Ch'ung and Tung Chung-shu of the Han.

36. See *Kuan wu-liang-shou ching* (The sutra of contemplation of Amitāyus), T.12.345c; translated in Lu K'uan-yü (Charles Luk), *The Secrets of Chinese Meditation: Self-cultivation by Mind Control as Taught in the Ch'an, Mahāyāna, and Taoist schools in China* (London: Rider, 1964), pp. 103–4.

37. On the Ch'an patriarchy, see Philip B. Yampolsky, *The Platform Sutra of the Sixth Patriarch: The Text of the Tun-huang Manuscript with Translation, Introduction, and Notes* (New York: Columbia University Press, 1967), pp. 1–57. On the importance of the Master in Ch'an, see Wm. Theodore de Bary et al., *Sources of Chinese Tradition*, paperback ed. in 2 vols. (New York: Columbia University Press, 1964) 1:346–50, and Richard H. Robinson, *The Buddhist Religion: A Historical Introduction* (Belmont, Cal.: Dickenson, 1970), pp. 94–95.

38. Hsiao, *Tao-chia yang-sheng-hsüeh*, pp. 333–37.

39. *K'ung-men hsin-fa* was used by Lin to describe his method of mind-cultivation. In the writings of Chu Hsi, however, it had a different meaning. In his introduction to the *Doctrine of the Mean*, Chu remarked, "This is the central way (*hsin-fa*) in which the doctrines of the Confucian school have been transmitted." *Ssu-shu chi-chu* (Collected commentary to the Four Books) (Taipei: T'ai-p'ing shu-chü, 1968), *Chung-yung chang-chü*, 1.

In Buddhism the term implied direct transmission from mind to mind, but Chu Hsi understood it as the "central way," thus emphasizing the doctrinal content of the transmission rather than the method. See Wing-tsit Chan, trans. and comp., *A Source Book in Chinese Philosophy* (Princeton: Princeton University Press, 1963), p. 97.

Lin Chao-en's interpretation followed that of Yüan dynasty Taoist Huang Yüan-ch'i, who taught that the oneness of the Three Teachings is in the preservation of centrality (*shou-chung*). Huang held that *hsin-fa* was a doctrine of the mind, transmitted from Yao and Shun down the line of the Confucian school, embodying the teachings of centrality. See Hsiao, *Tao-chia yang-sheng-hsüeh*, p. 128. Lin interpreted *hsin-fa* as *shih-hsin chih fa*, lit., serving the mind, here regulating the mind. He followed Huang in emphasizing the doctrine as the Confucian teachings on centrality transmitted from the sages, but he also emphasized the word *fa* (method or system) to highlight its function as a way of praxis.

40. On the distinction between religious and classical healing, I am indebted to Professor Nathan Sivin of the University of Pennsylvania, who kindly lent me a draft MS on popular medicine and classical medicine in China. However, the discussion has been recast to serve the purposes of this chapter, and I do not claim to represent accurately Sivin's view. On the classical theory of healing, see Manfred Porkert, *The Theoretical Foundations of Chinese Medicine: Systems of Correspondence* (Cambridge: MIT Press, 1974). On religious healing, see Raoul Birnbaum, *Bhaiṣajyaguru-tathāgata: The Buddha of Healing in the Indian and Chinese Traditions* (Berkeley: Shambala, 1979).

41. *Hsiao-shuo pu-cheng-ch'i* is from *Chu-tzu yü-lei* (Classified conversations of Master Chu) 140 *ch.*, ed. Li Ching-te (Taipei: Cheng-chung shu-chü, 1970; reproduction of 1473 ed.), 3.19b, in which someone enquired, "If there are correct principles, then there are heterodox principles; if there is right, there is wrong. The affairs of ghosts and spirits are similar. If in the world there are ghosts and spirits acting improperly, one cannot say they are without principle." Chu Hsi replied, "Lao Tzu said, 'They who by Tao ruled all that is under heaven did not let an evil spirit within them display its power.' If in this way the kingly Way is cultivated and clarified, such imbalanced [or: improper] vital force [i.e., ghosts and spirits] will all be dissolved." The reference is to *Tao-te ching*, LX, translation cited from Waley, *Way and Its Power*, p. 215.

Chu Hsi's statement was about governing the state, maintaining the macrocosm. Lin interpreted his statement in terms of governing the internal microcosm, keeping disruptive or imbalanced forces from emerging by maintaining moral balance.

IV. BIOGRAPHY OF LIN CHAO-EN   285

42. *Chronological Biography*, 9a–b. For a biography of Liu Hsün, see *Hsing-hua P'u-t'ien hsien-chih*, 23.3b–4a.
43. Chu Heng, T. Shih-nan, H. Chen-shan, held various offices until he asked to be allowed to retire because of the deterioration of ritual courtesies between subjects and ministers. *Ming shih*, 233.3a.
44. *Chronological Biography*, 10a–b.
45. Li Chih was discussed in the last chapter.
46. *Analects* 14:4; see Legge, *Four Books*, p. 194.
47. These are all traditional essay forms used in the government examinations. On disquisition and memorial, see James Robert Hightower, "The Wen Hsüan and Genre Theory," in *Harvard Journal of Asian Studies* 20 (1957):512–33. Commentaries explain the meanings of passages from the classics, and proposals were position papers on theoretical problems of government. There are examples of Lin's student essays in *Lin-tzu ch'üan-chi wen-lüeh*, L:18.
48. The record of attendance and activity calls to mind the records of daily activities and ledgers of merit and demerit (*kung-kuo ko*) kept by those in the morality book movement; see last chapter, discussion of Yüan Huang.
49. *Hsing-li ta-ch'üan-shu* (Great collection of the writings of Neo-Confucians), 70 *ch.*, comp. by Hu Kuang et al. (1415 ed.). *Tzu-chih t'ung-chien kang-mu* (Outline and digest of the General mirror for the aid of government) was compiled by Chu Hsi from the work by Ssu-ma Kuang. This Sung reexamination of Chinese history was very popular in the Ming.
50. *Tzu* was a courtesy name used by others as a polite form of address; it was normally selected when young men reached adulthood. *Hao*, a separate name, chosen by the man himself or given by others during or after his life, was very polite; it is an honorific name, often used in formal writing. In recommending that students use courtesy names, Lin was counselling against excessive familiarity and ostentatious formality.
51. *Ming-ching t'ang* (Hall for expounding the classics), XVII:1.1b–5b. Tseng Tien's delight is an allusion to the famous passage in which Confucius questioned his disciples about their pleasures, hopes, and dreams. *Analects* 11:25; see Legge, *Four Books*, pp. 150–55.
52. The niceties of Confucian socializing and its potential excesses were depicted in Wu Ching-tzu's novel *Ju-lin wai-shih* (Unofficial history of the Confucians), translated under the title *The Scholars* by Yang Hsien-i and Gladys Yang (Peking: Foreign Language Press, 1957).
53. In particular, *Ch'ung-li t'ang* (Hall in honor of rituals), D:VI; *Chu-tai li chi t'u-shuo* (Explanations with diagrams on setting out the generations' tablets for ancestral rites and sacrifices), D:III; and *Tiao-ku wen-wu li she t'u-shuo* (Explanation with diagrams in consideration of the ancient archery rite and drinking ceremony), D:V.
54. On the Japanese pirate raids on Fukien in the sixteenth century, see John T. Meskill, *Ch'oe Pu's Diary: A Record of Drifting Across the Sea* (Tucson: University of Arizona Press, for the Association for Asian Studies, 1965), pp. 18–19. A somewhat dated but classic work on the pirates is

Tomaru Fukuju and Mogi Shūichirō, *Wakō kenkyū* (Researches on Japanese pirates) (Tokyo: Chūō kōronsha, 1942). Authorities doubt whether all of the so-called *wakō* (Japanese pirates) were in fact Japanese; some seem to have been Chinese operating from Taiwan or other offshore islands.

55. My account is reconstructed from Lin Chao-en's records, in particular *Hsü-kao* (Manuscripts, continued), XIV:7.

56. *Chronological Biography*, 15a–b, and *True Record*, 5.1b. These accounts are confirmed in *Hsing-hua P'u-t'ien hsien-chih*, 34.7b, and *Min shu*, 129.21b.

57. On the ambivalent attitude of the Chinese toward their ancestors, see Jan Jakob M. de Groot, *The Religious System of China: Its Ancient Forms, Evolution, History and Present Aspect, Manners, Customs, and Social Institutions Connected Therewith*, 6 vols. (Taiwan: Literature house, 1964; originally Leiden: E. J. Brill, 1892–1910), Book 2, The Soul and Ancestral Worship; and Ch'ing-k'un (C. K.) Yang, *Religion in Chinese Society: A Study of Contemporary Social Functions of Religion and Some of their Historical Factors* (Berkeley: University of California Press, 1961), pp. 31–57.

58. For an extensive description of Chinese burial customs, rites, and laws, see de Groot, *Religious System*, 1:280–330, 356–60, 1391–1417. Lin was not the only figure in the Ming to engage in such activities. The Ming monk Te-ch'ing, for instance, buried epidemic victims as an act of spiritual compassion. See Sung-peng Hsu, *A Buddhist Leader in Ming China: The Life and Thought of Han-shan Te-ch'ing* (University Park: Pennsylvania State University Press, 1979), pp. 85–86. In later dynasties, since local government had little revenue for public relief, the burden of such activities fell on the shoulders of local gentry. See Hucker, *Chinese Government in Ming Times*, p. 21.

59. *Hsü-kao*, XIV:2.2b–3a. Sung-peng Hsu has noted that feasts for hungry ghosts were among the most important rituals of the Ming. They were generally performed by Buddhist monks. See Hsu, *Han-shan Te-ch'ing*, pp. 45–47, 86–87. Lin's services were similar, but he, of course, was not an ordained Buddhist.

60. *Hsü-kao*, XIV:2.3a–4a. The Chinese took elaborate measures to keep the body whole and unharmed, for the sake of the dead persons' happiness in the spirit world and so that they would shower blessings on their descendants. Death by dismemberment, injury to a corpse, or cremation were serious threats to the deceased—not as serious, however, as exposure and lack of spirit sacrifice.

61. The *Chronological Biography*, passim, records editorial work in some detail.

62. Allusion to *Mencius* 1A:7; see Legge, *Four Books*, p. 464.

63. *Hsü-kao*, XIV:7.1b–2b.

64. Chang Mei was a student who studied the nine stages of stilling in the back with Lin and traveled with Cho Wan-ch'un; *Fu-chien t'ung-chih* (Gazetteer of Fukien), ed. Ch'en I (Fukien: Cheng-fu chiao-yü-t'ang, 1938), sec. 47 on Taoists, 14a. Chang Ch'e studied stilling in the back; he was said

IV. BIOGRAPHY OF LIN CHAO-EN 287

to have a profound and independent mind when commenting on the classics. He excelled at calligraphy. He never married, although Lin firmly believed that marriage was essential. *Fu-chien t'ung-chih*, sec. 47, 1b. Li Hsüeh-shih practiced Lin's teaching and traveled expounding the techniques of nourishing life until he changed his name and disappeared (to lead a hermit's life). He wrote a colophon to one of Lin's essays, *Meng-chung-jen* (Man within a dream), III:6. *Fu-chien t'ung-chih*, sec. 47, 14b. Huang Chou abandoned examination studies to follow Lin. He practiced the nine stages for ten years, and wrote several works which were never published. *Fu-chien t'ung-chih*, sec. 47, 14a. He may be the same Huang Chou who was Lin's early disciple according to the *Chronological Biography*, but the characters for their names are different. Wang Hsing, a calligrapher and painter of Buddhist images (*Fu-chien t'ung-chih*, K'ang-hsi [1662–1722] ed., 50.3b) may be the disciple of the same name who figures in Lin's activities, writings, and cult. See *Chronological Biography*, 34b–35a and 59b; he is listed in an editorial capacity for over fourteen extant writings of Lin Chao-en.

Disciples Ch'en Chuan-hui, Ku Ta-lin, and Chia Tzu-li were said to be merchants, although there is no further information about their businesses. See *Shu-t'ien wen-kao* (Manuscripts of vows to heaven), XVI:3.21a, and *Chiu-kao* (Manuscripts), XIII:3.16a.

65. *True Record*, 1.32a. *Shih cha* (Ten letters), L:27.

66. Huang Tsung-hsi, *Lin san-chiao chuan* (Biography of Three Teachings Lin), in *Nan-lei wen-an* (Critical comments on literature by Huang Tsung-hsi) (1680 pref.), 9.2a. Tsou Yüan-piao, T. Erh-chan, H. Nan-kao, from Chi-shui, Kiangsi. *Ming shih*, 234.5b; *Ming-ju hsüeh-an*, 23.1a–2b; biography by Charles Hucker in *Dictionary of Ming Biography*. On Tsou Yüan-piao and the Tung-lin movement, see Charles O. Hucker, "The Tung-lin Movement of the late Ming Period," in *Chinese Thought and Institutions*, ed. John K. Fairbank (Chicago: University of Chicago Press, 1957), pp. 132–62, and Ray Huang, "Ni Yüan-lu: 'Realism' in a Neo-Confucian Scholar-Statesman," in de Bary, *Self and Society*, pp. 415–18.

67. *Keng T'ien-t'ai hsien-sheng wen-chi*, 2.16b ff. Keng Ting-hsiang, T. Tsai-lun, H. Ch'u-t'ung, was from Huang-an in present-day Hupei. See *Ming shih*, 221.5b; *Ming-ju hsüeh-an*, 35.1a; biography by Julia Ching in *Dictionary of Ming Biography*.

68. *True Record*, 1.32b. On Yüan Huang, see chapter three.

69. See, for instance, *Chronological Biography*, 36b–38a, 41a.

70. *Shu-t'ien wen-kao*, L:17.34b. Vows to heaven (*shu-t'ien*) were literally "petitions" (*shu*) to heaven, and these *shu* take their stylistic conventions from petitions to superiors. Hence the language about "braving death." I translate the word freely as "vows" to express their function in Lin's thought and practice.

71. *Shu-t'ien wen-kao*, XVI:3.2b–3b.

72. *Liang*, one Chinese ounce or tael of silver; *ch'ien, fen,* and *li* are tenth, hundredth, and thousandth parts of a tael, respectively.

73. *Shu-t'ien wen-kao,* XVI:3.8b–9b.
74. Ibid., 10a.
75. *Chronological Biography,* 53b–54a.
76. *True Record,* 1.44a. The eightieth birthday was a special occasion because of the Chinese respect for longevity. As Holmes Welch has written, "An abbot who reached his eightieth birthday had by that very fact given evidence of his sanctity." *The Practice of Chinese Buddhism, 1900–1950* (Cambridge: Harvard University Press, 1967), p. 336.
77. *True Record,* 1.44a.
78. *Chronological Biography,* 54b–55a.
79. Ibid., 55b.
80. Ibid., 55b–56a.
81. Hsieh Chao-che, *Wu tsa tsu* (Five miscellaneous sacrificial plates) (Japanese ed., 1789, based on original 1616 ed.) 8.44b–45a; Huang Tsung-hsi, *Lin san-chiao chuan,* 9.2a. Wolfgang Franke, "Some Remarks on Lin Chao-en (1517–1598)," *Oriens Extremus* 20 (1973):164, 168, translates the relevant passages. The Chinese term is *k'uang,* which in a general sense suggests "wild" or "crazy" in the colloquial sense of the term. In a personal communication, Nathan Sivin informed me that the specific meaning is "mania." Although it is unclear from the Hsieh passage how serious the *k'uang* was felt to be, Huang Tsung-hsi seems to have felt that Inner Alchemy caused mental problems in Lin Chao-en.
82. Holy men often predicted the moment of their death. A similar story is attributed to Confucius (see n. 86, below). Many Buddhist monks, including Chu-hung and Te-ch'ing, were said to have predicted the time of their demise. See Kristin Yü Greenblatt (Yü Chün-fang), "Yün-ch'i Chu-hung: The Career of a Ming Buddhist Monk," (Ph.D. diss., Columbia University, 1973), p. 43, and Sung-peng Hsu, *Han-shan Te-ch'ing,* pp. 97–98. The power to predict one's death demonstrated that one had conquered death by knowledge; one knew death and had peacefully accepted it.
83. Evidence of a lifelike appearance after death or the nonputrefaction of the body were signs of great sanctity. In the latter case, bodies were sometimes mummified and worshiped as "relics in the flesh" (*jou-shen*). See Welch, *Practice of Chinese Buddhism,* pp. 342–45, and Sung-peng Hsu, *Han-shan Te-ch'ing,* pp. 98–101. It does not seem that Lin's body became a "relic in the flesh," but his youthful and lifelike appearance at death were signs of his spiritual attainment.
84. Reference to the *Book of Rites, t'an-kung,* 1:44. The phrase is part of a song of Confucius:

> The great mountain must crumble;
> The strong beam must break;
> The wise man must wither away like a plant.

Confucius sang this song when he realized he was about to die; when he died a few days later, his disciples realized that he had been predicting his demise. For the translation, see James Legge, trans., *The Sacred Books of China, with Text, Prolegomenon, Notes, and Critical Appendices*, Sacred Books of the East, 39–40, ed. Max Müller (Oxford, 1891), pp. 138–39.

85. Lin was here identified with the sage Fu-hsi, who contemplated the images of heaven and earth and "invented the eight trigrams in order to enter into connection with the virtues of the light of the gods and to regulate the conditions of all being." Great Treatise of the *I ching*; see Wilhelm/Baynes, *I ching*, pp. 328–29.

86. *Chronological Biography*, 56a–56b.

V. THE SYSTEM OF MIND-CULTIVATION

1. On the basic teachings of the Buddha, see Walpola Rahula, *What the Buddha Taught*, rev. ed., with foreword by Paul Demiéville and a collection of illustrative texts translated from the original Pali (New York: Grove Press, 1974).

2. See Walter Y. Evans-Wentz, *Tibetan Yoga and Secret Doctrines: Or Seven Books of Wisdom of the Great Path, According to the late Lāma Kazi Dawa-samdup's English Rendering*, with a foreword by R. R. Marett and yogic commentary by Chen-chi Chang, 2d ed. (London: Oxford University Press, 1958).

3. On the significance and practice of the dialectical method, see Tirupattur R. V. Murti, *The Central Philosophy of Buddhism: A Study of the Mādhyamika System* (London: Allen and Unwin, 1970), and Frederick J. Streng, *Emptiness: A Study of Religious Meaning* (Nashville: Abingdon Press, 1967).

4. See Lu K'uan-yü (Charles Luk), *The Secrets of Chinese Meditation: Self-cultivation by Mind Control as Taught in the Ch'an, Mahāyāna, and Taoist schools in China* (London: Rider, 1964), pp. 81–108.

5. Ibid., pp. 15–42.

6. *Fu-chou Ts'ao-shan Pen-chi ch'an-shih yü-lu* (Recorded sayings of Ch'an master Ts'ao-shan Pen-chi of Fu-chou), 2 ch., ed. Genkei, T.47.538. Translated in Wm. Theodore de Bary et al., *Sources of Chinese Tradition*, paperback ed. in 2 vols. (New York: Columbia University Press, 1964), 1:366.

7. On kōan study, see Isshū Miura and Ruth Fuller Sasaki, *The Zen Koan: Its History and Use in Rinzai Zen* (New York: Harcourt, Harvest paperback, 1965). Daisetsu Suzuki's essays are classics in the field, but they dwell so intently on the paradoxical nature of the techniques that they serve more to heighten the reader's disillusionment with reason than to shed light on the issue. "Practical Methods of Zen Instruction," and "The Reason of Unreason: The Koan Exercise," in William Barrett, ed., *Zen Buddhism: Selected Writings of D. T. Suzuki* (Garden City, N.Y.: Doubleday, 1956), pp. 111–33, 134–56; also included in other collections of Suzuki's writings. Lu K'uan-yü emphasizes that the *kung-an* is not a riddle to be solved but a statement with a meaning that can be perceived only *after* the adept lets go of the normal flow of consciousness and reason and becomes one with the

problem, putting himself in the "host" position (that of the problem). *Secrets of Chinese Meditation*, p. 43 ff.

8. Kristin Yü Greenblatt (Yü Chün-fang), "Yün-ch'i Chu-hung: The Career of a Ming Buddhist Monk," (Ph.D. diss., Columbia University, 1973), pp. 303-4.

9. On Indian Yoga, see Mircea Eliade, *Yoga: Immortality and Freedom*, trans. Willard Trask, 2d ed., with corrections (Princeton: Princeton University Press, 1969), esp. pp. 117-42 and pp. 200-73. Yoga and alchemy were also linked in India, but in China yoga was reinterpreted in the native language of the Chinese alchemical tradition, which entailed a marked shift in symbologies.

10. The desires involved were not only sexual desires but also covetousness, fondness, and stupidity arising from sensory impressions. See Chao Pi-ch'en, *Hsing-ming fa-chüeh ming-chih* (The secrets of cultivation of essential nature and eternal life) (Taipei: Chen-shan-mei ch'u-pan-she, 1963; reissue of Peking, 1933 ed.; originally late nineteenth century), 4.2a-b; translated in Lu K'uan-yü, *Taoist Yoga: Alchemy and Immortality: A Translation, with Introduction and Notes, of The Secrets of Cultivating Essential Nature and Eternal Life (Hsin [sic] Ming Fa Chueh Ming Chih), by Taoist Master Chao Pi Ch'en, born 1860* (New York: Samuel Weiser, 1973), p. 28.

11. Eliade writes, "All of the yogic techniques invite to one and the same gesture—to do exactly the opposite of what human nature forces one to do." This entails, he continues, a progressive suppression of habits of living in order to unify the most important functions of life and, in the end, to homologize one's being with the deeper and truer life of the cosmos. Eliade, *Yoga: Immortality and Freedom*, pp. 96-97.

12. For a description of these circuits, see *Hsing-ming fa-chüeh ming-chih*, 1.4b-5a, and 11.12a-13a, translated in Lu, *Taoist Yoga*, pp. 13 and 24.

13. I. e., in various forms of yogic, tantric, alchemical, and brahmanical thought in India, plus d̲hikr in Islam. See Eliade, *Yoga: Immortality and Freedom*, passim and pp. 216-19. It may be that the Chinese, Islamic, and Indian strains of this practice all stem from one source, but the adaptation of the subtle physiology to native Chinese systems with different goals and metaphysical bases attests that the experience of this inner circulation of heat has the power to become a religious experience in a variety of traditions.

14. In classical Chinese medicine, the body was divided into five regions, each governed by a major organ and correlated with one of the Five Phases. Thus kidney and heart refer to the regions governed by these organs, and do not simply indicate the organs themselves; hence I have translated "kidney-orb" and "organ orb."

15. *Ch'i* is a difficult term to render into English because of its rich connotations. In Lin's system, *ch'i* shares many of the qualities of the *ch'i* (material force) of the Neo-Confucians; it is the substratum of all Being, a vitality or life force pervading all things. In a more general sense, it denotes breath or ether. Lin capitalizes on the connection between breath and air on the one hand, and *ch'i* as material force on the other, to make breath

V. THE SYSTEM OF MIND-CULTIVATION   291

control a technique of self-cultivation. Because *ch'i* (breath) is also *ch'i* (material force), the substratum of all Being, cultivation which begins in breath control ultimately expands the substance of the mind to include the universe. The translation "vital force" is an attempt to encompass both the meaning of ether or material force and the meaning of life force or vital breath, traditionally more connected with the Taoist tradition.

16. The description of the process which follows is based on the *Hsing-ming fa-chüeh ming-chih;* Lu, *Taoist Yoga;* Lu, *Secrets of Chinese Meditation,* pp. 163–214; Chang Chung-yuan, "An Introduction to Taoist Yoga," *Review of Religion* 20 (1956):131–48; Hsiao T'ien-shih, *Tao-chia yang-sheng-hsüeh kai-yao* (Essentials of Taoist theories of nurturing life) 2d ed. (Taipei: Tzu-yu ch'u-pan-she, 1971); and corroborated by examination of pertinent writings in the *Tao Tsang* (Taoist canon) and *Tao-tsang ching-hua* (Flowers of the Taoist canon), general ed. Hsiao T'ien-shih (Taipei: Tzu-yu ch'u-pan-she, continuing series).

Virtually all of the descriptions of the Inner Alchemy process which I have seen describe it solely in terms of the male body. Hsiao T'ien-shih (*Tao-chia yang-sheng-hsüeh,* pp. 343–45) informs us that there was a version of this process designed for women, but I have as yet been unable to locate any writings on Inner Alchemy meditation for females. Women figure in most histories of Taoism only as the partners for sexual yoga. However, assuming that Hsiao is correct, I have referred to "sexual fluids" rather than semen per se, and leave pending the exact interpretation of that term for female praxis.

As we shall see in the next two chapters, Lin's interpretation of Inner Alchemy techniques for his own system tended to avoid the physiological level of discussion. For instance, he never discussed retention of semen overtly. Thus we might surmise that there would be fewer obstacles to adapting the practice for females. In fact, although Lin preached to women and healed at least one (the teenage daughter of Huang Chou; see chapter four, "The Confucian Teacher," and n. 44), it is unclear whether he taught his nine stages of stilling in the back—or any part of them—to women. If he did, he would be cautious about publicizing it, for one of the most serious charges brought against religious groups or leaders in China was that they encouraged lacivious "mixing" of men and women. Lin, with his sensitivity to his public image, would have been very concerned about this. If there was a form of praxis for women, it was probably much simpler than that for men; and it is likely that there were limits on how far women could progress in the yogic process. However, we really do not know.

17. These are forms of traditional "internal hygiene," dating back at least to the period of disunion (third to fifth century C.E.); they are discussed briefly in Holmes Welch, *Taoism: The Parting of the Way,* rev. ed. (Boston: Beacon Press, 1965), pp. 105–12. Li Tao-ch'un's classifications of doctrines both give clues as to earlier Taoist sources of Inner Alchemy ideas and practices and represent one person's attempt to redefine the parameters of the tradition in light of the religious views of this school.

18. Hsiao, *Tao-chia yang-sheng-hsüeh,* pp. 55–59; citation is from pp.

292   V. THE SYSTEM OF MIND-CULTIVATION

57–58. Li Tao-ch'un was introduced in chapter three, in the discussion of Sung syncretism.

19. *Chang Heng-ch'ü chi* (Collection of Chang Tsai) (SPTK ed., based on Cheng-i t'ang ed.), 1.1a; see de Bary, *Sources*, 1:469. Chang Tsai, T. Tzu-hou, H. Heng-ch'ü, was from An-p'ing in Shantung. See *Sung shih* (History of Sung) (Wu-chou: T'ung-wen shu-chü, 1903), 427.1b, and *I-Lo yüan-yüan lu* (Record of the origins of the school of the two Ch'engs), Chu Hsi (Cheng-i t'ang ed.), 6.1a; there is a brief biographical sketch in English in Wing-tsit Chan, trans. and annotator, *Reflections on Things at Hand: The Neo-Confucian Anthology compiled by Chu Hsi and Lü Tsu-ch'ien* (New York: Columbia University Press, 1967), xxxi–xxxii.

20. *Ts'ui-yen* (Pure words), 2 *ch.*, in *Erh-Ch'eng ch'üan-shu* (Collected works of the two Ch'engs) (SPPY ed.), 1.7b; translated in de Bary, *Sources*, 1:475. Ch'eng I, T. Cheng-shu, H. I-ch'üan, was from the I river area in Honan. *Sung shih*, 427.9b; *I-Lo yüan-yüan lu*, 4.1a; Chan, *Reflections*, xxx–xxxi.

21. *T'ai-chi t'u-shuo* (Explanation of the Diagram of the Great Ultimate), in *Chou-tzu ch'üan-shu* (Collected works of Master Chou), ed. Tung Jung (Ch'ien-lung [1736–1795] ed.); see Wing-tsit Chan, trans. and comp., *A Source Book in Chinese Philosophy* (Princeton: Princeton University Press, 1963), p. 463. Chou Tun-i, T. Mao-shu, H. Lien-hsi, was a native of Tao-chou, Honan. *Sung shih*, 427.2b; *I-Lo yüan-yüan lu*, 1.1a; Chan, *Reflections*, xxviii–xxix.

22. Chu Hsi explained Ch'eng Hao's motives in shifting from quiescence to seriousness in *Chu-tzu yü-lei* (Classified conversations of Master Chu), 140 *ch.*, ed. Li Ching-te (Taipei: Cheng-chung shu-chü, 1970; reproduction of 1473 ed.), 94.17b.

23. Ch'eng I, *Chou I chuan* (Commentary on the Chou *Changes*), 4 *ch.*, in *Erh-Ch'eng ch'üan-shu*, 15.4a–4b; translated in Chan, *Reflections*, pp. 141–42. My discussion is indebted to Okada Takehiko, *Seiza to zazen* (Quiet sitting and Ch'an meditation) (Tokyo: Ōfūsha, 1970), esp. pp. 64–76.

24. For a succinct discussion of moral mind in reference to self-cultivation in Chu Hsi, see T'ang Chun-i, "The Development of the Concept of Moral Mind from Wang Yang-ming to Wang Chi," in Wm. Theodore de Bary and the Conference on Ming Thought, *Self and Society in Ming Thought* (New York: Columbia University Press, 1970), pp. 93–97.

25. Okada, *Seiza to zazen*, p. 121. *Chu-tzu yü-lei*, 11.1b, explaining how one scholar used quiet sitting to improve his scholarship.

26. *Chin-ssu lu* (Reflections on things at hand), 4.11b; translated in Chan, *Reflections*, p. 151.

27. *Hsing-li ta-ch'üan-shu* (Great collection of Neo-Confucianism), 70 *ch.*, comp. by Hu Kuang and others (1415). See Wing-tsit Chan, "The *Hsing-li ching-i* and the Ch'eng-Chu School of the Seventeenth Century," in Wm. Theodore de Bary and the Conference on Seventeenth-Century Chinese Thought, *The Unfolding of Neo-Confucianism* (New York: Columbia University Press, 1975), pp. 543–45.

V. THE SYSTEM OF MIND-CULTIVATION 293

28. See Wm. Theodore de Bary, "Neo-Confucian Cultivation and the Seventeenth-Century 'Enlightenment,' " in de Bary, *Unfolding*, p. 117.
29. *Hsing-li ta-ch'üan-shu*, 47.1b.
30. Ibid., 47. 16a–b; from *Chu-tzu yü-lei*, 96.10b; translated in Chan, *Reflections*, p. 151.
31. *Hsing-li ta-ch'üan-shu*, 47.19a. A saying of Li T'ung from the *Chu-tzu yü-lei*, 139.2b. Li T'ung was the teacher of Chu Hsi.
32. *I-shu* (Surviving works), in *Erh-Ch'eng ch'üan-shu*, 7.1a; translation adapted from Chan, *Reflections*, p. 137, to accord with the technical meanings of the terminology in Lin's thought. Ch'eng I simply taught keeping the mind in the body, within. For Lin, the *ch'iang-tzu-li* (within) refers specifically to the cavity of the back, as we shall see below.
33. *Ts'un-hsing kuei-t'iao* (Regulations for preserving the mind and self-examination), D:II.16a–b. (See appendix B).
34. Ibid., 17a–b.
35. Ibid., 18a.
36. Ibid., 18b, 20a.
37. Ibid., 20a–b.
38. The disciple who authored one colophon to "Direct Pointing to the Mind as Sage" recorded that he was only the second person to see the draft of the manuscript, and that he had studied with Lin for two years before he was allowed to see it. *Hsin-sheng chih-chih pa*, II:3.1b–2a (see appendix C).
39. See Sakai Tadao, *Chūgoku zensho no kenkyū* (Researches on Chinese morality books) (Tokyo: Kokusho kankōkai, 1960) and idem, "Confucianism and Popular Educational Works," in de Bary, *Self and Society*, pp. 331–66.
40. On the three bonds and five constant virtues, see n. 41, chapter three.
41. A legendary sage emperor, head of the Taoist celestial pantheon. Because he was more ancient, he had even more spiritual authority than Lao Tzu.
42. This seems to be an allusion to the Ch'ing-ming sect of Taoism, which emerged during the Yüan dynasty. Huang Yüan-ch'i, one of the giants of the sect, sought to integrate Taoism with Confucian morality, teaching the four virtues cited here as a basis for all Taoist doctrine. Lin spoke highly of Huang's doctrines. See *San-chiao hui-pien* (Joint chronicle of the Three Teachings), XII:5.26b–27b.
43. Four elements, i.e., *mahābhūta*: earth, water, fire, and air. These four represent solid, liquid, heat, and motion as components of matter.
44. Allusion to *Analects* 4:5; see James Legge, *The Four Books: Confucian Analects, The Great Learning, The Doctrine of the Mean, and The Works of Mencius* (New York: Paragon, 1966; unaltered reprint of Shanghai, 1923 ed.), p. 40.
45. I.e., *Sheng-hsüeh t'ung-tsung san-chiao kuei-ju chi*, comp. 1567. See appendix B.
46. Ancestral tablets were kept in a separate hall or in a special place in

the house. Lin once wrote an essay describing how poor families could maintain an ancestral altar without straining their finances. *Chu-tai li chi t'u-shuo* (Explanations with diagrams, setting out the generations' tablets for ancestral rites and sacrifices), D:III.21a–30b.

47. Although the realization of the highest stages of mind-cultivation involves sexual abstinence, such abstinence is not recommended for young men and women bound by the filial responsibility of continuing the family line. Lin's teaching bears resemblance to the Hindu system of the four stages of life, in which people were encouraged to fulfill social and secular responsibilities, putting off entry into religious life until a later stage.

48. This seems to be a reference to practices of millenarian Buddhists, who often wore turbans. There was growing concern in the Ming and Ch'ing about the potential social threat posed by these sects, who believed that the secular order and the state were about to end when Maitreya ushered in the eschaton. See Daniel L. Overmyer, *Folk Buddhist Religion: Dissenting Sects in Late Traditional China* (Cambridge: Harvard University Press, 1976).

49. *Chiu-hsü che-yen* (Selected sayings on the nine stages), XVI:1.5b–13b.

50. Ibid., 1a.

51. *Mencius* 6A:11; see Legge, *Four Books*, p. 879.

52. See discussion of his meeting with the enlightened master, in chapter four.

53. The ruler traditionally faces south; hence south is the front.

54. The terms are hyphenated because their order does not reflect the grammar of the situation. Literally, the passage reads: the south of the Fire of the mind; yet it is not the south which is washed, but the mind with its Fire. A similar situation holds with back-Water-north. The terms are chains of correspondences, and the three are seen an interchangeable.

55. Great Treatise of the *Book of Changes*, 1:10; Richard Wilhelm, trans., *The I Ching or Book of Changes*, translated into English by Cary F. Baynes, corrected 3d ed. with a foreword by C. G. Jung and preface by Hellmut Wilhelm, Bollingen Series, 19 (Princeton: Princeton University Press, 1967), p. 316. (Hereafter referred to as Wilhelm/Baynes, *I ching*.) I will follow the section numbers given in the *Shih-san ching so-yin* (Index to the thirteen classics) when those do not agree with Wilhelm/Baynes, to facilitate reference to the Chinese text.

56. *Hsin-sheng chih-chih*, II:2.1a–1b.

57. *Ken* hexagram; translation adapted to fit Lin's system from Wilhelm/Baynes, *I ching*, pp. 652–53.

58. Ibid., adapted from p. 653.

59. Ibid., adapted from p. 653.

60. Ibid., cf. p. 654.

61. Ibid., p. 201.

62. *Great Learning*, 3: see Legge, *Four Books*, pp. 318–20.

63. *T'ung-shu* (Penetrating the *Book of Changes*) (SPPY ed.), 4.21b–22a. Translated in Chan, *Reflections*, p. 272.

64. *Chu-tzu yü-lei*, 73.8b; translated in Chan, *Reflections*, p. 125.

V. THE SYSTEM OF MIND-CULTIVATION 295

65. *Mencius* 4B:26; cf. Legge, *Four Books*, p. 753.
66. *Ming-tao wen-chi* (Collected literary works of Ch'eng Hao), 59 *ch.*, in *Erh-Ch'eng ch'üan-shu*, 3.1a–b; translated in Chan, *Reflections*, pp. 39, 41.
67. *Ming-tao wen-chi*, 3.1b; translated in Chan, *Reflections*, p. 41.
68. *Chou I chuan*, 4.20a; translation adapted from Chan, *Reflections*, pp. 124–25.
69. *Chu-tzu yü-lei*, 73.12b; translated in Chan, *Reflections*, p. 125.
70. Huang Wan, T. Tsung-hsien, H. Chiu-an, was from T'ai-p'ing, Shansi. For biographical material, see *Ming shih* (History of Ming) (Taipei: I-wen yin-shu-kuan, 1961), 197.19b; *Ming-ju hsüeh-an* (Anthology of Neo-Confucians of the Ming), 62 *ch.*, ed. Huang Tsung-hsi (SPPY ed.), 13.5b; biography by Chaoying Fang and D. W. Y. Kwok, in *Dictionary of Ming Biography, 1368–1644*, ed. L. Carrington Goodrich and Chaoying Fang, 2 vols. (New York: Columbia University Press, 1976). See also Jung Chao-tsu, "Wang Shou-jen te men-jen Huang Wan" (Wang Yang-ming's disciple Huang Wan), *Yen-ching hsüeh-pao* 27 (1940):53–113.
71. Huang Wan, *Ming-tao pien* (On elucidating the Way), Chung-kuo ssu-hsiang shih tzu-liao ts'ung-k'an (Peking: Chung-hua shu-chü, 1959), 1.1; see Jung Chao-tsu, *Ming-tai ssu-hsiang shih* (History of Ming thought) (Taipei: K'ai-ming shu-tien, 1962), p. 174.
72. *Ken-chih ching-i chih chih* (The essential meaning of stilling in the *ken* hexagram), from *Wang Lung-hsi ch'üan-chi* (Collected works of Wang Chi), 3 vols. (Taipei: Hua-wen shu-chü, 1970; reproduction of 1822 ed.), 9.1a; see also Yamashita Ryūji, *Ō Yōmei no kenkyū: tenkaihen* (Studies on Wang Yang-ming: development of the school) (Tokyo: Gendai jōhōsha, 1971), p. 139 ff.
73. *Ming-tao pien*, 1.3; see also Yamashita, *Ō Yōmei*, p. 139.
74. *Ming-tao pien*, 1.2; see also Jung, *Ming-tai ssu-hsiang shih*, p. 175.
75. *Ken-chih ching-i chih chih*, 9.11a–12a.
76. Ibid., 12a.
77. Ibid., 11a.
78. *Wang Lung-hsi ch'üan-chi*, 3.14a, in a letter to Wang Nan-ming; see also Yamashita, *Ō Yōmei*, p. 40.
79. Liu Ts'un-yan marshaled evidence to suggest a Taoist genealogy for the term, but he ignored the fact that the only source which clearly juxtaposed the terms said that the theory was Confucian, not Taoist. "Lin Chao-en: The Master of the Three Teachings," *T'oung Pao* 53 (1967):273.

In chapter three, n. 15, I have defined the sense in which Inner Alchemy is Taoist. Of course, the Han system of correspondence was not simply Taoist; it was shared by all schools of thought. However, the use of these homologies in reference to an elaborate system of internal cultivation was by the Ming dynasty associated with the Inner Alchemy school.

80. Liu Ts'un-yan, "Lin Chao-en," pp. 271–72; cited from Yin Chen-jen, *Hsing-ming shuang-hsiu wan-shen kuei-chih* (Revealed doctrine of dual cultivation of nature and life store taught by the myriad spirits), 4 vols. (1615 pref.), 2.15a–b. The translation is Liu's, but I have capitalized Fire and Water to accord with the conventions of this book.

V. THE SYSTEM OF MIND-CULTIVATION

81. *Fen-che hsüan-tsung ta-tao* (Excerpts from the Great Way of the followers of Taoism), XV:6.2a. The Po Yü-ch'an citation is from *Hai-ch'iung ch'uan–tao lu* (Record of Po Yü-ch'an's transmission of the Way), TT. 1017.7b.
82. Liu, "Lin Chao-en," p. 272, citing *Ken-an shuo* (Discussions of the studio of stilling), in *Shang-ch'ing chi* (Collection of supreme purity), TT. 129.42.9b–10a.
83. *Chou-tzu ch'üan-shu*, 18.3a.
84. *Chiao-wai ming-yen* (Perspicacious sayings outside the written doctrine), in *Chung-ho chi* (Collection on equilibrium and harmony), 6 *ch.*, ed. Ts'ai Chih-i, TT. 118–19.6.24a–26b.
85. The other Taoists surveyed were Huang Yüan-ch'i, Chang San-feng, and Cho Wan-ch'un.
86. Sakai, *Chūgoku zensho no kenkyū*, p. 290.
87. The two texts, i.e., *Hsing-ming shuang-hsiu wan-shen kuei-chih*, 2.15a, and *Hsin-sheng chih-chih*, II:2.1b.
88. See chapter four, on the early years of his teaching career.
89. *Chin-ssu lu*, *ch.* 4; see Chan, *Reflections*, secs. 6, 53, 68, 69.
90. *Hsing-li ta-ch'üan-shu*, 47.19b–20a.
91. *Lin-tzu nien-p'u* (Chronological biography of Master Lin), ed. Lin Chao-k'o (1610), 43a (hereafter referred to as *Chronological Biography*). Biographical note on Yüan Tsung-tao in chapter three, section on Ming Neo-Confucian syncretism.
92. The Wilhelm/Baynes version follows the traditional interpretation: "In this way the holy sages purified their hearts, withdrew, and hid themselves in secret," p. 316.
93. *Hsin-sheng chih-chih*, II:2.23a–25a.
94. I have been unable to locate any such reference in the *Book of Changes*. It appears to be a mistaken reference to Great Treatise, 1:4; see Wilhelm/Baynes, *I ching*, p. 296: "Spirit has no direction, and the Changes have no form." The translation is adapted to highlight its affinities with Lin's statement.
95. Great Treatise, 1:10; cf. Wilhelm/Baynes, *I ching*, p. 316.
96. *Hsin-sheng chih-chih*, II:2.13b–14a.
97. See Chou Tun-i, *T'ai-chi t'u-shuo;* translated with the diagram in Fung Yu-lan, *A History of Chinese Philosophy*, 2 vols., trans. Derk Bodde (Princeton: Princeton University Press, 1952–1953) 2:435–51.
98. *Hsin-sheng chih-chih*, II:2.3b.
99. Ibid., 5a–b.
100. *Chronological Biography*, 44a–45a.
101. *Chiu-hsü che-yen*, XVI:1.2a.
102. *Hsin-sheng chih-chih*, II:2.12b.
103. Indirect allusion to Great Treatise, 1:4; see Wilhelm/Baynes, *I ching*, p. 298.
104. *Hsin-sheng chih-chih*, II:2.19b–20a. Mencius 7B:25; see Legge, *Four Books*, p. 995. Translation follows Chan, *Source Book*, p. 82.

V. THE SYSTEM OF MIND-CULTIVATION   297

105. *San-chiao ho-i ta-chih* (The meaning of uniting the Three Teachings), S:1.24b. See appendix D.
106. Ibid., 26a–b. "Conquering the mind" and "no place to abide" are both references to *Chin-kang ching* (The diamond sutra), T.8.748 ff.
107. *San-chiao ho-i ta-chih*, S:1.20b. Reference to *Analects* 2:4; see Legge, *Four Books*, p. 14.
108. This issue was a source of lively debate during the Ming, in the concrete form of a debate over the four axioms of Wang Yang-ming. See Wing-tsit Chan, trans. and annotator, *Instructions for Practical Living and Other Neo-Confucian Writings by Wang Yang-ming* (New York: Columbia University Press, 1963), pp. 241–46.
109. This has already been noted in articles on Lin Chao-en. See Sakai, *Chūgoku zensho no kenkyū*, p. 264, and Mano Senryū, "Rin Chōon to sono chosaku ni tsuite" (On Lin Chao-en and his writings) in *Shimizu hakushi tsuitō kinen Mindaishi ronsō* (Collection of articles on Ming history in commemoration of Professor Shimizu) (Tokyo: Daian, 1962), p. 432.
110. *Chiu-hsü che-yen*, XVI:1.1b.
111. *Lin Tzu* (Master Lin), XVI:6.18a.
112. Colophon, *Ch'iao-yang chiao-yen* (Instructions to disciples in Ch'iao-yang), A:VI.63a. Allusion to *Mencius* 6A:11; see Legge, *Four Books*, p. 879.
113. *Hsin-sheng chih-chih pa*, II:3.1a.
114. *Lin-tzu nien-p'u*, 19b–20b. "Melting the imbalanced" is from *Chu-tzu yü-lei*, 3.19b.
115. See Hsiao, *Tao-chia yang-sheng-hsüeh*, p. 174.
116. The feet were associated with images of water; there is an aperture in the feet called the bubbling spring (*yung ch'üan*). Hence the feet are a suitable place to cool the hot Metal of turbid vital force.
117. *Chronological Biography*, 40a–b.
118. In Ch'en Mei-kung, ed. *Yen-chien mi-lu* (The secret record of ease), of the Sonkeikaku Bunko (Ming ed.). This text does not appear in the Naikaku Bunko's *Yen-chien mi-lu*. Although it appears in the Sonkeikaku version, it carries no editorial information, as do the other volumes of the collection. However, in format, calligraphy, and other details, it appears to fit in with the larger work. Although the name of Lin Chao-en appears nowhere in this work, Sakai Tadao argues cogently on the basis of internal evidence that Master Lin must be Lin Chao-en. Moreover, up to p. 25b or 26a, the healing methods are consistent with examples in the *Lin-tzu nien-p'u*. However, after that point, the work suddenly shifts in both style and content, quoting from ancient medical texts and concentrating largely on sexual problems. In this later section, there is a general essay by Yü Ch'iao (fl. Chia-ching, 1522–1566), who may be the author of the second half. In any case, I am skeptical that the latter portion of the work may be ascribed with confidence to Lin Chao-en. Hence I will restrict my discussion to the material in the first twenty-five pages. For Sakai's argument on authorship, see *Chūgoku zensho no kenkyū*, p. 277 and n. 105.
119. *Lin-shih ch'üeh-ping kung-fu*, 17a.

120. Ibid., 11b.
121. See *San-feng hsien-sheng hsüan ko hsüan t'an* (Songs and talks on the mysterious Way by Master Chang San-feng), XX:6. On Chang San-feng's life, see Anna Seidel, "A Taoist Immortal of the Ming Dynasty: Chang San-feng," in de Bary, *Self and Society*, pp. 483–531.
122. Hsiao, *Tao-chia yang-sheng-hsüeh*, p. 34.
123. Ibid.
124. See discussions of classical versus popular medicine in chapter four.
125. *Ch'iao-yang chiao-yen*, A:VI.59a.

VI. THE NINE STAGES

1. *Chiu-hsü che-yen*, XVI:1; *Hsin-sheng chih-chih*, II:2. (See appendix C). For the sake of clarity it is necessary to divide up the two texts, and change the order of *Hsin-sheng chih-chih*, using it as a kind of commentary on *Chiu-hsü che-yen*. All passages from *Chiu-hsü che-yen* will be cited in the text as "Nine Stages"; all passages from *Hsin-sheng chih-chih* will be cited in the text as "Direct Pointing." Citations from other works will be footnoted in the usual fashion.
2. Allusion to *Mencius* 6A:11; see James Legge, *The Four Books: Confucian Analects, The Great Learning, The Doctrine of the Mean, and The Works of Mencius* (New York: Paragon, 1966; unaltered reprint of Shanghai, 1923 ed.), p. 879. Lin Chao-en often reinterprets terms from his allusions. For the sake of the reader I will, whenever possible, provide a reference to an English translation where the original context of the allusion may be checked.
3. Great Treatise of the *Book of Changes*, 1:10; see Richard Wilhelm, trans., *The I Ching or Book of Changes*, translated into English by Cary F. Baynes, corrected 3d ed. with foreword by C. G. Jung and a preface by Hellmut Wilhelm, Bollingen Series, 19 (Princeton: Princeton University Press, 1967), p. 316. (Hereafter referred to as Wilhelm/Baynes, *I ching*.) I will follow section numbers from the *Shih-san ching so-yin* (Index to the thirteen classics) when these differ from Wilhelm/Baynes to facilitate reference to the Chinese text. References to Wilhelm/Baynes will be made to provide a context for the citation or allusion, or a comparative translation; Lin's understanding of most passages reflects his own system of thought, so I will adapt the translation to convey its meaning in Lin's system.
4. *Wu-yen lu* (Record of the dialogues), XX:2.1b.
5. Allusion to the Great Treatise, 1:12. Translation adapted from Wilhelm/Baynes, *I ching*, p. 324.
6. Allusion to *Mencius* 6A:8; see Legge, *Four Books*, p. 870.
7. See chapter three, the discussion of Sung syncretism as seen in Li Tao-ch'un's *Chiao-wai ming-yen*.
8. *Mencius* 6A:15; see Legge, *Four Books*, pp. 884–85.
9. Allusion to *Analects* 9:4; see Legge, *Four Books*, p. 109. The translation

follows that of Wing-tsit Chan, trans. and comp., *A Source Book in Chinese Philosophy* (Princeton: Princeton University Press, 1963), p. 35, which is more economical and felicitous than Legge's.

10. *Hsin pen-hsü p'ien* (On the mind's original voidness), II:5.17b. Ch'eng I ascribed this saying to his teacher Chou Tun-i. *I-shu* (Surviving works), in *Erh-Ch'eng ch'üan-shu* (The collected works of the two Ch'engs) (SPPY ed.), 6.8b, translated in Wing-tsit Chan, trans. and annotator, *Reflections on Things at Hand: The Neo-Confucian Anthology compiled by Chu Hsi and Lü Tsu-ch'ien* (New York: Columbia University Press, 1967), p. 25.

11. See chapter five, Wang Chi's interpretation of *ken*.

12. *Ming-tao wen-chi* (Collected literary works of Ch'eng Hao), 59 *ch.*, in *Erh-Ch'eng ch'üan-shu*, 3.1a–b; translation adapted from Chan, *Reflections*, p. 41.

13. *Book of History, Wu-ch'eng* sec. See James Legge, trans., *The Chinese Classics: with a translation, critical and exegetical notes, prolegomena and copious indexes* (Oxford, Clarendon Press, 1893), 3:313.

14. *Ming-tao wen-chi*, 3.1a–b; translated in Chan, *Reflections*, p. 41.

15. As will become clear in the course of this chapter, Lin's nine stages control and remake the stream of consciousness. However, he tried with varying success to discuss this method not merely as a matter of mind-cultivation but in ethical as well as mystical terms.

16. *Mencius* 2A:2; cf. Legge, *Four Books*, p. 531. In citing this passage, Lin followed an alternate punctuation criticized by Chu Hsi, who claimed that the subject of the passage was *ch'i*, not the mind. See *Ssu-shu chi-chu* (Annotated version of the Four Books) (Hong Kong: T'ai-p'ing shu-chü, 1968), *Meng-tzu*, 40a–b.

17. Allusion to *Analects* 1:1; cf. Legge, *Four Books*, p. 1.

18. The sixth Ch'an patriarch Hui-neng wrote, "The *samādhi* of oneness is straightforward mind at all times, walking, staying, sitting, and lying." *Liu-tsu fa-pao t'an-ching*, T.48.352; translation cited from Philip B. Yampolsky, *The Platform Sutra of the Sixth Patriarch: The Text of the Tun-huang Manuscript, with Translation, Introduction, and Notes* (New York: Columbia University Press, 1967), p. 136. This passage is frequently alluded to by Inner Alchemy writers.

19. Confucius cited in *Mencius* 6A:8; cf. Legge, *Four Books*, p. 871.

20. "Cling to the body," i.e., *huo shen*. The most basic meaning of *huo* is to seize or catch, but commentators agree that the sense in this passage is to feel or perceive. I have chosen "cling to" in an effort to preserve both senses of the word. Wilhelm/Baynes, *I ching* (p. 652) translate "feels his body." The phrase is from the Judgment to the *ken* hexagram.

21. Allusion to *Analects* 15:9; cf. Legge, *Four Books*, p. 223.

22. Allusion to *Doctrine of the Mean*, 14; cf. Legge, *Four Books*, p. 367.

23. *Chu-tzu yü-lei* (Classified conversations of Master Chu), 140 *ch.*, ed. Li Ching-te (Taipei: Cheng-chung shu-chü, 1970; reproduction of 1473 ed.), 73.8b; translated in Chan, *Reflections*, p. 125.

24. I.e., they are in the front of the body. The emperor faces south; front and rear are defined from the point of view of the ruler.

25. *Chou-i pen-i* (Fundamental meaning of the Chou *Changes*), in 12 *ch.*, by Chu Hsi (Chou-i ch'ing-shu t'ang ed.), 2.39a.
26. Reference to *Analects* 6:9 and 7:15; cf. Legge, *Four Books*, p. 69 and 85, respectively. See also Chan, *Reflections* (p. 50) for Chu Hsi's discussion of the significance of this passage. Lin Chao-en, like Chu Hsi, would argue that these disciples of Confucius did not find their happiness in some external place, but in a place of contentment within themselves.
27. *Fen-che tsung-K'ung hsin-yao* (Excerpts from Essentials of the mind for followers of Confucius), XV:4.18b.
28. *Ch'uan-hsi lu* (SPTK reproduction of 1572 ed.), 1.4a; cited from Wing-tsit Chan, trans. and annotator, *Instructions for Practical Living and Other Neo-Confucian Writings by Wang Yang-ming* (New York: Columbia University Press, 1963), p. 64.
29. *Book of History, I pai* sec.; cf. Legge, *Chinese Classics*, 3:78.
30. *Ts'an t'ung ch'i ch'an-yu* (Explanations of obscure points of the Homology of the Triad), annotator Chu Yüan-yü (Taipei: Chen-shan-mei ch'u-pan-she, 1971; reprint of Ch'ing ed., pref. 1669), 1.32b.
31. *Ken* hexagram; see Wilhelm/Baynes, *I ching*, pp. 655–56.
32. Ibid.
33. *Ch'ien* hexagram; cf. Wilhelm/Baynes, *I ching*, p. 373.
34. Great Treatise, 1:10; see Wilhelm/Baynes, *I ching*, pp. 316–19.
35. *Hsin-sheng chih-chih*, II:2.18b–19a.
36. Allusion to *Analects* 17:17; cf. Legge, *Four Books*, p. 266.
37. Allusion to Great Treatise, 2:6; cf. Wilhelm/Baynes, *I ching*, p. 343.
38. Great Treatise, 2:8; cf. Wilhelm/Baynes, *I ching*, pp. 351–52.
39. I have been unable to locate any such reference in the *Book of Changes*. It appears to be a mistaken reference to Great Treatise, 1:4: "Spirit has no direction, and the Changes have no form." Translation adapted from Wilhelm/Baynes, *I ching*, p. 296, to highlight the similarities with Lin's statement.
40. Great Treatise, 1:10; cf. Wilhelm/Baynes, *I ching*, p. 316.
41. *Ch'ien* hexagram; cf. Wilhelm/Baynes, *I ching*, p. 373.
42. Ibid.
43. An allusion to the description of penetration in the Great Treatise, 1:10; see Wilhelm/Baynes, *I ching*, p. 318.
44. *Lin-tzu nien-p'u* (Chronological biography of Master Lin), ed. Lin Chao-k'o (1610), 43a (hereafter referred to as *Chronological Biography*).
45. As one Taoist source described it, "The means by which one is able to seize the rectified vital force of heaven and earth is exhaling and inhaling through the two nostrils." This was a means of purifying the body and mind and eventually of refining the elixir, the seed of a new self. From Yin Chen-jen, *Hsing-ming shuang-hsiu wan-shen kuei-chih* (Revealed doctrine of dual cultivation of nature and life store taught by the myriad spirits), 4 vols. (1615 pref.), 2.16a.
46. Great Treatise, 2:3; cf. Wilhelm/Baynes, *I ching*, p. 338. All references in this paragraph of "Direct Pointing" are to this passage of the Great Treatise.

VI. THE NINE STAGES   301

47. Allusion to *Analects* 17:10; cf. Legge, *Four Books*, p. 266.
48. *Ch'ien* hexagram; cf. Wilhelm/Baynes, *I ching*, pp. 382–83.
49. Ibid.
50. *Yin-shih-tzu ching-tso fa* (Yin-shih-tzu's method of quiet sitting), in *Ching-tso fa chi-yao* (Summary of methods of quiet sitting), *Tao-tsang ching-hua* (Flowers of the Taoist canon), general ed. Hsiao T'ien-shih (Taipei: Tzu-yu ch'u-pan-she, continuing series), ser. 2, no. 12 (1962), p. 83; translated in Lu K'uan-yü (Charles Luk), *The Secrets of Chinese Meditation: Self-cultivation by Mind Control as Taught in the Ch'an, Mahāyāna, and Taoist schools in China* (London: Rider, 1964), p. 174.
51. *Chronological Biography*, 43a.
52. Po Yü-ch'an, cited in *Wu-chen p'ien san-chu* (On awakening to the truth, with three sets of annotations), 5 *ch.*, ed. Hsüeh Tao-kuang, Lu Shu, and Ch'en Chih-hsü, TT.63.3.5a.
53. Travail, i.e., *k'un:* distress, difficulty, labor. Outer travail is an allusion to *Analects* 16:9 (Legge, *Four Books*, p. 247), where Confucius contrasts those who were born with knowledge, those who attain it through study, and those who must learn through personal hardship or travail. Inner travail is, I believe, an allusion to the *Book of History*, *P'an-keng*, sec. 2, discussing the travail of the mind in worry. See Legge, *Chinese Classics*, 3:236.
54. Reference to the *Book of Rites*, *K'ung-tzu hsien-chü*, 6. See James Legge, trans., *Li Chi: Book of Rites: An Encyclopedia of Ancient Ceremonial Usages, Religious Creeds, and Social Institutions*, 2 vols., ed. Ch'u Chai and Winberg Chai (New Hyde Park, N.Y.: University Books, 1967), 2:282.
55. Great Treatise, 1:10; cf. Wilhelm/Baynes, *I ching*, p. 317.
56. See *Ch'i-ch'iao ta-wen* (Answers to questions on the seven apertures), I:13.1a.
57. *Tao-ho yü-t'an* (Vague discussions on controlling the river [of life force]), XVII:14.8b.
58. Allusion to Lao Tzu, *Tao-te ching*, LXXI; see Arthur Waley, trans., *The Way and its Power: A Study of the Tao Te Ching and its Place in Chinese Thought* (New York: Grove Press, 1958), p. 231.
59. *Ch'i-ch'iao ta-wen*, I:13.4b.
60. Ibid., 6a.
61. Great Treatise, 1:4; see Wilhelm/Baynes, *I ching*, p. 295; italics are mine.
62. Mount Heng is in present-day Hopei; Moung Heng of the South in Hunan; Mount T'ai in Shantung; Mount Hua in Shensi; and Mount Sung in Honan. They are important as the five sacred peaks of the five directions. See Michael Saso, *Taoism and the Rite of Cosmic Renewal* (Pullman, Wash.: Washington State University Press, 1972), pp. 53–54.
63. See *Shih chi* (Records of the Grand Historian), Ssu-ma Ch'ien (Han dynasty), *Feng-ch'an shu*.
64. *Shuo kua* (Discussion of the trigrams), 3; cf. Wilhelm/Baynes, *I ching*, p. 274.
65. *K'un* hexagram; cf. Wilhelm/Baynes, *I ching*, p. 395.

66. *Ken* hexagram; cf. Wilhelm/Baynes, *I ching*, p. 653.
67. Yin,*Hsing-ming shuang-hsiu wan-shen kuei-chih*, 2.16a.
68. *K'un* hexagram; see Wilhelm/Baynes, *I ching*, p. 395, which says, "The superior man is yellow and moderate." The translation is adapted to accord with Lin's system of correspondences.
69. Ibid.
70. Indirect allusion to the Great Treatise, 1:4; see Wilhelm/Baynes, *I ching*, p. 298.
71. True yin is the core which can restore damaged yin (impure *ming* in the form of vital essence [*ching*] and vital force [*ch'i*], and *k'an* as the damaged form of *k'un*) to its original form. See Hsiao T'ien-shih, *Tao-chia yang-sheng-hsüeh kai-yao* (Essentials of Taoist theories of nurturing life) 2d ed. (Taipei: Tzu-yu ch'u-pan-she, 1971), p. 262.
72. *Hsien-hsüeh tz'u-tien* (Dictionary of Taoist studies), ed. Tai Yüan-chang (Taipei: Chen-shan-mei ch'u-pan-she, 1970), p. 173.
73. *Doctrine of the Mean*, 1; see Legge, *Four Books*, p. 349.
74. Great Treatise, 1:5; cf. Wilhelm/Baynes, *I ching*, pp. 297–98.
75. Great Treatise, 1:11; see Wilhelm/Baynes, *I ching*, pp. 318–19.
76. See Hsiao, *Tao-chia yang-sheng-hsüeh*, passim and p. 262. This is also the process of creation symbolized in the movements of the Diagram of the Great Ultimate; see discussion of that diagram in chapter five.
77. *Mencius* 7A:42; cf. Legge, *Four Books*, p. 971.
78. *Analects* 6:27; cf. Legge, *Four Books*, p. 76.
79. *Analects* 12:1; see Legge, *Four Books*, p. 155.
80. *Mencius* 7A:42; cf. Legge, *Four Books*, pp. 971–72.
81. *Book of History, Ta Yü mo*; cf. Legge, *Chinese Classics*, 3:61–62.
82. *Analects* 2:4; cf. Legge, *Four Books*, p. 14.
83. *Mencius* 7A:15; cf. Legge, *Four Books*, p. 885.
84. *Analects* 15:33; cf. Legge, *Four Books*, pp. 232–33. I have condensed the literal translation of Lin's Chinese slightly, for the sake of English prose style; the meaning is unaffected.
85. *Analects* 6:20; cf. Legge, *Four Books*, p. 73.
86. Great Treatise, 1:5; cf. Wilhelm/Baynes, *I ching*, p. 303.
87. Great Treatise, 1:4; cf. Wilhelm/Baynes, *I ching*, p. 298.
88. *Mencius* 7B:25; cf. Legge, *Four Books*, p. 995; translation follows that in Chan, *Source Book*, p. 82.
89. *Mencius* 4B:19; cf. Legge, *Four Books*, p. 744.
90. Ibid.
91. Indirect allusion to Great Treatise, 1:4; see Wilhelm/Baynes, *I ching*, p. 298: "The people use it day by day and are not aware of it."
92. Indirect allusion to Great Treatise, 1:4: "He is content with his circumstances and generous in his kindness." (Wilhelm/Baynes, *I ching*, p. 298). The same passage may also be rendered, "He rested in Earth, and sincerely nurtured humanity," which forms the theme of Lin's stage four.
93. Continued discussion of *Mencius* 7B:25; cf. Legge, *Four Books*, p. 995 ff.

94. *Book of History, Yao tien;* see Legge, *Chinese Classics,* 3:15.
95. *Book of History, T'ai shih,* 3; cf. Legge, *Chinese Classics,* 3:295-96.
96. *Analects* 7:34; cf. Legge, *Four Books,* p. 93.
97. *Mencius,* 7B:25; see Legge, *Four Books,* p. 995.
98. "Direct Pointing," 16b.
99. *Analects* 7:34; cf. Legge, *Four Books,* p. 93.
100. *Mencius* 6A:11; cf. Legge, *Four Books,* p. 879.
101. *Yang Kuei-shan chi* (Collection of Yang Shih), 2 vols. (TSCC ed.; based on the Cheng-i t'ang ed.), 2.32. Yang Shih, T. Chung-li, H. Kuei-shan, was from Chiang-lo, near present-day Chien-an, Fukien. See *Sung shih* (History of Sung) (Wu-chou: T'ung-wen shu-chü, 1903), 428.7b; *I-Lo yüan-yüan lu* (Record of the origins of the school of the two Ch'engs), Chu Hsi (Cheng-i t'ang ed.), 10.1a.
102. *Ko-wu,* investigation of things. Lin's interpretation as "ridding the mind of things" is different from that of most Neo-Confucians; he interprets *ko* as *ko erh ch'ü chih,* to govern or control things in the sense of "ruling them out," getting rid of them. See *Shu-sheng* (On the study of the sages), B:I.16a.
103. It was both life-giving and life-affirming. See Chan, *Source Book,* pp. 788-89.
104. Allusion to *Tao-te ching,* V; cf. Waley, *Way and its Power,* p. 147.
105. Yen Yüan and Jan Niu were disciples of Confucius distinguished for their virtuous conduct. In *Mencius,* it is recorded: "Jan Niu, the disciple Min, and Yen Yüan had all the members of the sage, but in small proportions" (2A:2; see Legge, *Four Books,* p. 535). The sage refers to Confucius; the general meaning is that these three possessed the virtues of their teacher, but not as strongly and clearly.
106. *Great Learning,* 1; see Legge, *Four Books,* pp. 311-12.
107. *Mencius* 2A:2; cf. Legge, *Four Books,* p. 531. Note Lin's punctuation is different from Legge's.
108. *Great Learning,* 1; see Legge, *Four Books,* p. 312.
109. *Analects* 9:4; which Legge (*Four Books,* p. 109) translates as "no arbitrary opinion."
110. See Fung Yu-lan, *A History of Chinese Philosophy,* 2 vols., trans. Derk Bodde (Princeton: Princeton University Press, 1952-1953), 2:11 ff., for an enumeration of these correspondences.
111. See Chao Pi-ch'en, *Hsing-ming fa-chüeh ming-chih* (Taipei: Chen-shan-mei ch'u-pan-she, 1963; reissue of Peking, 1933 ed.; originally late nineteenth century), 5.12b; translated in Lu K'uan-yü (Charles Luk), *Taoist Yoga: Alchemy and Immortality: A translation, with introduction and notes, of The Secrets of Cultivating Essential Nature and Eternal Life (Hsin [sic] Ming Fa Chueh Ming Chih) by the Taoist Master Chao Pi Ch'en,* born 1860 (New York: Samuel Weiser, 1973), p. 54. See also n. 16 to chapter 5.
112. *Hsing-ming fa-chüeh ming-chih,* 2.4a-5b, 3.2b-3a; trans. in Lu, *Taoist Yoga,* pp. 14-15, 23-24.
113. Tai, *Hsien-hsüeh tz'u-tien,* p. 108.

114. Lao Tzu, *Tao-te ching*, VI; cf. Waley, *Way and its Power*, p. 149.
115. Chao, *Hsing-ming fa-chüeh ming-chih*, 8.7a; translated in Lu, *Taoist Yoga*, p. 83.
116. *Chu-tzu yü-lei*, 98.11a; see Chan, *Reflections*, p. 75.
117. Yin, *Hsing-ming shuang-hsiu wan-shen kuei-chih*, 2.15b–16a.
118. *Mencius* 2A:2; cf. Legge, *Four Books*, pp. 527–30.
119. Such is the opinion of Wing-tsit Chan; see *Source Book*, p. 63.
120. *Mencius* 7A:1; cf. Legge, *Four Books*, p. 933.
121. *Lin Tzu* (Master Lin), XVI:6.36b–37a.
122. *Yü jen p'ien* (On humaneness and human desires), I:21.4b.
123. *Hsing-ming ta-yü* (Replies on human nature and life store), I:15.3a–b.
124. *T'ai-chi t'u-shuo* (Explanation of the Diagram of the Great Ultimate), in *Chou-tzu ch'üan-shu* (Collected works of Master Chou), ed. Tung Jung (Ch'ien-lung [1736–1795] ed.); translation adapted from Fung Yu-lan, *History of Chinese Philosophy*, 2:433–44. See the diagram and a discussion of its symbolical relationship to the process of cultivation in chapter five.
125. This is a Chinese view of Nonbeing (*wu*), dating back at least to the time of the Neo-Taoists in the period of disunion; see Fung Yu-lan, *History of Chinese Philosophy*, 2:168–236, esp. pp. 180–84.
126. The *sha-li* ray is somewhat obscure. *Sha-li* was a term used to denote relics of the Buddha or a hall or pagoda in which such relics were enshrined. Pagodas and their relics were sometimes reputed to emit a golden ray, especially at night, which was a sign of the spiritual power of the Buddha. See, for instance, Wu Ch'eng-en, *Hsi-yu chi* (Journey to the West) trans. in part by Arthur Waley as *Monkey* (New York: Grove Press, 1958), and in full by Anthony C. Yu, *The Journey to the West, edited and translated by Anthony C. Yu*, 2 vols. (Chicago: University of Chicago Press, 1976, 1978). It seems that the ray is here identified with the spiritual light of the mind.
127. *Great Treatise*, 1:11; cf. Wilhelm/Baynes, *I ching*, p. 318.
128. A reference to Mencius' *hao-jan chih ch'i*, 2A:2; see Legge, *Four Books*, pp. 529–30.
129. See Hsiao, *Tao-chia yang-sheng-hsüeh*, p. 249.
130. For a similar discussion in more detail, see *Liu Po-tzu p'ien* (On disciple Liu Po-tzu), D:I.9b–11a.
131. *Ssu-shu piao-che cheng-i* (Correct interpretation of the Four Books, by topic), VI:2.22a.
132. *Hsin-ching chih-mi* (Pointing to delusions with the parable of the mind as mirror), I:8.4b.
133. Chao, *Hsing-ming fa-chüeh ming-chih*, 16.2b–3a; see Lu, *Taoist Yoga*, p. 176.
134. *Great Treatise*, 2:5; cf. Wilhelm/Baynes, *I ching*, p. 338.
135. *Analects* 9:4; cf. Legge, *Four Books*, p. 107.
136. I.e., Masters of the Three Teachings: Confucius, Lao Tzu, and Śākyamuni.
137. *Doctrine of the Mean*, 20; cf. Legge, *Four Books*, p. 396.

138. Great Treatise, 1:9; cf. Wilhelm/Baynes, *I ching*, p. 315.
139. *Doctrine of the Mean*, 1; cf. Legge, *Four Books*, p. 351.
140. *Book of History, Ta Yü mo*; see Legge, *Chinese Classics*, 3:61–62.
141. Great Treatise, 2:5; cf. Wilhelm/Baynes, *I ching*, p. 338.
142. *Doctrine of the Mean*, 15; cf. Legge, *Four Books*, p. 369.
143. *Analects* 14:35; cf. Legge, *Four Books*, pp. 211–12.
144. *Analects*, 2:4; cf. Legge, *Four Books*, p. 14.

VII. THE TRUE TRANSMISSION OF THE THREE TEACHINGS

1. See chapter four, the discussion of Lin's early years of teaching.
2. *Lin Tzu* (Master Lin), XVI:6.1a–3a. (See appendix C.)
3. Allusion to *Mencius* 3B:9, in which Mencius decries Mo Tzu's doctrine because it denied the unique affection due to a father. The meaning of the term has shifted in this case to suggest the irreconcilability of celibacy with filial piety. See James Legge, *The Four Books: Confucian Analects, The Great Learning, The Doctrine of the Mean, and the Works of Mencius* (New York: Paragon, 1966; unaltered reprint of Shanghai, 1923 ed.), p. 678.
4. *I-hsüan Tao Shih jen-lun shu-kao* (Draft petition on Buddhists and Taoists and the laws of human relationships), in *Hsü-kao* (Manuscripts, continued), XIV:3.1a–b.
5. *Mencius* 4A:26; see Legge, *Four Books*, p. 725.
6. *I-hsüan Tao Shih jen-lun shu-kao*, XIV:3.1a.
7. Ibid., 1b–2a; the law is recorded in *Ta-Ming lü* (Great Ming code) (Japanese ed., Kyōhō period [1716–1735]), 12.5a.
8. *I-hsüan Tao Shih jen-lun shu-kao*, XIV:3.4a.
9. *Liu-mei t'iao-ta* (Replies on the six items for improvement), XVII:13.4b.
10. *Ta-Ming lü*, 6.4b.
11. *I-hsüan Tao Shih jen-lun shu-kao*, XIV:3.5a.
12. See chapter one for a discussion of the psychology of syncretism. The syncretist will strive to prove his or her "orthodoxy" in order to confirm a self-identification with a specific tradition.
13. It is noteworthy that the notice of disciples teaching members of all religions appears in this work. "Disciple [Huang] Ta-pen gathered a crowd of followers of all Three Teachings to instruct them. He went to P'u-t'ien to inform Master Lin and to ask about the methods of teaching." *Hsia-yü* (Sayings on *hsia*), XVI:7.25b–26a.
14. *Hsia-yü*, XVI:7.9b.
15. *Chiu-kao* (Manuscripts), XIII:1.6a–b. (See appendix C.) Since the *Chiu-kao* was compiled in 1554, this letter should be no later than that.
16. Ibid., XIII:2.6a–7a; this letter can be dated by internal evidence as having been written in 1552. Lo Hung-hsien was introduced in chapter four. The one thread is from *Analects* 15:2; see Legge, *Four Books*, p. 220. "Obtaining the one" is a reference to Lao Tzu, *Tao-te ching*, XXXIX; see Arthur Waley, trans., *The Way and its Power: A Study of the Tao Te Ching and Its Place in Chinese Thought* (New York: Grove Press, 1958), p. 191. The

exact reference of returning to the one is unclear. It is most likely a reference to Hui-neng's *Liu-tsu fa-pao t'an-ching*, T.48.351b: "Athough explanations are made in ten thousand ways,/ If you combine them with the principle, they return to one." Translation adapted to highlight the allusion from Philip B. Yampolsky, *The Platform Sutra of the Sixth Patriarch: The Text of the Tun-huang Manuscript, with Translation, Introduction, and Notes* (New York: Columbia University Press, 1967), p. 160.

17. See, for instance, commentary on stage two in *Hsin-sheng chih-chih* (Direct pointing to the mind as sage), II:2.13b–14a, chapters five and six.

18. *San-chiao hui-pien yao-lüeh* (Joint chronicle of the Three Teachings), XI:1.1a.

19. Liu Mi, *San-chiao p'ing-hsin lun* (On viewing the Three Teachings with a balanced mind) (TSCC ed.), p. 1. *Tsun* refers to the T'ien-tsun (heavenly worthies), venerated as Taoist deities. *Ta* is *mahā*, as in *mahāprajñāparamitā* (great perfected wisdom). This greatness entails the ability of the Buddha-nature to contain all things. See *Liu-tsu fa-pao t'an-ching*, T.48.339c; translated in Yampolsky, *Platform Sutra*, p. 146. I have been unable to locate any biographical data on Liu Mi.

20. *San-chiao p'ing-hsin lun*, p. 1. Lin is citing the *Yüan-tao p'ien* from the Liu Mi essay; the same is true of the other statements on the Three Teachings in this passage.

21. Ibid., p. 2. No biographical information has been located on Li Shih-ch'ien.

22. Ibid., p. 1. Chang Shang-ying, T. T'ien-chüeh, was from Shu-chou in present-day Szechuan. *Sung shih* (History of Sung) (SPPY ed.), 351.2a–3b.

23. *San-chiao hui-pien*, ch. 9, XII:5.28b–29a.

24. Ibid., ch. 5; XII:1.9b. Reference to *Liu-tsu fa-pao t'an-ching*, T.48.353; see Yampolsky, *Platform Sutra*, p. 159.

25. *San-chiao hui-pien*, ch. 5; XII:1.10a; T.48.352; see Yampolsky, *Platform Sutra*, p. 136. *Ching-ming ching* is an alternate name for *Vimalakīrti-nirdeśa Sūtra*, T.14 (No. 475), but as Yampolsky has noted (p. 136), the citation does not appear in this form in that sutra.

26. *San-chiao hui-pien*, ch. 4; XI:6.31a–31b. Fo T'u-teng is said to have come to China around 310; he was known for his magical powers and his ability to produce rain. Kenneth K.S. Ch'en, *Buddhism in China: A Historical Survey* (Princeton: Princeton University Press, 1964), pp. 79–80.

27. *San-chiao hui-pien*, ch. 3; XI:5.36a.

28. In particular Ch'en T'uan (fl. 956–984), who is said to have been a key figure in the transmission of the Diagram of the Great Ultimate to Chou Tun-i; Lü Tung-pin (1154?–1269), who is said to have started the Inner Alchemy tradition; Chang Po-tuan (983–1082), author of the *Wu-chen p'ien* (On awakening to the truth), a major Taoist classic; Po Yü-ch'an, discussed in chapter three as a major patriarch of the school; Ch'en Chih-hsü (Yüan, n.d.); and Huang Yüan-ch'i (Yüan, n.d.), whose thought bears striking similarities to that of Lin Chao-en (or rather Lin's to his).

29. *San-chiao hui-pien*, ch. 3; XI:5.36b. The Neo-Taoists and their con-

cerns are succinctly described in Richard Mather, "The Controversy over Conformity and Naturalness During the Six Dynasties," *History of Religions* 9 (1969–1970):160–81.

30. It has generally been assumed by scholars that Taoist influence on Neo-Confucianism would have come via the route of Neo-Taoism, because of the philosophical subtlety of that school, their interest in cosmological speculation and the *Book of Changes*, and their dialogues with early Buddhists. See, for instance, Jen Yu-wen, "Ch'en Hsien-chang's Philosophy of the Natural," in Wm. Theodore de Bary and the Conference on Ming Thought, *Self and Society in Ming Thought* (New York: Columbia University Press, 1970), pp. 53–92. I am not disputing the potential of Neo-Taoist influence on Neo-Confucians, but we have erred in not looking to contemporary Taoists who had interests in syncretic dialogue with other traditions.

31. Shao Yung, T. Yao-fu, H. K'ang-chieh, called Master An-lo, was originally from Fan-yang, south of present-day Ting-hsing county in Chihli; but he moved south and settled in Honan. See *Sung shih* (History of Sung) (Wu-chou: T'ung-wen shu-chü, 1903) 427.27b; *I-Lo yüan-yüan lu* (Record of the origins of the school of the two Ch'engs), by Chu Hsi (Cheng-i t'ang ed.), 5.11a; a brief biographical sketch in English is found in Wing-tsit Chan, trans. and annotator, *Reflections on Things at Hand: The Neo-Confucian Anthology Compiled by Chu Hsi and Lü Tsu-ch'ien* (New York: Columbia University Press, 1967), xxxi–xxxii.

32. *San-chiao hui-pien*, ch. 7; XII:3.18b–19b.

33. Ibid., ch. 9; XII:4.21b–22a. Li T'ung, T. Yüan-chang, H. Yen-p'ing, was from Nan-chien in present-day Fukien, Nan-p'ing county. He was the teacher of Chu Hsi and a strong advocate of quiet sitting. See *Sung shih*, 428.14b.

34. *San-chiao hui-pien*, ch. 9; XII:5.1b–2b.

35. On the Ming attitude toward cosmological and metaphysical speculation, see Wing-tsit Chan, "The Ch'eng-Chu School of Early Ming," in de Bary, *Self and Society*, pp. 29–52, esp. p. 33.

36. See, for instance, the discussion of Han Yü's memorial on the Buddha's bone in chapter two. Huang Yü-p'ien (fl. 1830–1840), in his *P'o-hsieh hsiang-pien* (Detailed refutations of heresies), attempted to "persuade" followers of millenarian Buddhism to return to the true Way of Confucius, but he was so sectarian and vicious in his criticisms of their views that his writings served only to widen the gap between the two views. He forms a striking contrast with Lin Chao-en, whose "correction of errors" is much gentler and moves gradually from old ideas to new ones. Granted, Lin's arguments would seldom convince Taoists or Buddhists set in their ways; but if they are open, he attempts to make the transition painless. See my article, "When They Go Their Separate Ways: Preliminary Reflections on Eighteenth Century Syncretism," in revision for a volume from the Conference on Eighteenth Century Thought, Asilomar, California, Tu Wei-ming ed., forthcoming.

37. *I-hsüan Tao Shih jen-lun shu-kao*, XIV:3.2a–3b.

38. See Ch'en, *Buddhism in China*, p. 83.
39. *Fen-che tsung-K'ung hsin-yao*, XV:3–4; *Fen-che hsüan-tsung ta-tao*, XV:5–6; *Fen-che hsing-k'ung tsung-chih*, XV:7–8.
40. *Pen-t'i chiao* (Instructions on original nature), I:10.1a. Allusion to *Analects* 9:8; see Legge, *Four Books*, p. 111.
41. *Pen-t'i chiao*, I:10.1b–2a. "What is still and unmoving in original nature" is an allusion to Great Treatise of the *Book of Changes*, 1:9; translation adapted from Richard Wilhelm, trans., *The I Ching or Book of Changes*, translated into English by Cary F. Baynes, corrected 3d ed. with a foreword by C. G. Jung and a preface by Hellmut Wilhelm, Bollingen Series, 19 (Princeton: Princeton University Press, 1967), p. 315, which says, "The Changes have no consciousness, no action; they are quiescent and do not move." (Hereafter referred to as Wilhelm/Baynes, *I ching*.) "What is spirit-like and boundless in original nature" is from Great Treatise, 1:4, adapted from Wilhelm/Baynes, *I ching*, p. 296: "Therefore the spirit is bound to no one place, nor the *Book of Changes* to any one form."
42. *Pen-t'i chiao*, I:10.2a, 2b.
43. Ibid., 3b.
44. *San-chiao wu-che ta-hui* (The unlimited meeting of the Three Teachings), I:18.7b.
45. *Ssu-shu piao-che cheng-i hsü* (Correct interpretation of the Four Books, by topic, continued), VIII:2.39b.
46. *Lin Tzu*, XVI:6.9b. Conquering the mind is an allusion to *Chin-kang ching* (Diamond Sutra), T.8.748c ff. Emptying minds and filling bellies is an allusion to Lao Tzu, *Tao-te ching*, III; see Waley, *Way and its Power*, p. 145. Washing the mind and hiding it is an allusion to Great Treatise, 1:10; see Wilhelm/Baynes, *I ching*, p. 316.
47. *P'o-mi* (Breaking down delusions), IV:3.8b–9a.
48. See *Chuang Tzu*, 4; translated in Burton Watson, trans., *The Complete Works of Chuang Tzu* (New York: Columbia University Press, 1968), pp. 57–58.
49. *Ch'ih-chai pien-huo* (Discussion of doubts about fasting), IV:4; passim.
50. *San-chiao hui-pien, ch.* 1; XI:3.3a.
51. See Wilhelm/Baynes, *I ching*, appendix on consulting the oracle, pp. 721–23.
52. *Yü-yen* (Parables), IV: 2.2a–b.
53. *San-chiao hui-pien, ch.* 4; XI:6.32a–b. On the Bodhidharma legend, see Heinrich Dumoulin, *A History of Zen Buddhism*, trans. Paul Peachey (Boston: Beacon Press, 1969; originally New York: Pantheon, 1963), pp. 67–72.
54. The original is found in *Ching-chieh hsien-sheng chi* (Collection of Master T'ao Ch'ien) (SPPY ed.), 6.1a ff.
55. *Yü-yen*, IV:2.14a–15b.
56. Outstanding examples are the Commentaries on the Four Books (V:1–VIII:2), *Shu-sheng* (On the study of the sages, B:1; see appendix B), and speculative works such as *San-chiao wu-che ta-hui*, I:18.

VII. THE TRUE TRANSMISSION 309

57. *Ssu-yin yü*, I:12; other simple works include *Yü-yen* (IV:2), and *P'o-mi* (IV:3).
58. *Hsien-yen* (The a priori abundant), II:2.
59. *San-kang kua* (Tetragrams of the three bonds), XVII:15.
60. *San-chiao tao-t'ung chung-i ching* (Scripture of the one in the Center in the line of the Three Teachings), XVIII:9–11.
61. *I-chieh li-yü*, S:72.1a (See appendix D).
62. *Lin-tzu nien-p'u* (Chronological biography of Master Lin), ed. Lin Chao-k'o (1610), 29b (hereafter referred to as *Chronological Biography*).
63. *Ssu-shu piao-che cheng-i*, VI:2.27b–28a.
64. *Hsin pen-hsü p'ien* (On the mind's original voidness), II:5.34a.
65. Ibid., 34b–35a.
66. *Hsin-sheng chih-chih* (Direct pointing to the mind as sage), II:2.26b; allusion to *Analects* 14:35; see Legge, *Four Books*, pp. 211–12.
67. Allusion to *Analects* 8:9; see Legge, *Four Books*, p. 100, in which Confucius says, "The people may be made to follow a path of action, but they may not be made to understand it." Lin interprets this as a distinction between a way which can be followed, which has a means of praxis, and a way hard to understand because it is couched in the transcendent terms of philosophy.
68. Allusion to *Book of Odes*, 235, cited in the *Doctrine of the Mean*, 33; cf. Legge, *Four Books*, p. 526.
69. Yen Hui was Confucius' most ardent and beloved disciple. Min was listed as one of the three disciples distinguished for virtue (*Mencius* 2A:2; see Legge, *Four Books*, p. 535). However, I have not yet discovered the precedent for singling out these two as a pair to be "counted first."
70. Allusion to *Analects* 8:9; see Legge, *Four Books*, p. 100.
71. Allusion to *Analects* 9:1; see Legge, *Four Books*, p. 107.
72. *Hsü-kao*, XIV:4.3b–5a.
73. *Yüan-shen shih-i* (The true meaning of original spirit), III:5.13a–b.
74. *Hsü-kao*, XIV:4.1a–1b.
75. Ibid., XIV:4.1b–2b.
76. Allusion to *Analects* 12.5; cf. Legge, *Four Books*, p. 160.
77. *Chang Heng-ch'ü chi* (Collection of Chang Tsai) (SPTK ed., based on Cheng-i t'ang ed.), 1.1a; translated in full in Wm. Theodore de Bary et al., *Sources of Chinese Tradition*, 2 vol. paperback ed. (New York: Columbia University Press, 1964), 1:469.
78. *Ssu-shu piao-che cheng-i hsü*, VII:3.16a–b.
79. *Shuo hsia* (Discussions of *hsia*), I:6.1a.
80. Ibid., 2b.
81. Ibid., 3a.
82. *Chronological Biography*, 22b.
83. William E. Soothill and Lewis Hodous, comps., *A Dictionary of Chinese Buddhist Terms with Sanskrit and English Equivalents, a Chinese Index, and Sanskrit-Pali Index* (London: Kegan, Paul, Trench, Trubner, 1937), p. 382.
84. *San-chiao wu-che ta-hui*, I:18.1b.

310   VII. THE TRUE TRANSMISSION

85. Ibid., 2b.
86. Allusion to *Mencius* 4A:1; see Legge, *Four Books*, p. 688: "Virtue alone is not sufficient for the exercise of government; laws alone cannot carry themselves into practice."
87. *San-chiao wu-che ta-hui*, I:18.6a.

VIII. THE LEGACY OF LIN CHAO-EN

1. Ho Ch'iao-yüan, *Ming-shan tsang* (Storehouse of the mountain of names), 20 vols., written 1586 (1640 ed.), *Pen-shih chi*, 9b. Ho Ch'iao-yüan, T. Chih-hsia, H. Fei-i, was from Chin-chiang, in the area of present-day Ch'üan-chou or the Amoy region of Fukien. He is best known for his historical writings. See *Ming shih* (History of Ming) (Taipei: I-wen yin-shu-kuan, 1961), 249.9b; biography by Lee Hwa-chou and L. Carrington Goodrich in *Dictionary of Ming Biography, 1368–1644*, ed. L. Carrington Goodrich and Chaoying Fang (New York: Columbia University Press, 1976).

2. *Lin san-chiao chuan* (Biography of Three Teachings Lin), in *Nan-lei wen-an* (Critical comments on literature by Huang Tsung-hsi), 10 *ch.* (Hsi-shuang t'ang ed., 1680 pref.), 9.1b–2a. Huang Tsung-hsi, T. T'ai-chung, H. Nan-lei and Li-chou, was a native of Yü-yao, Chekiang. For a detailed biography with Chinese sources, see Lienche Tu Fang, in Arthur Hummel, ed., *Eminent Chinese of the Ch'ing Period* (Washington: U.S. Government Printing Office, 1943), pp. 352–54.

3. *Lin-tzu nien-p'u* (Chronological Biography of Master Lin), ed. Lin Chao-k'o (1610), 26a, 26b, 29b, 33b, 36a, 38b (hereafter referred to as *Chronological Biography*). Mano Senryū has described the teaching activities in some detail in his latest book, *Mindai bunkashi kenkyū* (Studies on Ming cultural history) (Kyoto: Dōhōsha, 1979), esp. pp. 451–52. Lin first began teaching when people pressed him to explain his ideas as he traveled.

4. From 1584, shrines of the cult were erected with increasing regularity. *Chronological Biography*, 58b ff. Mano Senryū has published a convenient chart of the dates and locations of the shrines recorded in that work. "Mindai ni okeru sankyō shisō; toku ni Rin Chōon o chūshin to shite" (Three Teachings thought in the Ming dynasty, with special reference to Lin Chao-en), *Tōyōshi kenkyū* 12 (1952):439–40.

5. *Chronological Biography*, 53b–54a.

6. We know that there were such assemblies in the cult shortly after Lin's death; see below.

7. *Chronological Biography*, 23a.

8. *Sung-chang* (Hymns), III:9.

9. See discussion of the simpler and simplified writings in chapter seven.

10. See chapter four, discussion of Lin's struggle with superintendent of education Chu Heng.

11. In *Chüeh-mi li ts'e* (A calabash measure for awakening from errors), 3 *ch.* (1600 pref.), 1.27a. Kuan Chih-tao was introduced in chapter three, in

VIII. THE LEGACY OF LIN CHAO-EN 311

the discussion of conservative reaction against the excesses of the T'ai-chou school in the Ming.

12. *Wu tsa tsu* (Five miscellaneous sacrificial plates), 16 *ch.* (Japanese ed., 1789; original pub. 1616), 8.45a. Hsieh's passage is translated in full in Wolfgang Franke, "Some Remarks on Lin Chao-en (1517–1598)," *Oriens Extremus* 20 (1973):162–64. Hsieh Chao-che, T. Tsai-hang, was from Ch'ang-lo near Fuchow, Fukien. He was a man of broad erudition with a reputation as a good local official. See *Ming shih*, 186.2a.

13. Huang, *Lin san-chiao chuan, Nan-lei wen-an*, 9.1b–2a.

14. Chu I-tsun, *Ching-chih chü shih-hua* (Discussions of poetry by one who abides in the quiescent will), 24 *ch.* in 20 vols., ed. Yao Liu-i (1820 ed., from the Fu-li shan fang), 14.35a.

15. Okada Takehiko has cited the *Li-shih shuo-shu* (Discussions of writings by Li Chih), attributed to the editorship of Li Chih, with Lin Chao-en cited as publisher. The book appears to be a mixture of their teachings on the Four Books, although all of the sayings are attributed to Li Chih. See Okada Takehiko, *Ō Yōmei to Minmatsu no jugaku* (Wang Yang-ming and late Ming Confucianism) (Tokyo: Kōmeisha, 1970), pp. 244–49. Since Li and Lin were so different, I can only postulate that the book is a forgery from the hand of someone familiar with the writings of both men; I doubt very much that either Li or Lin would have consented to have his name linked with the other.

16. *Chronological Biography*, 22a. Ch'i Chi-kuang, T. Yüan-ching, was from Ting-yüan in present-day Wu-sheng county of Szechuan. His family held a hereditary military post. See *Ming shih*, 212.11a; *Ming-shan tsang*, 24.26; biography by J. F. Millinger and Chaoying Fang in *Dictionary of Ming Biography*.

17. In his *Yü-yü kao* (Manuscripts of ignorance about ignorance), in *Chih-chih t'ang chi* (Collection from the hall of stopping stopping) (pub. 1888; original pref., 1574), 1.11a.

18. See preface to *Chung-i hsü-yen chi* (Collection of introduction to the Center and the one) by Lu Wen-hui, S:63 (see appendix D).

19. *Ming-ching t'ang* (Hall for expounding classics), XVII:1.5b. These regulations were discussed in chapter four.

20. Hsieh, *Wu tsa tsu*, 8.45a.

21. See, for example, *P'o-mi* (Breaking down delusions), IV:3.20a–b, in which Lin criticizes the use of spells and talismans.

22. Wolfgang Franke, "Some Remarks on the 'Three-in-One Doctrine' and its Manifestations in Singapore and Malaysia," *Oriens Extremus* 19 (1972):130, and illustration 8.

23. *Chronological Biography*, 58b–59a. I have found no biographical information on Lin Chih-ching.

24. *Ming-hsia chi* in 4 *ch.* (1598 preface). Preserved in the Naikaku Bunko, Foreword, 1b–2a.

25. Ibid., Foreword, 1a. The *Fen-nei chi* (Collection on the world as my family), in 12 *ch.*, by Lin Chao-en, L:22 (see appendix E).

26. *Ming-hsia chi*, 4.24b–32b, records how Lin Chih-ching used this method to heal a variety of cases.
27. Ibid., 1.16a–17b. *Hun* and *p'o* were heavenly and earthly souls which constituted the self. At death the heavenly soul returned to heaven and the earthly soul returned to the soil.
28. Ibid., 2.28a.
29. Ibid., 2.29b.
30. Ibid., 2.32a.
31. Ibid., 3.29a. The Queen Mother of the West ruled the peach garden in heaven and figures dominantly in folk religion; she seems to have influenced the Holy Mother figure in Buddhist millenarian cults. Yüan-shih T'ien-tsun (Heavenly Worthy of the Primordial Beginning) was one of the three major deities (Heavenly Worthies) in many ritual Taoist texts. See Edward T. C. Werner, *A Dictionary of Chinese Mythology*, introduction by Hyman Kublin (New York: Julian Press, 1961), pp. 609–11.
32. *Chung-i hsü-yen chi*, S:63.
33. *Chronological Biography*, 55b.
34. Ibid., 58b.
35. For the significance of the robe and the bowl, see Philip B. Yampolsky, trans. and annotator, *The Platform Sutra of the Sixth Patriarch: The Text of the Tun-huang Manuscript with Translation, Introduction, and Notes* (New York: Columbia University Press, 1967), pp. 86–87, 129, 137. Preface to *Chung-i hsü-yen chi* by K'o Shou-k'ai, 2a, in S:63.
36. *Chung-i hsü-yen chi*, pref. by Chai Hsin; charts, and text, passim.
37. *Chung-i hsü-yen chi*, S:63.2a–b.
38. Ibid., 10b–11a.
39. Ibid. I have been unable to locate this statement in *T'ai-hsüan ching chi-chu* (The book of the great mysterious, with notes), 6 *ch.*, by Yang Hsiung of the Han dynasty, with notes by Ssu-ma Kuang of the Sung, TT.860–62.
40. *Chung-i hsü-yen chi*, S:63.10a–b. "Neither forgetting nor helping" is an allusion to *Mencius* 2A:2; see James Legge, *The Four Books: Confucian Analects, The Great Learning, The Doctrine of the Mean, and The Works of Mencius* (New York: Paragon, 1966; unaltered reprint of Shanghai, 1923 ed.). "Washing and hiding it" is an allusion to Great Treatise of the *Book of Changes*, 1:10; see Richard Wilhelm, trans., *The I Ching or Book of Changes*, translated into English by Cary F. Baynes, corrected 3d ed., with a foreword by C. G. Jung and preface by Hellmut Wilhelm, Bollingen Series, 19 (Princeton University Press, 1967), p. 316.
41. Lu Wen-hui, *Hsing-ling shih* (Poems on the spiritual luminosity of human nature), S:64.11b–12b, in which he wrote about Confucius, Lao Tzu, Śākyamuni, and Hsia-wu-ni.
42. Huang, *Lin san-chiao chuan, Nan-lei wen-an*, 9.2b.
43. For biographical information, see chronological biography in *Ch'eng-shih ts'ung-shu* (Reprinted writings of Ch'eng Chih), preserved in the Nai-

VIII. THE LEGACY OF LIN CHAO-EN 313

kaku Bunko (Ch'ing ed.), and Sakai Tadao, *Chūgoku zensho no kenkyū* (Researches on Chinese morality books) (Tokyo: Kokusho kankōkai, 1960), pp. 282–83.

44. This allegation is found in Lu Shan-huang, *Ta-yü chi* (Record of the great trial), preserved in *Shuo k'u* (Storehouse of sayings), 60 vols., comp. Wang Wen-ju, 3d carving (Taipei: Wen-ming shu-chü, 1925), 60.5a, and in Hsü K'o, *Ch'ing-pai lei-ch'ao* (Classified documents of Ch'ing legend), 48 vols. (Shanghai: Sheng-wu yin-shu-kuan, 1917), *Tsung-chiao lei*, pp. 60–63. The remarks in these sources seem to be based on Huang Tsung-hsi's statement.

Lin visited Lo Hung-hsien before giving up examination studies. Although Lin never openly aligned himself with any school of Neo-Confucians, it is possible that his contacts with Lo were well known. Mano Senryū discusses the basis for the identification of Lin with this school in his *Mindai bunkashi kenkyū*, pp. 467–68.

45. Lu, *Ta-yü chi*, *Shuo-k'u*, 60.6b. Note the similarity in phrasing to the remark in Huang's biography of Lin.

46. This is the view of Sakai Tadao, in *Chūgoku zensho no kenkyū*, p. 281.

47. *Ch'eng-shih ts'ung-shu*, 1.35b, 36b.

48. See the discussion of the interpretation of *ken* in chapter five.

49. Sakai Tadao disagrees. See above, n. 46. On the T'ai-ku sect, see Ma Yu-yüan, "Ch'ing-chi T'ai-ku hsüeh-p'ai shih-shih shu-yao" (Brief discussion of the historical events surrounding the T'ai-ku sect of the Ch'ing), *Ta-lu tsa-chih* 28, no. 10 (May 1964):13–18; Lu Chi-yeh, "T'ai-ku hsüeh-p'ai chih yen-ko chi ch'i ssu-hsiang" (Successive changes in the T'ai-ku sect and its thought), *Tung-fang tsa-chih* 24 (1927):71–75; Liu Tzu-hou, "Chang Shih-ch'in yü T'ai-ku hsüeh-p'ai" (Chang Shih-ch'in and the T'ai-ku sect), *Fu-jen hsüeh-chih* 9 (1940):81–124. Liu's article is particularly valuable in that it quotes extensively from the writings of Chou T'ai-ku, the founder, and Li Ching-feng, the founder of the southern branch. Unfortunately, I have not had the opportunity to see primary documents of the cult.

50. Liu Tzu-hou, "Chang Shih-ch'in," pp. 96–101.

51. On Lin's use of such symbols, see chapter seven, the discussion of pedagogical methods, and the Hsia-wu-ni scriptures (XX:7–8; see appendix C).

52. Liu Tzu-hou, "Chang Shih-ch'in," pp. 101–7.

53. Ibid., p. 93.

54. Ibid., p. 105.

55. Ibid., pp. 107–8; on the life of Li Ching-feng, see ibid., pp. 94–95.

56. Ibid., pp. 110–12.

57. Ibid., p. 113.

58. Ibid., p. 102.

59. Ibid., pp. 101–7.

60. Hsü, *Ch'ing-pai lei-ch'ao*, *Tsung-chiao lei*, p. 60.

61. This is Liu's contention, in "Chang Shih-ch'in," pp. 121–24.
62. Ibid., pp. 116–18, and Sakai, *Chūgoku zensho no kenkyū*, p. 281 and chapter 7.
63. Lin Chao-en's thought bore certain similarities to strains of Taoism in his day; it may be that there was a bridge between his ideas and those of the T'ai-ku school through some Taoist intermediary. Whether or not scholarship can establish direct influence of Lin on these later religions, it is clear that the ideas he proposed were not an isolated and short-lived phenomenon but part of a larger trend of religious thought.
64. *Ta-Ch'ing li-ch'ao shih-lu* (Veritable record of the successive reigns of the Ch'ing dynasty), 94 vols. (Taipei: Hua-lien ch'u-pan-she photocopy, 1964), 218.8a.
65. Wolfgang Franke reported on the modern remnants of the cult in "Three-in-One Doctrine," p. 123.
66. Because of Lin's activities during the pirate raids, the cult became associated with anti-Japanese resistance, as we shall see below. Perhaps this anti-Japanese feeling of the cult forced it to go underground or disband during the Japanese occupation of Taiwan.
67. Franke, "Lin Chao-en," p. 162.
68. Idem., "Three-in-One Doctrine," pp. 125–26.
69. Ibid., p. 128.
70. Ibid., p. 121, and figure 1.
71. Ibid., p. 123. *San-feng hsien-sheng hsüan ko hsüan t'an* (Songs and talks on the mysterious Way by Master Chang San-feng), XX:6.
72. *San-feng hsien-sheng* (Master Chang San-feng), S:66, pref., 1b.
73. On the legends surrounding this man, see Anna Seidel, "A Taoist Immortal of the Ming Dynasty: Chang San-feng," in Wm. Theodore de Bary and the Conference on Ming Thought, *Self and Society in Ming Thought* (New York: Columbia University Press, 1970), pp. 483–531.
74. Franke, "Three-in-One Doctrine," figure 6.
75. For my information on books now preserved in temples of the cult, I am indebted to Professor Wolfgang Franke, who kindly sent me copies of unpublished notes he made at the temples.
76. I.e., *San-chiao cheng-tsung t'ung-lun* (Discussions on the combination of correct principles of the Three Teachings), described in appendix D.
77. Franke, "Three-in-One Doctrine," where the inscription records that during the Japanese occupation the Master Immortal prophesied the end of the war, which had interrupted the construction of a cult grotto. It is possible that the Master Immortal designates someone outside the cult, but the text seems to imply that everyone reading the inscription would recognize the title; hence I suspect that it had become a priestly title within the cult.
78. Ibid., figure 8 and p. 124. On Maitreya Buddha, see Werner, *Chinese Mythology*, p. 303; on Chia-lan, p. 57; on Wei-t'o, p. 533. Ho Hsin-yin, T. Fu-shan, H. Kuei-ch'ien, original name Liang Ju-yüan, was a native of Yung-feng, Kiangsi. See *Ming shih*, 18.130; *Ming-ju hsüeh-an* (Anthology of Neo-Confucians of the Ming), 62 *ch.*, ed. Huang Tsung-hsi (SPPY ed.),

VIII. THE LEGACY OF LIN CHAO-EN

32.1a, and biography by Wu Pei-yi and Julia Ching in *Dictionary of Ming Biography*.

79. *San-i chiao-chu shuo Mi-le tsun-fo pao-ching* (Precious sutra honoring Maitreya Buddha preached by the Lord of the Three-in-One), XX:7.

80. See Werner, *Chinese Mythology*, for Kuan-yin, p. 228; for Kuan-kung, p. 229; for Sheng-mu, p. 373.

81. Yang Shu-liang, "Hsia-wu-ni-shih tao-t'ung chung-i san-chiao tu-shih ta-tsung-shih chuan-lüeh" (Brief biography of Hsia-wu-ni, savior and master of the line of the Center and the one of the Three Teachings), *Fu-chien wen-hua* 3 (1935):42.

82. See Ronald G. Dimberg, "The Life and Thought of Ho Hsin-yin: 1517–1579" (Ph.D. diss., Columbia University, 1970), pp. 55–56. Dimberg has published a revision of the dissertation, which does not include this material: *The Sage and Society: The Life and Thought of Ho Hsin-yin* (Honolulu: University of Hawaii Press, 1974).

83. See Wm. Theodore de Bary, "Introduction," to *Self and Society*, on the situation of the Ming intellectual, pp. 5–8.

84. *Chronological Biography*, 56a.

GLOSSARY

Names of persons and deities who do not appear in the bibliography as authors.

Chai Hsin 祭新
Chan Ling 詹陵
Chang Ch'e 張徹
Chang Hung-tu 張洪都
Chang Mei 張美
Chang Po-tuan 張伯端
Chang Shang-ying 張商英
Chen-ming Tzu 禎明子
Ch'en Chih-hsü 陳致虛
Ch'en Chuan-hui 陳轉惠
Ch'en Chung-yü 陳衷瑜
Ch'en Hsien-chang 陳獻章
Ch'en Su-k'un 陳素悃
Ch'en Tao-ch'ing 陳道清
Ch'en T'uan 陳摶
Ch'eng Yün-chang 程雲章
Chi Yün 紀昀
Chia-lan 伽藍
Chia Tzu-li 叚子利
Ch'ien Ch'ien-i 錢謙益
Chih-i 智顗
Ch'ih Ho-ch'un 池鶴椿
Ch'in 秦
Cho Wan-ch'un 卓晚春

Chou T'ai-ku 周太谷
Chu Fang-tan 朱方旦
Chu Heng 朱衡
Chu Ho-ling 朱鶴齡
Chu I-tsun 朱彝尊
Chuang Tzu 莊子
Erh-hsü-tzu 爾虛子
Fo T'u-teng 佛圖澄
Fu-hsi 伏羲
Genkei 玄契
Han-shan Te-ch'ing 憨山德清
Ho Hsin-yin 何心隱
Honda Wataru 本田濟
Hsi-wang-mu 西王母
Hsia-wu-ni 夏午尼
Hsing-ju Tzu 性如子
Hsüeh Tao-kuang 薛道光
Hu Chü-jen 胡居仁
Huang Chou 黃州
Huang Chou 黃冑
Huang Yü-p'ien 黃育楩
Hui-chiao 慧皎
Hui-ti 惠廸
Hun-hsü-shih 混虛氏

Hung Hsiu-ch'üan 洪秀全
Hung Tzu-wen 洪子文
Ko Hung 葛洪
Ku Ta-lin 顧大琳
Ku Ying-t'ai 谷應泰
Kuan Kung 關公
Kuan-yin 觀音
Jan Niu 冉牛
K'o Shou-k'ai 柯壽愷
Lao Tzu 老子
Li Ching-feng 李晴峯
Li Hsüeh-shih 李學仕
Li Shih-ch'ien 李士謙
Li T'ung 李侗
Lieh Tzu 列子
Lin Chao-chü 林兆居
Lin Chih-sheng 林之盛
Lin Fu 林富
Lin Wan-ch'ao 林萬潮
Lin Wan-jen 林萬仭
Liu Ching-pang 劉經邦
Liu Hsün 劉勳
Lo Ch'in-shun 羅欽順
Lo Hung-hsien 羅洪憲
Lu Hsiang-shan 陸象山
Lu Shu 陸墅
Lü Tsu-ch'ien 呂祖謙
Lü Tung-pin 呂洞賓
Min 閔
Mo Tzu 墨子
Mochizuki Shinkō 望月信亨
Mogi Shūichirō 茂木秀一郎
Morohashi Tetsuji 諸橋轍次
Ni Yüan-lu 倪元璐
P'an-ku 盤古
Po Chü-i 白居易
Ryūchi Kiyoshi 龍池清
Shao Yung 召雍
Sheng-mu 聖母
Shih 奭
Shimizu Taiji 清水泰次
Shun 舜

Ssu-ma Kuang 司馬光
Sung I-tsu 宋藝祖
Ta-hui Tsung-kao 大慧宗杲
Ta-kuan 達觀
Tao-an 道安
Tao-hsüan 道宣
Tao-yüan 道原
T'ao Hung-ching 陶弘景
Te-ch'ing 德清
Tomaru Fukuju 登丸福壽
Ts'ao-shan 曹山
Tseng Tien 曾點
Tsou Yen 鄒衍
Tsou Yüan-piao 鄒元標
Tu Ta-kuei 杜大珪
Tung Chung-shu 董仲舒
Tzu-po Ta-kuan (Chen-k'o) 紫柏達觀(眞可)
Wang An-shih 王安石
Wang Che 王嚞
Wang Ch'ung 王充
Wang Hsing 王興
Wang Ken 王艮
Wang K'o-shou 汪可受
Wang Nan-ming 汪南明
Wei Po-yang 魏伯陽
Wei-t'o 韋馱
Wu Ch'eng-en 吳承恩
Wu Ching-tzu 吳敬梓
Yang Ch'i-yüan 楊起元
Yao 堯
Yao Liu-i 姚柳依
Yao Min 饒民
Yen Hui 顏回
Yen Yüan 顏淵
Yü, T'ang, Wen, Wu 禹湯文武
Yü Ch'iao 俞樵
Yü Ch'ien 臉謙
Yüan Huang 袁黃
Yüan-shih T'ien-tsun 元始天尊
Yün-ch'i Chu-hung 雲棲袾宏
Yün-ku 雲谷

GLOSSARY

Chinese terms which appear in the text and the footnotes, including place names and proper names (of schools, sections of classics, etc.) which appear in the text of the book.

chai, chai-hsin 齊, 齊心
Ch'an 禪
chen-jen chin-tzu 眞人進子
cheng 正
cheng-ch'i 正氣
Cheng-i 正一
ch'eng 誠
Ch'eng-Chu 程朱
ch'eng-jan 澄然
chi-ting 寂定
chi-tse 極則
ch'i 氣
ch'i-chih chih hsin 氣質之心
ch'i-hsüeh 氣穴
Chia-ching 嘉靖
ch'iang-tzu-li 腔子裏
chiao san tao i 敎三道一
Ch'iao-yang 樵陽
chien 間
ch'ien (hexagram) 乾
ch'ien (silver) 錢
Ch'ien-lung 乾隆
chih 止
chih-chih (direct pointing) 直指
chih-chih (knowing where to stop) 知止
chih-chung 執中
chin-hsing 盡性
Chin-ling 金陵
chin-shih 進士
chin-tan 金丹
chin-tzu 進子
ching (quiescence) 靜
ching (reverence) 敬
ching-tso 靜坐
ch'ing-ching 清淨
Ch'ing-ming 清明
chiu-huan tan 九還丹
ch'iu fang-hsin 求放心

Chou 周
chu-ching 主靜, 主敬
chuan 傳
chüan 卷
Ch'üan-chen 全眞
chüeh-tuan 決斷
chün-tzu 君子
chung 中
fa-ch'en 法塵
fang-sheng hui 放生會
fang-wai 方外
fen 分
Fen-nei 分內
Feng-ch'an shu 封禪書
fu 復
fu-tzu 夫子
hai 亥
Han-lin 漢林
han-yang 涵養
hao 號
hao-jan chih ch'i 浩然之氣
Heng (mt., North) 恒
Heng (mt., South) 衡
ho-ssu ho-lü 何思何慮
hsi 洗
hsi-hsin (t'ui-ts'ang) 洗心 (退藏)
hsia 夏
Hsia-wu-ni 夏午尼
hsiang-fu ch'i hsin 降伏其心
hsiao-hsi chen-chi 消息眞機
hsiao-shuo pu-cheng-ch'i 銷鑠不正氣
hsieh-ch'i 邪氣
hsien-hsing 見性
hsien-shih 仙師
hsin 心
hsin-fa 心法
hsin t'u yeh 心土也
hsing 性
hsing-ch'a 省察

GLOSSARY

Hsing-hua 興化
hsiu-ts'ai 秀才
hsü-hsin shih-fu 虛心實腹
hsüan 玄
Hsüan-cheng 宣政
hsüan-kuan 玄關
hua 化
Hua (Mt.) 華
hua-hu 化胡
huan-tan 還丹
huang-chung 黃中
huang-t'ing 黃庭
hui-chien 慧劍
hun 魂
hun-jan 混然
huo shen 獲身
i (medicine) 醫
i (will) 意
I pai 益稗
i-tien ling-kuang 一點靈光
jen 仁
jou-shen 肉身
ju-men 入門
k'an 坎
K'ang-hsi 康熙
ken 艮
ken-pei 艮背
ko erh ch'ü chih 格而去之
ko-i 格義
ko-wu 格物
k'o-shih-yu chih tao 可使由之道
kou 姤
k'ou-chüeh 口訣
kuan 觀
k'uang 狂
k'un (hexagram) 坤
k'un (travail) 困
K'un-lun 崑崙
kung-an 公案
kung-kuo ko 功過格
k'ung-chung 空中
K'ung-men hsin-fa 孔門心法

K'ung-tzu hsien-chü 孔子閒居
li (hexagram) 離
li (distance) 里
li (ritual) 禮
li (principle) 理
li (of silver) 釐
li-pen 立本
liang 兩
liang-chih 良知
ling-kuang 靈光
Lo 洛
mieh 滅
ming 命
mo-fa 末法
mu-yü 沐浴
Nei-tan 內丹
Ni 尼
ni-wan 泥丸
nien 念
nien-fo 念佛
nien-p'u 年譜
Pai-sha 白沙
p'an-chiao 判教
P'an-keng 盤庚
pen-i 本義
Pen-shih chi 本士記
pen-t'i 本體
P'eng-lai 蓬萊
pi-ch'iu 比丘
p'o 魄
pu-cheng-ch'i 不正氣
P'u-t'ien 莆田
san-chiao ho-i 三教合一
san-chiao t'iao-ho 三教調和
san-chiao tz'u 三教祠
san-i chiao-chu 三一教主
san-kang wu-ch'ang 三綱五常
sha-li 舍利
Shao 召
shao wen-tz'u che 少文詞者
Shao-wu 召武
sheng (arising, birth) 生

GLOSSARY   321

sheng (pint) 升
shih 事
shih-chung 時中
shih-hsin chih fa 事心之法
shou-chung 守中
Shuo-kua 說卦
ssu 巳
Sung (Mt.) 嵩
ta 大
Ta-ch'eng chiao (completion) 大成教
Ta-ch'eng chiao (vehicle) 大乘教
Ta Yü mo 大禹謨
t'ai (hexagram, mt.) 泰
T'ai-chou 泰州
T'ai-ku 太谷
T'ai-p'ing 太平
T'ai shih 泰誓
tan-hsin 丹心
tan-t'ien 丹田
T'an-kung 檀弓
te 德
T'ien-ch'i 天啓
T'ien-t'ai 天台
t'ien-ti chih hsin 天地之心
t'ien-ti chih ken 天地之根
ting-hsing 定性
ting-tsai 定在
tou 斗
tsao 造

ts'e 冊
tsun 尊
ts'un 寸
ts'un-hsing 存性
ts'un-yang 存養
Tsung-chiao lei 宗教類
t'ui 退
Tung-lin 東林
tzu (earthly branch) 子
tzu (honorific name) 字
tzu-jan 自然
tzu-jan sheng-li 自然生理
tzu-te 自得
wang 妄
wei-fa chih chung 未發之中
wu (earthly branch) 午
wu (Nonbeing) 無
Wu-ch'eng 武成
wu hsing 五行
wu so chu 無所住
wu-wei 無爲
yang 陽
Yao-chiang 姚江
Yao tien 堯典
yeh-ch'i 夜氣
yin 陰
yü-yen 寓言
Yüeh-hsiu 岳秀
yung ch'üan 湧泉

Titles which do not appear in the bibliography,
including titles of essays of Lin Chao-en.

Ch'ang-ch'ing-ching ching 常清靜經
Ch'ang-ch'ing-ching ching shih-lüeh 常清靜經釋略
Ch'ang-ming chiao 常明教
Ch'ang-tao p'ien 常道篇
Ch'ang-tao shu-ch'i t'iao-ta 倡道疏啓條答
Ch'ang-tao ta-chih 倡道大旨
Chen-wo ch'ang-yen 眞我昌言
Cheng-tsung yao-lu 正宗要錄
Ch'i-ch'iao ta-wen 七竅答問

GLOSSARY

Chiao-wai pieh-ch'uan 教外別傳
Ch'iao-yang chiao-yen 樵陽教言
Chieh-shu wen-pien 戒疏問辨
Ch'ih-chai pien-huo 持齊辯惑
Chin-kang ching 金剛經
Chin-kang ching kai-lun 金剛經概論
Chin-kang ching t'ung-lun 金剛經統論
Ch'in-ting Ssu-k'u ch'üan-shu tsung-mu 欽定四庫全書總目
Ching-chih chü shih-hua 靜志居詩話
Ching-ming ching 淨名經
Ching-te ch'uan-teng lu 景德傳燈錄
Ching-t'ien 井田
Ching-tso fa chi-yao 靜坐法輯要
Chiu-hsü che-yen 九序摘言
Chiu-kao 舊稿
Cho hsiao-hsien shih 卓小仙詩
Chou-i ts'an t'ung ch'i 周易參同契
Chu-tai li chi t'u-shuo 著代禮祭圖說
Ch'u-hsüeh p'ien 初學篇
Ch'üan-shih 權實
Ch'un-ch'iu 春秋
Chung-i hsü-yen 中一緒言
Chung-yung 中庸
Chung-yung chang-chü 中庸章句
Ch'ung-li t'ang 崇禮堂
Daikanwa jiten 大漢和辭典
Erh-chiao lun 二教論
Fei san-chiao 非三教
Fen-che hsing-k'ung tsung-chih 分摘性空宗旨
Fen-che hsüan-tsung ta-tao 分摘玄宗大道
Fen-che sheng-hsüeh hsin-yao 分摘聖學心要
Fen-che tsung-K'ung hsin-yao 分摘宗孔心要
Fen-nei chi 分內集
Fen-nei chi fen-che pien-lan tzu-hsü 分內集分摘便覽自序
Fo p'u-sa i 佛菩薩義
Fu-chou Ts'ao-shan Pen-chi ch'an-shih yü-lu 撫州曹山本寂禪師語錄
Fu hsin ching shih-lun chiu-cheng hsiao-chien 附心經釋論就正小束
Hai-ch'iung ch'uan-tao lu 海瓊傳道錄
Han-shan ta-shih nien-p'u su-chu 憨山大師年譜疏註
Ho-i ta-yao 合一大要
Ho-ssu ho-lü chieh 何思何慮解
Hsi-yu chi 西遊記

Hsia i 夏一
Hsia-wu-ni pen-t'i ching 夏午尼本體經
Hsia-yü (fu-hsü) 夏語（附續）
Hsiang-shan yü-lu 象山語錄
Hsiao-ching 孝經
Hsien-hsing p'ien 見性篇
Hsien-yen 先衍
Hsin-ching chih-mi 心鏡指迷
Hsin ching kai-lun 心經概論
Hsin ching shih-lüeh 心經釋略
Hsin-nan p'ien 信難篇
Hsin pen-hsü chih-chih 心本虛直指
Hsin pen-hsü p'ien 心本虛篇
Hsin-shen hsing-ming t'u-shuo 心身性命圖說
Hsin-sheng chiao-yen 心聖教言
Hsin-sheng chih-chih 心聖直指
Hsin-sheng t'u-shuo 心聖圖說
Hsin-sheng tzu-hsü, hsiao-hsü, mu-lu 心聖自序，小序，目錄
Hsin yao 心爻
Hsing-hsin shih che-chu 醒心詩摘註
Hsing-hsin shih (chüeh-chü) 醒心詩（絕句）
(Fen-che) Hsing-k'ung tsung-chih （分摘）性空宗旨
Hsing-li ching-i 性理精義
Hsing-ling shih 性靈詩
Hsing-ming jen-tan 性命仁丹
Hsing-ming ta-yü 性命答語
Hsing shih 行實
Hsü-kao 續稿
Hsü shih chen-hsin 須識眞心
Hsü Tsang ching 續藏經
(Fen-che) Hsüan-tsung ta-tao （分摘）玄宗大道
Hsüeh-tao yao shen hsün-shih chu-sheng 學道要甚訊示諸生
Hsün Tzu 荀子
Huang-ming ying-shih ming-ch'en pei-k'ao lu 皇明應諡名臣備考錄
I chiao 易教
I-chieh li-yü 易解俚語
I ching 易經
I-hsüan Tao Shih jen-lun shu-kao 擬選道釋人倫疏稿
I-tuan pien-cheng 異端辯正
Jen-wang ching 仁王經
Ju-ching 儒經
Ju-lin wai-shih 儒林外史

Kao-seng chuan; *Hsü* . . . , *Fu-hsü* . . . , *Hsin-hsü* . . . , *Sung* . . . 高僧傳; 續; 附續; 新續; 宋
Ken-an shuo 艮庵說
Ko-hsüeh chieh 歌學解
Kuan-kung hsing-chuang 管公行狀
Kuan-kung mu-chih ming 管公墓誌銘
Kuang hung-ming chi 廣弘明集
K'un-chih chi 困知記
Leng-yen ching 楞嚴經
Li chi 禮記
Li Chih nien-p'u 李贄年譜
Li-pen 立本
Li-shih shuo-shu 李氏說書
Liang shu 梁書
Lien-chü 聯句
Lin Tzu 林子
Lin-tzu ch'üan-chi 林子全集
Lin-tzu ch'üan-chi wen-lüeh 林子全集文略
Lin-tzu fu-ch'u chi 林子復初集
Lin-tzu sheng-hsüeh t'ung-tsung san-chiao kuei-ju chi 林子聖學統宗三教歸儒集
Liu mei t'iao ta 六美條答
Liu Po-tzu p'ien 劉伯子篇
Lo hsien-sheng chuan 羅先生傳
Lu t'an 鹿談
Lun-yü 論語
Meng-chung-jen 夢中人
Meng Tzu 孟子
Mi-le tsun-fo pao-ching 彌勒尊佛寶經
Mindai ni okeru shūkyō yūgō to kōkakaku 明代に於ける宗教融合と功過格
Mindai no Sōkan 明代の僧官
Ming-chi 明紀
Ming-ching t'ang 明經堂
Ming shih 明史
Ming-shih chi-shih pen-mo 明史紀事本末
Mochizuki Bukkyō daijiten 望月佛教大辭典
Mu-chai ch'u-hsüeh chi 牧齋初學集
Nien-ching pien-huo 念經辯惑
Pa-Min t'ung-chih 八閩通志
Pei-ching jen-wen yen-chiu-so tsang shu-mu 北京人文研究所藏書目
Pen-t'i chiao 本體教
P'o-hsieh hsiang-pien 破邪詳辯
P'o-mi 破迷

San-chiao cheng-tsung t'ung-lun 三教正宗統論
San-chiao ching lüeh 三教經略
San-chiao ho-i ta-chih 三教合一大旨
San-chiao hui-pien yao-lüeh 三教會編要略
San-chiao tao-t'ung chung-i ching 三教道統中一經
San-chiao wu-che ta-hui 三教無遮大會
San-chiao yüan-pien 三教原編
San-feng hsien-sheng (hsüan ko hsüan t'an) 三峯先生 (玄歌玄譚)
San-i chiao-chu Hsia-wu-ni pen-t'i ching 三一教主夏午尼本體經
San-i chiao-chu shuo Mi-le tsun-fo pao-ching 三一教主說彌勒尊佛寶經
San-kang kua 三綱卦
Shan-jen 山人
Shang-ch'ing chi 上清集
Sheng-hsüeh t'ung-tsung san-chiao kuei-ju chi 聖學統宗三教歸儒集
Shichō 史潮
Shih cha 十札
Shih chi 史記
Shih ching 詩經
Shih ch'u-shih fa 世出世法
Shih-san ching so-yin 十三經索引
Shih-wen lang-t'an 詩文浪談
Shina bukkyōshigaku 支那佛教史學
Shu ching 書經
Shu Liu Tseng erh-sheng chu-shih yü 書劉曾二生註釋語
Shu-sheng 述聖
Shu-t'ien wen-kao 疏天文稿
Shuo hsia 說夏
Shuo kua 說卦
Ssu-pu pei-yao 四部備要
Ssu-pu ts'ung-k'an 四部叢刊
Ssu-shu cheng-i (tsuan) 四書正義 (纂)
Ssu-shu cheng-i hsü 四書正義續
Ssu-shu hsün-erh su-shuo 四書訓兒俗說
Ssu-yin yü 絲銀喻
Sung-chang 頌章
Sung shih 宋史
Ta-hsüeh 大學
Taishō shinshū daizōkyō 大正新脩大藏經
T'an-ching hsün-shih 壇經訊釋
T'ang shu 唐書
Tao-ho yü-t'an 導河迂談
Tao Shih jen-lun shu-kao 道釋人倫疏稿

Tao-te ching 道德經
Tao-te ching shih-lüeh 道德經釋略
Tao Tsang 道藏
Tao-tsang ching-hua 道藏精華
Tao-t'ung lun 道統論
Tao yeh cheng-i p'ien 道業正一篇
Tiao-ku wen-wu li she t'u-shuo 酌古文武禮射圖說
T'ien jen i-ch'i 天人一氣
(Lin-tzu) Ts'un-ch'u tsung-chi hsü (林子)存初挩集序
Ts'un-hsing kuei-t'iao 存省規條
(Fen-che) Tsung-hsüan ta-tao (分摘)宗玄大道
Tsung-K'ung t'ang 宗孔堂
Ts'ung-shu chi-ch'eng 叢書集成
Tu-shih 度世
Tung-jih chi 東日記
T'ung-shu 通書
Tzu-chih t'ung-chien kang-mu 資治通鑑綱目
Tzu-shu Ssu-yin yü chüan-tuan 自書絲銀喻卷端
Tz'u Shang-pao shao-ch'ing Yüan-kung chuan 贈尚寶少卿袁公傳
Wakō kenkyū 倭寇研究
Wang Shou-jen te men-jen Huang Wan 王守仁的門人黃綰
Wang Wen-ch'eng kung ch'üan-shu 王文成公全書
Wen Hsüan 文選
Wu-chen p'ien 悟眞篇
Wu-chen p'ien san-chu 悟眞篇三註
Wu ch'ieh-pu-k'o shih-chieh chu-sheng 五切不可示戒諸生
Wu-sheng fen-che pien-lan 無生分摘便覽
Wu-sheng p'ien 無生篇
Wu-yen lu 寤言錄 (寤 is a mistake for 寤; 寤言 is used for 晤言)
Yen-ching hsüeh-pao 燕京學報
Yü-an hsiao-chi 愚菴小集
Yü-chang hsü-yü 豫章續語
Yü-chang ta-wen (ta-yü) 豫章答問(答語)
Yü jen p'ien 欲仁篇
Yü-shu ching 玉樞經
Yü-yen 寓言
Yüan-chiao 原教
Yüan-chüeh ching 圓覺經
Yüan-shen shih-i 元神實義
Yüan-tao p'ien 原道篇
Yüan-tsung t'u (shuo) 元宗圖(說)

SELECTED BIBLIOGRAPHY

This bibliography is by no means comprehensive. It includes only those works which were most valuable in researching this work and those which would be valuable for the reader interested in further explorations of Chinese syncretism. Complete source citations are included in the notes and appendices.

I. EARLY WORKS
(Pre-1900, including modern editions of such works)

Chang San-feng 張三丰. *Chang San-feng hsien-sheng ch'üan-chi* 張三丰先生全集 (Collected works of Master Chang San-feng). *Tao-tsang chi-yao* 道藏輯要 (Selections from the Taoist canon). Edited by P'eng Wen-ch'in 彭文勤 et al. Taipei: K'ao-cheng ch'u-pan-she, 1971. Based on photoreproduction of 1906 edition.

Chang Tsai 張載. *Chang Heng-ch'ü chi* 張橫渠集 (Collection of Chang Tsai). 12 *chüan*. Ssu-pu ts'ung-k'an edition. Based on the Cheng-i t'ang edition.

Chao Pi-ch'en 趙避塵. *Hsing-ming fa-chüeh ming-chih* 性命法訣明旨 (The secrets of cultivation of essential nature and eternal life). Taipei: Chen-shan-mei ch'u-pan-she, 1964. Reedition of Peking, 1933. Originally late nineteenth century.

Ch'eng Chih 程智. *Ch'eng-shih ts'ung-shu* 程氏叢書 (Reprinted writings of Ch'eng Chih). Ch'ing edition of the Li-yen t'ang. Preserved in the Naikaku Bunko.

Ch'eng Hao 程顥. *Ming-tao wen-chi* 明道文集 (Collected literary works of Ch'eng Hao). 59 *chüan*. Ssu-pu pei-yao edition. In *Erh-Ch'eng ch'üan-shu* 二程全書 (Collected works of the two Ch'engs). Ssu-pu pei-yao edition.

328 SELECTED BIBLIOGRAPHY

—— *Erh-Ch'eng ts'ui-yen* 二程粹言 (Pure words of the two Ch'engs). 2 *chüan.* Edited by Yang Shih 楊時. In *Erh-Ch'eng ch'üan-shu* 二程全書 (Collected works of the two Ch'engs). Ssu-pu pei-yao edition.

Ch'eng I 程頤. *Chou I chuan* 周易傳 (Commentary on the Chou Changes). 4 *chüan. Erh-Ch'eng ch'üan-shu* 二程全書 (Collected works of the two Ch'engs). Ssu-pu pei-yao edition.

Ch'i Chi-kuang 戚繼光. *Yü-yü kao* 愚愚稿 (Manuscripts of ignorance about ignorance). In *Chih-chih t'ang chi* 止止堂集 (Collection from the hall of stopping stopping). Shan-tung shu-chü, 1888. Based on the Ming reprint in the Ssu-k'u Library. Original preface, 1574. Preserved in the Tōyō bunko.

Chiao Hung 焦竑. *Chiao-shih pi-ch'eng* 焦氏筆乘 (The vehicle of Mr. Chiao's pen). 6 *chüan*. Shanghai: Sheng-wu yin-shu-kuan, 1935. Original edition, 1606.

—— *Kuo-ch'ao hsien-cheng lu* 國朝獻徵錄 (Record of distinguished officials presented at court). 120 *chüan*. 1594 preface.

Chiao-wai ming-yen. See Li Tao-ch'un.

Chin-lien cheng-tsung hsien-yüan hsiang-chuan 金蓮正宗仙源像傳 (Biographies of immortals in the true school of the golden lotus). By Liu T'ien-su 劉天素 and Hsieh Hsi-ch'an 謝西蟾 of the Yüan. *Tao Tsang* 道藏 76.

Chou Ju-teng 周汝登. *Tung-yüeh cheng-hsüeh lu* 東越證學錄 (Record of advances of studies in Eastern Kwangtung). 16 *chüan*. 2 vols. Ming-jen wen-chi ts'ung-k'an series, no. 25. Taipei: Wen-hai ch'u-pan-she, 1970.

Chou Tun-i 周敦頤. *Chou-tzu ch'üan-shu* 周子全書 (Collected works of Master Chou). Edited by Tung Jung 董榕. Ch'ien-lung (1736–1796) edition.

—— *I-shu* 遺書 (Surviving works). In *Chou-tzu ch'üan-shu*.

—— *T'ai-chi t'u-shuo* 太極圖說 (Explanation of the Diagram of the Great Ultimate). In *Chou-tzu ch'üan-shu*.

—— *T'ung-shu* 通書 (Penetrating the *Book of Changes*). Ssu-pu pei-yao edition.

Chu Hsi 朱熹. *Chin-ssu lu* 近思錄 (Reflections on things at hand). With Lü Tsu-ch'ien 呂祖謙. 14 *chüan*. Edited by Chang Po-hsing 張伯行. Ssu-pu pei-yao edition.

Chu Hsi 朱熹. *Chou-i pen-i* 周易本義 (Fundamental meaning of the Chou Changes). 12 *chüan*. Chou-i ch'ing-shu t'ang edition.

—— *Chou-i ts'an t'ung ch'i chu* 周易參同契註 (Notes to the Homology of the triad of the Chou Changes). 3 *chüan. Tsao Tsang* 623.

—— *Chu-tzu yü-lei* 朱子語類 (Classified conversations of Master Chu). 140 *chüan*. Edited by Li Ching-te 黎靖德. Taipei: Cheng-chung shu-

chü, 1970. Reproduction of 1473 edition.
—— *I-Lo yüan-yüan lu* 伊洛淵源錄 (Record of the origins of the school of the two Ch'engs). 14 *chüan*. 2 vols. Ts'ung-shu chi-ch'eng edition.
—— *Ssu-shu chi-chu* 四書集註 (Collected commentary to the Four Books). Hong Kong: T'ai-p'ing shu-chü, 1968.
—— *T'iao-hsi chen* 調息箴 (Exhortations on breath control). In *Chu-tzu wen-chi* 朱子文集 (Collected literary works of Master Chu). Ssu-pu pei-yao edition. 85.6a.
—— *Yin-fu ching k'ao-i* 陰符經考異 (Researches on the book of spirit charms). In *Chu-tzu i-shu* 朱子遺書 (Surviving works of Master Chu). 25 *chüan*. 12 vols. Taipei: I-wen yin-shu-kuan, 1969. Based on the K'ang-hsi (1662–1722) edition of the Pao-kao t'ang.
Chu-hung 袾宏. *Chu ch'uang sui-pi fu erh-pi san-pi* 竹窗隨筆附二筆三筆 (Miscellaneous notes from the bamboo window, with addenda). Taipei: Chung-kuo fo-chiao wen-hua kuan, 1972. Reprint of Chin-ling k'o-chin-ch'u, 1897 edition.
—— *Yün-ch'i fa-hui* 雲棲法彙 (Collection of teachings of Chu-hung). 1897 edition.
Fu-chien t'ung-chih 福建通志 (Gazetteer of Fukien). Edited by Ch'en I 陳儀. Fukien: Cheng-fu chiao-yü-t'ang, 1938.
(*Ch'ung-tsuan*) *Fu-chien t'ung-chih* 重纂福建通志 (Revised Fukien gazetteer). 278 *chüan*. Reedited by Chen Shou-ch'i 陳壽祺 from the Cheng-i shu-yüan, 1868.
Han Yü 韓愈. *Ch'ang-li hsien-sheng chi* 昌黎先生集 (Collected works of Han Yü). 40 *chüan*. Edited by Li Han 李漢. Ssu-pu pei-yao edition.
Hang-chou fu-chih 杭州府志 (Hangchow gazetteer). 100 *chüan*. Edited by Ch'en Shan 陳善. 1686 edition. Original, 1579.
Ho Ch'iao-yüan 何喬遠. *Min shu* 閩書 (Book of Fukien). 154 *chüan*. 1965. Photoreproduction of 1630 edition.
—— *Ming-shan tsang* 名山藏 (Storehouse of the mountain of names). 20 vols. 1640 edition. Written in 1586.
Hsieh Chao-che 謝肇淛. *Wu tsa tsu* 五雜組 (Five miscellaneous sacrificial plates). 16 *chüan*. 1789 Japanese edition. Originally published in China, 1616.
Hsing-hua fu-chih 興化府志 (Hsing-hua gazetteer). 26 *chüan*. Edited by Lü I-ching 呂一靜 and K'ang Ta-ho 康大和. 1575 preface.
Hsing-hua P'u-t'ien hsien-chih 興化莆田縣志 (Gazetteer of P'u-t'ien, Hsing-hua). 36 *chüan*. By Wang Ta-ching 汪大經. New edition by Liao Pi-ch'i 廖必琦. 1879 supplement of 1758 edition.
Hsing-li ta-ch'üan-shu 性理大全書 (Great collection of the writings of Neo-Confucians). 70 *chüan*. 14 vols. Compiled by Hu Kuang 胡廣 et al. in 1415. Taipei: Sheng-wu yin-shu-kuan, 1974. Photoreproduction of

original from the Wen-yüan ko.
Hsing-ming fa-chüeh ming-chih. See Chao Pi-ch'en.
Hsing-ming shuang-hsiu wan-shen kuei-chih. See Yin Chen-jen.
Hsü K'o 徐珂. *Ch'ing-pai lei-ch'ao* 清稗類鈔 (Classified documents of Ch'ing legend). 48 vols. Shanghai: Sheng-wu yin-shu-kuan, 1917.
Huang Tsung-hsi 黃宗羲. *Lin san-chiao chuan* 林三教傳 (Biography of Three Teachings Lin). In *Nan-lei wen-an* 南雷文案 (Critical comments on literature by Huang Tsung-hsi). 10 *chüan*. 1680 preface. Hsi-shuang t'ang edition. In Columbia University library.
—— *Ming-ju hsüeh-an* 明儒學案 (Anthology of Neo-Confucians of the Ming). 62 *chüan*. Ssu-pu pei-yao edition. Originally published 1667.
Huang Wan 黃綰. *Ming-tao pien* 明道編 (On elucidating the Way). Chung-kuo ssu-hsiang shih tzu-liao ts'ung-k'an. Peking: Chung-hua shu-chü, 1959.
Huang Yüan-ch'i 黃元吉. *Ch'ing-ming chung-hsiao ch'üan-shu* 清明忠孝全書 (Collected writings on purity, illumination, loyalty, and filiality). 6 *chüan*. Tao Tsang 757.
Hui-neng 慧能. *Liu-tsu fa-pao t'an-ching* 六祖法寶壇經 (Platform sutra of the sixth patriarch). *Taishō shinshū daizōkyō* 48. No. 2008.
I-Lo yüan-yüan lu. See Chu Hsi.
Keng Ting-hsiang 耿定向. *Keng T'ien-t'ai hsien-sheng wen-chi* 耿天台先生文集 (Collected literary works of Keng Ting-hsiang). 20 *chüan*. Ming-jen wen-chi ts'ung-k'an, 20. Taipei: Wen-hai ch'u-pan-she, 1970. Based on 1598 edition.
Kuan Chih-tao 管志道. *Chüeh-mi li ts'e* 覺迷蠡測 (A calabash measure for awakening from error). 3 *chüan*. 1600 preface. In the Naikaku bunko.
Kuan wu-liang-shou ching 觀無量壽經 (The sutra of contemplation of Amitāyus). *Taishō shinshū daizōkyō* 37. No. 1750.
Kuo-ch'ao hsien-cheng lu. See Chiao Hung.
Li Chih 李贄. *Hsü Fen-shu* 續焚書 (A book to burn, continued). Peking: Chung-hua shu-chü, 1959. Originally sixteenth century.
—— *San-chiao p'in* 三教品 (Classification of the Three Teachings). Ming edition. In Naikaku bunko.
Li-shih chen-hsien t'i-tao t'ung-chien 歷世眞仙體道通鑑 (General mirror of the true immortals who embodied the Way throughout the generations). 53 *chüan*. By Yüan Taoist Chao Tao-i 趙道一. *Tao Tsang* 139–48.
Li Tao-ch'un 李道純. *Chiao-wai ming-yen* 敎外明言 (Perspicacious sayings outside the written doctrine). In *Chung-ho chi* 中和集 (Collection on equilibrium and harmony). 6 *chüan*. Edited by Ts'ai Chih-i 蔡志頤. *Tao Tsang* 118–19.
Lin Chao-en 林兆恩. See appendices A through F.
—— *Lin-tzu ch'üeh-ping kung-fu* 林子却病工夫 (Master Lin's art of healing).

In *Yen-chien mi-lu* 燕間秘錄 (The secret record of ease). Edited by Ch'en Mei-kung 陳眉公. Ming edition. Only in the Maeda Sonkeikaku Bunko version of the collection.

Lin Chih-ching 林至敬. *Ming-hsia chi* 明夏集 (Collection on illumining hsia). 4 *chüan*. 1598 preface. Preserved in Naikaku bunko.

Lin-tzu nien-p'u 林子年譜 (Chronological biography of Master Lin). 1 *chüan*. Edited by Lu Wen-hui 盧文輝 and Ch'eng Chung-yü 陳衷瑜. 1655. Preserved in the Hōsa bunko.

Liu Mi 劉謐. *San-chiao p'ing-hsin lun* 三教平心論 (On viewing the Three Teachings with a balanced mind). 1 *chüan*. Ts'ung-shu chi-ch'eng edition.

Liu-tsu fa-pao t'an-ching. See Hui-neng.

Lu Shan-huang 盧山黃. *Ta-yü chi* 大獄記 (Record of the great trial). In *Shuo-k'u* 說庫 (Storehouse of sayings). 60 vols. Compiled by Wang Wen-ju 王文濡. 3rd carving. Shanghai: Wen-ming shu-chü, 1925.

Lu Wen-hui 盧文輝. *Chung-i hsü-yen* 中一緒言 (Introduction to the Center and the one). See appendix D, S: 63.

Min shu. See Ho Ch'iao-yüan.

Ming-hsia chi. See Lin Chih-ching.

Ming-ju hsüeh-an. See Huang Tsung-hsi.

Ming T'ai-tsu 明太祖. *San-chiao lun* 三教論 (On the Three Teachings). In *Yü-chih wen-chi* 御製文集 (Collection of imperial compositions). 20 *chüan*. From *Chin-ling fan-ch'a chih* 金陵梵利志 (Record of temples in Nanking). Edited by Ko Yin-liang 葛寅亮. Nanking: Photoreproduction of Seng-lü ssu-k'an-pen, 1936. Originally published by the Nanking Central Buddhist Registry, 1627.

Mou Tzu 牟子. *Li-huo lun* 理惑論 (Discussion of doubts). In *P'ing-chin-kuan ts'ung-shu* 平津館叢書 (Collections of the P'ing-chin hall). Vol. 1. 1884 preface.

P'an Ching-jo 潘鏡若. *San-chiao k'ai-mi kuei-cheng yen-i* 三教開迷歸正寅義 (Romance of the Three Teachings exposing delusions and returning to the truth). 100 *chüan*. Written about 1615. Preserved in Tenri University library.

Po Yü-ch'an 白玉蟾. *Hai-ch'iung Po chen-jen yü-lu* 海瓊白眞人語錄 (The recorded sayings of Realized Man Po Hai-ch'iung). 4 *chüan*. Edited by Hsieh Hsien-tao 謝顯道. *Tao Tsang* 1016.

P'u-feng ch'ing-lai chi 莆風清籟集 (Collection of pure music in P'u-t'ien style). 60 *chüan*. Edited by Cheng Wang-ch'en 鄭王臣. Published in Fukien. 1722 preface. In Naikaku bunko.

San-chiao lun. See Ming T'ai-tsu, Liu Mi.

Ta-Ch'ing li-ch'ao shih-lu 大清歷朝實錄 (Veritable record of the successive reigns of the Ch'ing dynasty). 94 vols. Taipei: Hua-lien ch'u-pan-she photoreproduction, 1964.

Ta-Ming lü 大明律 (Great Ming code). 30 *chüan*. Japanese edition. Kyōhō period (1716–1735).

T'ai-hsüan ching chi-chu 太玄經集註 (The book of the great mysterious, with notes). 6 *chüan*. By Yang Hsiung 揚雄 of the Han dynasty. Sung edition with notes by Ssu-ma Kuang 司馬光. *Tao Tsang* 860–62.

T'ao Ch'ien 陶潛. *Ching-chieh hsien-sheng chi* 靖節先生集 (Collection of Master T'ao Ch'ien). 10 *chüan*. Ssu-pu pei-yao edition.

Ts'an t'ung ch'i ch'an-yu 參同契闡幽 (Explanations of obscure points of the *Homology of the Triad*). *Homology of the Triad* attributed to Wei Po-yang 魏伯陽. Commentary by Chu Yüan-yü 朱元育. 1669 preface. Taipei: Chen-shan-mei ch'u-pan-she, 1971; reprint of Ch'ing edition.

Tsung-mi 宗密. *Yüan-jen lun* 原人論 (On the original nature of man). *Taishō shinshū daizōkyō* 45. No. 1886.

Wang Chi 王畿. *Ken-chih ching-i chih chih* 艮止精一之旨 (The essential meaning of stilling in the *ken* hexagram). In *Wang Lung-hsi ch'üan-chi* 王龍溪全集 (Collected works of Wang Chi). 3 vols. Taipei: Hua-wen shu-chü, 1970. Reproduction of 1822 edition.

—— *Wang Lung-hsi ch'üan-chi*. See last entry.

Wang Yang-ming 王陽明. *Ch'uan-hsi lu* 傳習錄 (Instructions for practical living). Ssu-pu pei-yao edition.

—— *Wang Wen-ch'eng kung ch'üan-shu* 王文成公全書 (Collected works of Wang Yang-ming). 38 *chüan*. Edited by Hsü Ai 徐愛. 1568 preface.

Yang Ch'i-yüan 楊起元. *Yang Fu-so ch'üan-chi* 楊復所全集 (Collected works of Yang Ch'i-yüan). 14 vols. Edited by Chao Hou 趙厚. 1599 edition.

Yang Shih 楊時. *Yang Kuei-shan chi* 楊龜山集 (Collection of Yang Shih). 2 vols. Ts'ung-shu chi-ch'eng edition. Based on Cheng-i t'ang edition.

Yin Chen-jen 尹眞人. *Hsing-ming shuang-hsiu wan-shen kuei-chih* 性命雙修萬神圭旨 (Revealed doctrine of the dual cultivation of nature and life store taught by the myriad spirits). 4 *chüan*, or *chi* (collections). Preface 1615. In Kyoto Jinbun Kagaku Kenkyūjo.

Yüan Tsung-tao 袁宗道. *Pai Su-chai lei-chi* 白蘇齋類集 (Categorized collection of Pai Su-chai). 22 *chüan*. Chung-kuo wen-hsüeh chen-pen ts'ung-shu series. Shanghai: Shanghai tsa-chih kung-ssu, 1935.

II. MODERN WORKS IN ASIAN LANGUAGES
(Post-1900)

Araki Kengo 荒木見悟. *Mindai shisō kenkyū* 明代思想研究 (Researches on Ming thought). Tokyo: Sōbunsha, 1972.

——*Bukkyō to jukyō* 佛教と儒教 (Buddhism and Confucianism). Kyoto: Heirakuji shoten, 1972.

Ashikaga Enjutsu 足利衍述. "Sō igo ni okeru sankyō chōwa no kōgai to sono sankō shomoku" 宋以後に於ける三教調和の梗概とその参考書目 (An outline of the blending of the Three Teachings from the Sung on, with a list of sources). *Tōyō tetsugaku* 東洋哲学 16 (1909): no. 2, 61–65; no. 3, 54–58.

Ch'en Yüan 陳垣. "Nan-Sung ch'u Ho-pei hsin tao-chiao k'ao" 南宋初河北新道教考 (Researches on the new Taoism in Hopei in the early Southern Sung). *Fu-jen ta-hsüeh ts'ung-shu* 輔仁大學叢書 8 (1941).

Hsiao T'ien-shih 蕭天石. *Tao-chia yang-sheng-hsüeh kai-yao* 道家養生學概要 (Essentials of Taoist theories of nurturing life). 2d edition. Taipei: Tzu-yu ch'u-pan-she, 1971.

Hsien-hsüeh tz'u-tien. See Tai Yüan-chang.

Jao Tsung-i 饒宗頤. "San-chiao lun yü Sung Chin hsüeh-shu" 三教論與宋晉學術 (The Three Teachings theory and scholarship in the Sung and Chin). *Tung-hsi wen-hua* 東西文化 11 (May 1968): 24–32.

Jung Chao-tsu 容肇祖. *Ming-tai ssu-hsiang shih* 明代思想史 (History of Ming thought). Taipei: K'ai-ming shu-tien, 1962.

Koyanagi Shigeta 小柳司氣太. "Minmatsu no sankyō kankei" 明末の三教関係 (Relations of the Three Teachings in the late Ming). In *Takase hakushi kanreki kinen shinagaku ronsō* 高瀬博士還曆紀念支那学論叢 (Volume commemorating the sixtieth birthday of Professor Takase). Tokyo: Kōbundō, 1928. Pages 349–70.

Kubota Ryōon 久保田量遠. *Shina judōbutsu kōshōshi* 支那儒道佛交渉史 (The history of interactions of Chinese Confucianism, Taoism, and Buddhism). Tokyo: Daitō, 1943.

Liu Tzu-hou 劉滋厚. "Chang Shih-ch'in yü T'ai-ku hsüeh-p'ai" 張石琴與太谷學派 (Chang Shih-ch'in and the T'ai-ku sect). *Fu-jen hsüeh-chih* 輔仁學誌 9 (1940): 81–124.

Lu Chi-yeh 盧冀野. "T'ai-ku hsüeh-p'ai chih yen-ko chi ch'i ssu-hsiang" 太谷學派之沿革及其思想 (Successive changes in the T'ai-ku sect and its thought). *Tung-fang tsa-chih* 東方雜誌 24 (1927): 71–75.

Ma Yu-yüan 馬幼垣. "Ch'ing-chi T'ai-ku hsüeh-p'ai shih-shih shu-yao" 清季太谷學派史事述要 (Brief discussion of the historical events surrounding the T'ai-ku sect of the Ch'ing). *Ta-lu tsa-chih* 大陸雜誌 28 (May 1964): 13–18.

Mano Senryū 間野潜龍. *Mindai bunkashi kenkyū* 明代文化史研究 (Studies on Ming cultural history). Kyoto: Dōhōsha, 1979.

—— "Mindai ni okeru sankyō shisō; toku ni Rin Chōon o chūshin to shite" 明代に於ける三教思想; 特に林兆恩を中心として (Three Teachings thought in the Ming dynasty; with special reference to Lin

Chao-en). *Tōyōshi kenkyū* 東洋史研究 12 (1952): 18–34.

—— "Rin Chōon to sono chosaku ni tsuite" 林兆恩とその著作について (On Lin Chao-en and his writings). *Shimizu hakushi tsuitō kinen Mindaishi ronsō* 清水博士追悼記念明代史論叢 (Collection of articles on Ming history in commemoration of Professor Shimizu). Tokyo: Daian, 1962.

Okada Takehiko 岡田武彦. *Ō Yōmei to Minmatsu no jugaku* 王陽明と明末の儒学 (Wang Yang-ming and late Ming Confucianism). Tokyo: Kōmeisha, 1970.

—— *Seiza to zazen* 静坐と坐禅 (Quiet sitting and Ch'an meditation). Tokyo: Ōfūsha, 1970.

Sakai Tadao 酒井忠夫. *Chūgoku zensho no kenkyū* 中国善書の研究 (Researches on Chinese morality books). Tokyo: Kokusho kankōkai, 1960.

—— "Shushi to dōkyō" 朱子と道教 (Chu Hsi and Taoism). *Shushigaku nyūmon* 朱子学入門 (Introduction to Chu Hsi studies). Shushigaku taikei series, no. 1. Edited by Abe Yoshio 阿部吉雄. Tokyo: Meitoku shuppansha, 1974. Pages 411–26.

Sawada Mizuho 沢田瑞穂. "Sankyō shisō to heiwa shōsetsu" 三教思想と平話小説 (Colloquial novels and Three Teachings thought). *Biburia* 16 (1960): 37–39.

Shigematsu Shunshō 種松俊章. "Shina sankyōshi jō no jakan no mondai" 支那三教史上の若干の問題 (Certain problems regarding the history of the Three Teachings in China). *Shien* 史淵 21 (1939): 125–52.

Shimada Kenji 島田虔次. *Chūgoku ni okeru kindai shii no zazetsu* 中国に於ける近代思惟の挫折 (The frustration of thinking in recent China). Tokyo: Chikuma shobō, 1970.

Tai Yüan-chang 戴源長. *Hsien-hsüeh tz'u-tien* 仙學辭典 (Dictionary of Taoist studies). Taipei: Chen-shan-mei ch'u-pan-she, 1970.

T'ang Yung-t'ung, Hsi-yü 湯用彤, 錫予. *Han-Wei liang-Chin Nan-pei ch'ao fo-chiao shih* 漢魏兩晉南北朝佛教史 (History of Buddhism in Han, Wei, the two Chins, and the North-South dynasties). 2 vols. Taipei: Sheng-wu yin-shu-kuan, 1965. Reprint of 1938 original.

Tokiwa Daijō 常盤大定. *Shina ni okeru bukkyō to jukyō, dōkyō* 支那に於ける佛教と儒教道教 (Buddhism, Confucianism, and Taoism in China). Tōyō bunko ronsō, 13. Tokyo: Tōyō bunko, 1930.

Wang Wei-ch'eng 王維誠. "Lao-tzu hua-hu-shuo k'ao-cheng" 老子化胡說考證 (Researches on the theory of Lao Tzu converting the barbarians). *Kuo-hsüeh chi-k'an* 國學季刊 4, 2 (1934): 1–222.

Yamashita Ryūji 山下龍二. *Ō Yōmei no kenkyū: tenkaihen* 王陽明の研究: 展開編 (Studies on Wang Yang-ming: development of the school). Tokyo: Gendai jōhōsha, 1971.

Yang Ch'i-ch'iao 楊啓樵. "Ming-tai chu-ti chih ch'ung-shang fang-shu chi ch'i ying-hsiang" 明代諸帝之崇尚方術及其影響 (The veneration of Ming emperors for magicians, and their influence). From *Ming-tai tsung-chiao* 明代宗教 (Ming religion). Ming-shih lun-ts'ung series, 10. Taipei: Hsüeh-sheng shu-chü, 1963. Pages 203–97.

Yang Shu-liang 楊樹楳. "Hsia-wu-ni-shih tao-t'ung chung-i san-chiao tu-shih ta-tsung-shih chuan-lüeh" 夏午尼氏道統中一三教度世大宗師傳略 (Brief biography of Hsia-wu-ni, savior and master of the line of the Center and the one of the Three Teachings). *Fu-chien wen-hua* 福建文化 3 (1935): 41–44.

Yin-shih-tzu 因是子. *Yin-shih-tzu ching-tso fa* 因是子靜坐法 (Yin-shih-tzu's method of quiet sitting). *Tao-tsang ching-hua* 道藏精華 (Flowers of the Taoist canon). Edited by Hsiao T'ien-shih 蕭天石. Taipei: Tzu-yu ch'u-pan-she, continuing series. Ser. 2, no. 12 (1962).

Yoshioka Yoshitoyo 吉岡義豊. *Dōkyō to bukkyō* 道教と佛教 (Taoism and Buddhism). Vols. 1 and 2 of a continuing series. Tokyo: Toshima shobō, 1959, 1970.

——— *Eisei e no negai* 永生への願い (The search for long life). Sekai no shūkyō, no. 9. Kyoto: Tankōkai, 1970.

III. WESTERN LANGUAGE SOURCES

Araki Kengo. "Confucianism and Buddhism in the late Ming." In Wm. Theodore de Bary and the Conference on Seventeenth-Century Chinese Thought. *The Unfolding of Neo-Confucianism.* New York: Columbia University Press, 1975. Pages 39–66.

Baird, Robert D. *Category Formation and the History of Religions.* Religion and Reason Series, no. 1. The Hague: Mouton, 1971.

Chan, Wing-tsit, trans. and annotator. *Instructions for Practical Living and Other Neo-Confucian Writings by Wang Yang-ming.* New York: Columbia University Press, 1963.

——— trans. and annotator. *Reflections on Things at Hand: The Neo-Confucian Anthology compiled by Chu Hsi and Lü Tsu-ch'ien.* New York: Columbia University Press, 1967.

——— *Religious Trends in Modern China.* The Haskell Lectures at the University of Chicago, 1950. New York: Columbia University Press, 1953.

——— trans. and compiler. *A Source Book in Chinese Philosophy.* Princeton: Princeton University Press, 1963.

Chang Chung-yuan. "An Introduction to Taoist Yoga." *Review of Religion* 20 (1956): 131–48.

Ch'en, Kenneth K. S. *Buddhism in China: A Historical Survey.* Princeton: Princeton University Press, 1964.

―――― *The Chinese Transformation of Buddhism*. Princeton: Princeton University Press, 1973.
Ch'ien, Edward T. "Chiao Hung and the Revolt against Ch'eng-Chu Orthodoxy." In Wm. Theodore de Bary and the Conference on Seventeenth-Century Chinese Thought. *The Unfolding of Neo-Confucianism*. New York: Columbia University Press, 1975. Pages 271-303.
Ching, Julia. "The Goose Lake Monastery Debate." *Journal of Chinese Philosophy* 1 (1974): 161-78.
―――― *To Acquire Wisdom: The Way of Wang Yang-ming*. New York: Columbia University Press, 1976.
Dictionary of Ming Biography, 1368-1644. 2 vols. Edited by L. Carrington Goodrich and Chaoying Fang. New York: Columbia University Press, 1976.
de Bary, Wm. Theodore. "Individualism and Humanitarianism in Late Ming Thought." In Wm. Theodore de Bary and the Conference on Ming Thought. *Self and Society in Ming Thought*. New York: Columbia University Press, 1970. Pages 145-248.
―――― "Neo-Confucian Cultivation and the Seventeenth-Century 'Enlightenment.'" In Wm. Theodore de Bary and the Conference on Seventeenth-Century Chinese Thought. *The Unfolding of Neo-Confucianism*. New York: Columbia University Press, 1975.
―――― et al., eds. *Sources of Chinese Tradition*. 2 volume paperback edition. New York: Columbia University Press, 1964.
Eliade, Mircea. *Yoga: Immortality and Freedom*. Translated by Willard Trask. 2d edition, revised. Princeton: Princeton University Press, 1969.
Fang, Lienche Tu. "Lin Chao-en." *Dictionary of Ming Biography, 1368-1644*. 2 vols. Edited by L. Carrington Goodrich and Chaoying Fang. New York: Columbia University Press, 1976.
Fung Yu-lan. *A History of Chinese Philosophy*. 2 vols. Translated by Derk Bodde. Princeton: Princeton University Press, 1952-53.
Franke, Wolfgang. "Some Remarks on Lin Chao-en (1517-1598)." *Oriens Extremus* 20 (1973): 161-74.
―――― "Some Remarks on the 'Three-in-One Doctrine' and its Manifestations in Singapore and Malaysia." *Oriens Extremus* 19 (1972): 121-30.
Greenblatt, Kristin Yü. "Chu-hung and Lay Buddhism in the Late Ming." In Wm. Theodore de Bary and the Conference on Seventeenth-Century Chinese Thought. *The Unfolding of Neo-Confucianism*. New York: Columbia University Press, 1975. Pages 93-140.
―――― "Yün-ch'i Chu-hung: The Career of a Ming Buddhist Monk." Ph.D. dissertation, Columbia University, 1973. Published in book form as *The Renewal of Buddhism in China: Chu-hung and the Late Ming Synthesis*, by Chün-fang Yü (New York: Columbia University Press, 1980).

Groot, Jan Jakob M. de. *Sectarianism and Religious Persecution in China: A Page in the History of Religions.* 2 vols. Amsterdam: J. Miller, 1903-4.
Haeger, Jonathan Winthrop. "The Intellectual Context of Neo-Confucian Syncretism." *Journal of Asian Studies* 31 (1972): 499-513.
Hartman, Sven S. *Syncretism.* Based on Papers read at the Symposium on Cultural Contact, Meeting of Religions, Syncretism, held at Åbo, September 8-10, 1966. Included in Scripta Instituti Donneriani Aboensis. Stockholm: Almqvist and Wiksell, 1976.
Hsu Sung-peng. *A Buddhist Leader in Ming China: The Life and Thought of Han-shan Te-ch'ing.* University Park: Pennsylvania State University Press, 1979.
Hucker, Charles O., ed. *Chinese Government in Ming Times: Seven Studies.* New York: Columbia University Press, 1969.
Hurvitz, Leon. "Chu-hung's One Mind of Pure Land and Ch'an Buddhism." In Wm. Theodore de Bary and the Conference on Ming Thought, *Self and Society in Ming Thought.* New York: Columbia University Press, 1970. Pages 451-81.
Legge, James. *The Four Books: Confucian Analects, The Great Learning, The Doctrine of the Mean, and The Works of Mencius.* New York: Paragon, 1966; unaltered reprint of 1923 Shanghai edition.
Leeuw, Gerardus van der. *Religion in Essence and Manifestation: A Study in Phenomenology.* Translated by J. E. Turner. New York: Macmillan, 1938.
Liu Ts'un-yan. "Lin Chao-en: Master of the Three Teachings." *T'oung Pao* 53 (1967): 253-78.
—— "Taoist Self-Cultivation in Ming Thought." In Wm. Theodore de Bary and the Conference on Ming Thought, *Self and Society in Ming Thought.* New York: Columbia University Press, 1970. Pages 291-330.
Lu K'uan-yü. *The Secrets of Chinese Meditation: Self-cultivation by Mind Control as Taught in the Ch'an, Mahāyāna, and Taoist schools in China.* London: Rider, 1964.
—— *Taoist Yoga: Alchemy and Immortality: A translation, with introduction and notes, of The Secrets of Cultivating Essential Nature and Eternal Life (Hsin [sic] Ming Fa Chueh Ming Chih) by the Taoist Master Chao Pi Ch'en, born 1860.* New York: Samuel Weiser, 1973.
Porkert, Manfred. *The Theoretical Foundations of Chinese Medicine: Systems of Correspondence.* Cambridge: MIT Press, 1974.
Saso, Michael. *Taoism and the Rite of Cosmic Renewal.* Pullman, Wash.: Washington State University Press, 1972.
Seidel, Anna. "A Taoist Immortal of the Ming Dynasty: Chang San-feng." In Wm. Theodore de Bary and the Conference on Ming Thought, *Self and Society in Ming Thought.* New York: Columbia University Press, 1970. Pages 483-531.

T'ang Chun-i. "The Development of the Concept of Moral Mind from Wang Yang-ming to Wang Chi." In Wm. Theodore de Bary and the Conference on Ming Thought, *Self and Society in Ming Thought*. New York: Columbia University Press, 1970. Pages 93–120.

Tu Wei-ming. *Neo-Confucian Thought in Action: Wang Yang-ming's Youth (1472–1509)*. Berkeley: University of California Press, 1976.

Welch, Holmes. *The Parting of the Way*. Revised edition. Boston: Beacon Press, 1957.

—— *The Practice of Chinese Buddhism: 1900–1950*. Cambridge: Harvard University Press, 1967.

Wilhelm, Richard, trans. *The I Ching or Book of Changes*. Translated into English from German by Cary F. Baynes. 3d edition, revised, with a foreword by C. G. Jung and preface by Hellmut Wilhelm. Bollingen series, 19. Princeton: Princeton University Press, 1967.

Wu Pei-yi. "The Spiritual Autobiography of Te-ch'ing." In Wm. Theodore de Bary and the Conference on Seventeenth-Century Chinese Thought, *The Unfolding of Neo-Confucianism*. New York: Columbia University Press, 1975. Pages 67–92.

Yampolsky, Philip B. *The Platform Sutra of the Sixth Patriarch: The Text of the Tun-huang Manuscript with Translation, Introduction, and Notes*. New York: Columbia University Press, 1967.

Yü Chün-fang. See Kristin Yü Greenblatt.

Zürcher, Erik. *The Buddhist Conquest of China: The Spread and Adaptation of Buddhism in Early Medieval China*. 2 vols. Leiden: E. J. Brill, 1959.

INDEX

Abe Yoshio, 266n
Academies, 64, 68, 199
Alchemy, Han, 39–40; laboratory procedures, 96–97, 127, 165; technical symbols, 67; see also Inner Alchemy; (Chou-i) Ts'an t'ung ch'i
Apertures of the mind, 165, 166, 167 ff.
Araki Kengo, 267n, 275n, 276n, 277n, 278n, 279n

Baird, Robert, 7
Bodhidharma, 209
Bodhisattva, 92
Book of Changes (I-ching): and Han correspondences, 21; and Han alchemy, 22; and Neo-Confucian cosmology, 36, 38; importance of ken hexagram, 120; in Lin's Nine Stages, 125, 128, 132, 133, 135, 146, 148, 155, 159 ff., 161, 162 ff., 164, 166, 168, 169, 172, 173, 174, 187, 193, 225, 228, 238
Book of History (Shu-ching), 120, 151
Book of Rites (Li-chi), 166
Boundaries and boundary anxiety, see Orthodoxy
Buddhāvataṃsaka-sūtra, 123
Buddhism, 91–94; and Han correspondences, 23; accommodations with Chinese thought, 23–28; Mahāyāna, 26, 92; objections to, 30 ff., 46, 48, 51, 53, 54, 55 (see also Three Teachings, errors of); influence on other schools, 41, 53, 54–57; reverence for life, 57 ff., 202; Ming revival of, 57–61; in Lin Chao-en's thought, 71, 77, 90, 111, 113, 154, 190, 198, 199, 201–2, 204, 207, 208, 215, 216, 228, 236, 238; tensions with Neo-Confucianism, 104, 135, 151; Lin's criticisms of, 153, 202, 205, 211, 237; Lin's defense of, 196; T'ai-ku school's criticisms of, 230; see also Ch'an school; Pure Land school; T'ien-t'ai school; Celibacy; Lay Buddhism; Mind, absolute; Nature, human; Original nature; Recitation of the name(s)
Burial of pirate victims, 78–80, 198, 286n

Cavity of vitality (ch'i-hsüeh), 183–84; see also Center
Celibacy, objections to, 114–15, 196–98, 202, 205, 214, 294n
Center (chung): in Inner Alchemy, as elixir fields (tan-t'ien), 97, 100; as Mean, 109, 126, 127, 132, 134, 180, 191 ff., 212 (illustration); holding to (shou-chung), 120, 127, 176, 179, 192, 207; in Lin's chains of correspondences, 126 ff.; in macrocosm/microcosm, 128; as Great Ultimate and mind, 132, 160 ff., 162, 176; as Earth within, 133, 168; mind as ruler, 142, 159, 161, 167, 169, 178; as no fixed place (ting-tsai) or space between

Center (*chung*) (*Continued*) (*chien*), 148 ff., 171 ff.; as interior of the self (the back) or "within" (*ch'iang-tzu-li*), 158 (*see also* Ken hexagram, "within"); being centered, 170 ff. (*see also* Equilibrium); as womb (cavity of vital force, *ch'i-hsüeh*), 183–84
Chains of correspondence: Han, 20 ff., 181 ff.; Inner Alchemy, 98; in Lin's Nine Stages, 126, 142, 207; *see also* Syncretism, reconciliation
Chan Ling, 54; *see also* Neo-Confucianism, Ch'eng-Chu school
Chan, Wing-tsit, 292n
Ch'an school of Buddhism, 33–35, 42, 49, 51, 70, 92–93, 94, 202–3, 283n, 284n, 299n; and Pure Land, 58, 59, 94; and Lin Chao-en, 67 ff., 135, 155, 204, 226, 227, 228; versus Neo-Confucianism, 106–7
Chang Po-tuan, 306n
Chang San-feng, 140, 232, 196n, 314n; *see also* Inner Alchemy
Chang Shang-ying, 201
Chang Tsai, 104, 134; *see also* Neo-Confucianism, Ch'eng-Chu school
Chao Pi-ch'en, 290n, 303n, 304n; *see also* Inner Alchemy
Ch'en Chih-hsü, 306n; *see also* Inner Alchemy
Ch'en Hsien-chang, 54
Ch'en Su-k'un, 225; *see also* Lin Chao-en, disciples
Ch'en Tao-ch'ing, 86; *see also* Lin Chao-en, disciples
Ch'en T'uan, 271n, 272n, 306n; *see also* Inner Alchemy
Ch'en Yüan, 272n, 273n
Cheng-i (Correct and Single) school of Inner Alchemy Taoism, 273n
Ch'eng, see Sincerity
Ch'eng Chih, 228
Ch'eng-Chu school, *see* Neo-Confucianism, Ch'eng-Chu school
Ch'eng Hao, 44, 107, 118 ff., 123, 151; *see also* Neo-Confucianism, Ch'eng-Chu School
Ch'eng I, 104, 108, 118 ff., 123, 186; *see also* Neo-Confucianism, Ch'eng-Chu school
Ch'eng Yün-chang, 228

Ch'i, 290n; *see also* Vital force; Material force
Ch'i Chi-kuang, 223
Ch'i-chih chih hsin, see Mind, of physical endowment
Ch'i-hsüeh, see Cavity of vitality
Ch'iang-tzu-li (within), 108, 149, 158, 293n; *see also* Ken hexagram; Center
Chiao Hung, 51; *see also* Neo-Confucianism, School of Mind
Ch'iao-yang, 83
Ch'ien hexagram, 98, 102, 128, 130, 158, 159, 160, 164, 169, 175, 181, 183; *see also* Inner Alchemy, human nature and life store, copulation
Chih-chih, see Direct Pointing; Stopping; Knowing where to stop
Chih-i, 23, 269n
Chih yü chih-shan, see Stopping, at highest good
Ch'ih Ho-ch'un, 137
Chin-ling, 221
Chin-ssu lu, see Reflections on Things at Hand
Ching, see Quiescence; Quiet sitting; Reverence or seriousness; Vitality
Ching, Julia, 272n, 276n, 277n
Ching-ming ching, see Vimalakīrti-sūtra
Ch'ing dynasty, 231–32
Ch'ing-ming school of Inner Alchemy Taoism, 293n
Chiu-hsü che-yen (Selected sayings on the nine stages), 145
Ch'iu fang-hsin, see Seeking the Lost Mind; Mencius
Cho Wan-ch'un, 65 ff., 148, 232 ff., 242, 282n, 296n; *see also* Inner Alchemy
Chou dynasty, 14–19
Chou-i Ts'an t'ung ch'i, see Ts'an t'ung ch'i
Chou Ju-teng, 51; *see also* Neo-Confucianism, School of Mind
Chou-t'ien, see Revolutions of heaven
Chou Tun-i, 104–5, 150, 203; *see also* Neo-Confucianism, Ch'eng-Chu school
Chronological Biography, see Lin-tzu nien-p'u
Chu Fang-tang, 228
Chu Heng, 75, 76
Chu Hsi, 2, 36 ff., 105–7, 118, 119 ff., 156, 184 ff., 203, 266n, 284n, 292n; *see also*

INDEX 341

Neo-Confucianism, Ch'eng-Chu school
Chu-hung, see Yün-ch'i Chu-hung
Chuang Tzu: and early Taoism, 16; in Lin Chao-en, 63, 203; in the Taoist tradition, 268n, 281n
Chung, see Center; Mean
Chung-i hsü-yen chi (Empty words on the Center and the One), 226
Chung-yung, see Doctrine of the Mean
Ch'üan-chen (Perfect Realization) school of Inner Alchemy, 40
Chün-tzu (gentleman, superior man), 36 ff., 117
Classic of filial piety (Hsiao-ching), 197
Collected works of Master Lin, see Lin-tzu ch'üan-chi
Collection on Illuminating Hsia, see Minghsia chi
Confucianism, and Buddhism, 58; see also Confucius; Neo-Confucianism
Confucius: basic teachings, 15–16; as a Sage of the Three Teachings, 31, 52, 55, 88, 150, 216; as model in Lin Chao-en's thought, 50, 288n; as sage in Lin's thought, 53, 69, 85, 111–12, 117, 147; Analects of, 71, 97; as teacher, 77, 224; Hall of (in Lin's school), 86; in Lin's thought, 134–35, 152, 176, 189, 200, 201, 209, 215, 216, 217, 218, 227; Lin's correction of superstitions about, 209
Conversion of the barbarians (hua-hu), 27

de Bary, Wm. Theodore, 271n, 277n, 278n, 279n, 282n, 293n, 315n
Direct pointing (chih-chih), 68, 70 ff., 80
Direct Pointing to the Mind as Sage, see Hsin-sheng chih-chih
Disunion, period of, 23–28, 203, 291n, 304n
Doctrine of the Mean, 174, 191, 192, 193, 230, 284n

Earth (as one of Five Phases), 133, 177, 183–84
Eclecticism, defined, 5; different from syncretism, 4, 9
Eliade, Mircea, 290n
Elixir (tan): in Han alchemy, 22, 23; 165 ff.; ninefold refined, 65, 281n; as seed of sage embryo, 96, 98, 100, 130, 185, 300n; in Inner Alchemy, 99, 102–3, 122–23, 132, 165 ff., 181; as spark of spiritual light (i-tien ling-kuang), 126, 133, 169, 170, 173 ff., 176, 181, 187 ff., 192, 227; as seed of goodness, 126, 173 ff.; as seed of humanity (jen), 133, 168–81, 184, 191, 208, 212; as seed of sagely mind, 144, 177 ff., 184, 191, 206; as spirit or light of spirit, 183, 191; in Lin's Nine Stages, 183–84, 187
Elixir field (tan-t'ien), 99, 126, 127, 130, 179; defined, 97; see also Center; Ni-wan
Embryonic breathing, see Fetal breathing
Empty Words on the Center and the one, 226
Enlightened master (ming-shih), 68–71, 96, 124, 196, 199
Equilibrium, 108–9, 154; see also Center; Mean
Examination studies, 62, 64, 65, 73 ff., 77, 80, 84, 198, 199, 200

Fang, Lienche Tu, 241, 281n, 310n
Fang-sheng hui (Associations for Releasing life), 59 ff.
Fetal breathing: in Inner Alchemy, 100–1; in Lin's Nine Stages, 173
Fire and Water: union of, 100; in Lin's Nine Stages, 102, 103, 173; balancing of, 117, 121–23, 125, 146 ff.; in Inner Alchemy, 122; Fire and the elixir, 132; see also Inner Alchemy, human nature and life store; Ken hexagram, balancing Fire and Water
Five Phases (wu-hsing): defined, 21 ff., 268n, 269n; in Diagram of Great Ultimate, 128; in Inner Alchemy, 130; and healing, 142
Five virtues, defined, 23
Fo T'u-teng, 202, 306n
Forgetting (wang), 44 ff., 118–19, 123 ff., 149, 151, 152, 155, 156, 157, 189, 191, 193
Four Books (ssu-shu): identified, 36, 282–83n; in Lin's writings, 69, 158, 159, 211, 243; in Lin's curriculum, 74 ff.
Franke, Wolfgang, 240–41, 288n, 311n, 314n
Fu hexagram, 171, 181–82
Fu-hsi, 209
Fung Yu-lan, 271n, 303n

Gentleman, see Chün-tzu
Great Learning (Ta-hsüeh), in Lin's writings, 178, 180, 230, 283n
Great Ultimate (t'ai-chi), 126, 130, 132, 134, 158, 159, 162, 163 ff., 170, 173, 174 ff., 176, 183, 187, 217; diagram of, 38, 128–29 (figure, 129), 186 ff.; in Inner Alchemy, 103; see also Center; Chains of correspondence, in Lin's Nine Stages
Great Void (t'ai-hsü), 87, 102, 103, 135–36; see also Nonbeing
Groot, Jan Jakob M. de, 275n, 286n

Haeger, Jonathan Winthrop, 270
Han dynasty, 19–23, 268n, 279n; Confucians in, 70
Han-shan Te-ch'ing, 57 ff., 68, 286n, 288n; see also Ch'an school of Buddhism; Buddhism, Ming revival
Han Yü, 30–31, 55
Healing: and Lin Chao-en, 69, 73, 80, 132, 137–43, 165, 204, 221 ff., 225, 229, 297n; in Buddhism, 71–72; religious vs. classical, 71–73, 141, 284n; Chu Hsi's dissolving imbalanced vital forces (hsiao-shuo pu-cheng-ch'i), 72, 138; Taoist, 138; in Lin's cult, 224
Heaven and earth, see Inner Alchemy, human nature and life store
Hiding in secret place, see Ken hexagram
Ho Ch'iao-yüan, 220
Ho Hsin-yin, 234–35
Ho-ssu ho-lü, see No-thought
Homology of the Triad, see Ts'an t'ung ch'i
Hsi-hsin, see Washing the mind
Hsi-wang-mu, see Queen Mother of the West
Hsia, 217, 219, 225, 227, 229, 231; see also Way
Hsia-wu-ni, 225, 227, 232
Hsia-yü (Sayings on Hsia), 199
Hsiao T'ien-shih, 273n, 283n, 284n, 291n, 297n, 301n, 302n, 304n
Hsiao-ching, see Classic of Filial Piety
Hsiao-shuo pu-cheng-ch'i, see Healing
Hsieh Chao-che, 222, 224, 242
Hsin, see Mind
Hsin-sheng, see Sagely mind
Hsin-sheng chih-chih (Direct pointing to the mind as sage), 145
Hsing, see Nature, human

Hsing-li ta-ch'üan (Great collection of writings of Neo-Confucianism), 76, 124, 285n, 292n, 293n
Hsing-ming (shuang-hsiu wan-shen) kuei-chih (Revealed doctrine of the dual cultivation of nature and life store taught by the myriad spirits), 55 ff., 170, 185, 273n, 278n, 295n, 300n
Hsing-t'ing, see Moving in the chamber; Ken hexagram
Hsu, Sung-peng, 279n, 286n, 288n
Hsüan-kuan, see Mysterious pass; Light of spirit; Inner Alchemy
Hu Chü-jen, 54; see also Neo-Confucianism, Ch'eng-Chu school
Hua-hu (converting the barbarians) controversy, 27
Huang Chou, 73; see also Lin Chao-en, disciples
Huang-ti, see Yellow Emperor
Huang-t'ing, see Yellow Chamber
Huang Tsung-hsi, 220, 222, 242, 288n
Huang Wan, 119, 152; see also Neo-Confucianism, Ch'eng-Chu school
Huang Yü-p'ien, 307n
Huang Yüan-ch'i, 284n, 293n, 296n; see also Inner Alchemy
Hui-neng (Sixth Patriarch), 35, 202, 299n, 306n; see also Ch'an school of Buddhism
Hui-ti, 86
Humanity (jen), 104, 127, 135, 155, 176 ff., 186, 191; see also Elixir, as seed of humanity
Hung Tzu-wen, 86

I-chieh li-yü (Plain and simple explanations), 213
I-ching, see Book of Changes
I-tien ling-kuang, see Spark of spiritual light; Mysterious Pass
Immortality, 94, 101, 138, 142, 186, 208, 223
Innate good-knowing (liang-chih), 49, 52, 107–8, 144, 231; see also Original nature, as sagely mind
Inner Alchemy (nei-tan): origins and definition, 39 ff.; and Confucianism, 41, 49; and Buddhism, 42, 91; macrocosm/microcosm, 66; and enlightened master, 70; as system of meditation, 94–103, 131–37, 172 ff., 175;

INDEX   343

human nature (*hsing*) and life store (*ming*) and corresponding terms, 95 ff., 98, 130, 170, 173 ff., 175; and laboratory procedures from alchemy, 96 ff., 165; light of vitality, 99, 132 ff., 173; light of spirit (mysterious pass), 99, 133, 173, 174; copulation of ingredients of elixir, 100, 122, 181–83; gestation of sage embryo and fetal breathing, 101, 173, 183–84; and Diagram of Great Ultimate, 130; and Lin Chao-en, 145, 146, 170, 172, 187, 190, 202; as "Taoism," 272*n*; for women, 291*n*; *see also* Cheng-i school; Ch'ing-ming school; Ch'üan-chen school
Investigation of things (*ko-wu*), 105, 107, 185, 303*n*

Jan Niu, 180, 303*n*
Jen, see Humanity
Joint Chronicle of the Three Teachings, see San-chiao hui-pien
Jung Chao-tsu, 295*n*

K'an hexagram, 98, 130, 160, 173, 174, 181, 182–83, 302*n*
Ken hexagram, 44 ff., 116–21, 123, 162; and forgetting, 44, 45, 118–19; stilling in the back (*ken-pei*), 45, 69, 71, 116–21, 146–58; not clinging to the body, 45, 117; stopping in place (at highest good, knowing where to rest), 45, 117, 118, 120, 156 ff., 162, 163; moving in the chamber (*hsing-t'ing*), 45, 119, 155, 161 ff., 170 (*see also* Yellow chamber; Center); "within" (*ch'iang-tzu-li*), 108, 149, 158; hiding in the secret place, 119, 125, 146, 207, 209, 227, 228; stilling thoughts, 121, 125, 126, 149 ff., 154, 159, 163; North Star, 121, 126 ff.; balancing Fire and Water, 122, 146
Ken-pei, see Stilling in the back
Keng Ting-hsiang, 84; *see also* Neo-Confucianism, School of Mind
Knowing where to stop (*chih-chih*), 118; *see also Ken* hexagram
Ko Hung, 39
Ko-i, see Matching meanings
Ko-wu, see Investigation of things
K'o-shih-yu chih tao, see Way
Kou hexagram, 181–82

K'ou-chüeh, see Oral secret
Kuan Chih-tao, 54, 222; *see also* Neo-Confucianism, School of Mind
Kuang-t'a temple, 86
Kubota Ryōon, 239, 267*n*, 269*n*, 270*n*, 273*n*
Kumārajīva, 205
K'un hexagram, 98, 100, 102, 128, 130, 158, 160, 169–70, 175, 181, 183, 302*n*
Kung-an (Jap. *kōan*), 93 ff., 289*n* ff.; *see also* Ch'an school of Buddhism

Lao Tzu: and early Taoism, 16; and *hua-hu*, 27; as a Sage of the Three Teachings, 27, 31, 52, 55, 88, 150, 200, 209, 216, 218, 227; in Inner Alchemy 95 ff., 272*n*; in Lin's thought, 179, 203, 205; in Taoism 268*n*
Lay Buddhism, 111, 202, 205; associations for releasing life, 59 ff.
Lead and mercury, 130, 181; *see also* Inner Alchemy; Chains of correspondence
Leng-yen ching (*Surāngama*), 57
Li, see Principle; Ritual
Li hexagram, 78, 130, 160, 173, 174, 181, 182–83; *see also* Inner Alchemy, human nature and life store, copulation
Li-chi, see Book of Rites
Li Chih, 52–54, 58, 74, 223, 311*n*; *see also* Neo-Confucianism, School of Mind
Li Ching-feng, 230
Li Shih-ch'ien, 201
Li Tao-ch'un, 41 ff., 123–24, 127, 150, 152, 291*n*; thirteen vehicles of Inner Alchemy, 101–3
Li T'ung, 203; *see also* Neo-Confucianism, Ch'eng-Chu school
Liang-chih, see Innate good-knowing
Lieh Tzu, 208
Life store (*ming*), in Inner Alchemy, 95, 98, 99, 103, 130, 170, 173, 175, 186; in Lin's Nine Stages, 157, 174, 175; *see also* Inner Alchemy, human nature and life store
Light of spirit, mysterious pass (*hsüan-kuan*): in Inner Alchemy, 99; in Lin's system, as spark of spiritual light, 133, 173, 174; *see also* Inner Alchemy, light of vitality, light of spirit
Light of vitality, in Inner Alchemy, 99; in Lin's Nine Stages, 132 ff., 173; *see also* Inner Alchemy

INDEX

Lin Chao-en: disciples of, 73 ff., 82 ff., 88, 137–38, 224–28, 241; school of, 74–77, 85, 196; teaching practices, 81, 83, 198–99, 200, 204–13; attacks on 84, 222–23; religious organization of, 220–23; divinization of, 223 ff., 232; scriptures of, 223, 224, 226, 233, 245
Lin Chih-ching, 224–28
Lin-shih ch'üeh-ping kung-fu (Master Lin's art of healing), 139–40, 297n
Lin Tzu (Master Lin), 196
Lin-tzu ch'üan-chi (Collected works of Master Lin), 224, 232, 243, 244, 248 ff., 258 ff.
Lin-tzu nien-p'u (Chronological biography of Master Lin), 224, 241, 242, 244
Liu Ching-pang, 138
Liu Mi, 201
Liu Ts'un-yan, 240, 266n, 295n
Lo Ch'in-shun, 55; see also Neo-Confucianism, Ch'eng-Chu school
Lo Hung-hsien, 63 ff., 136, 200, 228, 313n; see also Neo-Confucianism, School of Mind
Lord on High (*Shang-ti*), 113
Lu Hsiang-shan, 38, 49, 203, 245; see also Neo-Confucianism, School of Mind
Lu K'uan-yü, 274n, 289n, 290n, 291n, 301n, 303n
Lu Wen-hui, 224–28, 233, 241, 243; see also Lin Chao-en, disciples
Lü Tung-pin, 39, 273n, 306n; see also Inner Alchemy

Macrocosm/microcosm, 95 ff., 127 ff., 148, 157, 160, 168, 207, 289n
Mahāyāna Buddhism, 26, 35, 42 ff., 70, 92; vow of Bodhisattva, 58; see also Buddhism
Mano Senryū, 240, 243, 275n, 297n, 310n, 313n
Master Lin's Art of Healing, see *Lin-shih ch'üeh-ping kung-fu*
Master of the Three Teachings (*san-chiao hsien-sheng*): as title of Lin Chao-en, 88, 111–13, 138
Matching meanings (*ko-i*), 25, 26, 29
Material force (*ch'i*), 37, 104, 105; see also Vital force
Mean (*chung*), 128, 176, 180, 191, 271n; see also Center; Equilibrium; Doctrine of the Mean
Mencius: in Lin's thought, 69, 71, 85, 86, 133, 135, 137, 146, 149, 150, 155, 176, 177–78, 185, 186, 188, 227; in Neo-Confucianism, 119
Mind (*hsin*): of heaven and earth (*t'ien-ti chih hsin*) or mind of Tao (*Tao-hsin*), 37, 100, 105; of physical endowment (*ch'i-chih chih hsin*), 37, 105; chasing after external things (runaway flow of consciousness), 108, 116, 119 ff., 137, 146, 151, 152, 153, 157, 175, 176; substance vs. function, 120 ff., 136, 152, 190; as ruler, 161, 167, 169 (see also Center); as mirror, 189; absolute mind, as in Buddhism, 190–91; see also Sagely mind; Seeking the lost mind
Ming, see Life store; Inner Alchemy
Ming dynasty, 3, 46–61, 91, 92, 94, 106, 107–8, 120–21, 136, 196, 273n, 279n, 297n, 307n; policies on Three Teachings, 47 ff., 196–98, 203
Ming-hsia chi (Collection on illuminating *hsia*), 225, 233
Ming-shih, see Enlightened master
Ming T'ai-tsu, 3, 46–48, 52, 60, 115, 277n
Morality books (*shan-shu*), 56 ff.; ledgers of merit and demerit (*kung-kuo ko*), 285n
Moral retribution, 56 ff., 279n; see also Vows to heaven; Morality books
Mou Tzu, 24 ff., 269n
Moving in the chamber (*hsing-t'ing*): interpretation of in *ken* hexagram, 45, 119; in Lin's Nine Stages, 155, 161 ff., 169, 170, 172; see also Ken hexagram
Mysterious pass (*hsüan-kuan*), 99, 102, 103, 174, 181; see also Light of Spirit; Inner Alchemy
Mu-yü (bathing), see Washing the mind

Nature, human (*hsing*): Neo-Confucian, 37; Buddha-nature, 43; in Inner Alchemy, 95 ff., 175; in Lin's thought, 176, 177, 186, 193, 209; see also Original nature; Inner Alchemy
Nei-tan, see Inner Alchemy
Neo-Confucianism: Ch'eng-Chu school, 36–38, 50, 104–7; School of Mind, 38, 49 ff., 107–8, 136, 203, T'ai-chou school, 50 ff.; Lin's criticisms of, 194; his

boundary tensions with, 198–99; see also Confucius
Neo-Taoism, 24, 203, 304n, 306–7n
Nien-fo, see Recitation of the name(s)
Ni-wan, 102, 132, 179, 181; see also Elixir field; Inner Alchemy
Nine Stages, 145–94; summarized, 116–37; in three sections, 216
Non-action (wu-wei), 17–19, 164
Nonbeing (wu), 24, 26, 89; ultimate of (wu-chi) or Great Void (t'ai-hsü), 128, 130 ff., 134, 186–90, 304n
No-thought (ho-ssu ho-lü), 121, 149, 151, 190, 192

Okada Takehiko, 292n, 311n
Oral secret (k'ou-chüeh) or secret oral transmission, 39, 70, 224, 225, 226, 273n
Original nature, Buddha-nature (original face), 94, 123, 188; Taoism, as original self, infant, 95; Inner Alchemy, as sage embryo, 96; Confucian, as mind of heaven and earth, 103, 105; as sagely mind, originally present, 121, 136, 190; Lin's original nature, 177, 192, 219; as empty, 193; Lin's, as sincerity, 206; Lin's original mind, 219
Orthodoxy, religious: levels of, 10; internal, 10, 38, 57; and boundaries of traditions, 10–11, 196–200; official, 49; in School of Mind, 50, 51, 54–55; as authority, 54–55, 198, 221
Outline and Digest of the General Mirror for the Aid of Government, see Tzu-chih t'ung-chien kang-mu
Overmyer, Daniel, 275n, 294n

Paisha, 222
Pantheon of Lin's cult, 232 ff.
P'an Ching-jo, 244
Peach Blossom Spring, 210
Pen-t'i, see Substance; Mind, substance vs. function; Original nature
Philanthropy, of Lin Chao-en, 63, 78, 80, 83, 85, 86 ff., 199, 222
Pirate raids, 78, 80, 285–86n
Plain and Simple Explanations, 213
Po Chü-i, 30
Po Yü-ch'an, 40 ff., 101, 122, 296n, 301n, 306n; see also Inner Alchemy

Popular writings of Lin Chao-en, 211–13, 237
Prayers for the comfort of the soul, 27, 79 ff., 198, 286n
Principle (li), 37, 42, 46, 49, 105, 107, 126, 130, 132, 156, 190 ff., 193, 275n; natural life (tzu-jan sheng-li), 121, 164, 183; of nature (t'ien-li), 157; as unceasing life will, 178; moral, 184 ff.
P'u-t'ien, 62, 78, 81, 85 ff., 197, 223
Pure Land Buddhism, 34, 58, 59, 79, 92, 94, 131, 202, 270n; see also Recitation of name(s); Ch'an Buddhism

Queen Mother of the West (Hsi-wang-mu), 226, 312n
Quiescence (ching), 104, 107
Quiet sitting (ching-tso), 105–7, 109, 292n

Recitation of the name(s): Pure Land, 34, 94, 131; Lin Chao-en, 131, 150, 152
Reflections on Things at Hand (Chin-ssu lu), 106, 124
Religious interaction, xiii, 5 ff., 14, 17; as dialogue, 19; see also Syncretism
Revealed Doctrine of the Dual Cultivation of Nature and Life Store as Taught by the Myriad Spirits, see Hsing-ming Kuei-chih
Reverence or seriousness (ching), 105
Revolutions of heaven (chou-t'ien), 97, 131–32, 137, 140, 158–65, 173, 181; see also Ken hexagram; Moving in the chamber; Fetal breathing
Ritual (li): in Confucius, 16–17; in Lin's thought, 76, 77
Romance of the Three Teachings Exposing Delusions and Returning to the Truth, 244

Sage (sheng), ideal of, 37, 103, 237; see also Original nature; Sagely mind
Sage embryo (sagely fetus): in Inner Alchemy, 101; in Lin's Nine Stages, 173, 183–84
Sagely mind (lit. mind as sage, hsin-sheng), 49 ff., 55, 90, 108, 135, 183, 185, 218; see also Original nature
Sakai Tadao, 240, 266n, 275n, 278n, 279n, 292n, 297n, 383n
Śākyamuni, see Shakyamuni
San-chiao, see Three Teachings

San-chiao hsien-sheng, see Master of the Three Teachings
San-chiao hui-pien (Joint chronicle of the Three Teachings), 80, 200–4
San-chiao k'ai-mi kuei-cheng yen-i (Romance of the Three Teachings exposing delusions and returning to the truth), 244
San-chiao kuei-ju chi (Collection of the Three Teachings returning to Confucianism), 114
San-chiao lun (On the Three Teachings), 46
San-chiao p'ing-hsin lun (On viewing the Three Teachings with a balanced mind), 201
San-chiao wu-che ta-hui (Unlimited meeting of the Three Teachings), 218
San-kang wu-ch'ang, see Three bonds and five constant virtues
Sayings on Hsia, see Hsia-yü
School of Mind, see Neo-Confucianism
Seeking the lost mind (ch'iu fang-hsin), 106, 135, 137
Selected Sayings on the Nine Stages, see Chiu-hsü che-yen
Shakyamuni, 91, 92 ff.; as Sage of the Three Teachings, 31, 52, 55, 88, 158, 205, 209, 216, 218, 227; in Ch'an Buddhism, 70; as sage in Lin's system, 113, 200
Sha-li ray, 187, 304n
Shan-shu, see Morality books
Shang-ti, 113
Shao Yung, 203; see also Neo-Confucianism, Ch'eng-Chu school
Shao-wu, 85 ff.
Shen, see Spirit
Sheng, see Sage
Shigematsu Shunsō, 270
Shou-chung, see Center, holding to
Shu-ching, see Book of History
Shu-t'ien, see Vows to heaven
Sincerity (ch'eng), 104, 109, 126 ff., 134, 152, 166, 191, 192 ff., 206; in Inner Alchemy, 103; as single-mindedness, 112–13, 152, 155, 156, 192; as absence of falsehood (wang), 150 ff.; of will, 180
Sivin, Nathan, 266n, 268n, 282n, 284n, 288n
Six Dynasties, see Disunion, period of

Sixth Patriarch, see Hui-neng
Spark of spiritual light (i-tien ling-kuang), see Mysterious pass; Light of spirit; Inner Alchemy, human nature and life store
Spirit (shen): in Inner Alchemy, 95, 98, 174, 176, 184; light of, 125, 173, 181, 191 (see also Mysterious Pass); in Lin Chao-en, 148, 157, 183, 209; see also Light of Spirit
Spontaneous (tzu-jan), 24; see also Principle, natural life
Ssu-shu, see Four Books
Stilling in the back (ken-pei), 45, 69, 71, 116–21, 141, 146–58, 196, 199; false stilling, 154; see also Ken hexagram
Stopping: at highest good (chih yü chih-shan), 45, 118; in place, 156; finding peace in, 157; at proper time, 162, 163; see also Ken hexagram
Strickmann, Michel, 268n
Substance (pen-t'i), in Lin Chao-en, 136; see also Mind, substance vs. function; Original nature
Subtle or spiritual physiology, 94 ff., 97–98, 99
Sung dynasty, xiv, 2, 12, 32–46, 48, 56, 58, 92, 104–6, 118–20, 122, 196, 201, 203, 270n, 272n
Sung Neo-Confucianism, see Neo-Confucianism, Ch'eng-Chu school; Lu Hsiang-shan
Suraṅgama-sūtra, see Leng-yen ching
Suzuki, Daisetsu, 289n
Syncretism: redefinition of religion, xiii, 10, examples of, 16, 17, 34, 39–40, 46, 151, 154, 168, 177, 204–13; and sectarianism, 2, 28 ff.; objections to, 4; reconciliation in, 5, 9–10, 11, 12, examples of, 22–23, 25, 28, 122–26; etymology, 6; intention, 8; defined, 9–13; selectivity, 9–10, 11–12, 28, examples of, 45, 90, 111, 143, 200–4; in Buddhism, 23, 29, 33–35, 57–61; acculturative, 24; adversary, 27; defensive, 28; accommodative, 32; in Sung, 33–46; in Neo-Confucianism, 35–58, 49–55; in Taoism, 38–40, 55–57; in Ming, 46–61; shift in Lin's, 198–200; general theories about, 265n

INDEX   347

Ta-ch'eng chiao, 228
Ta-hsüeh, see Great Learning
Ta-hui Tsung-kao, 58; see also Ch'an school of Buddhism
T'ai hexagram, 171
T'ai-chi, see Great Ultimate
T'ai-chou school, 52, 54, 68, 222, 276n; see also Neo-Confucianism, School of Mind
T'ai-hsü, see Great Void; Nonbeing
T'ai-hsüan ching, 227
T'ai-ku school, 228–32, 314n
T'ai-tsu, see Ming T'ai-tsu
Tan, see Elixir
Tan-t'ien, see Elixir fields
T'ang Chun-i, 292n
T'ang dynasty, 28–31, 122, 272n
Tao, see Way
Tao-an, 28
Tao-hsin, see Mind
Taoism: syncretism in, 38–40, 55–57; objections to, 48, 67; in Lin's thought, 71, 77, 90, 112, 116, 145, 146, 154, 155, 167, 198, 201, 205, 207, 208, 215, 216, 236, 238; mind-cultivation in, 94–103 (see also Inner Alchemy); lower paths of Inner Alchemy, 101–3; Lin criticized for, 137–38, 223; in tension with Neo-Confucianism, 151; Lin's criticisms of, 153, 214, 237; Lin's defense of, 196; T'ai-ku criticisms of, 230; problems of definition, 266n, 268n, 272n; see also Lao Tzu; Chuang Tzu; Neo-Taoism; Morality books; Inner Alchemy
T'ao Ch'ien, 210
T'ao Hung-ching, 39
Te-ch'ing, see Han-shan Te-ch'ing
Tetragrams of the Three Bonds, 211–12
Three bonds and five constant virtues (san-kang wu-ch'ang), 47, 112, 114, 153, 154, 165, 211, 275n
Three-in-One Cult (modern cult of Lin Chao-en), 231–35
Three Teachings (san-chiao): tradition of, 8, 13, 14, 200–4; shrines, 14, 32, 224, 226; debates, 29 ff.; dramas, 29 ff.; sages of, 32, 52, 55, 58, 87, 88, 150, 152, 227, 238, 304n; harmony (unity) of, 40, 42, 45, 46 ff., 52 ff., 55, 60, 199 ff., 213–19, 222, 227, 229, 233; and Ming T'ai-tsu, 46 ff., 52; errors of, 67, 110–11, 153 ff., 180,
195, 209, 214, 230; in Lin Chao-en, 80, 81, 88, 90, 199, 201, 206; Ch'ing persecutions of, 231–32; see also San-chiao lun; San-chiao p'ing-hsin lun
T'ien-li, see Principle, of nature
T'ien-t'ai school of Buddhism, 29, 42, 58, 274n
T'ien-ti chih hsin, see Mind
Tokiwa Daijō, 267n, 271n, 273n
Triad of heaven, earth, and man, 20, 21, 22, 127 ff., 148
Ts'an t'ung ch'i (Homology of the triad), 22, 40, 158, 202, 266n, 269n; see also Alchemy, Han
Ts'ao-shan, 93, 289n; see also Ch'an school of Buddhism
Tsou Yen, 21
Tsou Yüan-piao, 84; see also Neo-Confucianism, School of Mind
Tsung-mi, 31
Tu Wei-ming, 271n, 276n
Tung-lin party, 84
Tzu-chih t'ung-chien kang-mu (Outline and digest of the General mirror for the aid of government), 76
Tzu-jan, see Spontaneous
Tzu-jan sheng-li, see Principle, natural life
Tzu-po Ta-kuan (Chen-k'o), 58, 68; see also Ch'an school of Buddhism; Buddhism, Ming revival

Ultimate of Nonbeing (wu-chi), see Nonbeing
Unlimited Meeting of the Three Teachings, 218
Upper elixir field, see Ni-wan

Vimalakīrti-sūtra, 202, 205, 306n
Vital force (ch'i), 98, 131, 137 ff., 140, 142, 149, 165, 166, 168, 173, 176, 182, 183, 185 ff., 187, 188, 202, 206, 218, 284n, 290–91n, 302n
Vitality (ching, vital essence): in Inner Alchemy, 95, 98, 99, 102, 103, 175, 181, 184; light of, 99 ff., 125, 132, 133; in Lin's Nine Stages, 157, 302n; see also Light of Vitality; Inner Alchemy, human nature and life store
Void, see Great Void; Nonbeing
Vows to heaven (shu-t'ien), 84–87, 110–16, 145, 221, 237, 242, 287n

Wang, see Forgetting; Sincerity, as absence of falsehood
Wang Che, 39; *see also* Inner Alchemy
Wang Chi, 51, 147 ff., 151, 152, 158; *see also* Neo-Confucianism, School of Mind; T'ai-chou school
Wang Ken, 50, 54; *see also* Neo-Confucianism, School of Mind
Wang Yang-ming, 49 ff., 107–8, 157; *see also* Neo-Confucianism, School of Mind
Washing the mind (*hsi-hsin*) or bathing (*mu-yü*), 103, 117, 122, 123, 125, 146, 148, 156, 207, 209, 227, 228
Water, *see* Fire and Water
Way (Tao): Taoist, 16–17, 24, 217; undifferentiated, of Inner Alchemy, 40, 131; transcendent, 51, 180, as absolute, 191; as mind, 52; sagely, 64 ff.; misuse of, 85; unknowable, in Lin Chao-en, 173; simple and followable (*k'o-shih-yu chih tao*), 213, 215 ff., 217, 219, 220, 236–37, 309*n*; moral, 217; all embracing, 217 ff. (*see also* Hsia)
Welch, Holmes, 288*n*, 291*n*
White Lotus Sect, 224
Women, in Inner Alchemy, 291*n*; and Lin's Nine Stages, 291*n*
Wu, see Nonbeing
Wu-chi, see Nonbeing
Wu-hsing, see Five Phases
Wu-wei, see Non-action

Yamashita Ryūji, 295*n*
Yang Ch'i-yüan, 51; *see also* Neo-Confucianism, School of Mind

Yang Shih, 303*n*
Yao Min, 86; *see also* Lin Chao-en, disciples
Yellow Chamber (*huang-t'ing*), 97, 99 ff., 126, 130, 170; *see also* Chains of correspondence; Center; *Ken* hexagram; Moving in the chamber
Yellow Emperor (Huang-ti), as age in Lin's system, 112, 203, 205, 234, 293*n*
Yen Hui, 309*n*
Yen Yüan, 180, 303*n*
Yin Chen-jen, 122, 123, 124, 273*n*, 278*n*, 295*n*, 300*n*
Yin and yang: defined, 21; in Inner Alchemy, 95, 173; and Diagram of Great Ultimate, 128, 187; in Lin's Nine Stages, 173, 181, 182–83, 187, 209
Yoshioka Yoshitoyo, 267*n*, 273*n*, 279*n*
Yü Chun-fang, 270*n*, 271*n*, 280*n*, 288*n*, 290*n*
Yüan dynasty, 200, 273*n*, 284*n*
Yüan Huang, 56
Yüan-shih T'ien-tsun, 226, 312*n*
Yüan-tao p'ien, 201
Yüan Tsung-tao, 51, 125, 132, 162, 165; *see also* Neo-Confucianism, School of Mind
Yüeh-hsiu, 225
Yün-ch'i Chu-hung, 59, 94, 288*n*; *see also* Ch'an school of Buddhism; Buddhism, Ming revival
Yün-ku, 56

Zürcher, Erik, 269*n*

Neo-Confucian Studies

Instructions for Practical Living and Other Neo-Confucian Writings by Wang Yang-ming, tr. Wing-tsit Chan	1963
Reflections on Things at Hand: The Neo-Confucian Anthology compiled by Chu Hsi and Lü Tsu-ch'ien, tr. Wing-tsit Chan	1967
Self and Society in Ming Thought, by Wm. Theodore de Bary and the Conference on Ming Thought. Also in paperback ed.	1970
The Unfolding of Neo-Confucianism, by Wm. Theodore de Bary and the Conference on Seventeenth-Century Chinese Thought. Also in paperback ed.	1975
Principle and Practicality: Essays in Neo-Confucianism and Practical Learning, ed. Wm. Theodore de Bary and Irene Bloom. Also in paperback ed.	1979
The Syncretic Religion of Lin Chao-en, by Judith A. Berling	1980

Translations from the Oriental Classics

Major Plays of Chikamatsu, tr. Donald Keene	1961
Four Major Plays of Chikamatsu, tr. Donald Keene. Paperback text edition.	1961
Records of the Grand Historian of China, translated from the *Shih chi* of Ssu-ma Ch'ien, tr. Burton Watson, 2 vols.	1961
Instructions for Practical Living and Other Neo-Confucian Writings by Wang Yang-ming, tr. Wing-tsit Chan	1963
Chuang Tzu: Basic Writings, tr. Burton Watson, paperback ed. only	1964
The Mahābhārata, tr. Chakravarthi V. Narasimhan. Also in paperback ed.	1965
The Manyōshū, Nippon Gakujutsu Shinkōkai edition	1965
Su Tung-p'o: Selections from a Sung Dynasty Poet, tr. Burton Watson. Also in paperback ed.	1965
Bhartrihari: Poems, tr. Barbara Stoler Miller. Also in paperback ed.	1967
Basic Writings of Mo Tzu, Hsün Tzu, and Han Fei Tzu, tr. Burton Watson. Also in separate paperback eds.	1967
The Awakening of Faith, Attributed to Aśvaghosha, tr. Yoshito S. Hakeda. Also in paperback ed.	1967
Reflections on Things at Hand: The Neo-Confucian Anthology, comp. Chu Hsi and Lü Tsu-ch'ien, tr. Wing-tsit Chan	1967
The Platform Sutra of the Sixth Patriarch, tr. Philip B. Yampolsky. Also in paperback ed.	1967
Essays in Idleness: The Tsurezuregusa of Kenkō, tr. Donald Keene. Also in paperback ed.	1967

The Pillow Book of Sei Shōnagon, tr. Ivan Morris, 2 vols. 1967
Two Plays of Ancient India: The Little Clay Cart and the Minister's Seal, tr. J. A. B. van Buitenen 1968
The Complete Works of Chuang Tzu, tr. Burton Watson 1968
The Romance of the Western Chamber (Hsi Hsiang chi), tr. S. I. Hsiung. Also in paperback ed. 1968
The Manyōshū, Nippon Gakujutsu Shinkōkai edition. Paperback text edition. 1969
Records of the Historian: Chapters from the Shih chi of Ssu-ma Ch'ien. Paperback text edition, tr. Burton Watson 1969
Cold Mountain: 100 Poems by the T'ang Poet Han-shan, tr. Burton Watson. Also in paperback ed. 1970
Twenty Plays of the No Theatre, ed. Donald Keene. Also in paperback ed. 1970
Chūshingura: The Treasury of Loyal Retainers, tr. Donald Keene. Also in paperback ed. 1971
The Zen Master Hakuin: Selected Writings, tr. Philip B. Yampolsky 1971
Chinese Rhyme-Prose: Poems in the Fu Form from the Han and Six Dynasties Periods, tr. Burton Watson. Also in paperback ed. 1971
Kūkai: Major Works, tr. Yoshito S. Hakeda 1972
The Old Man Who Does as He Pleases: Selections from the Poetry and Prose of Lu Yu, tr. Burton Watson 1973
The Lion's Roar of Queen Śrīmālā, tr. Alex and Hideko Wayman
Courtier and Commoner in Ancient China: Selections from the History of The Former Han by Pan Ku, tr. Burton Watson. Also in paperback ed. 1974
Japanese Literature in Chinese. Vol. I: Poetry and Prose in Chinese by Japanese Writers of the Early Period, tr. Burton Watson 1975
Japanese Literature in Chinese. Vol. II: Poetry and Prose in Chinese by Japanese Writers of the Later Period, tr. Burton Watson 1976
Scripture of the Lotus Blossom of the Fine Dharma (The Lotus Sūtra), tr. Leon Hurvitz. Also in paperback ed. 1976
Love Song of the Dark Lord: Jayadeva's Gītagovinda, tr. Barbara Stoler Miller. Also in paperback ed. Cloth ed. includes critical text of the Sanskrit. 1977
Ryōkan: Zen Monk-Poet of Japan, tr. Burton Watson 1977
Calming the Mind and Discerning the Real: From the Lam rim chen mo of Tsoṅ-kha-pa, tr. Alex Wayman 1978
The Hermit and the Love-Thief: Sanskrit Poems of Bhartrihari and Bilhaṇa, tr. Barbara Stoler Miller 1978
The Lute: Kao Ming's P'i-p'a chi, tr. Jean Mulligan. Also in paperback ed. 1980

Modern Asian Literature Series

Modern Japanese Drama: An Anthology, ed. and tr. Ted T. Takaya	1979
Mask and Sword: Two Plays for the Contemporary Japanese Theater, by Yamazaki Masakazu, tr. J. Thomas Rimer	1980
Nepali Visions, Nepali Dreams: The Poetry of Laxmiprasad Devkota, tr. David Rubin	1980

Studies in Oriental Culture

1. *The Ōnin War: History of Its Origins and Background, with a Selective Translation of the Chronicle of Ōnin,* by H. Paul Varley — 1967
2. *Chinese Government in Ming Times: Seven Studies,* ed. Charles O. Hucker — 1969
3. *The Actors' Analects (Yakusha Rongo),* ed. and tr. by Charles J. Dunn and Bunzō Torigoe — 1969
4. *Self and Society in Ming Thought,* by Wm. Theodore de Bary and the Conference on Ming Thought. Also in paperback ed. — 1970
5. *A History of Islamic Philosophy,* by Majid Fakhry — 1970
6. *Phantasies of a Love Thief: The Caurapañcāśikā Attributed to Bilhaṇa,* by Barbara Stoler Miller — 1971
7. *Iqbal: Poet-Philosopher of Pakistan,* ed. Hafeez Malik — 1971
8. *The Golden Tradition: An Anthology of Urdu Poetry,* by Ahmed Ali. Also in paperback ed. — 1973
9. *Conquerors and Confucians: Aspects of Political Change in Late Yüan China,* by John W. Dardess — 1973
10. *The Unfolding of Neo-Confucianism,* by Wm. Theodore de Bary and the Conference on Seventeenth-Century Chinese Thought. Also in paperback ed. — 1975
11. *To Acquire Wisdom: The Way of Wang Yang-ming,* by Julia Ching — 1976
12. *Gods, Priests, and Warriors: The Bhṛgus of the Mahābhārata,* by Robert P. Goldman — 1977
13. *Mei Yao-ch'en and the Development of Early Sung Poetry,* by Jonathan Chaves — 1976
14. *The Legend of Semimaru, Blind Musician of Japan,* by Susan Matisoff — 1977

Companions to Asian Studies

Approaches to the Oriental Classics, ed. Wm. Theodore de Bary	1959
Early Chinese Literature, by Burton Watson. Also in paperback ed.	1962

Approaches to Asian Civilizations, ed. Wm. Theodore de Bary and
Ainslie T. Embree 1964
The Classic Chinese Novel: A Critical Introduction, by C. T. Hsia. Also
in paperback ed. 1968
Chinese Lyricism: Shih Poetry from the Second to the Twelfth Century,
tr. Burton Watson. Also in paperback ed. 1971
A Syllabus of Indian Civilization, by Leonard A. Gordon and Barbara
Stoler Miller 1971
Twentieth-Century Chinese Stories, ed. C. T. Hsia and Joseph S. M.
Lau. Also in paperback ed. 1971
A Syllabus of Chinese Civilization, by J. Mason Gentzler, 2d ed. 1972
A Syllabus of Japanese Civilization, by H. Paul Varley, 2d ed. 1972
An Introduction to Chinese Civilization, ed. John Meskill, with the assistance of J. Mason Gentzler 1973
An Introduction to Japanese Civilization, ed. Arthur E. Tiedemann 1974
A Guide to Oriental Classics, ed. Wm. Theodore de Bary and Ainslie
T. Embree, 2d ed. Also in paperback ed. 1975

Introduction to Oriental Civilizations
Wm. Theodore de Bary, *Editor*

Sources of Japanese Tradition	1958	Paperback ed., 2 vols.	1964
Sources of Indian Tradition	1958	Paperback ed., 2 vols.	1964
Sources of Chinese Tradition	1960	Paperback ed., 2 vols.	1964